D0854146

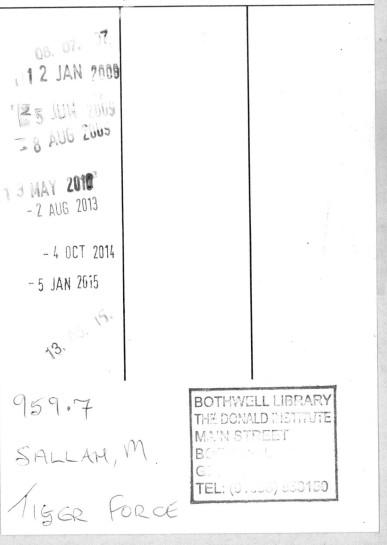

MICHAEL SALLAH & MITCH WEISS

TIGER
FORCE

HODDER

First published in Great Britain in 2006 by Hodder and Stoughton
A division of Hodder Headline
This edition published in 2007

A Hodder paperback

1

A CIP catalogue record for this book is
available from the British Library

ISBN 978 0 340 75250 0
ISBN 0 340 75250 5

Printed and bound in Great Britain by Mackays of Chatham Ltd,
Chatham, Kent

Hodder Headline's policy is to use papers that are natural, renewable
and recyclable products and made from wood grown in sustainable
forests. The logging and manufacturing processes are expected to
conform to the environmental regulations of the country of origin.

Hodder and Stoughton
A division of Hodder Headline PLC
338 Euston Road
London NW1 3BH

To Our Wives and Children

There is nothing concealed that will not be revealed, nor secret that will not be made known.

LUKE 12:2

CAST OF CHARACTERS

TIGERS:

SERGEANT JAMES BARNETT
January 1967 to January 1968

PRIVATE EDWARD BECK
June 1967 to September 1967 (KIA: September 29, 1967)

SERGEANT GERALD BRUNER
August 1967 to September 1967

SPECIALIST WILLIAM CARPENTER
January 1967 to December 1967

PRIVATE DANIEL CLINT
August 1967 to May 1968

PRIVATE JAMES COGAN
June 1967 to September 1967

SERGEANT ROBERT DIAZ
April 1966 to September 1967

SERGEANT BENJAMIN EDGE
June 1967 to August 1967

SERGEANT CHARLES FULTON
June 1967 to September 1967

SPECIALIST KENNETH "BOOTS" GREEN
June 1967 to September 1967 (KIA: September 29, 1967)

SERGEANT JAMES HAUGH
May 1967 to March 1968 (KIA: March 27, 1968)

SERGEANT LEO HEANEY
December 1966 to October 1967

PRIVATE JERRY INGRAM
June 1967 to September 1967 (KIA: September 27, 1967)

PRIVATE KENNETH KERNEY
May 1967 to December 1967

PRIVATE TERRENCE KERRIGAN
May 1967 to May 1968

PRIVATE GARY "LITTLE SKI" KORNATOWSKI
September 1966 to October 1967

PRIVATE JAMES MESSER
August 1967 (KIA: August 22, 1967)

SERGEANT ERNEST MORELAND
September 1966 to October 1967

SERGEANT TERRY LEE OAKDEN
September 1967 (KIA: September 20, 1967)

PRIVATE CECIL PEDEN
June 1967 to September 1967

PRIVATE FLOYD SAWYER
July 1967 to October 1967

PRIVATE SAM YBARRA
April 1967 to January 1968

TEAM LEADERS:

SERGEANT WILLIAM DOYLE
June 1967 to November 1967

SERGEANT ERVIN LEE
July 1966 to October 1967

SERGEANT DOMINGO MUNOZ
May 1967 to July 1967 (KIA: July 28, 1967)

SERGEANT MANUEL SANCHEZ JR.
December 1966 to July 1967

SERGEANT HAROLD TROUT
March 1967 to February 1968

SERGEANT ROBIN VARNEY
November 1966 to September 1967
(KIA: September 27, 1967)

MEDICS:

PRIVATE MICHAEL ALLUMS
January 1967 to April 1968

SPECIALIST BARRY BOWMAN
May 1967 to September 1967

PRIVATE RION CAUSEY
October 1967 to March 1968

PRIVATE HAROLD FISCHER III
September 1967 to January 1968

PRIVATE RALPH MAYHEW
August 1967 to December 1967

SERGEANT FORREST MILLER
May 1967 to May 1968

PRIVATE DOUGLAS TEETERS
May 1967 to December 1967

OFFICERS:

LIEUTENANT COLONEL HAROLD AUSTIN
June 1967 to August 1967

LIEUTENANT COLONEL JOSEPH COLLINS
September 1966 to June 1967

LIEUTENANT GARY FORBES
March 1967 to May 1967

LIEUTENANT JAMES HAWKINS
July 1967 to November 1967

CAPTAIN CARL JAMES
June 1967 to November 1967

CAPTAIN HAROLD McGAHA
November 1967 to January 1968 (KIA: January 21, 1968)

LIEUTENANT COLONEL GERALD MORSE
August 1967 to December 1967

CAPTAIN BRADFORD MUTCHLER
November 1966 to November 1967

CAPTAIN LARRY NAUGHTON
May 1967 to June 1967

LIEUTENANT STEPHEN NAUGHTON
June 1967 to July 1967

LIEUTENANT EDWARD SANDERS
August 1967 to November 1967

LIEUTENANT DONALD WOOD
June 1967 to August 1967

C COMPANY:

PRIVATE JOHN AHERN
July 1967 to March 1968 (KIA: March 16, 1968)

PRIVATE GARY COY
August 1967 to November 1967

CID:

WARRANT OFFICER GUSTAV APSEY
CAPTAIN EARL PERDUE
CHEIF WARRANT OFFICER FRANK SUGAR
COLONEL HENRY TUFTS
COLONEL KENNETH WEINSTEIN

TIGER FORCE

INTRODUCTION

1975

The sun glared off the hood of his blue Buick as Gustav Apsey peered through the windshield at the white clapboard shack. Rust stains ran down the sun-bleached wood, and scattered around the home were beer cans, cardboard boxes, and a rusty tailpipe from a pickup truck. There were no mansions on the San Carlos Indian Reservation, just miles of scrub and cacti and rows of shacks built on dry sand and clay. It was one of the poorest and most desolate areas of southeastern Arizona, a no-man's-land where generations of Native Americans survived on food stamps and other government handouts.

Apsey slowly pulled into the gravel driveway and turned off the ignition.

For a moment, he stared at the shack's door and then at its windows, trying to catch any movement through the flimsy sheer curtains and cracked glass masked with tape. Just two days earlier, shots were fired over the top of a police car that had pulled into the drive on a disturbance call. Instead of radioing for backup, the patrol officer turned his car around and left. "It's just Crazy Sam," he said to the dispatcher at the reservation.

3

The police had long known to ignore the man who lived in the shack at the end of the road. And you certainly did not want to encounter Sam Ybarra when he was drunk.

For Apsey, an Army investigator, it was important to get the tribal police to accompany him, since he was a federal agent on their land now, on their reservation. But when he had gone to the police station, the officers had been less than thrilled to help. They were Apache, just like Ybarra, and there wasn't exactly a long history of benefits for the tribe when they helped out white guys from the U.S. Army.

Reservation police chief Robert Youngdeer told the investigator about Ybarra's drinking and warned that he might even fire his gun at Apsey's car. But Apsey was undeterred. He had waited too long for this and traveled too far. He assured Youngdeer he was only going to question Ybarra — not arrest him. Besides, Apsey didn't want to have to come back with more agents. There was already bad blood between the feds and Native American activists on other reservations, and no one needed any trouble at San Carlos.

Youngdeer agreed to assign reservation police sergeant Frank Cutter to follow the agent's car to Ybarra's home; he couldn't spare any more officers. He had only thirty to cover one of the largest reservations in the Southwest, an expanse of land that could have been an entire state: 1.8 million haunted acres.

Apsey opened his car door and stepped onto the driveway, while fellow investigator Larry Pereiro bounded out the passenger side. Cutter, who trailed the investigators in another car, joined the men.

The three walked slowly to the door.

Apsey knocked and peered through a torn screen at a dark figure on a couch just inside.

"What do you want?" asked the man without getting up.

Apsey responded, "Are you Sam Ybarra?"

The man didn't move.

Apsey knew it was Ybarra. He had seen pictures of him and knew this is where he lived.

"We're here to talk to you," Apsey said.

After a moment of tense silence, Apsey saw the man raise his hand and motion for the men to enter.

Apsey slowly opened the door and stepped in, followed by the others. It was sweltering inside. The air reeked of urine and sweat, and flies swarmed over a table covered with beer bottles and food that had been left out for days.

Ybarra's face was gaunt and yellowish as he leaned back on the sofa, his hollow eyes expressionless. He was unshaved, and his soaked T-shirt and shorts clung to a body that had shriveled from 200 pounds in the Army to about 145 pounds. To Apsey, the man on the couch hardly bore a resemblance to the once burly Vietnam paratrooper whose battlefield exploits had been written about in *Stars and Stripes*.

Apsey introduced himself, flashing a badge from the Army's Criminal Investigation Command, and then introduced Pereiro, who flipped open a wallet showing his Army badge.

Ybarra didn't flinch. Instead, he sat motionless, his eyes darting from one man to the other. Targeting. He had been visited by Army investigators before and had always refused to cooperate — three times before.

Apsey opened a notebook, jotted down the date — March 21, 1975 — and began, "You are a suspect in a military investigation and are under investigation for murder, body mutilations, and conduct unbecoming a soldier."

Apsey waited for a response, but Ybarra sat stone-faced. Apsey stood in silence, listening to the flies buzz and his own breathing.

Finally Ybarra slowly rose to his feet, prompting the police sergeant to move closer to him. The former paratrooper looked at Apsey for a moment and then quietly said, "I want a lawyer."

The Army investigator closed his notebook and stared at Ybarra. "Are you sure?" he asked. Ybarra nodded without saying a word.

Apsey stood for a moment, knowing this was his last chance.

"I was hoping we could talk," he said. "I came a long way to see you."

Ybarra folded his arms and turned away. There was no use in trying to ask any more questions. Apsey hesitated momentarily, his frustration apparent to the others, then turned and walked out the door as the others followed.

As he climbed back into his car, Apsey realized this was the end. No more interviews and no more trips around the country.

During the drive to the Phoenix airport, Apsey's mind began to drift back over the endless hours he had spent on the case: The nights he was hunched over a Royal typewriter at his office — alone — writing questions for agents to ask suspects. The reports he was forced to write for commanders. The trips he made around the clock to the mimeograph machine to copy files.

For three years, he lived and breathed this case. For three years, he had descended into an unimaginable nightmare, thirty-six months of blood and fear and ghosts. Trips to the grocery store or restaurants with his wife weren't the same anymore, his mind wandering to the images described over and over in sworn statements. Even to grizzled war-crimes investigators like Apsey, the details were outrageous, and no one in the story was as frightening as the man back in that shack — a half Apache, half Mexican soldier who, among other things, had once worn necklaces of human ears and tied a scalp on the end of his rifle as a trophy.

"I wanted him to talk to me," Apsey wistfully told the other investigator in the car. Perhaps Ybarra could have explained what happened.

Apsey shook his head, just as he did so many other times. An Austrian immigrant who was educated by Jesuits in his native country, he was appalled by what he had learned over the past several years. It was counter to everything he knew about the people of his adopted country.

Apsey pulled into the airport, his mind drifting to the same question he had grappled with every spare moment since beginning the case. And after an investigation that had led agents to more than sixty-three Army bases and cities around the world, he didn't have the answer. Perhaps it was right there in front of him, but the darkness was too profound to make it out.

In the night gloom, Sam Ybarra stumbled toward his mother's trailer, just beyond the scrubland that covered one end of the San Carlos Indian Reservation.

Though he was drunk, he knew the road by heart. Since his dishonorable discharge from the Army in 1969, this was his world — a desolate area one hundred miles east of Phoenix and home to thousands of Native Americans for generations. Most of his days began with a beer and a joint, if he could get a young Apache to score for him. By late afternoon, he was passed out.

Ever since Apsey and Pereiro had left his house earlier in the day, Ybarra had been restless, pacing the floor. He began downing bottles of Coors shortly after his visitors departed and hadn't stopped until he walked out the door of his shack to go to his mother's.

He reached his mother's home and opened the back door. Therlene Ramos kept the door open for her son even when she wasn't home. He plopped down on a couch in the living room, hoping the thoughts would fade, or end altogether. But each time he closed his eyes, the memories would rush back. The more he tried to forget, the more he remembered.

The door opened, and suddenly Therlene walked into the home. She flicked on a light to find her son once again in her living room. He was curled on the couch, tears in his eyes.

"What's wrong?" she asked.

He responded, "It's my life. What I did. What I did. I killed people, Mama. I killed regular people. I shouldn't have. My God, what did I do?"

Therlene had seen her son shake and cry before, but not like this. Maybe it had something to do with the visit by the Army investigators, word of which was already making the rounds on the reservation.

7

Therlene knew that when Sam was like this, the best thing she could do was listen. She didn't want to push him; she didn't want to know the details, or why the Army kept returning to his home to ask him questions about a war that ended for her when her son returned.

But for Sam, the war was always there, and nothing could make him forget, especially after investigators showed up. This time, they hadn't even asked him about the others: Hawkins, Trout, Barnett, Doyle. But every time he closed his eyes, he saw their faces — and the faces of those they killed.

He had promised his family he would never talk about what happened when he served with Tiger Force. Never. That was part of his past. But in the darkness, he would wake up sweating, and sometimes the slightest noise would roust him from his sleep. His wife would reassure him he was not in Vietnam, that he was home — in his own bed. Still, there were times she would watch him as he cried in his sleep, or as he jumped up in bed and acted like he had a rifle in his hand, "in his fighting stance," recalled Janice Little.

Sitting on his mother's sofa, Ybarra began sobbing uncontrollably. With all the beer he had been drinking, he should have been passed out by now, but he was too upset by the people who came to his door.

"He said to me, 'Oh, I really feel bad. I asked God to forgive me for what I did, for killing all those people, all those civilians, all those children,'" recalled his mother.

As he always did when facing the nightmares, Ybarra would bring up his best friend, Kenneth "Boots" Green. The memories of Boots lying in the dirt, blood gushing from his head, haunted Ybarra. "Why did he have to die?" he asked his mother between tears. "Why?"

Because when it all got crazy, when Boots went down in an ambush on September 29, 1967, that's when Ybarra really lost control. And now he was afraid everyone would know what he had been trying to lock away for years.

CHAPTER 1

1967

Even through the haze of smoke in the dimly lit lounge, Sam Ybarra glimpsed Ken Green as he walked through the door. "Kenny, over here!" shouted Ybarra over the music blaring from a tape deck. Meeting, the two friends hugged as the other soldiers looked up from their beers and shot glasses.

It had been nearly a year since they arrived in Vietnam, and this was one of the few weekends the two could meet on a break. They'd been waiting it out, and now at long last it was time to down beers and later slip into the brothels that lined the streets of Kontum. Green introduced Sam to two buddies, Leon Fletcher and Ed Beck. For days, Ken had been telling them about his time with "Crazy Sam" — cruising the streets of Globe, Arizona, in Green's blue 1964 Chevelle SS, guzzling Ripple with the Rolling Stones' "Satisfaction" crackling over the radio. And now, in this sad and near corner of Southeast Asia, the two old friends were together again.

To most people, they were as opposite as they were close: Green was boyish, good-looking, and cocky — the type of guy who could turn heads in a crowded room. Ybarra was dark skinned, with a round, pockmarked face — awkwardly shy unless he was drinking. But for all their differences, they shared something in common: they were constantly in trouble.

Green was known for his temper — quick to start fights with other students at Globe High School, regardless of their age and size. Though he stood only five feet, five inches, he rarely backed down. Everyone knew to stay away from him. As a junior, Green had brutally attacked another student who was a year older and a foot taller for looking at him the wrong way in the hallway. Dozens of classmates watched in horror as he pummeled the student senseless on the floor. It took three teachers to pull him away.

Back home, on some summer nights, Green would sneak out of the house with his .22 rifle and head for a ridge overlooking a dam on nearby Lake Roosevelt. Patiently, he would wait for Sheriff Dutch Lake to drive onto the roadway over the dam, and then Green would shoot out the lights on the road before fleeing into the darkness. The sheriff suspected it was Green but could never prove it. Nor could the sheriff prove that Green was the one who rolled a boulder onto the dirt runway at the tiny Lake Roosevelt airstrip, shutting down flights for hours. By the time authorities arrived to remove the large rock, Green and the two buddies who carried out the prank had vanished. But they left their calling card on the boulder: the words "Fuck You," painted in black.

His father, Melvin, was a laborer for the state highway department who also ran Carson's Café, a diner on Lake Roosevelt. He was quick to discipline his son for misbehaving, sometimes beating him in front of his friends, but those beatings only made Green more defiant. Once, his father grounded him for coming home with alcohol on his breath, ordering him to work extra hours at the diner with his sister and older brother. Instead of washing dishes, Green stole his father's boat, later flipping the craft in a race on the other side of the lake. The beatings that followed his pranks only seemed to make him more aggressive, and by his late teens, he was getting into fights almost weekly.

Ybarra was angry, but for more obvious reasons: he was painfully aware of his own physical appearance and never felt accepted in the small mining community that looked down on Mexicans and Native Americans. Sam was burdened with the shame and angst of being a "half-breed," and his longing for a father who had died when Ybarra was five was profound. (Manuel Ybarra was a truck driver for the Inspiration Consolidated Copper Company when he stopped at a bar on the way home and was stabbed to death in a brawl.)

Besides getting into fights, he was arrested three times for underage drinking and once for disorderly conduct. At sixteen, he had dropped out of high school, guzzling beer and wine behind Mark's or Pinky's — the two nightspots in town that catered to Native Americans. He was too young to go inside, so he would wait outside the door and ask elders from the reservation to buy him a Coors or a pint of Thunderbird.

In Globe, Indians and whites weren't supposed to socialize. It had been that way for generations. But by the 1960s, some of those rules began to be challenged. Though Ybarra and others from the reservation went to "Indian schools" during their grade-school years in the 1950s, they were now attending the white public schools. Whites and Indians were at this point playing on the same football and basketball teams, and even joined in school dances. Still, the older Indians would tell Ybarra to stay out of the white bar, The Huddle.

Green and Ybarra didn't meet until high school, where they began hanging out in the parking lot before classes. Though they came from different worlds, they found something in common: they were angry and were quick to pick fights. Ybarra was an outcast, and Green was becoming one.

Their bond became deeper after Green began driving, and the two started skipping school and drinking. "No one knows the shit that Sam has gone through," Green told family members who tried to discourage him from associating with Ybarra. It was them against the world, as ferocious as suns.

And now, here they were in late May 1967, ten thousand miles from home and oblivious to the soldiers around them in the bar. They ordered Black Labels and toasted each other.

"At least we're both still alive," said Green.

The night before they had enlisted, the two friends had sat in Green's car downing beers when they heard a radio broadcast about the war. They began talking about joining the Army. Sam had challenged his friend: "If you do it, I'll do it."

Green had agreed. As a boy growing up along Lake Roosevelt, he was spellbound at the sight of the paratroopers dropping from the sky during training exercises. And when Green and Ybarra hunted deer and quail in the nature preserves near the lake, they often talked about what it would be like to be soldiers. Besides, there was nothing for them in Globe, except working in the copper mines. Ybarra knew all about that life: his relatives had toiled underground for years, and he didn't want any part of it.

The next day, they showed up at the local recruiting office and enlisted under the Army's buddy system. Together they entered the 101st Airborne in January 1966 and, after jump training at Fort Benning, Georgia, were sent to Vietnam, Ybarra in July and Green a month later.

It had been about ten months since they arrived in Vietnam, leaving behind their lives in Arizona, and for most of that period, they were assigned to different units. Green was in a mortar platoon but spent most of his time humping in the mountains in the heart of South Vietnam with heavy equipment and only sporadic contact with the enemy. Ybarra's experiences were different — and it showed even in his uniform. Unlike the others in the lounge that night, he wasn't wearing the traditional olive green. Instead, he was dressed in tiger-striped fatigues and a soft-brimmed jungle cap, and he carried his own sidearm and hunting knife.

Tiger Force, the 101st Airborne's version of Special Forces. Badass of the badass.

Ybarra had actually been sent to a signal corps after arriving in Vietnam, but quickly grew bored and asked to be transferred to the Tigers in early 1967. He didn't regret his move. As soon as he joined the platoon of forty-five men, he felt part of a special team of soldiers who were treated differently than the grunts in the line companies. He remembered the first time a battalion commander addressed his platoon in Phan Rang: "You're the Tigers, men," he reminded them before they went on a reconnaissance mission. "The Tigers always get it done, no matter how many gooks you see." It was an exceptional group that allowed no exceptions.

Tiger Force was founded in November 1965 by Major David Hackworth to "outguerrilla the guerrillas," a platoon known as a "recondo unit" because it was to carry out reconnaissance and commando functions. The model for *Apocalypse Now*'s Colonel Kilgore, Hackworth was a hell-for-leather soldier of savage brilliance who had revealed himself as a daring hero during the Korean War. In Vietnam, he had realized that conventional warfare was a dead end. Following his lead, his commanders found the best way to locate the new enemy was to blend into the jungle terrain. That meant breaking into small teams, donning camouflage, and carrying enough rations and supplies to last several weeks. They would leave themselves behind.

Such was Hackworth's answer to an enemy that moved in intricate underground tunnels and carried out hit-and-run tactics.

Beyond surveillance, the Tigers were often ordered to perform impossible maneuvers, such as acting as a blocking unit for retreating guerrilla forces and often relieving much larger line companies trapped in firefights. In February 1966 at My Canh II, an area covered by rice paddies and mountains in the Central Highlands, the Tigers were trapped by a well-fortified enemy until the unit's own commander, Lieutenant James

Gardner, heroically charged three bunkers. Gardner was killed, but his actions allowed his platoon to escape, and he was posthumously awarded the Medal of Honor. At Dak To, a city just thirty-five kilometers from Laos, eleven Tigers were killed on June 11, 1966, when they pursued a fleeing North Vietnamese Army (NVA) regiment. In that case, as it would be often, they had been the first unit sent to face the enemy. Let the other guys mop up — the Tigers wanted fresh blood, even if it meant some of it might be their own.

Only forty-five men were accepted in the Tigers, and that was only after three months of combat experience and a screening process by commanders that included a battery of questions, mostly centered on the soldiers' willingness to kill.

Ybarra had impressed the officers. With cold, steely eyes, he said he could kill without hesitation — using a knife, M16, or even his own hands. It made no difference. Ever since jump school at Fort Benning, Georgia, he had been looking for a home. He hated the structure of the line companies — the chain of command, the rules, the officers. The Tigers were different, part Green Beret, part line company. They would break into small teams, two or three men at a time, creep deep into the jungles, "and do whatever the hell you want to do," he was fond of saying. When the commanders told him he was accepted into the platoon, he was "thrilled."

After several rounds of beer, Sam sank down into his chair. There was so much smoke in the lounge it was almost impossible to see across the room. Not that there was anything special worth noticing. The room was a typical makeshift military bar, with round Formica-top tables, folding chairs, and thin wood walls built on a raised bamboo platform, and filled with the stench of cigarettes and whiskey. There were hundreds of these cheap versions of nightspots in South Vietnam that were supposed to remind American soldiers of the watering holes they left behind. The only prop in the lounge was the flickering Black Label neon light dangling over the bar.

Ybarra guzzled the last of his beer, leaned over, and began telling Green and the others about the Tigers' most recent battle. On May 15 Ybarra and the Tigers were called to a valley west of Duc Pho in the heart of the Central Highlands — Quang Ngai province — where another Army reconnaissance unit, the Hawks, was pinned down by enemy fire. In the late morning, with a dozen Tiger Force soldiers at the bottom of the valley, the enemy launched a surprise attack. "They were fuckin' all over the place," Ybarra angrily recalled. Well-fortified enemy bunkers at the top of the valley suddenly opened up, and NVA soldiers began shelling the helpless Tigers below.

Led by the Tigers' commander, Lieutenant Gary Forbes, the platoon members charged the bunkers but were forced down by a flurry of mortars and .50-caliber machine-gun fire. For hours, the platoon was at the bottom of the basin, dodging artillery, grenades, and bullet fire. Tiger Force radioed for helicopters to evacuate the wounded, but each time a chopper tried to land, it was forced to leave because of enemy artillery. One helicopter was able to land in a rice paddy but was immediately hit by fire and destroyed.

By early afternoon, Tiger Force was no closer to escaping and was running low on ammunition. But the platoon finally caught a break when the soldiers found a new position and were able to call in American air strikes without being hit. For two hours, U.S. jets dropped bombs on the bunkers. The combination of air strikes and the arrival of some additional American troops allowed the Tigers to escape. By the end of the day, two were dead and twenty-five wounded. For some of the injured, including Lieutenant Forbes, the war was over.

Because of the losses, Sam admitted the Tigers "were down" and unable to go back out on maneuvers until they could find reinforcements. The battalion officers were trying to bring in new volunteers. Now Ybarra did his part. He turned to Green. "You need to come with me, Kenny. You need to be a Tiger."

Green always knew when Ybarra was serious; his smile would disappear and his eyes would narrow. He had seen the look many times before, and he saw it now.

Vietnam in early 1967 was still vastly different from what it was to become at year's end. There was still a sense of patriotism that had not yet been eroded by the bitterness of the Tet Offensive and casualties that would soon turn most Americans against the war. Until now, most of the conflict had been marked by skirmishes and, if not wild optimism, at least a sense of inevitable triumph.

Through most of the conversation, Green's friend Leon Fletcher was quiet. But after several minutes, he grew agitated. "You don't want to join these guys, Kenny," he said. "You're going to get yourself killed."

Fletcher had looked up to Green. Ken had been the one who took the time to show Leon the basics of survival, from throwing him to the ground during sniper attacks to teaching him how to avoid booby traps. And now Fletcher thought it was time to return the favor.

Green was quiet for a moment, and then he turned to Fletcher. "At this point, I just want to kill a lot of them. My job is to kill."

Ed Beck joined in. After several months in South Vietnam, he was looking for real action — not just maneuvers or air strikes with no real targets. He had come to Vietnam to escape, not just from the boring western suburbs of Chicago but from a wife who was making his life miserable. "How do we get in?" he asked.

Before Ybarra could answer, Fletcher interrupted again. "You guys are crazy. You're supposed to be trying to stay alive. Why do you want to join a fucking recon unit?"

Ybarra quickly cut him off. "Look, man, stay out of this," he said, jabbing a finger at Fletcher. "Don't be telling Kenny what he's going to do. We go way back." There was not a trace of friendliness in his comment.

Ybarra's anger may have been what Green most admired,

especially when his fury involved protecting Ken's right to do whatever the hell he wanted to do. Green turned to his friend. "I'm in, man. Tell me what I need to do."

"If you're going, I'm going," Beck said.

For Green and Beck, it was their way of finally taking part. Like so many others in the bar that night, they had been in high school when the first U.S. fighting units arrived in Da Nang in March 1965, and had watched the television reports of a war that was supposed to stop the spread of Communism.

Green, Beck, and Ybarra felt they were the next generation to carry on the traditions of their fathers and grandfathers who fought against evil in two world wars. Army recruiters were hawking the Vietnam War as a conflict of good versus evil, Democracy versus Communism. And to Green, Beck, and Ybarra, that was good enough. They grew up in the throes of the Cold War and recalled the hundreds of times they were told to duck under their desks at school during bomb drills. The Russians would attack without warning. The Red Chinese would swarm into all of Asia. Latin America and Mesopotamia were all on the verge of Marxist descent. To Green, it was a familiar message. He would listen to customers at his father's diner talk endlessly about how the United States was losing the Cold War and how the nation needed to get tougher on the "Commies." World War II veterans would come into the diner still wearing GOLDWATER FOR PRESIDENT buttons long after the 1964 election ended, complaining bitterly that if Goldwater had won the race for the White House, North Vietnam would have been bombed into the Stone Age.

The French had learned the hard way. For nearly six decades, Vietnam had been a French colony. They introduced their language and culture, and Saigon became the Paris of the Orient, with rows of elegant storefronts and cast-iron balconies overlooking wide boulevards and roundabouts. Street-corner bistros served chardonnay and shrimp gratiné. But the Vietnamese hated the French, and they wanted their country back. They saw their chance after World War II. Led by the legendary

Ho Chi Minh, the Vietnamese guerrillas — known as the Vietminh — battled French soldiers for nine years using weapons and ammo provided by the Chinese and Soviets, though at this point, Ho claimed only to be a nationalist.

The Vietminh attacked French strongholds at will, forcing their occupiers from several key provinces. The cluster of tiny villages at the foothills of the mountains at Dien Bien Phu became the scene of one of the most historic battles in Vietnamese history. In 1954, with the French troops trapped in the low ground, the Vietminh pummeled them with heavy artillery for days until the French surrendered. The United Nations interceded and, in July 1954, a peace treaty was signed.

As part of the agreement, the country was temporarily divided at the 17th parallel, with two nations emerging — South Vietnam and North Vietnam. Ho Chi Minh would command the North, while the South would be led by Emperor Bao Dai, who appointed Ngo Dinh Diem as his prime minister. Ho agreed to the plan only because it called for free elections in June 1956. He was confident he would win a fair vote and then be able to reunite the country.

But in 1955, Diem, with the backing of the United States, seized power from the emperor and unilaterally rejected the treaty, canceling elections. The action infuriated Ho, who then declared war against the South and announced to the world he was a Communist. The coup revealed that the South, he declared, was simply a puppet of the United States — another in a long line of nations that had tried to divide the Vietnamese. No one, Ho swore, would ever subjugate his people again.

In the ensuing years, armies from the North and South clashed, with the South Vietnamese losing most of the battles to Ho's soldiers, who were now quietly backed by the Soviet Union and China.

With his country in danger of collapsing, Diem found an ally in President John F. Kennedy, a fellow Roman Catholic and a Cold War hard-liner who sent American advisers to prop up the South Vietnam troops. The soldiers Kennedy was sending to South Vietnam were doing more than lending advice. In fact, many were fighting side by side with their new allies. Kennedy knew, as did the two presidents before him, that he would be judged by his success in the Cold War. Allowing South Vietnam to fall to the Communists would be a political disaster, especially after his criticism during the 1960 race for the White House, when he had claimed the United States was losing the arms race to the Soviets in what the Democratic candidate characterized as a "missile gap." By 1962 there were twelve thousand American advisers in South Vietnam, but there was growing unrest in the South with Diem and the American presence. Buddhist monks began protesting in the streets — some committing suicide by lighting themselves on fire — to stop the war and end U.S. involvement.

Diem was killed in a coup on November 1, 1963, and just three weeks later, Kennedy was assassinated in Dallas. But American policy stayed the same. President Lyndon Johnson increased aid to the country, though he resisted pressure to send combat troops until the Gulf of Tonkin incident.

On August 2, 1964, two North Vietnamese patrol boats fired on the USS *Maddox,* a destroyer on an intelligence-gathering mission in the waters off North Vietnam. Two days later, another attack on the destroyer, this time involving North Vietnamese torpedoes, was reported. In fact, there was no evidence to support the claim. But Johnson accused the North Vietnamese of a blatant attack on a U.S. ship, and he convinced Congress to pass a special resolution granting him the extraordinary power to take retaliatory action. In the next several months, U.S. warplanes dropped thousands of bombs over North Vietnamese military targets, and in March 1965, the first ground forces arrived.

There was little debate among Americans over whether the country should be involved in the conflict. Soldiers such as Green, Ybarra, and Beck were oblivious to the history of Vietnam. All they knew was that the Communists were trying to take over another country — just like they had taken over Eastern Europe and China. Like so many other new arrivals, they were convinced American firepower would force the enemy to surrender and American troops would soon be home. They were all going to be heroes.

CHAPTER 2

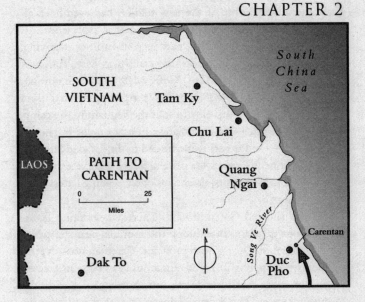

The veterans who served with Ybarra knew he liked to be alone. He ate by himself and slept in his own tent. Even on patrols, he walked alone. Most of the Tigers learned after a few weeks to stay out of his way, because you never knew which Sam you were going to get. He could be surly, other times, cool. Ybarra once pulled a knife on another soldier because he thought the soldier was laughing at him. He rarely smiled, but when he spotted Green hopping off the

21

arriving convoy truck, he jumped up and threw his arms around his old friend.

It had been three weeks since Ybarra convinced his buddy to join the Tigers. Green was the last replacement for a platoon that had not been at full strength since what they were now calling the Mother's Day Massacre. For Green, it was easy to get into the platoon, partly because eager commanders had scrapped the more rigorous screening process in order to get the Tigers back into action. Some of the new soldiers had even been allowed into the Tigers with little or no combat experience.

Over the past several days, new recruits had been arriving, and for the first time in weeks, the camp was busy. Transport trucks were bringing in M16s, M60s, M79s, and ammunition, while UH-1 and CH-47 helicopters were dropping off rations and other supplies. It was easy to spot the veterans in the camp. Some wore beards — a rule violation in other units, but not in Tiger Force — and others were dressed in dirty, faded fatigues. Some of the new Tigers were playing poker with veterans, and others were in their tents, door flaps open, reading letters from home.

Ybarra showed Green around. There was nothing glamorous about the base. Built along the foothills near the white sandy beaches of Quang Ngai province, Carentan was a typical temporary camp, consisting of numerous rows of tents erected along dirt roads that turned into muddy trenches during the monsoon season. There were a dozen makeshift buildings for the officers, but otherwise it was a sea of canvas.

Named after a town in France captured by the 101st Airborne during the invasion of Normandy, Carentan was home to the Army's 1st Brigade — "The Nomads of Vietnam" — a legendary unit of the 101st. No one could ever say this unit stayed in one place too long. Like mercenaries, the brigade's soldiers were constantly sent from one hot spot to another. In the first two years of the war, they had been pulled to six different provinces, always leaving a trail of enemy casualties. They put down an insurrection in the coastal province of Phu

Yen. They engaged the NVA in the Central Highlands of Kontum province.

The brigade was made up of three battalions: the 2nd Battalion/327th Infantry, the 2nd Battalion/502nd Infantry, and the 1st Battalion/327th Infantry. In all, there were 3,500 soldiers. Each battalion had roughly 900 men and was similarly structured. Each had a reconnaissance platoon with about 45 soldiers. Then there were the three to four line companies, each with 150 men. They were considered the fighting units, the grunts, the guys who did the dirty work, the ones who humped through some of the most treacherous terrain ever encountered by American combat units, and all the while were targets of snipers, booby traps, and ambushes. The rest of the battalion soldiers were in what was known as "the rear" — the support and headquarter companies, with officers and sergeants carrying out most of the duties. The S-1 officers took care of the paperwork: soldiers' records, payroll, and supply services. The sergeants made sure the grunts had enough ammo, weapons, and rations. The S-2 officers gathered and interpreted intelligence information and tipped off top commanders about new developments. The S-3 officers were in charge of training. The S-4 officers took care of logistics, making sure vehicles and equipment arrived as needed. The S-5 officers carried out civil affairs, such as listening to complaints from villagers. The headquarter company officers were the big shots who gave the orders.

The Tigers were the reconnaissance platoon in the 1st Battalion/327th Infantry. But unlike other recon units, the Tigers had additional responsibilities. Not only were they supposed to find the enemy but they were to engage the enemy, at times acting as a commando unit. They were there not just to search but to destroy.

Carentan looked out of place along a coastline sprinkled with thatched huts crowded along the narrow, dusty roadways that hugged the South China Sea — as third world as any area of Vietnam. The people were poor and were growing more dependent on American troops for food and menial jobs. It wasn't uncommon to see skinny, barefoot children standing at the edge of the base begging for food scraps and Life Savers.

Before Green had a chance to unpack and settle into his tent, a battalion sergeant called for the men to gather. It was early for a real briefing but not too early for an announcement from headquarters, usually delivered by commanders who said their piece and left before any real action began. Slowly the soldiers moved into the mess area and, without standing in formation, gathered around a sergeant. For the first time in six months, most of the Tigers were new. They had not been trained in the exigencies of guerrilla warfare, or surviving a terrain with a dozen species of poisonous snakes and spiders. For this Tiger Force platoon, it would be on-the-job training.

Those lessons would be held in one of the most dangerous provinces of South Vietnam: Quang Ngai. The briefing sergeant was clear: "You will listen to your team leaders!" he shouted to the men. "If you want to come back alive, you will listen to what they say."

Harold Trout had heard all the pep talks before. A stocky, tough-talking thirty-year-old soldier from southeastern Missouri who was now in his eleventh year in the service, he knew more about survival than most of the young officers sent to lead platoons in Vietnam. His men considered him a "born soldier."

Trout could be caustic and stubborn, demanding the men under his watch do things his way. Like a flinty big brother, he kept the younger soldiers alive, but he could also be ruthless, knocking them upside the head when they were out of line. Wounded a month earlier by a booby trap that killed a point man, he was fully recovered from his injuries. Like other soldiers injured in battle, Trout could have finished his first tour in Vietnam in a safer unit, but he missed the action and wanted to get back to his Tigers.

Standing at the opposite end of the circle from Trout that morning was James Barnett, a tall, strapping Tennessean — six feet, four inches tall and two hundred pounds — with a tattoo on his left arm of a devil and pitchfork and the words BORN TO

RAISE HELL. Like Trout, he had a short fuse and could also be a bully. He would push around the new Tigers, seeing if they would stand up to him. But while Barnett liked to brag about his toughness, the truth was that, under fire, he was the first one to dive for cover. Only twenty-two, he didn't share Trout's years of experience in the Army, nor perhaps his blunt confidence. The two men loathed each other.

The newest team leader was a wiry, balding sergeant: William Doyle, at thirty-four, was the oldest Tiger. He had joined the Army in 1950 after he was told by a Kansas City judge to either suit up or go to jail for beating a teenager with a bicycle chain in a park. (Doyle said he attacked the victim after the victim called Doyle's girlfriend an "ugly bitch.") It seemed as if everyone who worked in Kansas City's juvenile justice system had run into the wiry, foulmouthed teenager who had been on the streets since he was twelve. His mother died in a car accident when he was six, and his father, a switchman in the local rail yards, routinely came home drunk and beat the youngster. When the old man contracted tuberculosis and was sent to a sanitarium for three years, Doyle caught a break and was placed in a foster home while his sister was sent to a convent. While she stayed with the nuns, William found that his living arrangements didn't last, and he began running with an Irish street gang. "We were getting into fights all the time," he recalled. "That's how you survived." In the end, he said, it was "good training for the infantry."

Covered with tattoos, Doyle stood five feet, nine inches, weighed 150 pounds when he enlisted, and went by the nickname Scar. He had left the Army in 1953 and bragged about being a mercenary who had fought with Fidel Castro against Cuban dictator Fulgencio Batista, but no one knew for sure. Doyle rejoined the U.S. military in 1956 and eventually went to South Vietnam, where he expressed a hatred for Vietnamese people almost from the start.

As team leaders, Doyle and the others would be there to help the newcomers deal with booby traps, spider holes, and impending ambushes — all of which were likely. The briefing sergeant tried to explain the upcoming dangers. "This is like no place you've been before," he said, reminding them that Quang Ngai was a Vietcong (VC) stronghold — twice the size of Rhode Island — with the enemy hiding in underground tunnels that resembled ant farms. The enemy could be right under the feet of American soldiers, and they would never know until it was too late. In addition, snipers had been attacking U.S. soldiers every day since their arrival in the province on May 3 — a dozen ambushes in the first fourteen days.

Bill Carpenter, who had been with the platoon five months, didn't need the briefing. To him, Quang Ngai was a "hellhole" that he wanted to forget. "You had VC crawling all over the place," he recalled. "You'd walk up to these villages, and they were flying VC flags over the huts." He scanned the circle of newcomers and shook his head. They were about to discover there was a big difference between shooting a stationary target at Fort Campbell and firing at a sniper you couldn't see.

Newcomers such as Private Ken Kerney hadn't taken that into consideration when they joined up. Like so many others in the early years of the war, Kerney enlisted for adventure and patriotism. It was 1967, and despite fifteen thousand killed in two years of fighting, most Americans supported the war. But now, standing in the sweltering heat with the enemy lurking beyond the hills, Kerney was jittery. For the first time, he wondered whether he made the right decision.

He had grown up in a Catholic blue-collar family in a bungalow in Berwyn, Illinois, just outside Chicago, where pictures of John F. Kennedy adorned living room walls. It was a neighborhood where the events of the day were followed on television and where people — swept up by Cold War rhetoric — argued that the spread of Communism must be stopped or the Soviets could someday take over America.

But for Kerney, the reality seemed a bit less clear when viewed from Carentan. After two months in country, he began to think about his mother and her parting words. "I worked hard so you didn't have to do this." Ever since his father died when he was ten and his mother took a job with U.S. Steel as a secretary — working her way up to become a sales rep — Kerney was supposed to be a businessman, not a soldier. He had tried to follow his mother's wishes, studying business for a year at Morton Junior College, but he dropped out. It was all because of one friend, Art Voelker, who returned from the early war, filling Kerney's head with stories of a faraway exotic place. Kerney was seduced and off he went.

Fellow midwesterner Barry Bowman had no idea what the conflict in Vietnam — or the Tigers — was all about. Sure, he had read the newspapers and watched the TV news from his home in Chicago, but he'd never paid close attention to the details. To the twenty-two-year-old medic, it was still a war of patriotism that was merely a continuation of World War II and victories over the Nazis and Japanese. Another evil force needed to be stopped, and America was going to do it.

But it was one thing to be sitting at the dinner table with families in small towns talking about a distant war. Standing in the circle that day, Bowman realized for the first time that he would be going on reconnaissance missions — and he might not come back.

Before the briefing, the newcomers were told the Tigers would be joining the rest of the battalion to "clear the land" and to "take the fight to the VC." If the U.S. Army was going to win the war, the briefing sergeant said, it was crucial to secure Quang Ngai. "This is going to be your job to go out there and take it back." Like a football coach, he paced back and forth, repeating the phrase "We're going to take the fight to the enemy."

Nothing more detailed was specified, and the briefing sergeant wasn't much help: "You're going to be going into a place where no Americans have ever been," he said. "This ain't Saigon. They're not going to welcome you with open arms." That was a bit of an understatement.

Just as the sergeant began to unfurl a large map showing the grid coordinates of the province, two officers interrupted, announcing that the commander had arrived. The veterans looked at one another, puzzled, but everyone quickly jumped to attention, and the group was joined by scores of other soldiers. It was not, as had been expected, Battalion Commander Lieutenant Colonel Harold Austin but rather the commander of all U.S. forces in Vietnam, General William Westmoreland. Dressed in his familiar starched fatigues, Westmoreland walked briskly to the head of the formation and turned toward the men. The lean, steely eyed general was known for showing up unexpectedly in the field, most of the time to deliver pep talks. This was a visit he had been eager to make. These were the soldiers from what he referred to as his "fire brigade," and he made no bones about his affection for the unit, which he considered a crucial part of the 101st Airborne. Westmoreland had been the commander of the 101st from 1958 to 1960 and kept close ties with the commanders. Now, his eyes moving along the front row of soldiers, the four-star general reminded the men that he was counting on them. "You are here for a reason," he said, "and I can't stress that enough." Along with soldiers from the 196th Light Infantry Brigade and the 25th Infantry Division, the 1st Brigade would be part of what was known as Task Force Oregon, created in February 1967 to take complete control of the area. In all, there were twenty thousand troops.

The general was well aware that the Central Highlands, stretching from the Laotian border eastward to the South China Sea, had been a contentious area since the French occupation. To Westmoreland, it was a key geographic area. The Buddhist farmers who occupied the mountainous region had always felt they were neglected by South Vietnamese leaders, and now with the American invasion, they felt threatened. They were stubborn and independent and had no more allegiance to Saigon than Hanoi.

Westmoreland and others at the Military Assistance Command in Vietnam (MACV), including General William Rosson, feared that the guerrillas would set up an armed line from Laos to the sea, cutting South Vietnam in half. If that occurred, they believed, Americans would not be able to move supplies to troops in the demilitarized zone — the area that divided South and North Vietnam. Westmoreland argued that in order to control the Central Highlands, especially Quang Ngai, thousands of civilians needed to be moved to relocation centers so they wouldn't support the enemy. For the last two years, the U.S. military and South Vietnamese government had been setting up temporary camps throughout the province, but, as the Marines had learned, forced relocation was not an easy or popular policy to implement. Earlier that year, the Marines had been assigned to herd 300,000 people from the province to relocation camps — about half the province's population — and soon discovered that people would only leave kicking and screaming. Protests erupted, and many, forced from their homes, escaped the camps. Not surprisingly, the Vietcong was gaining support among the people and had already set up a network of clandestine routes that allowed the North Vietnamese Army to carry guns and ammunition to the area to battle U.S. troops.

One of the Tigers, Douglas Teeters, tensed up as the general brushed by him, pacing. For years Teeters had heard about the man who was handpicked by President Lyndon Johnson to run the war, but now here he was in the flesh. Teeters wanted to turn and look at the most powerful military leader in South Vietnam but was afraid to move a muscle. So he stared ahead, rigid as bone, and listened as the commander shouted to the men from just a few feet away.

Westmoreland warned them their toughest days were still ahead. They were to look for the enemy and destroy everything in their path. "Wear down the enemy," he ordered. "They will surrender."

Before the general left, he described a color code to help the soldiers on patrol identify the people of Quang Ngai. "If the people are in relocation camps, they're green, so they're safe," he explained. "We leave them alone. The Vietcong and NVA are red, so we know they're fair game. But if there are people who are out there — and not in the camps — they're pink as far as we're concerned. They're Communist sympathizers. They were not supposed to be there."

The men listened.

Private Terrence Kerrigan tossed in his sleeping bag. It wasn't the heat or the mosquitoes buzzing in his ears that kept him up. He was just hours away from his first reconnaissance mission — and the rush of adrenaline was already starting. No sense in even trying to sleep.

It was the same feeling the surfer had before sunrise on those glorious mornings in Southern California when the twelve-foot waves were breaking. You couldn't quite explain it. It was a feeling of exhilaration and fear — riding a wave but knowing you could wipe out at any moment and get sucked into the powerful vortex. You might pop back up or you might never come out from under.

Ever since arriving at Carentan a week earlier, the lanky six-footer with short brown hair and green eyes had been pacing, waiting. Sometimes he would trek to the closest foothills and stare in the distance, knowing the enemy, too, was waiting.

When he enlisted in 1966, Kerrigan had known this moment might come. He just didn't know he would be so scared. The recruiters hadn't told him about going to South Vietnam when he joined. Instead, they said he could end up in West Germany and, by serving for a few years, could go to college on the GI Bill. His mother, Joan, a single mom raising Kerrigan and his brother, Keith, on a bookkeeper's salary, told him he was giving up his freedom. He was only nineteen — a year out of San Gabriel High School.

"You're not going to be going to the beach on weekends,"

she pleaded with him. "I don't want you to go." But while Kerrigan relished his weekends on Redondo Beach, he knew his mother struggled to support her two boys. On the beach, everyone was equal. They shared their surfboards, towels, and sometimes their girlfriends. But away from the surf, there were two worlds in his hometown of San Gabriel and everyone knew it: the rich kids and the ones who mightily struggled to keep afloat. There were those who tooled around in shiny Alfa Romeos and those who drove beat-up Impalas. Kerrigan was in the latter group, and very conscious of it. He never shared his secret, but he loathed being on the outside and hated that his mother had to work so hard. He told his friends the only way he was ever going to get into one of those Mediterranean-revival homes that sat behind wrought-iron gates was to go to law school, and the only way to pay for it was to join the Army.

Several friends begged him to reconsider. He wasn't a soldier. He was a beach kid whose favorite song was "I Get Around" and who never talked about fighting. You ride the wave given you and you paddle in.

Once he learned he was being sent to South Vietnam, he made up his mind he was going to serve his tour, come back home, go to college — UCLA — and then attend law school. Now, sitting in his tent, he wondered whether he made the right decision. Once in country, Terrence had tried to tell himself that South Vietnam wasn't such a bad place. It reminded him a little of San Gabriel: the palm trees, the ocean just miles away — and the sun, the endless, glaring sun. He even nervously joked with another soldier about surfing the South China Sea. He tried to convince himself the villagers near the base seemed harmless, and he would walk to the edge of the base to toss tubes of Life Savers to the kids. He didn't think about dying.

Kerrigan wasn't the only restless soldier. A light was still on in Sergeant Manuel Sanchez Jr.'s tent. The twenty-one-year-old had spent the last hour packing his gear: three canteens of water, a bag of rice, eight cans of C rations, two rolls of toilet paper, a tube of insect repellent, malaria tablets, a poncho, a toothbrush, and several hundred rounds of ammo for his M16.

While growing up on a farm in Roswell, New Mexico, "Junior," as he was called, learned to be prepared. He never knew when his father was going to roust him from sleep to go into the fields. If he didn't bring enough water and clothes, he was stuck — once in the fields, you didn't go home until the work was done.

Raised with seven siblings, Junior and everyone else in the Sanchez home pitched in. But he was the oldest male in a traditional Mexican-American family, so the burden seemed to fall on him. His father would look sternly into his son's deep brown eyes and tell him, "Look out for your younger brothers and sisters. You're the oldest." And the old man meant it. If the younger kids couldn't get out in the fields to work, Junior had to carry their load.

During the week, the children went to school and worked the farm, but on weekends, the family hosted barbecues with cousins, aunts, and uncles at nearby Lake Van. There, Junior and his father would break out their guitars and serenade the entire countryside with Tejano music.

Sanchez was now sitting up, writing another letter to his sixteen-year-old girlfriend. He hated being away from Mary Delfina, but he knew this wasn't going to last forever. The Army would win the war. It was just a matter of time.

He was now, he wrote Delfina, in a new province and didn't know what to expect or when the operations would end. He asked her to be patient, promising that someday they would be married. Sanchez told Mary he might not be able to write anytime soon, since it was difficult to send letters from the field. Then he ended the letter like the others: "I love you."

Two tents away, Bill Carpenter had turned off his light. In five months, he had learned not to think about the next day, only the moment. That was the way to survive.

It took him a while to stop dwelling on his roots in the rolling hills of southeastern Ohio, with its steel mills belching smoke into the pale winter sky. That was in the past, and he knew it didn't do any good to get homesick. To a gangly country boy who had rarely ventured far from home, South Vietnam was an exotic world he had glimpsed only in movies and magazines. The unrelenting heat and rain and palm trees and wild monkeys and strange-looking people burning incense by the roadside — it was a long, long way from the Buckeye State.

A bit of a braggart, Carpenter would never admit he was awestruck by his new surroundings. He had joined the Tigers by convincing the screening officers he could be a real killer, but the reality was that he was frightened by this new place. And no matter how long he stayed in South Vietnam, he would never quite understand the people and culture. Carpenter's home was a microcosm of small-town Ohio, where life centered around football, Grandma's farm, and openings at the steel mills. Hunting was a way of life and everyone dreamed of bagging a five-point deer with antlers the size of chandeliers. There were no Buddhists or Vietnamese in Jefferson County.

Bill had played football on his high school team, boasting he was good enough to play for Woody Hayes. But the six-foot, one-inch 165-pounder was never offered a scholarship to play for Ohio State, so after graduating from high school in 1965, he joined his father in the railroad yards. Carpenter soon grew bored. Despite his own provincialism, he knew there was another world beyond southern Ohio. His big brother, Tom, had enlisted a year earlier in the Army and was now in South Vietnam, and Bill wanted to join him in this new adventure. "I'm going to Vietnam," he would boast to his friends. And so he did.

He found out after he arrived in December 1966 that he couldn't hook up with his brother's unit because of a rule banning siblings from serving together. But Bill found something better: the Tigers. He heard stories about the reconnaissance unit. "They had the reputation for being elite," he recalled. If you wanted to rule the jungle, Tiger Force was your crew.

In another tent, most of the medics were sleeping, but Douglas Teeters stared into the darkness. Just hours earlier, he had passed around a joint with others while listening to the album *The Doors* on a battery-powered turntable one of the medics had brought back from Hong Kong. The haunting strains of "Light My Fire" kept playing in his mind as he tossed and turned, unable to forget that he would soon be jumping onto a chopper.

To pass the time, he got up and packed and repacked his medical kit. He had more than enough bandages, syringes, scissors, and antidiarrheals. There was something else, too. Teeters had been in combat — two months with Company B, treating soldiers with their limbs blown off and, in some cases, watching them die. It was so hard for him to forget the faces of men begging him to make the pain go away. The only thing he could do was shoot them up with morphine. Restocking his kit, he made certain there was sufficient liquid morphine; he had a dreadful feeling about Quang Ngai that perhaps no amount of pain killer would be enough. Returning to his sleeping bag, Teeters tried once again to sleep.

CHAPTER 3

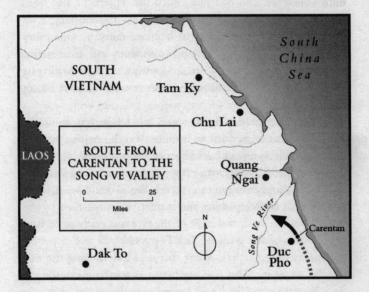

South
China
Sea

SOUTH
VIETNAM

Tam Ky

Chu Lai

LAOS

ROUTE FROM
CARENTAN TO THE
SONG VE VALLEY

0   25

Miles

Quang
Ngai

N

Carentan

Dak To

Duc
Pho

red sun rose over the South China Sea as helicopters departed the base camp carrying the newest "class" of Tiger Force. Three Hueys, each carrying men, circled Carentan and veered west, soaring over endless foothills that seemed to rise higher as the aircraft flew farther away from the coast. From the air, everything seemed blanketed by trees, a great green expanse that faded gradually only where it scaled the slopes of the oncoming mountains. After they passed over the first row of peaks, the land suddenly opened — and in the distance was a wide valley with lush green rice paddies cut by waterways glistening in the sun.

From his seat near the open doorway, Donald Wood scanned the scene below: farmers toiling in a field, their conical hats protecting them from the rays. Water buffalo herded along a dike leading to the riverbank, where children splashed in the water.

Wood knew all about the Song Ve Valley. As a forward artillery observer who had just joined the Tigers, he had been studying maps of the four-mile-wide-by-six-mile-long river basin for days. His job was to become familiar with every crevice of the valley so he could confidently call in air strikes when the platoon located Vietcong positions. If he made one mistake — one miscalculation — fellow soldiers could be hit by friendly fire.

A remote, timeless basin some ten kilometers from the coast, the Song Ve had always been low on the Army's priority list of trouble spots, but intelligence reports were starting to show that the Vietcong were extorting rice from Song Ve farmers. As his chopper began to descend, Wood could see that the wide stretch of rice paddies and hamlets was unscathed by the war. It was late June, and most of the rice was ready to be harvested. One of the goals of Task Force Oregon was to cut off the enemy's food supply, and if that meant destroying the rice paddies, so be it. "This is as important as anything else we can do," Westmoreland had said several months earlier during a planning session at the MACV.

That point had been driven home during yesterday's briefing. Even before the choppers departed the base camp that morning, Lieutenant Colonel Harold Austin had stressed to his men the goal of the Song Ve campaign. "The farming needs to stop. The VC are moving the rice on sampans along the river to enemy camps," he said. But the Tigers had no clue just how much farming they needed to stop until they saw the expanse of green rice paddies on the valley floor. It was like trying to count the stars in the night sky.

Thus, in order to curtail the harvest, they would have to take drastic measures. That meant clearing the entire valley and moving everyone out — all seven thousand inhabitants in seven known villages. In South Vietnam, there were several definitions for populated areas. But in general, a village was larger than a hamlet and, in many cases, plotted on government maps. Scattered throughout the Song Ve were hamlets, some with just four or five huts.

Colonel Austin declared that the battalion's three line companies, known as A, B, and C, would move the people and their livestock to the Nghia Hanh relocation center just west of the valley, while the Tigers would break into small teams and look for Vietcong and rice caches.

As Wood's chopper landed in a rice paddy, he watched as several farmers leaned over their plows in a nearby field, barely looking up. This had been their land for generations, and Wood wasn't expecting an easy campaign, no matter how many pep talks the men got. The twenty-two-year-old officer was one of the few Tigers who had studied the Vietnamese culture — both in Officer Candidate School at Fort Sill, Oklahoma, and later on his own. During his first two weeks at the base camp, he had talked to South Vietnamese translators about the people of the Song Ve. Most of the inhabitants were Buddhist farmers whose families had grown rice in the valley for hundreds of years. Wood and other battalion officers had been told in briefings that the province had always been difficult to control for the South Vietnamese government, partly because the people were fiercely independent. Some of the village elders were active in what was known as the Struggle Movement — an active campaign to bring peace to North and South Vietnam. Wood was told the people of the valley were pacifists and had tried to remain independent in the war, but it was getting more difficult. The VC had been trying to recruit, touting a fairer distribution of land ownership, while the government of South Vietnam had done very little to win any sort of support. That lack of effort was all the more telling since the people of the Song Ve had a grim recent history with the South Vietnamese. During a program launched by the government in 1958 to move rural people into "strategic hamlets," the occupants of the Song Ve refused to move, and eventually the program was scuttled, though not before the South Vietnamese government killed some of the villagers.

When the United States began sending fighting units to South Vietnam in 1965, parts of the strategic hamlet program were resurrected. Under the new plan, the peasants would no longer have a choice: To keep them from joining the Vietcong, they would be forced to live in relocation camps. Instead of growing their own rice, the government would feed them. In order to notify the people about the new program, the U.S. military came up with a system of dropping leaflets from aircraft, ordering locals to leave and promising food and shelter at the camps. This was very similar to a leaflet program, known as "Chieu Hoi," that was offered to enemy combatants, but this one specifically targeted civilians, with millions dropped in various provinces.

As a team of four soldiers gathered around Wood in the paddy, they looked up and watched as a chopper broke through the morning fog, the first wave of leaflets fluttering downward. Other choppers began circling the valley, releasing trails of paper. Over the next few minutes, the leaflets began covering the hamlets like freshly fallen snow.

Wood and four soldiers headed for the south side of the valley to set up a command post, while three other teams began moving in different directions for their first patrol.

As Wood and the men reached a row of huts, shots were fired in their direction. The soldiers quickly scrambled for cover, but no one knew where the snipers were hiding. Wood radioed the platoon commander, Lieutenant Stephen Naughton, to let him know his position. The firing ceased, but it was clear the Vietcong had been watching the Tigers since they arrived in the valley. For more than a dozen rookie Tigers, it was the first time they had ever been shot at.

Suddenly Ybarra began talking about opening fire if they found any civilians in the huts. Wood jumped in. "No one is going to fire on anybody who's not armed," he said. Wood knew what it was like to go into combat, the sickening feeling in the stomach and the inability to stop shaking even when your hands were wrapped around an M16. But he had also learned from his Special Forces training that you had to stay in control. You had to know when to fire and when to hold back. It could make the difference between killing an enemy soldier or an unarmed villager.

When Wood had arrived in Vietnam, he had spent several months in the 1st Battalion/320th Field Artillery learning that firefights almost always begin without warning and that many times, there's no time to call in the supportive air strikes. "You got to keep moving" were the words he remembered most from Special Forces. That is, don't panic, don't be stupid, and finish the job on your own. Air strikes were icing.

For newcomers such as Barry Bowman, just talking about killing unarmed villagers made him nervous. Like most of the soldiers who served in Vietnam, he had received less than two hours of instruction on the Army's rules of engagement and the 1949 Geneva conventions, which prohibited the inhumane treatment of civilians and prisoners — a crash course on the rules of war. The Tigers were handed cards when they arrived in Vietnam defining eighteen war crimes, but no one ever talked about them and it wasn't clear if the cards had ever been read.

Bowman knew that if you saw a war crime, you were supposed to immediately report it to commanders. "I just hoped I wouldn't have to," he recalled. But if you weren't sure what constituted a war crime, how would you know what to report?

To stay safe, the team took cover and waited to ensure the snipers left. As they hid in the brush, Wood and others watched as several Vietnamese villagers, mostly old men and women, emerged from their huts. One by one, the people reached down and began examining the papers on the ground. More generic leaflets had been dropped all over the province for weeks, but the instructions on these papers were specific. By June 21, the people would have to evacuate the valley for a relocation camp. That meant they had to leave in two days. The leaflets' message was clear: "At Nghia Hanh you will be safe. There will be shelter for you and your family. Those of you who choose to remain in the area will be considered hostile and in danger."

Satisfied that the Vietcong snipers had given up, the men prepared to move on. Terrence Kerrigan looked toward the village but wasn't really paying attention. His hands were still shaking, and he was barely able to hold his rifle. In the first two weeks of June, the Tigers had spent most of their time guarding combat engineers repairing sections of Highway One, the national roadway that ran along the coast of South Vietnam. Occasionally they would hear a few stray shots but saw no major combat. The whole thing felt a bit like a game. The free-spirited Californian tried to calm himself, but he was overcome with a sense of foreboding. He looked around to see if anyone was looking at him, but they were walking toward the village. They were going in, and Kerrigan had no choice but to follow.

By late afternoon, more Hueys began arriving and dropping soldiers from the battalion line companies on opposite sides of the Song Ve River, the main waterway that cuts through the heart of the valley. Their job was to fan out across the basin and visit the seven villages in the company of translators who were to tell the locals they had to leave.

When some of the soldiers from C Company entered the Hanh Tin hamlet, they met two elders who immediately told them the people didn't want to move to a relocation camp. "This is our land," said one of the villagers. A translator with the soldiers angrily told the elders they didn't have a choice:

They had to evacuate or they would be considered the enemy. They would be safe if they went to the camp. Their wives and children would be cared for. If the men were of military age, sixteen through fifty-five, they would probably be drafted into the Army of the Republic of Vietnam to fight the Vietcong.

Lu Thuan was saddened as he watched the soldiers. For the first time, the war was coming to the Song Ve, something he had dreaded for two years. He had seen the men from the 101st Airborne — known as "chicken soldiers" because of the eagle patches on their sleeves — in other areas of Quang Ngai, but somehow he had hoped they would bypass his valley.

The thirty-one-year-old farmer knew that with the arrival of the American soldiers, it was just a matter of time before he and the others would get caught in the middle. A devout Buddhist who traveled every month to the pagodas — a house of worship — he had heard stories from the people along the coast who were forced to flee and the chaos and death that came with it. The VC would fire on the Americans, and the Americans would eventually retaliate by flying in planes with bombs. The valley — his valley, his home, his land, his wife, his children — none of it was safe any longer.

After one night in the field, planning, the Tiger teams had mapped out their patrol areas. The valley was divided into four quadrants — north, south, east, and west — with each team responsible for hunting Vietcong positions and rice caches in their own sections and, unless ordered, staying clear of the line companies.

Sergeant Sanchez insisted on teaching his team members a few tips about patrols — the same rules he learned when he joined the Tigers. As his soldiers passed through brush on the way to the west quadrant, he watched as Kerrigan moved toward two mangroves.

"Quick, stop," Sanchez said. Kerrigan looked at his team leader and froze.

Sanchez, motioning with his hand for the other five soldiers to follow, walked toward Kerrigan. As they circled the soldier, Sanchez pointed toward the two trees, located parallel to each other, two meters apart. "What do you see there?" he asked the men.

Sergeant Ervin Lee waited for someone else to answer, but everyone was silent, so he piped in. "It's a good place to put a trip wire," he answered.

Sanchez asked Lee to repeat what he just said to make sure everyone heard.

"Trip wire," Lee said.

Sanchez nodded. "There's nothing there now, but when you see two trees within a short distance of one another, don't walk between them. It's a perfect place to string a wire at foot level that can set off an explosive."

Over the next hour, Sanchez passed on more rules, knowing the soldiers had already been briefed about these safety measures but also knowing that even good soldiers sometimes forget the most basic instructions, even those that could make a difference between life and death. He told them not to smoke on patrol; the flash of a lighter or wisp of smoke was enough to give away a soldier's position. And then there was the rule about going to the bathroom: make sure you dig a hole to cover your excrement. "Your shit leaves a trail," Sanchez said.

Sanchez also told them about water. In the heat, a soldier could easily go through four canteens in twenty-four hours. If they happened to run out of water while on patrol, they should look for clusters of bamboo; there was a good chance a spring was nearby. As far as sleeping, he told them to use their poncho liners for sleeping bags. It would keep them dry and help protect them from spiders and other bugs.

Though he spoke of insects and arachnids in a cavalier manner, the same was not true for all creatures of the Vietnamese terrain. Sanchez was a stickler about one thing: leeches. "Check your bodies every few hours," he told the men. "They can latch onto you without you even knowing."

Five kilometers away, in the far west quadrant, Wood and his team came upon a thicket of bamboo. He stopped the men — mostly newcomers — and reached down to separate a single stalk from the others. "You see this?" he asked. "This is bamboo. It's more dangerous than a rifle."

The newcomers seemed puzzled. Wood explained that the VC cut a piece about a foot long and then sharpen one end, mash feces in the hollow opening, and insert the other end in the ground.

"The VC want you to step on this," Wood said. "It's a booby trap. And when it penetrates your boot, you will get an infection — count on it."

His team moved beyond the thicket and reached a rice paddy, when the soldiers spotted a thatched hut in the distance. Such huts were usually used to store rice, plows, and other tools, but as the Tigers moved closer, a man jumped out and, to the surprise of the soldiers, fired an AK–47.

The Tigers dropped to the ground as the man dashed back into the hut. Without hesitation, they opened fire with their M16s, blowing the hut to pieces. It was the first time outside of training that some of the soldiers had ever fired their M16s, and they weren't sure when to stop. After several minutes, they rose in unison and inched their way to what remained of the hooch. When they looked inside, they saw not only the dead man, his rifle laying across his torso, but a woman and baby whose bodies had been ripped apart by the barrage.

The deaths were unavoidable — no one had known the mother and child were inside — but Wood was clearly upset. He turned from the rest of his men and walked away. Bill Carpenter quickly approached his lieutenant and tried to console him, but Wood brushed him aside. He was the team leader and was ultimately responsible. And, of course, he had fired his M16 just like everyone else. Indeed, it may have even been his own bullet that ended the baby's life.

Though he had been in skirmishes with the enemy, this was the first time Wood had seen a child killed in a firefight. But as an officer, he had to remain in control of his emotions. There were too many newcomers, and he knew they would be looking to him for guidance. If he showed any signs of weakness, he could lose their confidence. And this was no place to let that happen. No doubt, they were going to run into more ambushes.

"Just forget it," he told Carpenter. "It's over. I just want to forget it." But for the next several hours, he was quiet. He couldn't shake the images. And there was no way he would ever tell his family what happened. They wouldn't understand. How could they? Their lives revolved around church, Friday night football games, and fish fries in the small town of Fridley, Minnesota. It suddenly seemed so long ago when he packed his bags on a bone-chilling January morning in 1965 and drove to the bus station to report for duty. He had been on the move ever since: Fort Leonard Wood, Missouri; Fort Benning, Georgia; Fort Bragg, North Carolina; Fort Sill, Oklahoma.

For most of his life, Donald Wood had been on the move.

His father, a Whirlpool engineer, was always being transferred. By the time Donald was eleven, he had lived in three cities, and each time it became harder to adjust. He and his twin sister, Helen, and younger brother, Jim, had to make new friends and attend new schools. Finally, in Fridley, he found a home. In high school, he had developed a close group of friends and even stayed in contact with them through letters after joining the Army. But he couldn't even tell them what happened. War was a series of brutal honesties that fostered a clot of terrible secrets. So it had long been, and so it would be.

That night, the Tigers regrouped near a bend in the river and set up camp. While one of the Tiger Force teams patrolled the perimeter of the area, the rest of the soldiers stretched out along the bank, some finally getting a chance to empty their bowels. Wood kept to himself, while some of the others began to open the mail that had been delivered earlier in the day by supply choppers. For several minutes, the men were quiet as they began reading their correspondence, and then suddenly one Tiger began reading a portion of his letter aloud. When he stopped, another followed, and then another. The men took turns reading letters aloud — some from girlfriends, others from parents and siblings.

Barry Bowman thought it remarkable that the Tigers — many of whom had only known one another for days — were sharing intimate details of their lives. "We read them and shared everything in them with our comrades as a way of coping with the danger we were in," he recalled. In these pauses, moments disorienting with a sense of frontier and temporary relief, the men could let down their guard. They were still tethered to their old lives via each letter read. But soon that tether would break.

CHAPTER 4

The sun was just rising as a steady stream of men, women, and children began walking down a slope toward the Song Ve River. On both sides of the trail were soldiers, making sure no one tried to run.

From a foothill, Don Wood peered through binoculars as the evacuation of the valley began. The ground was soaked from an early rain, the drops sparkling like jewels on the tall strands of grass. From the ground, the valley was as peaceful as anything he had seen in South Vietnam: coconut and banana trees, and clusters of thick mangroves. The elephant grass blanketing the basin was a kaleidoscope of greens — a bright spring color on the tops of the foothills and growing darker along the slopes until it became a dark olive along the river. Wood was struck by how beautiful it was — not just to the eye but to the ear. The sounds of songbirds filled the air.

While the scene was tranquil, the temperature was rising. Though it was early, Wood's shirt was already soaked from the heat and humidity — a virtual steam room that was relentless.

It was the beginning of the monsoon season, which would mean rain — lots of it — nearly every day. The mud along the river was now dry, but by afternoon, it would be thick and deep. Not even the villagers would walk through the muck, preferring instead to walk on the grass.

As a soldier, Wood knew the locals had to be moved and, in the end, believed they would be safer in Nghia Hanh than the valley. But he was disturbed at the sight of the people leaving their huts. This was their home. As Buddhists, they believed their connections to the land and their ancestors would be irrevocably shattered. Wood wondered whether they would ever return to the valley.

Other Tigers didn't share his concerns. For the past two days, Sam Ybarra, Ken Green, James Barnett, and William Doyle had been grousing that the evacuation was a waste of time. These Vietnamese were no better than the Vietcong, they said. They were all gooks, and none of them could be trusted.

Wood tried to ignore them. He knew the difference between villagers and the Vietcong, and refused to buy into the grunt talk about every Vietnamese being an enemy. He understood why some of the soldiers bitterly hated the Vietnamese. From the time they were in boot camp to their arrival in South Vietnam, the soldiers were told the native people were despicable. Sometimes it was subtle — "They don't grieve for their dead the way we do." Other times, overt — "They're not human." Drill sergeants and even officers used a litany of slurs to describe the people of Vietnam: gooks, dinks, and slant eyes. Boot camp even included an exercise in which soldiers carrying rifles with bayonets would charge targets and, with every thrust of the blade, scream the word "gook."

Unbeknownst to many soldiers — but not to Wood — the Army had been carrying out a subtle but powerful indoctrination program that was insidiously dehumanizing the enemy, stripping them of any human qualities, and thus making it easier for soldiers to kill them. In warfare, that's not unusual, but in

Vietnam, it had been a growing problem. Not all soldiers had been attempting to distinguish between Vietnamese combatants and noncombatants. "They all look alike," as the saying goes.

Wood watched as South Vietnamese soldiers carrying clipboards went to each evacuee, writing down his or her name. Some of the adults carried burlap bags stuffed with rice and clothes. Others balanced shoulder bars with buckets at each end filled with rice. They had taken everything they could from their huts.

As they reached the front of the line, the villagers were handed two slips of paper: a temporary relief payment for food, which equaled about eight cents a day, and a resettlement assistance voucher that guaranteed shelter. After each interview, they were moved single file to a larger clearing, where they gathered in groups, waiting for the soldiers to usher them aboard CH-47 helicopters, twenty-five in each chopper.

By the time the second village was emptied, with more than one hundred people now gathered near the processing tent, another phase of the evacuation had begun. At the far northeast corner of the valley, large groups of livestock — water buffalo and cattle — were being led from holding areas surrounded by poles and barbed wire. In a scene reminiscent of a cattle drive from the Old West, the animals were herded down a foothill and through a gap toward a dirt road that eventually led to the relocation center.

Other Tigers gathered on the foothill, chuckling at the scene below, some yelling, "Giddyup!" to the battalion soldiers passing by. To Carpenter, it was comic relief in what had been a tense three days. But to Wood, it was another reason for the Vietnamese to resent the soldiers. This was not a moment to be seen laughing.

Wood peered through his binoculars as the first helicopter took off, and within minutes, another CH-47 landed to pick up the next group. He had been told in Officer Candidate School that the Army was going to win the war by gaining the support of the peasants — to "win the hearts and minds" of the people under a policy touted by President Lyndon Johnson. But that meant treating them fairly and with decency. Wood didn't come to Vietnam to be a social worker, but he didn't come to watch peasants be belittled, either. It struck him as wrong — and against everything he was ever taught. Though he was expected to show disdain toward the people, it was just too hard for him to play that role. Maybe he was just too idealistic. Maybe he expected too much.

Just a few years earlier, he had toyed with the idea of joining the Peace Corps — swept up by the enthusiasm of a young Catholic president and an idealistic message of volunteerism. Wood wanted to go to Africa to set up schools, but here he was, in another third-world nation, with bullets instead of books.

As a youngster, Wood had relished his role as an altar boy in a town where there were few Catholics. Masses were celebrated in the middle of the Fridley High School gymnasium — with Wood serving as an altar boy. He would arrive early on Sundays to set up the altar and folding chairs and stay after services to put everything back in storage.

He continued going to Mass in high school, but he also began drinking, at first with friends after football games, and later, alone. A wild streak started to show his sophomore year, when he would jump into his Volkswagen Beetle and race through speed traps.

He went on to St. Thomas Aquinas College in Saint Paul but dropped out after one semester. To keep from disappointing his father, a Navy veteran of World War II and Korea, Wood volunteered for the 101st Airborne. "He wanted to make us proud," recalls his brother, Jim. The new enlistee invited his family to spend their vacations near his training bases at Fort Bragg and later Fort Sill. "We all came. We were excited about seeing him," says Jim. "He even worked it out so that I could spend a weekend with him in his barracks."

Wood wasn't the only one who had serious questions about what he was witnessing. Douglas Teeters, the Tiger Force medic, had been watching the villagers' reaction to the American presence and realized there was no way the Army was going to win their support, "not after the way we were treating their brothers and sisters and mothers and fathers," he recalled. A month earlier in Duc Pho, the medic watched as several soldiers from B Company surrounded an old man who was selling trinkets from a roadside stand, picked him up, and carried him to the side of a creek before tossing him in the water. He remembered the soldiers laughing as the man splashed around frantically. Teeters had been angry, but he didn't say anything. He didn't want the soldiers to know he felt any empathy for the old man. But he was bothered by the image of the man's children crying as they rushed to his side. Now, as he watched the evacuation of the Song Ve, he noticed tears running down the face of a child.

That same day, the Army issued a press release about the cattle drive, calling it Operation Rawhide:

> More than five thousand residents of the Song Ve Valley west of here
> regained their identity with the Republic of Vietnam government as
> Vietnamese and American military units concluded the largest civil affairs
> operation ever launched in the Quang Ngai province. As the villagers were
> evacuated, the joint military force collected cattle and livestock, initiating
> the second phase of the operation by driving the herd to Nghia Hanh.
> While helicopters whisked the villagers to Nghia Hanh, paratroopers began
> the cattle drive. They dubbed the overland route "The Chisholm Trail,"
> and cries of "Head 'em up; move 'em out" echoed throughout the valley.
> The Vietnamese forces sang folk tunes; the paratroopers replied with
> Western tunes.

By the time the sun was setting over the valley, only a few villagers were still milling around the clearing area. From the foothills, Lu Thuan watched sadly. No longer would he venture into the rice paddies to work, or watch his children play on the backs of water buffalo. From a crevice in the rocks, he had spent most of the day watching the people leave. Two days earlier, he said good-bye to his wife and two children, and fled with other men to the first mountain ridge west of the river.

Since they were all of military age, had they gone to Nghia Hanh, they would be forced to serve in the South Vietnamese Army.

As Lu watched, he wondered when he would ever see his family again, and how long he and others could survive in the Annamese Cordillera Mountains. It was just a matter of time before the Vietcong would return and fight for control of what was one of the most productive rice-growing valleys in the Central Highlands.

The following day, three Hueys swooped over the river basin to look for signs of life. No one was in the rice paddies in the Song Ve, and no one was along the river, but the pilots were surprised to see people walking openly along the trails leading to the Hanh Tin hamlet in the center of the valley, some carrying wood and buckets of water.

Immediately, the lead chopper radioed headquarters: *You got people crawling all over the place.* "I thought you cleared the hooches," the pilot said. Clearly the Army had missed scores of villagers who had successfully hidden from the American patrols.

At Carentan, Harold Austin, the lean, bespectacled lieutenant colonel who had assumed command of the battalion on June 10, was pacing as he talked on the radio. He didn't know what happened, he said, but would call his acting Tiger commander, Lieutenant Naughton, to find out.

Within minutes, he was on the phone with Naughton, who was with his own team in the valley. "No one is supposed to be there," he barked. General Westmoreland had made it clear: no more farming in the Central Highlands. "Get those people out of there," said Austin.

A former battalion executive officer who rarely left command headquarters, Austin didn't like the Tigers and made no bones about it. He didn't like their dress code and the fact that some platoon members didn't salute him. He was a by-the-book, starched-shirt officer who had just taken over for Lieutenant Colonel Joseph Collins, a gung ho soldier who often jumped into his helicopter to fly over troops in the middle of fire-fights. That chopper had been struck by enemy fire while hovering over the men during a skirmish on April 20, 1967, but the very next day, Collins was back in the air. "He's nuts," said a battalion officer. Collins had made his mark and was promoted to full colonel.

In Vietnam, commanding a battle unit was the way to move up the food chain. Austin was a soldier of a different color. The Colorado native had spent time at the Pentagon and arrived in Vietnam in August 1966 as an intelligence officer training advisers. He was about brains over brawn. But as much as Austin didn't like the Tigers, he knew he needed a small unit that could sneak into the villages to find the people and enforce the Army's orders.

He had taken the time to know the Tigers by interviewing each one before sending him into the Song Ve. Yet he couldn't control them, not like the line soldiers. The Tigers lived by their own rules. That's the way it had been since Hackworth had put the unit together. "I want forty swinging dicks," he once told a reporter. The less bureaucracy, the better. When you're sneaking up on a VC encampment, you're not supposed to radio the battalion commander for permission to piss.

As a result, the Tigers took orders from their lieutenant or team leaders. The only officer in the rear who had contact with the Tigers was the headquarter company commander, Captain Carl James, the designated point man for the battalion commander. It was a very weak link, which is just how Hackworth, now assigned to the Pentagon, had intended. Shortly after Tiger Force was created in 1965, some officers at the MACV argued that Special Force's units like the Tigers could be trouble. They worried that these kinds of units could get carried away and take the war into their own hands. But Westmoreland had insisted such autonomous units were needed in a guerrilla war, and that was the end of the debate.

Nevertheless, Austin was determined to keep tabs on the Tigers. He would meet with battalion officers every morning to talk about strategies and review intelligence reports on NVA and VC movements in the operations area, which covered the Song Ve and other trouble spots in Quang Ngai province. He would always ask the whereabouts of the fighting units, especially the Tigers, and would then draw up plans and relay orders to the units in the field. If possible, the Tigers would receive the orders, but most of the time they were out of contact with the rear. And in any case, they weren't necessarily going to listen even if they did hear the message.

Austin was required to report to officers from the MACV overseeing Task Force Oregon — the overall campaign to win the Central Highlands. As he received calls from the MACV about the Song Ve evacuation, he said the operation was moving smoothly. On June 22, he was proud to announce that the valley was cleared.

"Good job" was the curt response on the other line.

But the mission was far from over.

CHAPTER 5

Lieutenant Stephen Naughton broke the bad news to the Tigers: instead of hopping on choppers for the ride back to Carentan, the platoon would stay in the valley. It was typical Army — after all the press releases and planning and the maneuvers to clear the valley, the villagers had returned. The whole thing felt like pushing waves back into the ocean.

Some of the men grumbled, a few angrily and dramatically tossing down their rucksacks. Such open displays of discontent weren't found in just Tiger Force. By the summer of 1967, American troops across Vietnam were periodically questioning orders in the field. There was already plenty of racial unrest in combat units, a reflection of the social discord back home. But there was also mounting frustration with tactics and leadership. Troops would fight for a hill, give up numerous soldiers to casualties, and then, after winning the battle, move on — leaving the hill to the enemy. A week later, the troops would return and fight over the same hill. This kind of strategy wasn't lost on the grunts, who were bearing the burdens of battle, and throughout the Army, they were starting to speak up.

In the end, the strategy had a deep impact on the troops. Psychologically, soldiers risking their lives in firefights need to see some tangible form of victory, some evidence that what they are doing is making a difference in the war. Winning control of a village or a piece of land — and securing it. The Marines raising the flag at Iwo Jima became a powerful symbol of victory during World War II. The South Pacific island was won, boosting the morale of U.S. troops and Americans at home. But in South Vietnam, there were no such scenes.

Naughton understood that the men wouldn't be happy about the new assignment, but he was following orders. As he saw it, they were free to complain, but they weren't leaving the valley until it was cleared.

The Tigers' mission in the Song Ve had originally been to root out VC and rice supplies. Now they were being asked to serve as an escort service for stubborn villagers. But if they didn't have any choice about staying, they were going to do things their way. They would go hamlet to hamlet and escort the remaining people to a landing zone, where choppers would pick them up for the ride to the relocation camp. But unlike the line companies, the Tigers would not bring translators to each hamlet as they made the rounds. There was a universal language, and it was all they felt they needed: if the people insisted on staying, they would be removed by force. And as a show of force, the soldiers would take one more measure: they would burn the villages to the ground. If you torched the huts, the logic went, the people *couldn't* come back. Problem solved.

This tactic wasn't new but was part of a broader search-and-destroy strategy embraced by General Westmoreland as the only real way of bringing the country under control. By June 1967, it was common practice among the troops in South Vietnam "to break out the Zippos." It was the U.S. military's method of tearing down the will of the people. If the Vietnamese were going to defy the Americans, they would see there were irrevocable consequences. If they were assisting the enemy, their villages would be incinerated. If they refused to leave their land, their huts would be destroyed. Westmoreland's goal was to make it impossible for rural people to live anywhere but relocation camps — especially for the Vietnamese of the Central Highlands. They were "too independent," according to military strategists — always a problem if one demands agreement. President Ngo Dinh Diem had warned American military leaders years earlier that if rebellions were going to take place, they would be in those trouble spots: the Quang Ngai, Quang Tin, and Binh Dinh provinces. Concentrated into relocation camps, residents of these hot spots could be observed, influenced, and constricted.

Ironically, search and destroy would directly conflict with another strategy that was used by President Johnson to sell the war to the American people. During a speech, he declared that "ultimate victory will depend on the hearts and minds of the people who actually live out there." That meant treating the people with enough respect that they would support Saigon — and ultimately American ideologies — rather than succumbing to the pressure of Ho Chi Minh and Communism. But the policies of search and destroy were already having the opposite effect. The people deeply resented being forced off their land, and they began hating the Americans. It was hard to love the country that sent soldiers to yank you from your home, burn your village down, force you into a squalid refugee camp, and compel fathers and sons into the army of a visibly corrupt regime.

After carefully going over the details of the operation, the Tiger team leaders began talking to their men, and within a few minutes, the platoon broke into four groups.

Wood's unit headed to the cluster of huts closest to the river, about five hundred meters away. After reaching the entrance, the soldiers found close to a dozen people, including children, standing nearby. Some were locals whom the Army missed during the first sweep; others were villagers who hid from the soldiers.

Carpenter looked around the hamlet and shook his head. "These people just didn't get it," he recalled. "We dropped leaflets, we brought in translators. We did everything we could do, and they still didn't leave." Now, because these farmers couldn't follow simple instructions, he and the rest of Tiger Force had to be *here* doing this kind of shit work instead of getting hot showers back at the base — not to mention a beer and a good time at Mama San's, the brothel at the end of the dirt roadway in Duc Pho. The whorehouse was sandwiched between thatched huts, one of those wonders from the war with a bamboo frame and walls made from crushed beer cans, scented candles in every room, and beads hanging in the doorways. The smell was distinct: whiskey, cigarettes, and fish oil from the back room where the women were always cooking. For five dollars, the men could pick out a young girl and get laid on a bamboo cot and forget about the war.

Before Wood had finished explaining to the villagers the evacuation orders by holding up a leaflet, several Tigers walked to the first row of huts, removed their Zippos, and began lighting the dry thatch. With flames running up the sides of the huts, people bolted from their homes, some screaming. One elderly woman grabbed a bucket of water and threw it on the fire engulfing the door to her hut, but it was futile. As the other huts caught fire, some of the soldiers began laughing. One soldier even fired his M16 in the air, adding to the festive chaos.

Wood didn't like what he was seeing. He knew his men were frustrated, but he didn't expect them to act like desperadoes. He quickly ordered them to begin rounding up the villagers. Amid the flame and smoke, they complied.

Just two kilometers away, another group led by Manuel Sanchez was departing an empty hamlet when they spotted an elderly woman on a bicycle pedaling in their direction. Several Tigers cautiously raised their rifles, but as the woman came closer, Sanchez could see she wasn't armed. "Don't fire," he ordered, raising his hand.

Everyone on the team lowered his gun but James Barnett. The sergeant had been in South Vietnam six months and didn't trust anyone. The Vietnamese looked different. They smelled different. And he wasn't going to take a chance. Let your guard down and that smiling young girl could toss a grenade in your Jeep. Relax for a second and the kindly grandfather could shoot you in the back. If the enemy didn't wear uniforms, wasn't the safest thing to assume everyone held a knife behind his or her back?

As the old woman approached the soldiers, Sanchez raised his hand for her to stop, uttering one of the few phrases he knew: *"Dung Lai, Dung Lai."* She immediately began dragging a foot in the dirt until the bicycle came to a halt. As the soldiers moved closer, she began babbling nervously, pointing to the tree line beyond the hamlet. The only words the soldiers recognized were "Nghia Hanh," the name of one of the relocation camps.

Sanchez turned to the men. "She's harmless," he said, guessing she had once lived in the hamlet but was now trying to join the others at the camp. Everyone could see she posed no threat. Kerrigan walked over to get a closer look at her bicycle, rigged with a half-dozen burlap bags on the rear. After closer inspection, Sanchez decided not to call a chopper to transport her and instead waved her on.

Staring straight ahead, she started pedaling, but as she passed by Barnett, he jumped into the path and kicked her rear tire, sending her flying to the ground.

Before anyone could react, Barnett picked up her bike and heaved it into the brush as she began screaming in Vietnamese.

One of the bundles tied to the rear opened, and Barnett reached down and rummaged through her belongings. He pulled out a small roll of South Vietnamese currency and held it in the air. "See this?" he asked, waving the money as Sanchez approached. "She's VC. That's why she's got this money. She's VC."

Sanchez clenched his fists and growled. This was his team and he had already let her pass. He glared at Barnett and then turned around to pick up the woman while Kerrigan pulled her bicycle from the brush. The other team members quickly came over to see if Sanchez needed any help.

Kerrigan carefully tied the bag onto the rear. He then rolled the pedals with one hand while holding up the back of the bike with the other to make sure everything was still working.

Everyone on the team shared Sanchez's anger. There was no reason to hurt the woman. "You do that again, Barnett, you'll deal with me," said Sanchez.

Barnett shot back, "What the hell are you doing? She's a gook. She shouldn't have that money."

"I told her she could pass," Sanchez said.

Despite his time in South Vietnam, Sanchez wasn't jaded. He didn't believe that every villager was the enemy, especially an old lady who wasn't trying to hide. She had been forced from her hut and was heading to the place where she probably didn't want to go. Where was she supposed to leave her money — in a hut that would be burned down?

The two sergeants stared at each other for a moment but said nothing. It was clear Sanchez was not going to back down, even if Barnett was four inches taller and thirty pounds heavier. Barnett could get away with pushing around newcomers, but Sanchez wasn't a newcomer — he had served in the Tigers longer than Barnett and he had survived just as many firefights.

Barnett turned around and, stuffing the money in his pocket, walked away.

By noon, the chopper pilots noticed a layer of fog over the valley.

They called to battalion headquarters to report a strange haze shrouding the Song Ve, and they were quickly informed that the mist blanketing the valley was smoke. "The Tigers are burning the valley," a voice crackled over the radio. Four hours after the Tigers had broken into teams, nearly every structure along the river was ablaze. The four teams had lit more than two hundred huts, with only a few remaining.

For the most part, violence had been minimized. In one hamlet, six people were bound and dragged to a clearing, where they were placed on a transport chopper for the ride to Nghia Hanh. One man was struck several times when he tried to run. He was later tied and a burlap bag was forced over his head before he was whisked away by chopper for questioning at Go Hoi intelligence camp, about twenty-five kilometers away.

Had that been the end of it, perhaps everything would have been different.

There had been sporadic resistance. In one hamlet, Ybarra and Green had been forced to take cover on the ground when shots were fired toward them. Unable to determine the direction of the gunfire, they quickly began searching the huts but couldn't find anyone. "I'll kill all these gooks," Ybarra blurted out. After several platoon members joined the two friends, they began torching the huts.

Throughout the torching, Ybarra had cursed loudly, his face glowing red and his eyes narrowing into a deep, dark stare. God, how he did not want to be here. He had wanted to go into Duc Pho. He had wanted to go to the brothel. With money, he could buy a woman and feel normal. Now, instead, he was getting shot at during a futile attempt at pest eradication. When the Tigers were told they had to stay, he had taken it personally. Shortly after the announcement, one of the newcomers had inadvertently brushed Ybarra. Sam told the soldier he would kill him if he ever touched him again.

Ken Green had seen his friend's fury before, but not quite like this, not even when he was teased in high school. It was a rage that had been growing for years, born from rejection — a chubby teenager with acne and a broad, flat nose who never fit in. As he grew older, Ybarra had turned his anger inward. Three years before joining the Army, he had run away from home and hadn't returned until a week later, dirty and tired. He told his mother he hopped a freight train to Phoenix so he could be alone.

Green was one of the few people who really understood

him. Ybarra often fumed about his people being "treated like shit by white people," how they were forced from their land and relocated to reservations. It was never a good omen of things to come when Ybarra started turning inward, and here in the valley, Green was seeing the signs: the frequent outbursts mostly over minor problems, like a blister (common because of moisture seeping into the soldiers' boots, compounded by the heat and sun, which dried and shrank the leather), followed by silence.

CHAPTER 6

When the teams regrouped later in the afternoon, Ybarra pulled Green aside. Slowly, he opened the pouch he was carrying and nudged his friend to look inside. When Green peered down, he saw two bloody clumps of flesh.

"I cut the ears off a gook," Ybarra said.

Green looked at his friend and, without saying anything, shrugged his shoulders. He figured the ears were from a soldier killed in a firefight, and besides, if he was surprised, he wasn't going to show it. Both friends were always trying to outdo each other. When hunting near Lake Roosevelt, they would dare each other to see who could shoot the most game — deer, quail, and rabbit — and most of the time would leave their prey to rot. It wasn't about hunting.

Other times, they would see who could drink the most whiskey, and then challenge each other to a shooting match. With a friend driving, they would sit in the back of a pickup and fire at rabbits. If one still moved after it was shot, Ybarra would hop from the truck and snap the animal's neck with his teeth and hands. It was his way of outdoing Green.

Several Tigers were already talking about Ybarra's souvenirs, but no one was going to say anything. No one wanted to get on Ybarra's bad side. No one even knew when or where he acquired the ears. To be safe, the newcomers were starting to keep their distance from the point man. "It was better for all of us to stay out of his way," recalled Kerney.

It wasn't long after regrouping that the Tigers received another radio alert from Carentan: chopper pilots had just spotted two more clusters of huts in the valley, with people milling around. Some of the Tigers began cursing. They had just spent most of the day going from hamlet to hamlet, and now they were being ordered into the fray again.

Ybarra and Green were part of the first team to reach a row of huts that had not yet been searched — one of dozens of clusters of hooches scattered across the valley that didn't appear on military maps. Following a routine, one man approached the entrance, rifle drawn, to look inside, while two others stood behind aiming their rifles at the openings. They searched four huts, and it appeared the villagers were gone.

While Trout and other team members walked the perimeter, looking for Vietnamese, Ybarra and Green stayed behind.

After carefully walking around each hut, lifting up bags of rice and other objects to look for weapons, they decided to go back into the huts. There were simply too many supplies for the people to be gone. As they crept into the largest hooch, they surprised a man who was lying flat under a table. Quickly, they pointed their rifles at him and motioned for him to rise. As he stood up, they noticed he was wearing a black-and-white-checkered scarf. Ybarra and Green had seen the scarves before, mostly on prisoners. This wasn't a peasant. This was an NVA soldier.

Ybarra ordered the man to raise his hands, and as the prisoner lifted his arms over his head, Ybarra struck him on the side of the head with a rifle. When the man fell to the ground, Green dragged him outside and began kicking him. Soon both soldiers pounced on the man, beating him with their fists. As he lay motionless on the ground, Ybarra stood up and reached for his knife.

Suddenly Green stood up and backed away.

Before his friend could say anything, Ybarra reached down and lifted the man's head back, exposing his neck, and in one motion slit the man's throat.

For several seconds, the Vietnamese began kicking on the ground, grabbing his throat, making gurgling noises as the blood ran down his neck.

Ken was sickened. It was one thing to beat an enemy soldier, but Ybarra had killed the man without hesitation and in a manner that would mean an excruciating death. "Sam, what are you doing, man?" he asked.

Ybarra looked up but didn't answer.

Green again prodded his friend. "What did you kill him for?"

After wiping his knife on the ground, Ybarra stood up and stared angrily at Green. "This ain't the mortar platoon," he snapped. "This gook would have killed you. You better learn to kill them first, or you ain't never going home alive."

Green stood silent for a moment. This wasn't the guy he knew from Globe. Ybarra was crazy, especially when he was drinking. But he never knew his friend would just kill a defenseless human being so easily. Green knew Sam had been through a lot of bad shit in South Vietnam, but he didn't know how bad until now. He didn't know how far Sam had separated himself from the other Tigers, even the veterans. Soldiers go through several psychological stages when they are in combat: fear, anxiety, and anger among them. Sam was already well into the latter stage and becoming more enraged by the day.

When the other team members returned, they saw the body and the two friends standing nearby. For a moment, no one said anything. The newcomers looked at one another and then looked at their sergeants, Harold Trout and James Barnett, but they were quiet.

Carpenter asked Ybarra what happened. "I cut his throat," he said.

Ybarra calmly recounted the capture and beating of the prisoner while Green remained quiet.

The other soldiers continued looking at one another, but no one was going to say anything more — not when the team leaders were silent.

Before leaving, they knew they had to get rid of the body. Prisoners were supposed to be taken to the rear for interrogation — not summarily executed. Under Trout's orders, Carpenter dragged the body to the woods.

It wasn't the first time Carpenter saw a prisoner killed. Before the Mother's Day Massacre, the Tigers had captured a man with explosives near Duc Pho. Large and muscular, the prisoner looked to be Chinese. For two days, the Tigers beat him, while Carpenter tried to keep him alive. But for some reason, one of the soldiers got carried away and ordered the prisoner to run. As the man bolted, the soldier raised his M16 and shot the prisoner in the back. But the men had rationalized that the victim was undoubtedly the enemy, and they considered the shooting a killing, not a murder. Still, it was far from a source of pride, and usually unspoken.

Carpenter dug just deep enough into the ground to make sure the body would be hidden. He remembered the card he was handed when he arrived in country with the dos and don'ts of handling prisoners. Like most soldiers, he had discarded it, but he remembered the general message: You can't degrade a prisoner. You can't torture a prisoner. Most of all, you can't kill a prisoner. If you were caught, you could be court-martialed and tossed in the brig.

But in a place like South Vietnam, it seemed strange to have rules.

In fact, rules of war had been around a long time, with

some dating to medieval times and the code of chivalry. But few soldiers knew the history, and most didn't give a damn. The early conventions beginning in 1863 in Geneva created the rules of war, but it wasn't until the Geneva conventions of 1949 that most countries went along with the treaties. And by the time the Marines arrived in Da Nang in 1965, those countries involved in the conflict — the United States, North Vietnam, and South Vietnam — had signed the accords. The Nuremberg trials — highly publicized prosecutions of Nazi war criminals between 1945 and 1949 that saw two hundred defendants tried for violating the rules of war and for crimes against humanity — showed that such treaties could be enforced.

Most of the grunts in Vietnam realized they were supposed to keep prisoners alive; the Tigers certainly knew, having been told by commanders to remove prisoners from the field by calling in choppers. Prisoners were good sources of information. Furthermore, the laws of war offered the slim chance of keeping Americans alive if they were captured. If one army knew the other was killing prisoners and civilians, it opened the door for the other army to follow suit.

Carpenter dragged the Vietnamese by the legs into the fresh, shallow hole and began pushing dirt over the body until it was completely covered. He backed up for a moment and looked at the grave before turning around and returning to the village. He didn't always like what he saw in South Vietnam, but he learned a long time ago to keep his feelings in check. That's how you'd survive.

It was the same with killing enemy soldiers. After he shot his first NVA, he expected to feel the "thrill of the kill" — the rush other soldiers described after the firing stopped. But there was only sadness. He kept thinking of his grandmother, who would always lead prayers before Sunday dinner at her southeast Ohio farm, her voice cracking as she talked about how the Good Lord had sustained her through the hard times, the spring floods and droughts. After his first kill, he realized that he wasn't in her backyard playing war games during family gatherings. That he was now killing people. That he was now in a different world. "I couldn't get her out of my mind," he recalled. "I felt like I disappointed her, that I let her down in the worst way."

In time, he found the killing became easier.

Sanchez and Barnett weren't talking.

The team leader walked at the front of the line, while Barnett stayed in the rear. The soldiers in between could feel the tension, but they weren't going to get involved. They had to reach the last hamlet before dusk and didn't need distractions.

They had been walking the valley floor for nine hours and were nursing cuts from the razor-sharp edges of elephant grass along the river. At any other time of year, the grass was tolerable, but in monsoon season the blades grew seven feet high and were coarse enough to cut like a knife.

By late afternoon, the deep scratches on their faces, hands, and arms were burning from the sun and sweat, and all the Tigers wanted to do was jump into the river. It didn't help that some of the men were starting to show the early signs of jungle rot, a chafing that began in their crotches and inner thighs. The chafing from sweating and walking caused blisters and sores. The medics were already handing out pHisoHex, an antibacterial liquid soap, to keep the skin from infection.

Every now and then, Barnett, who was clearly in pain, would curse aloud, and everyone would stop to make sure he didn't drop. He was lugging a twenty-five-pound M60 machine gun in addition to his eighty pounds of gear and had stripped off his shirt several hours earlier. His wide shoulders were baked from the sun and were already starting to blister.

As the team members reached a trail leading to the hamlet known as Hanh Thien, they could hear the familiar whirl of helicopter blades. Sanchez raised his hand, and the soldiers stopped and looked up. They could see it was a command-and-control chopper.

Not a good sign. This was the battalion commander.

Suddenly, from a loudspeaker onboard the craft, a voice shouted, "Stay there! Keep your positions!"

The chopper circled for a few minutes and then landed in a clearing about one hundred meters away. Three figures emerged from the doorway, and as they approached the team, Austin was in the lead.

Over the din of the whirling rotors, he began screaming at Sanchez and pointing to an old Vietnamese woman behind him. The men recognized her as the woman who was on the bicycle earlier in the day.

His face red and veins bulging in his neck, Austin shouted, "You're a bunch of Genghis Khan barbarians! Who took her money?" Sanchez looked down and didn't say anything. Neither did Sergeant Ervin Lee, who was second in command of the team. The other soldiers, including Carpenter, didn't say a word. As much as they didn't like what Barnett did, they weren't going to turn on him. Austin took the woman down the line and asked her which one stole her money. When they reached Barnett, she began babbling and pointing at him.

Austin put his hands on his hips and faced Barnett. "Return her money, Sergeant," he ordered.

Barnett froze. He wasn't going to answer his commander or return the money. Austin moved closer and locked eyes with Barnett.

"I said give her the money."

Slowly, Barnett reached into his pants pocket and pulled out the wad of bills. "She's VC, Colonel," he said, looking down.

But Austin didn't respond. The woman had gone to the re-location camp, abiding by the Army's rules, and immediately reported the theft to a guard. Within hours, Austin was told about her complaint. Austin wasn't a soldier who easily breached Army regulations. He grabbed the money from Barnett's hand and passed it to the woman. Austin then ordered Barnett to apologize. Barnett shifted uneasily. He couldn't believe the order. Apologize. To a gook? He looked around and could see the other soldiers staring. He looked at Austin, mumbled something that resembled an apology, and turned away.

Barnett's hands began to shake as he fought back tears. It was like he had just lost a fight in the backyard of the family's old wood shack in Loretto, Tennessee. And now he had to face his father, who would be waiting for him with a stick of firewood. Lose a fight, and prepare for another ass kicking. That's the way his father, James Sr., treated his namesake.

The older Barnett used to justify the beatings to relatives by saying he was just trying to make a man out of his son. You had to be tough, and you had to remind people that if they messed up, they would pay dearly for it. The old man was a deaf-mute, and no one gave him any breaks. During the Depression, he had to beg to get a job at a local textile mill, where he was sometimes the brunt of jokes because of his inability to communicate. But it didn't stop him from taking swings at workers for making fun of him.

James Sr. would, in turn, take out his anger on his son. Sometimes he would try to make up for the beatings, which could be brutal. He would ask his son to go bass fishing on the Tennessee River, or hunting in the woods. James Jr. would reluctantly accept his father's overtures but, inside, hated spending time alone with the old man.

He preferred instead to gather after school with his friends and two older stepbrothers, drinking and raising hell at a place called the Dairy Barn, a 1950s-style soda shop next to a parking lot in the center of the small town on the Alabama border. They would sit in their cars, radios blaring, downing beers.

In his youth, Barnett was considered handsome — jut jawed, with a boyish smile that belied an anger that could erupt at any time. People knew to stay away from him when he was drinking, recalled his friend Sonny Beckman. "He was friendly and good-hearted, but there was always that mean streak that would surprise you," he said. "You didn't know which Jim you were going to get." More than anything, he joined the Army to escape his father. "He was tired of the old man and just wanted to get away," recalled his friend.

Army journalist Dennis Stout ripped open an envelope placed on his desk and smiled as he read the letter. No more tagging along with Army units repairing roads or building schools. No more riding along with the top brass on public relations tours for visiting dignitaries. He was now going to be covering Tiger Force.

For weeks, the twenty-one-year-old specialist had been in Quang Ngai but spent most of his time with the line companies in search of feature stories about "hometown soldiers" who, among other things, handed out candy to South Vietnamese children in relocation camps. He was ordered to look for the positive side of the war — American soldiers fighting for freedom alongside the South Vietnamese against the Communist invaders. "Make the soldiers feel good" was the mantra of his newspaper, *Diplomat & Warrior,* the official organ of the 101st Airborne Division.

Stout didn't disappoint his commanders. With his notebook in hand and a 35mm Canon camera around his neck, he had filed so many stories about brave grunts that he could now write them by heart. After almost two months, he knew what he could report and what he couldn't. "Every story had to go through five censors in Saigon before being published," he recalled. All the pieces were basically the same — all he had to do was change the names.

A paratrooper, Stout had arrived in Vietnam three months after the June 1966 battle at Dak To, and was initially assigned to B Company of the 1st Battalion/327th Infantry. For the first nine months of his tour, Stout was a line soldier who traveled with his battalion to numerous hot spots in South Vietnam. He was slightly wounded by shrapnel from a mine that killed a sergeant during a patrol west of Duc Pho and was recuperating in a hospital when he was told his newest assignment would be battalion public information officer. He wasn't a journalist by training, but a commander had found out that Stout had tried unsuccessfully to freelance articles for outdoors magazines before joining the Army. Since he had more writing experience than anyone in his battalion, he was tapped for the public information job.

Stout's new duties included tagging along with the dozens of U.S. and foreign journalists who were arriving each week in the country to cover the escalating war. He would also be charged with filing his own stories and taking his own pictures for the 101st Airborne weekly newspaper.

Stout had heard stories about Tiger Force, and to prepare had thumbed through back issues of *Stars and Stripes,* old news releases, and a few Army intelligence reports available to military reporters. He also already knew some of the Tigers from when they had been with the line companies, so he was confident he could get interviews right away. Stout excitedly penned a letter to his young wife, Marthann, who had just given birth three weeks earlier to their daughter, Denise. In the letter, he told her about his new assignment with the Tigers in a place known as the Song Ve Valley, and that he would be careful. "In some ways, I should have stayed at the base camp," he recalled. "I had a new baby and two months to go in my tour. But I just couldn't pass up the chance."

Even before dawn, the Tigers were put on alert: A riot had broken out in Nghia Hanh, and dozens of people had escaped into the darkness. No one knew where the refugees fled, but most were believed to be from the Song Ve, and it was natural to assume they would return home.

Wood, who took the radio call from battalion headquarters, wasn't surprised. He had heard for days from translators about how the people hated the camp. Surrounded by concrete walls, barbed wire, and armed soldiers, the Nghia Hanh facility resembled a prison. No one was allowed to leave during the day without permission, and at night the gates were locked.

Worse, there was little food or shelter. Most of the refugees were forced to sleep outdoors in monsoon season because there were few wooden barracks and only two latrines. Surrounded by rotting garbage, people sat around waiting for handouts, and when the rice supply dwindled, the refugees broke into a storage shed on June 26. A riot ensued, and two twelve-year-old boys were shot to death by guards. To calm the crowd, South Vietnamese soldiers fired tear gas. The effect had been far from relaxing.

Wood could have predicted this was going to happen. He had read Army civil operation reports about the dismal conditions in various camps in Quang Ngai province, and of the sixty-eight camps in the province, Nghia Hanh was among the worst. During the past week in the Song Ve, Wood had taken time to talk to translators, who told him the people at Nghia Hanh were constantly hungry and suffering from malaria, dysentery, and infectious hepatitis.

He was also hearing about another alarming trend: many of the new refugees were joining the Vietcong. To Wood, it was obvious the people felt no allegiance to the government of South Vietnam. How could they? The government had done very little to reach out to them over the years. And now this.

Wood did not like the Vietcong. They were Communists and they could be terribly oppressive to the people, stealing their rice and threatening their families. But he had also learned from talking to translators and refugees that the VC were offering a more equitable land reform than the leaders in Saigon, and the VC were not forcing everyone to leave his or her home. They were basic promises that created clear bonds.

The whole thing was a vicious circle, getting worse and worse. But Wood and the others had to carry out the orders passed on to them from battalion headquarters and Colonel Austin, even if, to a seasoned field officer, the mission was foolish and unbefitting the Tigers. After all, this was a Special Force

created to conduct surveillances of the enemy — a reconnaissance platoon with a short but celebrated history. He joined the
unit to be a part of that excitement. And as a forward artillery
observer — the man who calls in air strikes based on enemy
positions — he knew he had an important job. But it was clear
to him that the role of the Tigers was changing. The soldiers
were now being ordered to function as enforcers for the Army
commanders, not to serve as frontline spies and commandos.
They were no longer the eyes and ears, but the fist. The Tigers
were being let out of their cage.

CHAPTER 7

Despite the thousands of leaflets dropped on the valley and the evacuation that followed, the villagers simply weren't leaving. The battalion had already forced five thousand residents to Nghai Hanh, and the Tigers rounded up forty-three more before burning the huts, but that still left an estimated two thousand people unaccounted for. To Austin and other battalion commanders, this was a disappointment. They had already issued a news release touting the success of the evacuation. Now they ran the risk of the MACV finding out the truth. In particular, no one wanted General Westmoreland to know that the mission in the Song Ve was not going as planned. He was a stickler for results and had very little patience for failure.

It was time to kick into another mode. After requesting permission, Austin and his officers agreed to declare the once populated area of the valley — four miles wide by six miles long — a free-fire zone.

It was an extreme measure but well within the Army's tactics. The way it worked was simple: with the declaration, U.S.

74

troops were free to attack enemy targets in civilian areas, the usual safety precautions intended to minimize collateral damage put aside. This put the onus on civilians to get out; otherwise, they risked getting killed in the cross fire.

U.S. troops had to get the free-fire approval from their commanders and South Vietnamese provincial leaders. Legally, it was the only way to attack. But under no circumstances did troops have the right to deliberately fire on unarmed civilians, regardless of whether an area was a free-fire zone.

The MACV was willing to embrace free-fire zones in the Song Ve because of what was happening in the larger Quang Ngai province: the North Vietnamese Army was successfully infiltrating and setting up base camps. Despite intensive bombing, the enemy was actually gaining strength, and some thought it was just a matter of time before they would attack the American troops in the Song Ve. Indeed, two weeks earlier, the VC had waged a surprise mortar attack on an ammunition depot at Carentan, injuring several soldiers. Judging from other attacks in the Central Highlands, commanders agreed the enemy had the ability to strike anywhere, anytime. They also agreed a response was necessary. The free-fire request was approved.

As the Huey hovered overhead, Dennis Stout took a deep breath and looked down on the large sections of scorched earth, the river, and the sea of green below. From conversations with his translator, Nguyen Van Phoc, Stout had learned the Song Ve was a revered place to the Buddhist farmers, partly because their ancestors were buried there and partly because of the rich soil and abundant water. Though most of the topsoil in the province was replete with limestone, the valley was just the opposite: rich in nutrients and highly fertile.

At Stout's request, the pilot circled to give the journalist a bird's-eye view of the tree-covered foothills surrounding the valley and rising one thousand meters. He was struck by the breathless expanse of rice paddies rolling gently for miles in all directions.

As the Huey touched down in a clearing, two bearded soldiers wearing tiger-striped fatigues and soft-brimmed hats approached the chopper doorway. Without saying a word, they quickly escorted Stout to the edge of the river, where a team was huddled around a map as a sergeant drew up points along the grids. They watched carefully as the team leader instructed the soldiers to keep their eyes open for any stragglers. They were not going out there to make friends. Their job was to clear the valley, then burn the huts. That's all.

As Stout approached the team, some soldiers looked up and nodded, while others ignored him. Newcomers didn't mind reporters because they had never been exposed to them, but some veterans were leery. They had been with journalists in the field, and that always meant extra work. You had to make sure they were keeping up with the patrol, and you had to protect them if things heated up. They were baggage.

As the team walked toward the nearby foothills, Stout was told to stay in the middle of the line and not to veer anywhere else. The middle was always the safest. Those in the front usually ran into ambushes and booby traps first, and those at the end of the line would sometimes get picked off by snipers sneaking up from behind.

It wasn't long before the team leader began complaining about the Song Ve. The platoon should be hunting VC, and instead they were stuck looking for villagers. "They were pissed off," recalled Stout. "That was my first impression of the Tigers." The blisters on their feet were starting to break into open sores, and the men were constantly complaining of the overwhelming smell of manure blowing from the rice paddies, where the villagers used animal and human waste to fertilize the fields. Two of the newcomers had carelessly pulled leeches from their legs earlier in the day, leaving wounds so deep the medics were worried about infections setting in.

Private Gary Kornatowski was already hobbling from the

cuts in his shins left by the nasty green creatures. When he took off his boots earlier in the day, he had noticed his legs were covered and had quickly begun pulling off the leeches with his hands. The whole country was a collection of vampires, large and small.

As the team passed by piles of blackened thatch beyond the river, Stout asked the soldiers what happened. "We torched everything. We don't want the gooks coming back," the team sergeant responded.

No sooner had Stout asked the question than they spotted two Vietnamese running down a hill toward the soldiers, waving leaflets. Stout could clearly hear them yelling, "No shoot, GI, no shoot, GI!"

He froze. Stout expected the soldiers to wait for the peasants to reach them before questioning them. They looked like civilians and weren't carrying any weapons. He watched as two of the soldiers raised their M16s at the peasants, and figured it was just a precaution.

Suddenly Stout was startled by the instant, rapid sounds of the M16s. The peasants fell in a spray of bullets. "It happened so fast," recalled Stout. "They just shot them. I couldn't believe it." He looked at the other three soldiers who didn't fire their weapons, and could see the puzzled looks on their faces. One of the men turned around in disgust and blurted out, "Sarge, what happened?" The team leader glanced at Stout before motioning for the soldier to come over to talk to him privately.

Stout stared at the two men as they huddled, and knew he wasn't supposed to hear what they were saying. As their voices rose, Stout could hear the sergeant saying the words "free-fire zone. It's a damn free-fire zone, and you don't question that." Moments later, the men walked back and joined the rest of the team. Stout looked at the bodies and saw the leaflets in their hands. No guns or ammunition were found.

★ ★ ★

As the Tigers began to walk in a patrol line, Stout's mind kept churning. That didn't make sense. He knew the peasants clearly weren't VC. And after spending nine months with a line company — wounded three times — he knew when to fire at a target and when not to. But the Tigers were experienced soldiers, he mused. They must know what they're doing.

For the rest of the day, as the team walked through the foothills, Stout was quiet. He didn't take any notes, nor did he bother to ask any questions. He had thought about finding a soldier to profile but didn't bother.

By sundown, the entire platoon regrouped. The day's patrols were over. As the soldiers broke out their C rations, they began to talk. Stout learned that the only two villagers spotted by the teams that day were the two killed by his team. All other team members came up empty.

As they ate, several soldiers walked over to Stout and introduced themselves, joking that they wanted their pictures taken and stories written about "all the VC they were going to kill." Stout tried to be friendly — even snapping a few photos of the Tigers — but was still subdued. He didn't know what he would report about the day's events. Maybe it was better not to write anything. One thing was for certain: the next time they went out on patrol, he didn't want to be with the same team. Those guys were too trigger-happy. Stout wasn't sure how he would bring it up to Lieutenant Naughton, but before the end of the night, he was prepared to ask to be reassigned. He was done with this valley. But so were the Tigers.

Before the platoon finished their rations, a radio call came from battalion headquarters: the choppers were on their way to pick up Tiger Force. "We're heading back to Carentan," said Naughton. Since after the Tigers' most recent sweep there was now little perceived activity in the valley, the battalion commanders were going to redeploy them to a cluster of villages one thousand meters west of Duc Pho.

As they waited for the choppers, some of the soldiers talked about taking a shower and then tossing their uniforms in a bonfire, the accepted practice for soldiers in the bush. That way, the men were guaranteed a new set of clothes because no one carried extra uniforms on patrol. Besides, there was no other way to clean fabric soaked with two weeks' worth of sweat, blood, pus, and urine.

Later, the men would head to the whorehouses near Duc Pho and get drunk. Stout had no intention of joining the soldiers. All he wanted to do was go back to his tent.

From a ledge in the mountains, Lu Thuan and several villagers watched as the choppers flew out of sight, the lights receding into the blackness. Carefully, they scanned the valley floor, searching for any movement or even a flicker of light. There was nothing.

The men gathered closer and began to talk. They asked one another whether it was safe to go back to their homes.

Now that the hamlets were burned, there seemed to be no reason for the soldiers to return. But Lu wasn't so sure. His uncertainty was shared by others, and the villagers agreed to wait in the mountains until morning.

For several more hours, Lu Thuan thought about his family and whether they were still alive at Nghia Hanh. He wondered whether he would ever see his two children. For nearly two years, bombs had dropped everywhere in Quang Ngai — everywhere but the Song Ve. Lu couldn't understand why the Army turned its attention to his valley. His people were just simple farmers.

As dawn broke, he and the others gathered once again and looked down on the valley. There were no trucks or choppers. So far, no soldiers.

Some of the men proposed going back to rebuild their huts. Lu argued that it was too soon to know whether the Americans would be back. The helicopters could swoop over the valley at any time. There was no hurry as long as they still had rice, though admittedly, they only had enough to last two weeks.

But Lu could tell he was not going to convince those men who had already made up their minds. Some of the men agreed to stay with Lu, but most returned to the crevices along the ridge where they had been hiding, gathering their clothes and bags of rice. With the sun rising over the foothills, dozens of them walked slowly down the ridge toward the river, toward home.

Sitting at his desk, Dennis Stout stared at his black Underwood typewriter. After punching a few keys, he stopped. "What am I going to write?" he muttered to his translator, Nguyen Van Phoc. After spending a day on his new assignment, he had nothing — at least nothing the Army would publish. He had tried to think of a story during the helicopter ride to Carentan, but the images kept returning of the young men waving leaflets, gunned down on the hill.

Just a month earlier, he had witnessed the rape and execution of a woman by several soldiers in a bunker west of Quang Ngai City. Disgusted by the incident, he informed a chaplain about the atrocity but was told to go back to his job. It was too late to do anything, and it was, the chaplain argued, an isolated incident.

Stout had tried his best to get over it. He had to move on; otherwise, it would consume him. So he had argued with his editor for a new assignment because he didn't want to cover the same company, and his request was granted — he got the Tigers.

With paper littering the floor — balled-up pages of previous attempts to write something — Stout finally called it quits. If his editors wanted a story to fill the paper, they could take one of his surplus Warrior of the Week columns — vignettes written weeks in advance from field interviews with grunts.

He rose from his desk and turned around to talk to his twenty-one-year-old South Vietnamese translator. Nguyen was sleeping in a nearby cot. In the past six weeks, they had become close, sharing stories about their families and what the two men wanted to do after the war.

Stout debated waking him up so he could tell Nguyen about what he had seen earlier in the day. But he stopped himself. Why bring it up now? Let the man sleep.

Stout walked outside his tent and turned on a transistor radio, tuning in to the American Forces Vietnam Network radio broadcast from Saigon. He had hoped to listen to some music to get his mind off the day's events, but instead he got the news about Lyndon Johnson's meeting with Soviet prime minister Aleksey Kosygin in Glassboro, New Jersey. There was hope their talks would somehow be the first step toward a peace agreement for Vietnam, but it was clear from the report that nothing was going to happen.

Stout had already learned how to parse what he heard on the radio. Johnson and Westmoreland were telling reporters that the end of the conflict was within reach, and the enemy was losing its will to fight. It was, Stout was realizing, just the opposite. He had been in Vietnam for nearly a year, and the fighting was escalating, not decreasing. He had spoken frankly to South Vietnamese soldiers who told him that thousands of North Vietnamese Army regulars were infiltrating Quang Ngai every month. From the air, you could see their new bunkers and encampments going up, and American soldiers were running into NVA troops every day in the mountains west of Duc Pho.

Staring up at the stars, Stout wanted to be home. Back with his wife and daughter, and far away from this hot, brutal place where nothing seemed real. Uneasily, he was starting to loathe his life in the military. He was raised in a house where the men served — without question. His grandfather fought in France in World War I. His father fought in the South Pacific in World War II. His uncles fought in the war, too, and they weren't bashful about it; indeed, that's all they talked about at gatherings. His brother had already served in South Vietnam in the Navy, and just a week after high school graduation, Stout had walked to the recruiting office in Phoenix and signed the three white sheets of paper that had eventually landed him here. While

Stout had signed up to be a helicopter pilot, he never got out of the infantry. He always suspected someone mixed up the paperwork. Well, it was that kind of war.

Stout turned off the radio and went back into his tent. He tried to sleep, but after several hours of staring at the ceiling, he gave up.

Not far away, some Tigers were restless. Sanchez tossed and turned but couldn't sleep, so he sat up with a notebook to write another letter to his girlfriend. Two things bothered him: Barnett and word that other Tigers had killed two civilians that day.

He was not surprised that Barnett had flipped out. His fellow team member was always close to the edge, and Sanchez was getting tired of it. It was probably better, he thought, that they didn't serve together. More troubling was the killing of the two Vietnamese who were clearly unarmed. "I don't understand what's happening," he wrote Mary. "We never did things like that. Most of the time, we leave the civilians alone." He told Mary he was having second thoughts about serving in the Tigers. "Maybe I just need to get out," Sanchez concluded.

In another tent, Green was trying to finish a belated Father's Day letter to Melvin Green. A few hours earlier, he had told Ybarra to go on to Mama San's without him. He needed a break from Sam. His old friend was changing in a troubling way.

Green liked being a Tiger. He even had a new nickname: "Boots," he told Melvin, because he would fall asleep without removing his shoes — his way of wanting to be ready. After all, the Tigers were a far cry from the mortar platoon. Deep into enemy territory, they were always in danger of being hit.

He told his father not to worry, though, because he wasn't going to be in South Vietnam much longer. He had already been there almost a year. "I hope my boat is ready to be used," Ken wrote. "I really miss running around the lake. But I'll be back at it again. Sorry this is short. You don't have to write back. I'll be home before I would get it," he said. Green didn't share his concerns with his father.

The light in Harold Trout's tent was still glowing. He had finished a letter to his wife, Brigette, and reached for a worn notebook — one he had been carrying since joining the Tigers in March 1967. Few of his fellow soldiers knew that Trout would regularly compile a roster of the Tigers — their ranks and their positions. It was his way of keeping track.

In many ways, he considered the Tigers *his* unit, even if he wasn't an officer. He knew more than the officers and was older than everyone in the unit except for Sergeant Doyle. Everyone wanted to be on his team, partly because he never showed fear — a trait noted in his evaluations. He hated the Vietnamese and made no bones about it. He would every kill every last one of them if he had to.

Raised in a working-class family outside Saint Louis, Missouri, Trout had seen enlistment as his only escape. After high school, he joined the Army in February 1956 and knew the military was going to be his life. He served in Korea and Germany, but he needed combat experience to advance, and South Vietnam was his ticket.

An eleven-year veteran by the time he arrived, he was more seasoned than nearly everyone in Tiger Force. He could be gruff, but he also acted the protector — a comforting trait to newcomers. "They followed in his footsteps," Carpenter recalled, even if it meant occasionally getting dressed down. No one wanted to get on his bad side.

Trout scanned the list of soldiers in his notebook to make sure it was up to date. Every time someone was killed or injured or rotated out, he would draw a line through his name. So far, he hadn't had to cross out anyone since the Mother's Day Massacre, but he knew that wasn't going to last. Soon, he would be proved correct.

CHAPTER 8

Wearing his new tiger-striped fatigues with a lieutenant's bar patch, James Hawkins was on his way to
the battalion headquarters on July 2 to meet with
Austin when he caught the attention of platoon members
standing in the chow line.

They took a long look. For weeks, they had heard rumors
they would be getting a new leader, but like everything else in
the Army, they were always the last to officially know.

At six feet, two inches and 230 pounds, Hawkins was larger
than past commanders, and he looked out of place. Most of the
field officers were thin and agile, but Hawkins had a paunch,
stooped shoulders, and arms that swung back and forth as he
walked.

For most of Hawkins's military career, he had been a grunt,
working his way from infantry soldier when he joined in 1958
to second lieutenant eight years later. The Maysville, Kentucky,
native had arrived in Vietnam on April 17, 1967, and was
wounded a month later during maneuvers with B Company.
While recovering in a hospital, he volunteered to take over

Tiger Force, which had been looking for a permanent replacement since the Mother's Day Massacre.

For Hawkins, it was a break for his career. Serving as field lieutenant for Tiger Force was basically like being a commander. Everyone in the platoon would take orders from him; he would have great freedom, often spending weeks in the bush without any supervision; and ultimately, if he succeeded with the Tigers, he would be promoted to first lieutenant and be on a fast track to captain. There was nothing more he wanted. He was a soldier who came from a working-class family and who disdained West Pointers — "ring knockers" who, in his view, had it easy. They were college boys and were "handed" a commission when they graduated. Hawkins didn't have a four-year degree and hadn't gone to Officer Candidate School — the other alternative to receiving a commission. Instead, he had proudly earned his first stripe the "hard way," via field commission in September 1966.

In some ways, soldiering was a dream that began when he was a child growing up on the Ohio River, playing war games. As a young boy, Hawkins was quiet and generally unassuming but seemed to come to life when he patrolled — toy rifle in hand — along the water. Even when the other kids went home, he could be seen leading imaginary troops up a hill to face an imaginary German Army.

His father worked for Ashland Oil, moving the family to Owensboro, Kentucky, just before Hawkins started high school. As soon as he graduated in 1958, he volunteered for Army service. "I never saw myself doing anything else," he said.

Three years later, when he was married with a young child, his career was almost derailed. He and other soldiers had been drinking. With Hawkins driving, the men were headed to a horse farm near Fort Knox when they crashed. One of his passengers died, and Hawkins was hauled before a military hearing. He thought his career could be over, but in the end, his superiors found no cause to proceed to a court-martial.

For the next few years, Hawkins kept his nose clean, took

college courses, and found that the best way to rise through the ranks was to go to South Vietnam. Before reaching the headquarters at Carentan, he had stopped to meet Stephen Naughton, who was relieved to be giving up his acting command of the Tigers. It had been a long three weeks in a role Naughton never relished, and he was about to be reassigned within the battalion.

Naughton told Hawkins that many of the men in the platoon were relatively new with little combat experience, and that the Song Ve was a free-fire zone. Expect the Vietcong to put up a fight for control of the fertile basin, Naughton warned.

If Hawkins wanted to make it, he needed to know the unit's strengths and weaknesses. Donald Wood was his forward artillery observer — and a good one, Naughton said. Sam Ybarra was crazy, but he was one of the best point men he had ever worked beside. Just keep your eye on him, Naughton instructed. Harold Trout was a tough son of a bitch, Naughton concluded, but he was fair to his men and looked out for them. There was something else, the outgoing leader added. The job of Tiger commander was a bitch, with a history of past leaders being killed or wounded. Others were glad just to get out alive. With a handshake, Naughton left the camp.

Hawkins met Austin and several other battalion officers, including Captain Carl James, who had a direct supervisory role over the Tigers. They were immediately struck by his eagerness to go into the field without really knowing Quang Ngai.

By evening, Hawkins began introducing himself to the Tigers, talking in a deep Kentucky drawl about his prior combat experience and trying to act like he was one of the grunts. He even mentioned that he was anxious to get laid in the whorehouses in Duc Pho.

But his words were worth only so much. To the Tigers, he looked more like he belonged in the rear than leading a Special Force in the most dangerous area of South Vietnam. Carpenter and others were willing to give him the benefit of the doubt. "He was with B Company, and they saw some serious shit, so we figured he was going to be okay," he recalled. But the Tigers knew that if Hawkins turned out to be a dud, they might have to take matters into their own hands.

That night, Hawkins and a few of the men hopped in a Jeep and drove west toward Duc Pho. Just outside the town, they were stopped at a roadblock and warned by a military policeman to turn around. The Vietcong were all over Duc Pho at night and it wasn't safe. But Hawkins didn't care. "He stood up in the Jeep and said he was going to get laid and no one was going to stop him," Carpenter recalled. The MP shook his head and waved them through.

Even before the next morning's briefing, the rumors spread quickly through camp: contrary to plan, the Tigers were heading back to the Song Ve. The men were already packing their rucksacks when Hawkins walked into the camp area and confirmed the news. "Saddle up," he said. "It's time to ride." For a moment, the men looked at one another, some frowning at the commander's John Wayne imitation.

"What's this? Cowboys and Indians?" Carpenter mumbled to the others.

No one said anything during the chopper ride to the valley. The soldiers were preparing themselves for a firefight, or worse — an ambush. Adding to the tension were the heat and humidity. Like a slow burn, the temperature was already at 90 degrees, and by noon, it would reach 100. The soldiers' uniforms were soaked, and their eyes burned from the perspiration. It didn't help that they were lugging heavy gear. Though some had been in country for nearly a year, no one had gotten used to the temperatures. The air would hug the body like a heavy blanket on a summer day. And for those who rubbed insect repellent on their bodies, it was even hotter because the lotion closed their pores.

Ken Kerney felt his stomach churning and had the sinking feeling someone was going to die. Staring around the inside of the Huey, he could see the same dreadful look on the faces of the others.

Below, the valley was covered by patches of scorched earth where the hamlets had been torched, wisps of black smoke still rising from the embers. The Hueys carrying the Tigers circled the area before hovering above a clearing. As the forty-five soldiers jumped from the choppers, the men noticed Hawkins hesitate for a moment, unsure where to go, before Trout quickly ordered the group to follow him.

As they neared the river, the men broke into four teams: two consisting of ten men each, one with thirteen, and the other with twelve. One team bolted toward the high ground above the first ridge. Before reaching the tree line, they stumbled on the remains of a burned-out hamlet. They stopped and noticed cooking pots and clothing scattered on the ground, indicating that someone had just been there. Within view was a raised earthen mound — a telltale sign that someone had been digging a bunker.

Two of the Tigers crawled to the opening, while the others stood back with their guns raised, pointing to the entrance. *"Dua Tay Len!"* one of the soldiers yelled, a warning to those inside to come out with their hands raised.

There was no answer.

The soldiers waited sixty seconds before entering the twenty-foot-deep bunker. Though no one was inside, the soldiers emerged a few minutes later with three helmets worn by North Vietnamese Army regulars, along with rucksacks, ammunition, and other equipment. It took but a second to sink in: The Tigers weren't going to be fighting just the local militia. They were going to be taking on the NVA.

Another team walking along the first ridge found a hut and, inside, a cache of weapons, including 60mm mortar rounds, three rockets, grenades, and two North Vietnamese textbooks on military discipline. From the color of the green thatch, the huts appeared to have been built just two to three days earlier. That made it clear the NVA was settling in. The Tigers had been away from the valley for just a few days, and the NVA were already "crawling all over the place," recalled Carpenter.

Gradually, as planned, the four Tiger teams moved to the center of the first ridge, and by the time the sun was directly over the valley, the platoon was united. Wood estimated they faced "probably a company of NVA." That would mean they were outnumbered three to one.

Shortly after Wood's prediction, a Tiger team broke from the platoon and began walking the ridge north of the river. The VC had been systematically stealing the rice from the locals and stashing it, even keeping detailed maps of the hiding places. The Tigers knew this and, as part of their mission, were supposed to ferret out the rice caches, some of which might contain tons.

The soldiers came upon a thicket of brush and found two large wooden structures. Carefully, the soldiers looked inside. No one was there, but there was room for an entire regiment.

Wood immediately got on the radio and provided the map coordinates to the U.S. gunships off the coast. Quickly, the soldiers moved out of the way before the shells struck their targets.

The explosions were enough to draw the attention of NVA infantry soldiers in the foothills, and as the Tigers began walking toward the river, shots were fired at them. After falling to the ground for cover, Wood quickly scanned the perimeter with his binoculars and noticed the fire was coming from a thicket across the river — a safe enough distance to call in another strike without hitting the Tigers. But before he could order the assault, Hawkins was on the radio, providing coordinates to the gunships. Wood protested the order, saying the coordinates were wrong.

"Lieutenant, you're going to get us killed," said Wood.

Hawkins yelled back that he was the commander and he would give the orders, but Wood refused to obey, grabbing the

radio and halting the strike. Hawkins was furious. He didn't like
being shown up in front of his men, especially by another officer. Wood walked over to his commander and held up a grid
map of the valley, pointing to the coordinates on the map.
"Look, Lieutenant, the strike should be here," he said, his finger on the coordinates. Hawkins looked carefully at the map
and turned away. Wood immediately called in the correct numbers, and within minutes, the strikes began — directly hitting
the target across the river. No one said a word. That night, Carpenter and other veterans gathered at their campsite in the
foothills and began to talk among themselves. "He could have
gotten us killed," Carpenter said of Hawkins.

That night, they set up camp along the river. Shortly thereafter,
the first grenade was hurled down, exploding one hundred meters from where most of the Tigers were sleeping. Ybarra, on
watch duty, yelled for the men to take cover. As is, the Tigers
were sitting ducks. Quickly, some soldiers scurried to the riverbank but were forced to crawl back to the camp after additional
grenades began exploding in the water.

"Where the hell are they?" Green blurted out. No one
knew. Ybarra began firing his M16 into the foothills, but Wood
quickly shouted for the point man to stop firing; by shooting,
they were giving their positions away. Wood grabbed the receiver from the radio telephone operator and called headquarters, requesting an artillery strike at coordinates just north of a
major bend in the Song Ve River. It was the closest he could es-
timate the enemy's position. The voice on the other end of the
radio urged the Tigers to hang on. There were no planes in the
area, and those that were available were assisting troops thirty
kilometers north, near Chu Lai. "We need artillery now,"
Wood barked into the phone. "We need it now."

The soldiers waited on their stomachs in the grass for another
fifteen minutes before the air support came. Wood recognized
the sound of the blasts: 7-62mm miniguns opening up from

AC-47 aircraft. "The sky just lit up," recalled Carpenter. The blasts were so close the men could feel the earth shake as they huddled closer to one another for what seemed like an eternity.

As soon as the assault concluded, the Tigers bolted for the tree line about three hundred meters from the river and waited. For the rest of the night, they stayed awake, expecting another attack, jumping at every sound. But nothing happened.

The next morning, everyone was tired and edgy. The Tigers hoped the rest of their time in the Song Ve would pass more easily, but to Trout, the mission was a loser. The troops had to be on the valley floor to make sure the hamlets were clear, but being so low in an area without cover opened the soldiers to attacks from the high ground. "We were beginning," he said, "to get nickeled-and-dimed."

For the next few days, the valley was quiet. For whatever reason, there were no more attacks. The Tigers suspected some villagers were returning — possibly escaping from Nghia Hanh — but were hiding. To the soldiers, the more pressing concern was the whereabouts of the NVA and Vietcong.

"They're still here," Trout warned the men.

No one could really relax, especially at night. They knew from several days earlier that the enemy was capable of targeting them from the high ground, but the orders from headquarters were firm: stay on the valley floor.

Just as the men settled down for camp on the north side of the river — after a full week of patrols — they heard the haunting sound of a whistle echoing from the foothills. It was a mortar, and within seconds it exploded in the river, just fifty meters away. "Take cover!" Hawkins yelled.

Within fifteen seconds, another mortar exploded, this time on the other side of the river. Then another, this time landing along the bank closest to the Tigers.

The men gathered their gear and hugged the ground — they had nowhere else to go. Kerrigan shook in the darkness and whispered a prayer. Kerney, Bowman, and Teeters huddled close to one another. They waited for the next round, hoping it would miss the mark. For several minutes, nothing happened. One Tiger began to rise, but Wood ordered him to hit the dirt. They waited, but the only noise they heard was a splash in the river, nothing else. Once again, things were quiet.

The next morning, several Tigers openly talked about killing anyone they saw — including villagers. "I ain't taking anyone to any relocation camp," snarled Sergeant Doyle.

Wood heard Doyle but didn't say anything until he and his team separated from the rest. "No one's going to kill unarmed civilians," he said wearily. "We're all tired. We're pissed off. But we stay under control."

Already, fatigue was setting in, and that wasn't a good sign. Exhaustion in battle can cause soldiers to get anxious, even jumpy — just the opposite of someone in civilian life. One sound — a twig breaking under a soldier's foot — can cause a soldier to needlessly fire his gun. Simple orders are often forgotten and warning signs for booby traps and other obstacles are frequently overlooked. The Tigers were wearing down.

Kerney and others began to notice that the platoon members were starting to break into factions. Soldiers such as Ybarra and Doyle wanted to just start shooting. Others, like Wood and Sanchez, wanted to toe the line. Newcomers, including Kerney and Kerrigan and Bowman, found themselves caught in the middle.

Kerney kept telling himself over and over to stay strong. Don't get crazy. But Kerrigan was already on the verge of losing it. He would try to calm down by thinking about the nights in Southern California when he would walk the beach and stare at the sky. In the Song Ve, the stars were incredible: bright and sparkling against the darkness. He would close his eyes and make believe he was on the beach just to keep from shaking. As a surfer, he could ride into a storm on powerful waves and never think about dying. But nothing in his life had prepared him for this. Here, death could come from anywhere, at any time.

The Tigers were able to take their first real break when the entire platoon set up camp near a burned-out hamlet along the river on July 23.

The soldiers removed their rucksacks and watched a supply chopper fly over and drop several cases of Black Label beer, containers of hot food, and supplies. Not since leaving Carentan had the men been able to relax. "Everyone, including myself, was pretty well uptight," recalled Sergeant Forrest Miller.

With the sun glistening on the river, the men tossed cans to one another. The Black Label was warm, but they didn't care — it was beer and it tasted good. They opened their rations, removing hot plates of spaghetti, beef tips, and vegetables. The men watched as Hawkins drank one beer, then another. By dusk, he was loud and obnoxious. He staggered as he walked back and forth between the radio and the supplies, and at one point nearly tripped over another soldier.

To the soldiers, Trout looked like he was trying to keep up with Hawkins, downing beer after beer. They were like two country boys at a backyard barbecue. "He was acting funny — more brave than he actually was," said Miller. "After three beers, he was wiped out."

Hawkins and Trout started ranting about having to be in the Song Ve and "became loud and boisterous," recalled Sergeant Leo Heaney. Ybarra and Green, who had already guzzled several beers apiece, were also stumbling into a foaming incoherence.

Wood, who had been watching the men drink for hours, grew concerned and just hoped the Tigers would not need to fight the enemy that night. The best thing they could do was sleep. But as the sun set over the valley, a call came over the radio: Your break is over. Gear up. Get ready to go out on maneuvers.

★ ★ ★

Darkness set in, but Dao Hue knew the trail by heart.

The sixty-eight-year-old carpenter had walked the dirt path that wound around the river for most of his life, but it was getting harder. Because of pains in his joints, he had to frequently stop on trips to other villages.

At sunset, he left the hut he shared with his niece, Tam Hau, in what remained of Hanh Tin in the center of the valley, to walk to a hamlet a mile away to get geese from a peasant who had been trapping them along the river. He and his niece were glad to be back in the valley. Dao had escaped to the mountains while other family members were rounded up and whisked away in choppers to Nghia Hanh. For the past three days, Dao and others who had eluded the American dragnet had spent hours in the hot sun with their machetes, cutting bamboo and thatch from the brush. Even though he was in great pain, he wanted to use his skills to help rebuild the huts the Americans had incinerated.

Dao, whose wife died three years earlier, didn't like leaving his niece alone. But if he didn't get the geese, they might have to wait another day to eat. They had consumed their supply of rice, and it wasn't safe to harvest what was left in the fields.

He found the villager and accepted two geese in exchange for promises to help the man build a hut. Dao placed the dead animals in two baskets hanging from the ends of a shoulder bar he brought from his hut and began the trek back home. Instead of walking the trail, he decided to wade across the shallow end of the river to avoid any chance of being seen by VC or Americans.

Wood couldn't believe the orders: cross the river and set up an ambush. It was reckless to do this after drinking all afternoon. And to cross the Song Ve at night? Too many things could happen. Night patrols were dangerous enough with snipers along the riverbanks and pungi sticks planted in the ground along dikes and hidden by the rice plants. Sharp enough to pierce a man's foot and covered with enough human feces to infect a victim within hours, the sticks had been plaguing the line companies ever since they arrived in Quang Ngai.

For days, Wood had been avoiding Hawkins, but he knew he had to try reasoning with the platoon commander now. He jumped up and walked over to Hawkins as he was putting on his rucksack.

"You can't do this," he said, arguing that the men had been drinking and couldn't possibly function at their best on a night maneuver. Hawkins, clutching his carbine .15 rifle, ignored Wood and instead turned to the men. "Let's saddle up and ride," he bellowed.

Wood was undeterred. He jumped around Hawkins to face him again, saying the ambush was a stupid and dangerous move. But the tall, lanky commander — towering over the five-foot, nine-inch Wood — brushed by his forward artillery observer and headed toward the river with several others in tow.

Wood just shook his head and, instead of protesting again, went to the rear of the column. "I was second from last in line, feeling that this was the safest place to be considering the condition of most of the members of Tiger Force," he recalled.

They began wading across the waist-high water, but instead of keeping quiet, the men began talking among themselves, their voices rising in the darkness. Wood was furious. He felt that Hawkins should have been controlling the soldiers but instead was joining in with them.

Within a minute, Sergeant James Haugh surprised everyone by tossing a grenade in the water, the explosion loud enough to be heard across the valley. Some of the men burst out laughing, and now Wood knew the platoon was in trouble. For days, the VC and North Vietnamese had been infiltrating the valley. The sole reason the Tigers were on this maneuver was because of intelligence reports showing the enemy was expected to move rice in sampans down the river. The success of any ambush depended on the element of surprise. Drunk soldiers fooling around with explosives was a formula for disaster.

As the Tigers reached the other side, Leo Heaney picked four soldiers for a team to provide security while the rest of the men set up the ambush. As Heaney led the team down a trail, he came face-to-face in the darkness with Dao Hue. Heaney grabbed the old man. "He was terrified and folded his hands, and started what appeared to me as praying for mercy in a loud, high-pitched tone of voice," Heaney recalled.

Heaney could tell Dao was harmless but didn't have the authority to let him go, so he brought him back to the area where the Tigers were setting up the ambush. The sergeant watched as Dao trembled, pleading in Vietnamese to be left alone.

Standing a few feet away, Trout was annoyed. The old man shouldn't even be in the valley. Without warning, Trout stepped forward and clubbed Dao on the head with the barrel of his M16. The old man flew to the ground, moaning, blood running down the side of his face.

Hawkins, who heard the commotion, rushed over and saw Dao on the ground. "Shut this old fucker up or I'll kill him," he insisted.

Carpenter jumped to Dao's defense. "The old man's just a farmer. He can't hurt anyone!" he shouted. But Hawkins pushed Carpenter away with his left hand, admonishing the soldier for speaking up. "You chicken shit son of a bitch. If you don't shut up, I'll shoot you," Hawkins told him.

Medic Barry Bowman stepped forward to treat Dao, but Hawkins thrust his rifle up to the old man's head and pulled the trigger. There was a blast and Dao fell backward to the ground. Hawkins pulled the trigger again. At first, Carpenter thought *he* was the one who was shot because he was hit by pieces of the old man's skull and flesh, but quickly realized it was Dao. He looked down and saw the old man was dead. "Half of his head was blown off," he recalled.

Bowman, who was also hit by the pieces of flesh, was

stunned, and for several minutes was quiet. He had joined the Army as a medic to help save lives and was now wondering what was happening.

Wood ran from the riverbank and bolted toward the men as they stood around Dao's body. "What happened?" he asked as he neared the group. Before anyone could answer, Trout ran up behind Wood and struck him on the side of the head, knocking him to the ground. As Wood fell down, he heard someone fire a round over his head.

Feeling dizzy, Wood got back up and walked toward Hawkins. "I got one," Hawkins said, smiling. Wood turned around, still groggy, and staggered away, realizing that it had been Hawkins — his commander — who had fired a shot over his head.

Before he had a chance to confront Hawkins and Trout, shots were fired near the river. The commotion had caught the enemy's attention, and now the Tigers were in trouble. Their position was known, and there were more enemy soldiers in the valley than Tigers. For the next hour, they were forced to fend for themselves along the river, running from enemy fire and dodging grenades. "Luckily," said Carpenter, "no one was killed." But it was now obvious to him and Wood that Tiger Force was being led by a nut who would have allies, and that even if they survived, bad things were bound to be on the way.

CHAPTER 9

I n the morning, Wood kept his distance from everyone. Usually, he pored over maps with team leaders, but he was in no mood to talk, and he wanted nothing to do with Hawkins.

When the Tigers gathered up their gear and began walking in the direction of Hanh Tin, Wood stayed in the rear. He was still seething over the killing of the old man near the river. It was an unjustified shooting, but more than that, it was stupid. It gave the platoon's position away, leading to a firefight. If Hawkins was trying to keep the prisoner quiet, there were other ways.

"He's not fit to lead anything," Wood told Carpenter that morning.

Even the commander's drinking buddies from the night before had some concerns. Already, the Tigers were making snide remarks behind his back, several calling Hawkins "Jingles" because when he walked his pants would make noise from the many objects stuffed in his pockets.

As the platoon reached the outskirts of the hamlet, the soldiers could see a cluster of huts. Hawkins ordered the men to halt. He went down the line, picking several men to set up a perimeter around the area, with each one responsible for guarding a three-hundred-meter area. Anyone walking in or out of the area would be stopped, detained, and questioned by translators. The Tigers were determined to keep people from building more huts. "This is a free-fire zone," Hawkins said. "No one is supposed to be here."

Wood walked to the front of the perimeter where Hawkins was standing, but Wood didn't acknowledge him. The morning fog had already burned away, and the translators were in the hamlet talking to a few remaining villagers, getting them ready to be evacuated, when a Tiger spotted two women walking toward their position. "Two approaching!" the guard shouted. Hawkins looked over and told the men to open fire. As soon as he uttered the words, Wood blurted out with a hand raised, "No, hold your fire. Hold your fire."

Hawkins wheeled around, his face flushed, and angrily snapped, "You don't countermand my orders. This is my platoon."

Wood turned to Hawkins. "They're openly approaching our position. It looks like they want to communicate with us."

With the men waiting, their weapons drawn, Hawkins lifted his rifle, aimed at the women, and began firing, followed by another Tiger Force soldier. The two women fell to the ground, one screaming.

Wood couldn't believe what he had just seen. He pivoted around and faced Hawkins, who had just lowered his rifle. "What the hell are you doing?" he screamed. "These were just two old women!"

Without waiting for a response, Wood and two medics rushed to where the women fell. One was shot in the leg and arm; the other did not appear to be hurt but was shaking and crying on the ground.

As the medics leaned over the women, Wood rose and ordered a radio operator to call for a medevac. No one protested the command.

Wood was beside himself. He stormed to the opposite side of the hamlet. He was done with Hawkins. He was going to report everything when he got back to Carentan. There was no way Hawkins should be leading a platoon, and if the commanders didn't relieve him of duty, Wood would ask to be transferred.

"This isn't good," he told Carpenter later. "This isn't good. This isn't good for the Tigers. You tell me how a guy like this ends up becoming a commander."

As the sun set over the mountains, the Tigers slipped off their gear and settled down in the brush. There was not much left to do. Other than the two elderly women who were targeted, no one else had approached the perimeter. It was getting too late to move, and it was better to set up camp along the river just outside the entrance to Hanh Tin.

Just before dark, Wood and six others walked away from the camp, each stopping to dig a foxhole in the dry red soil around Hanh Tin — spaced seventy-five meters apart — with two Tigers posted along a large bend of the river. If the Tigers were going to get ambushed, it was going to be at night and they wanted to be ready.

For several hours, it was quiet, and many of the Tigers dozed off. One thing Carpenter noticed before falling asleep was the brightness of the moon, casting shadows on the valley floor as if it were a sun instead of a satellite. "It was like nothing I had seen in a long time," he recalled.

Sleeping in between Trout and Bowman, Carpenter was startled awake by shots. He jumped up and grabbed his M16 when he heard someone shout, "We need a medic!" He and Bowman ran fifty meters to the perimeter, where they saw a Vietnamese male in his early twenties rolling on the ground, holding his leg. Covered in blood, he was crying.

Bowman could see the man was seriously wounded. He

opened his medic kit to look for bandages as Trout arrived. The team sergeant asked what happened, and one of the soldiers on guard said he shot the man because he had approached the perimeter. Trout stared at the man on the ground and could tell he needed a medevac. But there was no way he was going to call in a chopper and give the Tigers' position away. As Bowman began wrapping bandages around the man's leg, Trout slipped next to the medic and removed a .45-caliber handgun from his side. He then thrust the gun in the medic's face. "C'-mon, Doc, break your cherry," he said.

Bowman knew what the sergeant meant. But that would mean crossing a line — one he didn't want to cross. He and Trout had been on maneuvers several times, and he knew the veteran sergeant wanted his soldiers to be tough. But this was different. This was murder. The man rolling around in the dirt in pain wasn't carrying a weapon. The men didn't even know if he was an enemy soldier. He could have been a villager returning home like so many others. "I couldn't do it," he recalled. "It was against everything I believed." He'd become a medic to save lives, not take them.

Trout shrugged his shoulders and pointed the .45 at the man, calmly firing three shots into his chest and head. Bowman stood speechless, too afraid to protest, too afraid to say anything.

For a minute, the men stood and stared at the man's body, twitching in the dirt. "No one bothered to check the body for an ID card," Carpenter recalled.

Wood, who arrived as the sergeant was pulling the trigger, didn't know what to say to Trout. Though he didn't always agree with the veteran, he respected him. Now he had watched the sergeant execute a wounded man. And Trout had done it in front of so many of the soldiers who looked up to him.

★　★　★

The medics were huddled in their own group along the river-bank, uncharacteristically quiet. Normally they would borrow supplies from one another and chat about what transpired with their teams. But no one wanted to say anything. They had heard about the killing of the old man by the river and the shooting of the wounded Vietnamese by Trout.

Teeters just wanted out of the Song Ve. Nothing good was happening here. Since joining the Tigers in February, he had never seen anything like this. Something was happening in Tiger Force that he couldn't quite put his finger on. It was no secret that everyone was pissed off. No one wanted to be in this hellhole. The heat was wearing on everyone, and so was the jungle rot.

The tension was keeping the men awake at night, and to carry out the day's mission, Teeters and other medics were passing out Black Beauties, amphetamines that would jack up the soldiers but also increase their stress — a dangerous combination. Now Teeters was dipping into the bag himself — it seemed the only way to get through the days.

He wondered whether he would ever get back to Oregon, particularly the pines and streams where he fished with his father, Don. He kept thinking more and more about his home — his mother, Gayle, and two brothers — something he knew he shouldn't do. *Don't lose your head. Don't think too much.* "Man, this is fucking nuts," he said to the others.

A soldier on edge isn't necessarily bad. The brain and body adapt to war: the senses become sharpened to every noise, every flicker of light, every smell. But when soldiers are artificially stimulated and are lacking sleep, they become agitated at the slightest thing. They are too tired to process every sound, sight, and smell. They become overwhelmed by their surroundings, and without rest, they are no longer capable of making sound decisions. The Tigers were teetering on the edge.

Lying under a cover of leaves, Nyugen Dam peeked out to make sure there were no soldiers. He had been hiding under the thick green underbrush, but with no one in sight, he rose slowly and walked a few feet to the water's edge to wait for another villager. Across the river, he saw his friend wading toward him, his head barely visible above the moonlit water.

Nyugen was irritated after waiting for hours and whispered to the man to hurry. Even after sunset, it was dangerous to be in the open. The American soldiers could be anywhere. As the two reached the riverbank, Nyugen grabbed a shovel hidden in the brush.

They crept along a dike and then to the edge of the hamlet where the soldiers had been earlier in the day, ever watchful of lights flickering in the darkness — a sure sign the soldiers were near. For the villagers, the only safe places were the old bunkers in the foothills. The Vietcong knew the locations of the underground shelters, but they weren't bothering the villagers, at least not now. Not with the Americans in the valley.

With each step, Nyugen and his companion could smell a familiar odor lingering in the night air. The man cupped his hand over his nose as he neared the tree line. Next to the remains of a hut was the body of the Vietnamese shot by Trout several hours earlier. Nyugen and his companion had known the smell of death before. They had buried fellow villagers and family members in the past.

Nyugen stood for a moment and stared at the corpse, the face unrecognizable and the shirt soaked in dark blotches of blood. Hours earlier, he had seen the body from a distance but was unable to move closer in fear of being spotted by the soldiers. He did not see the execution but heard the shots from the foothills.

It was hard to recognize the dead villager, especially in the darkness. It would be impossible to bury him in the nearby rice paddy, because the water would push the corpse back to the surface. Nyugen walked fifty meters to a clearing, bent over, and rubbed the soil between his fingers. It was dry, red clay — good enough to support a shallow grave. He handed the shovel to the other man and told him to dig a large, round hole, but not too deep. The man began digging while Nyugen walked back to the body.

Nyugen tried not to think about the victim, but it was difficult. As he lifted the arms of the man to carry him to the burial site, he noticed large gaping wounds on both sides of the man's head. Because it was dark, he peered closer to get a better look and noticed the ears were missing.

CHAPTER 10

Green and Ybarra couldn't sleep. It was like every other night: sweltering heat, with the air so heavy it was tough to breathe. The monsoon rains had just hours earlier soaked the valley floor. The friends were used to warm weather from growing up in Arizona, but nothing had prepared them for Vietnam's humidity — a constant steam room with little breeze. The Tigers had set up camp hours earlier, hoping to sleep, but the mosquitoes and saturated air made it impossible.

"I hate this place," Ybarra blurted out to several soldiers gathered around the camp. So did Green. So did Trout. So did Ed Beck, now so covered with sores and cuts that he visibly limped and staggered on maneuvers. He was waiting until early morning, when he would sneak a quick dip into the cool waters of the Song Ve for some relief, even though the medics had warned him to stay away from the water. His open sores, oozing with pus and blood, would only attract leeches, and the Song Ve was full of them. But what else could he do? Beck had been hounding the medics for more antibacterial salve and tetracycline, yet it never seemed enough. The only way to numb the pain was by popping Darvon, a sedative and painkiller. It helped but left Beck woozy when he needed to be focused and clearheaded.

Earlier in the day, air surveillance pilots had radioed battalion headquarters, saying they spotted a dozen enemy soldiers running down a foothill in the eastern end of the valley near a pagoda. Now, several hours later, the Tigers were camped just two hundred meters from that pagoda. Team leaders told the soldiers pulling security detail on the perimeter to be especially alert and quiet.

Just after midnight, the Tigers were startled by an explosion. No one knew where it came from, but it was close enough that they could feel the earth vibrate. As some of the Tigers rolled over, M16s in hand, another explosion sounded just fifty meters away from the camp. Teeters heard cries of "Medic, medic," then came another blast even closer, followed by a voice screaming in the darkness, "I'm hit!"

Hawkins stood up and peered across the river. "Where the fuck are those coming from?" he asked aloud, but before anyone could answer, enemy soldiers began spraying the campsite with bullets from AK-47 assault rifles. The Tigers were trapped.

To Wood, it was time to clear out. One medic, while bandaging the leg of a soldier, told Hawkins the small, sharp, slashlike wounds were from Chicom — Chinese Communist — grenades. It appeared the explosives were hand-tossed, indicating the enemy soldiers were close. The medics crawled to the four men struck by grenade fragments. The grenades seemed to be coming from a hill just beyond the pagoda, though no one knew for sure. Given that, Wood guessed the Tigers would have to move two kilometers west before it was safe to order an air strike.

Clutching his M16, Wood yelled for the men to follow him as he bolted for brush just beyond the campsite. "The grenades were just coming out of nowhere," recalled Bowman. Some of the soldiers ran to the medics to help them carry the wounded, and as the grenades exploded around the camp, the Tigers began moving westward.

They didn't feel safe until they could hear the grenades well behind them. When the platoon finally reached what remained of the Hanh Tin hamlet, Wood called battalion headquarters and requested an air strike, giving the coordinates of the areas north and south of the river from where he suspected the enemy launched the grenades. Within minutes, the gunships off the coast were firing their five-inch guns.

From across the valley, Company B soldiers were ordered to move to Hahn Tin hamlet to protect the Tigers. While the Tigers waited for the medevacs, they set up a security perimeter around the area. "It was a long, shitty night," said Carpenter.

Two medevacs arrived about the same time as the Company B soldiers. The Tigers quickly carried the wounded aboard. After the choppers departed, the platoon members and other battalion soldiers reinforced the perimeter and waited. For the rest of the night, no more shots were fired, but no one slept.

Most of the Tigers expected to return to Carentan to rest, while larger and better-equipped line companies moved in. But by sunrise, the Tigers received their orders: stay on the valley floor. Their new mission was to patrol the trails along the river, round up any civilian stragglers, and send them by choppers to the relocation camp.

No one liked the orders, not even Hawkins. By sheer geography, the Tigers were open targets from the high ground. "I began to question what the hell we were doing," Bowman recalled. Commanders were making decisions from the safety of Carentan, not the valley. "We're tired of being bait," Trout complained.

Soldiers are trained to go into battle, but there's a fundamental component to combat: the infantryman wants to know his commander is supportive and understands the risks. The soldier wants to know the commander would do the same thing — and has been called to do the same in the past. It wasn't lost on the Tigers that ultimately the orders — life-and-death decisions — were being made by officers in a base camp. The Tigers had been left to fend for themselves.

Gathering their gear, they began breaking into teams, and then huddled for their assignments. One team would walk the wide, twisting trail running north of the river; another would cross to the south side and cover the main path there. Two other teams would inspect the areas once covered by the valley's seven villages. Noticeably angry, Hawkins announced, "Anything in this valley is ours. There are no friendlies. Do you hear me? There are no friendlies. No one is supposed to be here."

Shouting, he gave the order "Shoot anything that moves!"

The first team, after wading across the river to the south side, found a trail tucked deep in the brush. Much of the path was covered over by elephant grass, so the soldiers began cutting through the thick green stalks with their knives. Warned to be on the lookout for booby traps, they took their time slicing through the thick morass still soaked by the morning dew until they came upon a clearing.

With the fog just lifting from the valley, the soldiers could spot three figures in the distance walking along a dike. The soldiers quickly jumped to the side of the trail and waited with rifles aimed. As the people came closer, the soldiers could see a young boy leading two men by the arms. The men, who appeared to be blind, were stumbling in the grass.

As the villagers walked by, medic Forrest Miller and two other soldiers jumped out of the brush and grabbed the three Vietnamese. Miller quickly determined they were unarmed.

"They're just peasants," he said.

The soldiers surrounded the boy and men, and took them back to the clearing. As they waited for the first chopper of the day to arrive in the Song Ve, another team joined them a few minutes later. With Miller standing by, the soldiers argued over what to do with the detainees.

Sergeant Ernest Moreland recalled that some of the Tigers

firmly believed the three were "trail watchers" alerting the Vietcong to the Americans. Some suggested the peasants had something to do with the attack on the Tigers' camp. Miller wasn't so sure. Two of the soldiers had already separated the two blind men from the boy and began pushing the men into a nearby rice paddy. They raised their rifles and fired. Both men fell to the ground. It happened so fast Miller didn't have time to react. He knew the two men shouldn't have been in the valley but asked why they were executed.

"They're VC, man," one of the soldiers said as he walked away.

Miller glanced at the boy, who was trembling. As the soldiers began arguing over what to do with the youth, who looked no older than twelve, they suddenly picked up the sound of a chopper in the distance. Another minute and things might have been different, but now they couldn't kill the boy — there might be witnesses from the Huey hovering overhead. Moments later, the chopper landed near the two bodies, and the boy was led to the open door and placed aboard for transport to Nghia Hanh.

Stepping back from the madness, Tiger Force was at a crucial juncture. If there was a moment when this unit needed to be reined in, it was now. Once commanders look the other way, the soldiers begin to take liberties. As combat intensifies, so does the frequency of attacks. Soldiers are capable of spinning into a frenzy — feeding on one another's anger and emotion. Without a strong leader to keep them in line, the attacks continue. Without a strong leader to impose consequences, nothing changes. That's what was starting to happen in Tiger Force. Hawkins was supposed to be the governor on the engine, ensuring the motor didn't rev too high. Instead, he was stepping on the gas.

While the chopper was leaving the valley, another team was entering a hamlet a half mile away where new huts had been erected in the shadow of a tree line. As the soldiers began checking the hooches, an elderly man wearing a gray robe and tassels emerged and began shouting in Vietnamese. Without a translator on the team, no one could understand him, but the man was clearly upset. Dressed in the robes of a Buddhist worshipper, he appeared to be a village elder. Carpenter guessed the man was riled about the destruction of his village. The soldiers just brushed by the old man. They needed to search the huts for people, rice, and weapons and then clear out, not listen to his gibberish. But the man was undeterred. He followed the soldiers and continued ranting as they went from hut to hut, until one of the Tigers wheeled around and, without warning, fired several rounds into the man's head and chest. As he fell to the ground, the Tigers rushed to the body and then looked around to see if anyone else was watching. They immediately began arguing among themselves: if the South Vietnamese translators or others saw that a holy man was shot, the Tigers could be in trouble. Someone might tell Colonel Austin or, worse, report the shooting to the Army's Criminal Investigation Division in Saigon.

Two of the soldiers came up with a solution: plant a grenade on the man to make him look like the enemy.

As much as any Tiger, Manuel Sanchez despised the Song Ve but was determined to keep his men in control. If he could just hang on for another two months, he could be rotated back to the States. *Just try to get through each day — each hour. Just think about Mary, how much you love her and want to be with her. How much you want to sit on her front porch, the sun setting, and sing to her.* The night before he joined the Army, he had reclined on her porch swing with his guitar and had sung "Sixteen Candles," watching her giggle. It was her birthday, and he had given her a sterling silver heart with a tiny diamond in the center so she would remember that his heart was with her while he was gone. Before leaving, she had pressed a crucifix into the palm of his hand. For much of his tour, he had kept the cross in his rucksack, but now, he found himself clenching it in his hand, leaving marks on his palm.

Say the Our Father, he would remind himself. *It will keep you safe. But whatever you do, don't pop those pills. They'll mess you up.*

He didn't like the way some soldiers treated the villagers. He was Mexican-American, and he was conscious of the way his own people were treated back in southern New Mexico. Growing up, he was called a wetback more times than he cared to remember. And this in a state where the whites who taunted him came from families who hadn't even heard of New Mexico when Spanish speakers had already settled the place.

After these two weeks, Sanchez considered Hawkins a redneck who mistreated the Vietnamese. He was particularly upset over the execution of Dao Hue. "It was cold-blooded," Sanchez told his team. "The man had no weapons and he offered no resistance." He also believed that when soldiers cross the line in the field, "bad things happen," he said. And bad things were already starting to happen, like the grenade attack the night before. When you stretched the definition of what was right too far, the band had a way of snapping back and slapping you in the face hard.

As his team was walking down a hill and into a rice paddy, Sanchez spotted two peasants running across the field. He ordered them in Vietnamese to halt, but they ignored him.

His soldiers raised their rifles, but Sanchez told them not to fire. "They're not armed," he said of the peasants. Instead, he bolted across the paddy, followed by his men, and after a short chase, they tackled the two Vietnamese. After searching the two for weapons, the soldiers led the detainees to a knoll just beyond the paddy.

Sanchez suspected the older man was probably Vietcong, and with the assistance of a translator, he began questioning him. After several minutes, the man — hobbling from an earlier shrapnel wound to his lower left leg — confessed to being VC and said the younger detainee was his thirteen-year-old brother. On Sanchez's order, a team member called battalion headquarters to report the capture of the prisoners and to ask what should be done with the injured detainee.

Over the radio, a voice responded, "What do you do with a horse with a broken leg?"

Sanchez shook his head. "I'm not going to kill him," he said. He was going to hold the line. He was intent on bringing the brothers back to camp as his prisoners, and that's what he was going to do — regardless of what headquarters suggested.

All the Tiger Force teams were directed back to a clearing near the Hanh Tin hamlet, where they would camp.

As darkness set over the valley, two of the teams reached the clearing, and the soldiers began unpacking. Wood agreed that he and five other soldiers would set up a security perimeter until midnight, and then another team would take over.

Sanchez and his team dragged themselves into the clearing, exhausted, with the prisoners in tow. He was going to personally guard them until a chopper could come in the next morning.

Ybarra wasn't happy about the Vietnamese brothers being brought into camp. To punctuate his discontent, he began bragging about capturing a prisoner earlier in the day. Several of his team members cringed when he started to recount the story. It was an unwritten rule to keep quiet about patrol activities, even with other teams. But Ybarra was intent on telling the story.

Green shifted uneasily but didn't say anything as Ybarra began describing how he jabbed a knife into the throat of the detainee, just wanting to break the skin to torture him. But, he said, after several minutes of Sam coaxing his Arizona buddy into finishing the job, Green plunged the knife into the man's neck.

Instead of silencing a horrified group, Ybarra's story simply encouraged others to unload. Two members from another team began by teasing Sergeant Robin Varney. "We call him 'One Punch,'" one soldier said.

Earlier in the day, the lone team with a translator had stopped a detainee. With the help of the interpreter, the soldiers began asking the man questions. Frustrated at the lack of response, the translator began cursing. Suddenly, Varney walked over and bet the soldiers he could knock the man out with one blow. Varney punched the man in the face, knocking him to the ground, but the prisoner was still conscious. The soldiers laughed, saying he lost his bet. The prisoner was forced back to his feet and then Ernest Moreland sneaked up behind the man, holding a bayonet in back of the prisoner's neck. Varney then pushed the prisoner's head into the blade, impaling him.

By talking about what happened that day, the Tigers were unconsciously taking part in a ritual that had been around since the beginning of warfare. In World War I, they called it a hot wash. In World War II, it was a debriefing. By talking about the day's events — usually combat — the soldiers are able to work their way through the memory and, in the process, minimize the emotions associated with the events. They were taking an important step toward justifying their actions in the field.

But the Tigers were taking it one step further. They were desensitizing themselves to the torture and execution of prisoners — not enemy combatants.

As Sanchez sat near his prisoners, two soldiers approached him and said they were ordered by Hawkins to take his prisoners down the hill just outside the camp. Sanchez decided he was going to accompany them.

Sanchez followed the soldiers as they led the brothers down the slope. When they reached the bottom, the two Tigers ordered the brothers to stand next to each other, and before Sanchez could act, the soldiers raised their M16s and shot the prisoners from five feet away. Sanchez was stunned. He had vowed to keep them alive until a chopper arrived, and now he felt betrayed.

He couldn't look at their bodies. He turned around and stormed back up the hill, cursing. When he reached the top, he stomped to the far end of the camp to be alone, turning his back to the soldiers.

One of the Tigers who led the prisoners away approached him, saying he was sorry. "I was just following orders," he said. "Get away from me," Sanchez snapped.

In the darkness, Nyugen Dam crawled into the rice paddy, running his hands through the muck in search of the bodies. He needed to move quickly. The NVA and American soldiers were encamped, and he had just a few hours before dawn to find the dead.

He barely knew the two blind men who were shot earlier in the day, but he knew the boy, Vo Cahn, and his parents. From a mountain perch a quarter mile away, he had watched as the soldiers led the two men into the field, certain they would be killed. He had hoped they would spare young Vo. In his mind, Nyugen could visualize the boy with the wide grin who often played along the dirt roads of the Van Xuan village. Nyugen had been happy to see the chopper swoop down and carry Vo away. At least he had a chance to survive at Nghia Hanh and maybe be reunited with his parents. This valley had turned into an abattoir.

The blind men were not from the Song Ve but had ended up there after their village was bombed outside Duc Pho. They were led to the valley by a relative who was later captured by battalion soldiers during the evacuation. For the last two weeks, the two blind men had been going from hamlet to hamlet, just trying to stay away from the soldiers. Nyugen knew Vo was attempting to help the men hide.

On his hands and knees, Nyugen brushed aside the rice plants as he moved along the paddy, looking for remains. Just before he reached a dike, he touched one of the bodies.

He had vowed that as long as he was in the valley, he would try to bury the people killed by the soldiers. It was disrespectful to leave their corpses rotting in the sun. But this was going to be difficult. He would have to drag each body across the length of the paddy to reach dry soil.

Over the next hour, he trudged through the muck, at times stopping to rest. After pulling the corpses to a clearing, he found the shovel he had hidden near a trail and began digging a shallow hole. Just then, two other Vietnamese men showed up, helping him cover the bodies with the soil.

With two hours to spare before sunrise, the three crept along the trail until they reached the edge of the foothills where other villagers had been hiding. Nyugen warned them to leave. If they wanted to stay, they would have to go deeper into the mountains. But some of the villagers were defiant. They were angry and determined to remain. This was their land, and they were not going to subject themselves to the humiliation of Nghia Hanh. Some had already been there and escaped. They hated the filth and the fear, the concrete walls, barbed wire, and armed soldiers. They weren't going back.

No one was going near Sanchez. It was better to leave him alone.

After his prisoners had been killed, he walked to the edge of the campsite and plopped down on the ground.

He felt responsible for the death of Dao Hue and was now blaming himself for failing to protect the Vietnamese brothers. The choppers would have been in the Song Ve in the morning and would have taken them to Go Hoi. It would have been no burden to the unit to watch over them for a few more hours. Killing the two was not only unnecessary — it was stupid. The VC could have been interrogated. Now he was a wasted opportunity.

In the campsite, all of the soldiers but one were sleeping in a circle known as a wagon wheel, their feet pointing to the center. That way, if they were attacked or if someone heard a suspicious sound, they could kick or nudge the person next to them. The exception was Sanchez, who stayed on the perimeter. He didn't know how long he could remain in the unit with Hawkins. He had been a Tiger for seven months. He had lived through more than a dozen battles, including the Mother's Day Massacre. He had always felt proud to do what he did. The Tigers were trained to be aggressive: that was the culture. But Sanchez was now seeing actions that went beyond the bounds of war.

"You don't kill civilians and you don't kill prisoners," he told his men. But that's what was happening, and no one else seemed to care.

As he sat staring into the darkness, he heard a thud close by in the brush, and before he had time to react, Sanchez was knocked backward by an explosion. Suddenly, he was rolling on the ground, with sharp, stinging pains in his legs and side.

"I'm hit!" he yelled out before another explosion shook the camp, and then another. Wood yelled for the soldiers to stay down, crawl to the hill, and then roll to the bottom. Not everyone heard him, and before Sergeant Domingo Munoz could escape the camp, fragments from a grenade ripped into his body. Immediately, two medics rushed to him as the other soldiers bolted for the hill. Wood was already on the radio to headquarters, calling for help. Another medic crawled to assist Sanchez, who could barely move.

Unlike the previous attack, the Americans could see the enemy's position just beyond the hamlet, and several Tigers on the perimeter began firing their M16s and M79 grenade launchers into the brush. The hamlet was lit up by the counterassault.

A half dozen Tigers stood their positions, blasting the thicket. The M79s appeared to be doing much of the damage, blowing out sections of trees. After several minutes, the Tigers stopped firing, waiting for the enemy to begin lobbing another round of grenades, but nothing happened. Except for the moans of the wounded, there was silence.

As the soldiers returned to the camp, a medevac headed out to pick up Sanchez, Munoz, and another wounded Tiger. Sanchez looked as if he would survive. As the medics wrapped tourniquets around his legs to stop the bleeding, he managed to reach his shirt pocket for his crucifix and clenched his teeth. "Please don't let me die," he said. Munoz was in worse shape; the medics could not stop the bleeding. Blood gushed out of his wounds, and with it, his life.

The "bad things" Sanchez had worried about were no longer hypotheticals. The clock had struck midnight.

CHAPTER 11

With bags of rice seedlings flung over their backs, Kieu Cong and the other farmers trudged down the mountain, swinging machetes to cut through the brush. For nearly an hour, they slashed through the thicket, cutting themselves on the sharp elephant grass and bamboo as they moved down the slope. Though some of the people complained, Kieu knew it was the only way. Indeed, he had told them as much before leaving their hideaway. They needed to reach the valley floor and plant the young green sprouts in order to grow more rice to survive. Their own supplies were dwindling and would be gone in ninety days — at best. There was an easier path to the valley floor, but the farmers were afraid the American soldiers would see them. So this was the only way.

After clearing the brush, the people reached a steep footpath where, a day earlier, they had tied two water buffalo to a tree. After throwing harnesses around the animals, the farmers slowly led the oxen down the slope. Without the animals, there was no way they could plow the field.

As the sun was rising, they reached the valley floor and traipsed onto the first rice paddy, the muck squishing between their toes. Kieu didn't waste any time. He turned around and motioned for the men to plow and the women to plant. They had two hours to insert as many seedlings in the ground as possible before returning to the mountains. If they were lucky no one would see them.

At sixty, Kieu was actually the youngest farmer on the field, but he was undoubtedly their leader. Raised in the Song Ve, he was seen as an elder, even if not the oldest, a likable fellow who had the respect of people from Van Xuan village.

A generous man who traveled frequently to the pagoda to pray, Kieu was known for teaching the tenets of Buddhism to all who asked him. But mostly, people sought his advice about growing rice. He took the time to teach younger villagers how to build dikes and how to know when seedlings were ready for planting. He would lead the young villagers into the paddies, patiently showing them how to plant the sprouts, never placing them too deep in the soil or too close to the dikes. During the harvest, he showed them how to toss the stalks onto round, woven trays to separate the grains from the husks. To his own five children, he made few demands other than that they observe their daily prayers and follow the teachings of Buddha, especially with regard to the need to be honest. "He told me not to steal," said his son Kieu Trak. "He encouraged me to avoid the bad things in life."

A small man with leathery, withered hands, Kieu reached down to make sure the water was five inches deep. If it was less than five inches, farmers ran the risk of their seedlings withering in the sun. If it ran over five inches, the dikes could break, or the seedlings would drown.

Kieu raised his hand and signaled for the men to begin plowing. As the buffalo started dragging the plows to make a smooth bed, the five women in the field walked quickly along the plow lines, planting the seedlings into the rich black muck. Under normal conditions, it would take nearly three days to cover the entire field, but they didn't have three days. Kieu knew from scouts in the mountains that the soldiers were camped just three miles away.

By dawn, the Tigers followed their daily ritual of breaking down their M16s, cleaning the cartridges, and reassembling them to ensure they didn't jam. After checking their ammo supplies and rations, they waited for their orders.

Several were still shaken from the ambush the night before when team leaders walked into the campsite after a meeting and broke the news: Munoz was dead and Sanchez was on his way to an Army hospital in Japan.

To the newcomers, Sanchez was one of the few team leaders who bucked the trend. Now he was gone.

Munoz was another story. They knew he had a wife in Texas from the letters he received from home, but didn't know much else about him. He had turned twenty-two just before joining the Tigers in May — days after the Mother's Day Massacre. But he was still a Tiger, and now he was dead.

Upon hearing the news, Doyle began ranting about "gooks" and that they should all die. To him, it was obvious: as long as villagers were still in the Song Ve, the Tigers weren't going anywhere. "You don't have to worry about anyone who's dead," he said. Ybarra and Green joined in, saying they wanted to be let loose in the mountains. If he couldn't be drinking beer back at the base, Ybarra wanted to be hunting. There was only one good thing about the Song Ve: "That's where the gooks are," he said.

Kieu Cong was worried the planting was taking too long. The five men and five women had been in the paddy two hours, and several hundred seedlings had yet to be placed in the soil. Part of the problem was that the field was too flooded, and the dike needed to be lowered to release an inch of water. But beyond the water level, the elderly farmers were tired, their footing slowed in the muck. For weeks, they had been hiding in the mountains and surviving on small rations of rice, sometimes a bowl a day. Kieu knew he couldn't push them any harder.

As the sun rose over the first ridge, Kieu and the others spotted a man walking across the paddy. At first, they froze and stared at the figure, but soon realized it was Kieu's son Kieu Trak. The thirty-four-year-old man had been keeping a look-out and had become alarmed because the farmers were taking too much time.

"I told them they needed to hurry," he recalled. "They were running out of time." But while his father was concerned, he ignored the warning, telling his son to go back to his post. "He told me that they needed to finish their work. He said this may be their only chance." There were just a few days left for optimum planting and no guarantees the seedlings would last. The farmers had been nurturing the sprouts thirty days in the mountains and needed to get them in the ground.

Kieu Trak was reluctant to leave. He felt a sense of obligation to take care of his father. Weeks earlier, he had decided not to join his brothers and sisters in a relocation camp but to stay with his father, who had refused to go. For the first two weeks, father and son had hidden together before being joined by Kieu Trak's wife, Mai Thi Tai, who escaped from Nghia Hanh.

Kieu Trak's father ordered him to go back to his lookout perch. Slowly, he turned around and walked toward the foothills, leaving his father in the middle of the field. As he reached the end of the paddy, Kieu Trak could hear a sound echoing across the valley floor. As the noise came closer, he realized it was the whirling blades of a helicopter.

His heart began to race as he turned around to look at his father, who was already motioning for his son to run away. "No, no!" Kieu Cong yelled. "Go back."

Kieu Trak obeyed and raced toward a cluster of trees near the footpath leading to the first ridge. Just as he reached the brush, the helicopter was within sight. He rolled on the ground and into a thicket of bamboo, peering at the figures of his father and the others in the field. They weren't running.

Kieu Trak yelled for the farmers to flee, but they continued planting seedlings. Maybe they — like he — hoped desperately the chopper would circle and leave, like they used to do before the great evacuation. But there was more than just a helicopter to fret over. Between the river and the field, Kieu Trak could see men walking toward the rice paddy. They appeared to be soldiers.

For the first time in days, the Tigers had broken camp as a full platoon. No teams. No instructions. No warnings.

As they had left the campsite, Barry Bowman had noticed the men were walking faster than usual in a single-file column. No one was talking. They were tired of the grenade attacks and even more upset at battalion commanders for leaving them on the valley floor another day.

There had been no shortage of volunteers to walk the point that morning, but Ybarra had been the first to jump in front — just where team leaders wanted him. By now, he was the designated point, but not through any official decision. His commanders knew that, unlike many newcomers, Ybarra wouldn't hesitate to pull the trigger and wouldn't turn away.

With Ybarra in front, the Tigers had moved down a hillside and spotted the burned-out remains of another hamlet. A small narrow dirt roadway twisted through the cluster of blackened bamboo and clay slabs.

The men had slowed their pace as Ybarra inched his way one hundred meters in front of the others, with Green leading the rest of the column. Ybarra had tiptoed over to the first hooch, using the barrel of his rifle to lift up a piece of wood that he thought might be covering an earthen bunker, but it was just wood.

Ybarra had moved on to the second hooch area, and then to the third a few yards away — seemingly unconcerned that the rest of the platoon was several paces behind.

When Ybarra had reached the last hooch, he had motioned for Green to catch up. So far, there were no signs of life.

Suddenly, before Green could join Ybarra, the point man had raised his hand and motioned for the platoon to halt. Crouching down, he had pointed toward a rice paddy about two hundred meters away. After staring a few more seconds at the field, Ybarra had sprung up and motioned for the others to follow.

He had turned around and, while still walking, whispered something to Green. Green then slowed down long enough to tell the man behind him what Ybarra had spotted.

The third man turned around and told the fourth, and the fourth turned and informed Hawkins. The commander hadn't hesitated. Instead, Hawkins had wheeled around and passed the word: "Fire on my orders."

After a couple of minutes, the soldiers were now well within sight of the villagers, but for some reason, the Vietnamese weren't moving. Several were hunched over, their backs to the soldiers. Two of the men continued to drive the water buffalo along the beds.

"They looked to be older, about half of them men, half women," Carpenter recalled. Shaking his head, he looked around to see the other soldiers' reactions to the order. Wood and others were dumbfounded. It was one thing to open up on enemy soldiers, or prisoners, or even people running away. But these people weren't moving — they were just farming.

Before anyone had a chance to say anything, Hawkins raised his CAR-15 and pulled the trigger. Immediately, Doyle, Barnett, and Green fired.

From the thicket of bamboo, Kieu Trak watched as his father and others initially looked up, appearing almost startled, before they began running. Some fell in the muck. Others made it to the dike before dropping. The helicopter soaring overhead began circling the rice paddy, then firing down on the chaos below.

Shaking, Kieu Trak could see the water buffalo running in

circles, their handlers nowhere in sight. He couldn't do anything. If he ran onto the field, he would be killed. He buried his head in his hands and began sobbing.

Less than a quarter mile away, Lu Thuan, a villager who had fled to the mountains, watched from a ledge as the helicopter zigzagged overhead, trying to follow three of the farmers bolting toward a dike. Suddenly, as the farmers tried to jump across the embankment, Lu could hear the rattling of the machine guns from above. All three dropped to the ground. "They were helpless," he recalled. "There was nowhere for them to go."

As the soldiers fired, Carpenter refused to lift his M16. "I couldn't believe it," Carpenter recalled. "I knew people were pissed off. The valley was a shitty place for all of us. But we didn't have to pick on civilians. We were the Tigers. We were above that."

Bowman was just as upset. "They were just working in the field. We all knew that. They had no weapons. I remember them running and falling. There was absolutely no place for them to hide. I just watched. I couldn't take part in it." But their reluctance meant nothing to those who now lay dead, and it began to mean something to those who had killed them.

Hidden by bamboo shoots, Kieu Trak waited for darkness. For hours, he wondered whether his father was alive or dead and agonized over whether he should go onto the field to find out. Every few minutes, he would stare at the bodies, hoping to see some movement. But the bodies were still.

That morning, he was in the rice paddy with his father, warning him about taking too long. He wished his father had heeded his advice, but Kieu Cong had always been stubborn. He was a man who took responsibility for others, and if the rice wasn't planted, the villagers would go hungry.

By late afternoon, Kieu could hear the voices of American soldiers. For a moment, he froze. Did they see him? But instead of checking the bamboo cluster, the men passed by and headed in the direction of the hamlet.

The soldiers' voices trailed off, until Kieu could only hear them faintly in the distance. He decided to take a chance and crawl into the field.

Just before the sun set below the ridge, Kieu could see the figures of two people creeping onto the rice paddy. They looked to be villagers, but he wasn't sure. As they moved toward the middle of the field, he noticed they were not wearing uniforms and did not appear to be as tall as soldiers. In fact, they were Vietnamese women. He knew there would be other villagers looking for their loved ones. He slowly brushed aside the bamboo shoots covering his body, rolled over, and stood up.

Staying low, he crept onto the paddy until he could see the faces of the two women — one his wife. They didn't say anything but immediately moved toward the first body in sight, which appeared to be a man facedown in the muck. They turned it over. It was Le Muc, a villager who had worked side by side with the Kieu family for years. They moved to the next body. It was Phung Giang, another well-known farmer. He, too, was dead.

Kieu then turned and saw another body a few yards away. As he moved closer, his heart sank. It was the body of his father lying faceup, his white shirt covered in blood. He went over and placed his hand on his father's chest, but knew he was already dead.

He tried to hold back the tears. This was no place to break down — the soldiers could be back at any time. He had to remove his father's corpse and carry it to the dry earth for burial. Kieu stood up and grabbed his father's arms and slowly dragged him across the paddy, his wife following. As they inched along, they could see other villagers begin to crawl onto the field and, moments later, hear their soft, muffled cries.

CHAPTER 12

The drone startled some of the Tigers camped along the river: Forward Air Control planes flying low, carrying out surveillance over the valley. Within minutes, the soldiers would know whether they would have to stay in the Song Ve. An empty village meant success. Based on the last two weeks, the men had little hope they would get out.

While the soldiers gathered around the radio to wait for their orders, Donald Wood turned around and walked to the edge of the river. He needed time to think. For a moment, he blocked out the noise. Wood dreaded another day but not because he feared losing his life. He feared that the Tigers would kill more civilians.

Wood's team members knew to leave him alone when he went off by himself. It was no different at home in Fridley, when he would slip into his room and close the door, or even sneak out of the house in the rain and walk for miles. That was his way to clear his mind. When the high school football coach told him he was too small to play, he backed out of the gym, red-faced, and walked to the edge of town, refusing to go home until 10:00 that night. And when he did get to his home, he didn't go into the house. Flushed with anger, he went directly to the garage and began lifting weights. That night he promised himself he would work out every night until he bulked up enough to play football. The next year, he made the team.

As a five-foot-nine, 160-pound halfback, Wood had tried to run over tacklers, instead of around them. He had never been a coward and he believed traversing the shortest distance between two points sometimes entailed the destruction of any obstacles in the way. Watching the water rush by, Wood came to the conclusion that he wasn't going to let the Tigers run amok. He was going to challenge Hawkins at every turn, even if it meant physically restraining him. "I gotta stop this guy," he told Carpenter. "It's all gotta stop now."

Wood reasoned that while Hawkins, Trout, Ybarra, Doyle, and Barnett had been killing villagers in their teams, not everyone had gone along. Even when Hawkins had ordered the entire platoon to open up on the farmers, Wood noticed that most of the newcomers didn't raise their rifles. That proved to him the platoon could be salvaged. Wood made up his mind: he would save the soul of the Tigers.

As he joined the men huddled around the radio, the call came from battalion headquarters: the Tigers were pulling out. Several soldiers pumped their fists in the air, exhilarated over the prospect of heading back to Carentan.

Wood saw his chance. He would go back to Carentan and talk to his commanders. Surely they would understand his concerns and would support his efforts to get rid of Hawkins. Wood was a soldier who always believed in the adage that what goes on in the field stays there. There was no room in the Army for snitches. But he didn't have any choice; it was his responsibility. Strangely enough, he felt a sense of relief. He jumped onto the chopper and scurried to the rear.

After jumping off the Huey, Wood headed to Lieutenant Naughton's tent. At first, Naughton wasn't around, but an hour later, wandering around the base, the men ran into each other.

In confidence, Wood unloaded, saying he was disgusted at the leadership of the Tigers — Hawkins in particular. Not only did Hawkins not know how to read maps but he had tried to call in air strikes at the wrong coordinates. Sooner or later, he was going to get the men killed, and Wood didn't want to be around to bear witness to a slaughter.

That wasn't all. He told Naughton about the killing of the old man, the shooting of the two old women, and the targeting of unarmed farmers. "These younger guys are impressionable," he told the lieutenant. "They're going to eventually go along, and when that happens, the Tigers will be nothing but an assassination squad."

Naughton listened without saying much. He knew Wood wasn't off the mark. When he had still been in the field, he had known Ybarra was collecting ears and that Doyle was crazy. But Naughton announced there was little he could do. He didn't have the authority to investigate the allegations by himself, and besides, the commanders were depending on the Tigers. "That's just the way it is," he said. As far as headquarters was concerned, the unit was "off-limits" to scrutiny. Naughton told Wood to hang in there and, if he really wanted to press the issue, take it to someone higher. (Unknown to Wood, Naughton was preparing to pass on the complaint, but not before returning to the United States.)

Disappointed, Wood was faced with a dilemma. He could stick to his plan and restrain Hawkins himself or keep going up the food chain until someone listened.

Just as when he had been told he was too small to play, he started to get angry. Why should he listen to Naughton? *The hell with it,* Wood concluded — he was going to go to the top. He marched to the battalion headquarters and there met with an executive officer, repeating the same story. "It's got to stop," he said.

The officer listened and then glared at Wood. "What do you expect me to do?" he asked. "We're in the middle of a war,

Lieutenant. And you want me to take our best unit out of action because a few guys are killing gooks?"

Wood was stunned. He paused and took a deep breath. "I'm only talking about the field commander. Getting him out. He's a lousy soldier and he's setting a bad example."

The officer shook his head. "I will take your request under consideration," he said, clearly wanting Wood to leave.

Wood could tell this wasn't going anywhere. He rose from his chair and left. He would have to take care of Hawkins himself.

Dennis Stout watched through his tent as the Tigers strutted into camp. He didn't think he would ever see the platoon members again, but there they were — back at Carentan — and suddenly he was anxious. He was supposed to have rejoined them after his first venture into the Song Ve but had always managed to find an excuse. Stout could have reported the shooting of the villagers to the Criminal Investigation Division. As a public information officer, he had access to Army officials above and beyond the battalion commanders. But he hadn't done so.

More frustrating was the war itself. He had started to get South Vietnamese soldiers to open up more to him about the enemy's real strength, and what he heard wasn't good. The NVA was setting up more camps each day in the Central Highlands. "Westmoreland is a bullshit artist," he told his translator after reading news accounts of the general's comments to Defense Secretary Robert McNamara on July 7. In a news story published in the *New York Times* and picked up by the Associated Press, Westmoreland was quoted as saying, "The war is not a stalemate. We are winning slowly but steadily. North Vietnam is paying a tremendous price, with nothing to show for it in return." The reality was that nearly five thousand Americans had been killed in just the last six months — half of them since

May. That was close to the same number killed in all of 1966. "How the hell can he possibly say we're winning?" Stout wondered.

Stout just wanted to go back to the United States and finish his time. But before leaving, he was going to document what he had seen. That night and into the early morning, he sat at his desk and wrote down everything he remembered about the shooting of the villagers who were trying to surrender. He knew what he was doing would be frowned upon by battalion commanders. And if soldiers found out, his life could be in jeopardy. But he had not been able to forget what he saw. He hadn't done the right thing earlier, but there was still time.

He tried to recall each and every name of the soldiers who could corroborate his account of what happened. He also pulled out the identification cards of the civilians who were executed. "I need to reconstruct everything," he told Nguyen. *Everything.*

Sitting on a slope overlooking his old hamlet, Nyugen Dam promised himself he would wait one more day before making the trek to rejoin the others who had left their hiding places in the foothills. So far, there were no signs of soldiers, no signs of helicopters, and no signs of other villagers. But he wasn't about to venture onto the valley floor. He had buried too many people.

As he sat on the hillside, he recalled his childhood, spending hours playing along the trails and splashing in the river. He remembered his parents and grandparents trudging each morning through the fog into the rice fields. The valley was his home, and he dreaded leaving. "It was as if I was giving up my life," he recalled.

Nyugen wasn't worried about catching up with the others. He could move faster by himself and knew the terrain well enough to find his way to the mountains west of the Song Ve Valley. But he knew he couldn't wait too long. He had enough rice to last a week and could find bananas and coconuts along the way. And he feared his wife or other family members would leave Nghia Hanh and come back, and he wouldn't be there to warn them about the soldiers with the stripes — men who fired their guns at will.

As the sun burned away the morning fog, he could see planes passing over the mountains, the drone growing louder as the aircraft approached. He reached over and grabbed for a piece of canvas he had been using to shield himself from the rain and pulled it over his body. If the planes spotted him, it was just a matter of time before the soldiers came.

Nyugen peered from under the canvas, and as the aircraft came closer, he could see a fine mist coming down — almost like rain, but different. He was sure it wasn't water. The mist omitted a strange, tingling odor that quickly became stronger and stung his nostrils. He pinched his nose, but it did no good. Suddenly, his head began to spin, his eyes burned, and he felt deeply sick.

The "mist" released by the four American twin-engine C-123 Provider transports overhead was a highly toxic herbicide — known as "Agent Orange" — that had been dumped on thousands of acres of Vietnamese jungle since 1962 to strip away the enemy's hiding places. The use of chemicals by the U.S. military began in World War I, but it was taken to a new and dangerous level in South Vietnam. Agent Orange destroyed entire habitats, but it also led to serious health problems for U.S. troops exposed to the herbicide. Seven major companies, including Dow Chemical and Monsanto, supplied the military with more than 20 million gallons of Agent Orange during the war.

Flying in a staggered, lateral formation, the planes went the length of the valley's six miles and then soared out of sight. With the river basin officially cleared of people, the military had received permission to put an end to the farming altogether by taking the most extreme measure: defoliating the rice fields. It was a final act to a campaign that began two months earlier, enough chemicals to kill every living plant and tree. Nothing could survive.

Nyugen waited until the noise subsided before pushing away the canvas. He stood up, dizzy and confused, wondering what had been sprayed. He staggered to the river, where he splashed water on his face and neck. After regaining his strength, he rose from the water and began walking slowly toward the trail leading out of the Song Ve.

CHAPTER 13

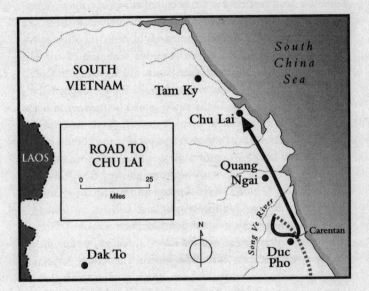

SOUTH
VIETNAM

Tam Ky

South
China
Sea

Chu Lai

LAOS

**ROAD TO
CHU LAI**

0   25
Miles

Quang
Ngai

Song Ve River

Carentan

N

Dak To

Duc
Pho

T he Tigers weren't given much time to unwind. Three
hours after arriving at Carentan, they were hustled to a
briefing in the mess area. Restless from their weeks in
the valley, they wanted to head into town, but Colonel Austin
and other officers were pressed for time, and the Tigers had no
choice. Out there, the rules could be ignored, but on the base,
the usual rigidity was maintained.

After they gathered, the briefing sergeant delivered the good news: the Tigers would not be returning to the Song Ve. That campaign was over. But the sergeant didn't hesitate with the next bit of information: they would have only a few days for stand-down. "Don't get too comfortable," he said. They would be pulling out of Carentan on August 10 and heading in a truck convoy thirty-five miles north to the sprawling Army air base at Chu Lai and a new province — Quang Tin.

Unlike other assignments, this was not coming merely from battalion headquarters but from commanders in Saigon. Westmoreland and others were growing increasingly frustrated over intelligence reports showing thousands of enemy soldiers moving into the province. Despite intensive bombing of the Ho Chi Minh Trail, enemy soldiers were still traveling unabated down the route with weapons and food. With the Tigers carrying out surveillance, the battalion would be moving into the jungle terrain northwest of the air base to find enemy encampments. Because the area was seen as critical to the control of the Central Highlands, Westmoreland was adamant about stopping the movements. Secret Army estimates showed that 7,500 enemy soldiers per month were slipping into the South — mostly on the trails that wound through Quang Tin.

The development was not good for several reasons. First, it showed that despite the massive losses sustained by the enemy, the war was far from over. The North Vietnamese were not backing down. Since various units had arrived in the region in May, at least seventeen enemy positions had been set up in Quang Tin alone. Second, the deployment — if reported in the press — would be a blow to Westmoreland's credibility with certain members of Congress and the American public, and generals rarely fought harder than when defending their own political turf.

The plan was for the Tigers to camp at Chu Lai and then break into teams on search-and-destroy missions. The new area of operations was much larger — ten times the size of the Song Ve Valley — and, in some ways, more treacherous. The terrain was covered by triple-canopy jungle, and most of the region was unknown even to the translators.

Beyond geography, Quang Tin was more challenging for two reasons: there were more North Vietnamese soldiers there than in Quang Ngai, and it was even more difficult to remove the civilians. In Quang Ngai, people lived in large population centers along the coast. Most of the villagers in Quang Tin were scattered across the province, with as many people living in the far western reaches, and for years the people had been building a system of earthen bunkers to stay safe from American sorties. The Vietcong had made significant inroads in the rural areas and had promised the people they wouldn't force the villagers to leave their hamlets. The province served as a major artery of the Ho Chi Minh Trail — a massive patchwork of jungle paths, bridges, and underground passages where thousands of enemy troops were moving to the South undetected. No amount of bombing could destroy the trail. Even when a bridge was blown up, a new one was erected in hours by an army of workers devoted to keeping the trail open. For the North Vietnamese, it was a noble cause worth dying for.

Added to this was the fact that the people of Quang Tin had long been abandoned by Saigon. That didn't mean they unanimously sided with the North. Indeed, many of the Buddhist leaders in the province had opposed the war. But such distinctions would matter little to the Tigers headed to the area. The enemy was more entrenched, and the villagers were less likely to leave on their own. And with Hawkins in the lead, there were only going to be more problems.

Before heading to the new operations area, the Tigers were given a day to get drunk and laid. Unfortunately for them, most huts selling alcohol in Duc Pho were sold out, and no new supplies were expected for days. After striking out, Carpenter and several Tigers stopped at a wood building that resembled a drive-through, with a large, open walk-up window and several picnic tables.

When Carpenter ambled to the window, a Marine behind the counter asked why the Tigers weren't wearing helmets. "We don't wear helmets," a Tiger snapped.

The Marine then asked why the men weren't wearing flags on their uniforms. Carpenter said the Tigers didn't have to wear them and added that he wasn't there to talk about uniforms.

"We just want some beer to last until tomorrow," he said.

With his arms folded, the Marine stepped back and said he wasn't going to sell them any beer. "Take off," he said. But the Tigers weren't going anywhere. They had been looking forward to getting drunk. Now that they had finally found beer, they weren't going to let this Marine get in their way. "Fuck you, Marines," said a Tiger. "You guys aren't in there fighting the war. We are."

Without warning, two Tigers hopped over the counter and started grabbing cases. When two Marines jumped into the fray to help their fellow soldier, the other Tigers stormed the building. They jumped on the Marines. Some grabbed chairs and began smashing them against the wall; others took out their Zippo lighters and held the flames up to the slats in the building. Within minutes, flames were running up the sides and to the roof.

As the soldiers ran outside and the building was engulfed by fire, the Tigers loaded the beer onto a Jeep and sped away.

Even after chugging Black Labels most of the night, Green and Ybarra couldn't sleep. They staggered to their tents and immediately began talking so loudly the other soldiers were awakened. With their tours over in a few weeks, they would be given the option of signing up for another six months. Before starting their new tours, they would get a month's R & R — anywhere they wanted to drag themselves. But they needed to make a decision soon.

From the briefing, Ybarra was looking forward to going to the new operations area. Green wasn't so sure. He couldn't see staying any longer than he had to in South Vietnam. He was already close to the edge, and he was looking forward to getting back to some form of sanity.

Ybarra glared at his friend. "What do you mean, man? You can't leave now," he snapped. Green wanted to tell Ybarra that it was over, that he just wanted to go home. But he couldn't. Once again, Ybarra was challenging Green's manhood, and Ken wasn't going to let Ybarra get his way. Besides, if they stayed together, they could keep each other alive.

Ybarra was excited. "There's more action up there," he said about the new operations area. Besides, what was Green going to do back in Globe? Did he want to work in the mines? There sure as hell wasn't much else. Here, he was part of something that was important. In Globe, he was nothing, and would always be nothing.

Green agreed. He hated the mines and didn't want to spend his life frying eggs in the family diner. Globe was a dead end in a dead land. Vietnam it would be.

On the morning of August 10, the 150 soldiers in B Company crowded into the transport trucks idling along Highway One, followed by C Company. Last came the Tigers. One by one, the men hopped on the canvas-covered vehicles. Of course staying on base was easier, but now that the game was on, the Tigers were ready for it. "Most of us couldn't wait to go," recalled Carpenter. As the men readied themselves for the trip, they looked around to see who was in the trucks. Conspicuously absent was Wood. What they didn't know was that the Tigers' forward artillery observer had been ordered to pack his gear. He was no longer a Tiger. He was being shipped to another unit. His efforts to counter Hawkins were over. Any hopes he held of winning over the men one by one — men such as Bill Carpenter, Ervin Lee, and Forrest Miller — were over. This was how the Army was going to deal with his complaints about atrocities: transfer the messenger. The move was significant on many levels. Wood was a leader who reminded the others that, even in war, there was a code of honor — and without one, the men were not warriors but murderers. In combat units, one such person can make a difference, partly because he keeps the "weaker" soldiers from crossing the line. He is a constant reminder of what's right. As the trucks pulled away, a key link in the chain connecting Tiger Force to the rule of law was severed.

CHAPTER 14

Most of the Tigers had never visited Chu Lai — ten miles long and five miles wide, bordered by a beach covered with white sand and palm trees, and in the distance, mountain islands rising over the horizon. It was once a thriving fishing village, but by now most of the huts that lined the shoreline had been leveled by the U.S. military to set up one of the largest air bases in the country.

As the Tigers arrived, they were led to a small area near the beach and away from the barracks. They were allowed to use the latrines and showers to the west of the barracks, but they were not assigned to their own building like other units. They pitched tents along the shore, while the pilots of the air base were allowed to sleep in bunks. To Carpenter and others, it felt as if they were being purposely isolated.

After unpacking their equipment, the Tigers were given permission to walk around. They were struck by the steady stream of F-4 Phantoms landing and taking off. Though the Tigers were technically on stand-down, several soldiers were fidgety. While walking along the roadways connecting the barracks, the Tigers noticed they were being watched by MPs.

What the Tigers didn't know was that a complaint had been filed days earlier over the looting and torching of the Marine service center. The Army had no intention of investigating. It needed the Tigers for the battalion's operations in the new province. Instead, battalion officers agreed to keep close tabs on the Tigers at their new base by notifying the military police at Chu Lai.

Most of the time, the Tigers were oblivious to the larger political and military decisions. They had no idea the commanders were putting so much emphasis on wresting control of Quang Tin to win the war, or that Westmoreland had promised victory by the end of the year — "light at the end of the tunnel." Recalled Kerney, "We were operating in a vacuum when we got there. We only knew what we had to do day to day."

Before leaving the base, the Tigers had been told they were being sent into the area to look for an enemy encampment believed to belong to the 26th Company of the 2nd North Vietnamese Army Division. From the air, the landscape of Quang Tin was noticeably different than that of the Song Ve. As the four Hueys carrying the platoon members swooped over the area twenty miles northwest of Chu Lai, there were no rice paddies below. "You got nothing but jungle down there," said Hawkins. In some places, the trees rose with the mountainous terrain. It took several minutes for the lead chopper to find a landing zone, and just beyond what appeared to be a stream, the choppers set down.

Intelligence reports said the unit was moving east toward the air base. The soldiers disembarked and headed for what they thought was a tree line. When they passed through the first row, however, they found a jungle path into an area so dense the trees almost completely blocked the sun's rays. Walking single file, the Tigers followed the trail, at times using their knives to slash through thick vines barring the way.

The men had been warned about snipers in trees and booby traps camouflaged by palm fronds and jungle orchids. They were also told to be on the lookout for hamlets that seemed to blend into the vegetation.

In the darkness of the jungle, Ybarra stumbled upon a dozen huts shrouded by palm trees and mangroves. He turned around and whispered to Green, who then passed the word down the line.

Following Ybarra, the soldiers stopped, raised their rifles, and inched toward the hamlet. There didn't seem to be any movement until two villagers surprised the men by jumping from a hut. Ybarra and Green opened fire, hitting the men and then spraying the hooches with bullets. The villagers fell to the ground, but as the Tigers approached, shots were fired at the Americans. Most of the Tigers jumped back into the brush and then scattered in several directions. Ybarra and Green fired back, but it was too dark to see from where the enemy rounds were fired, and the Tigers couldn't call in air strikes because the platoon was too close.

In the past, they would designate a spot to regroup, but there was no time to set up an area. Instead, the Tigers had to go on the offensive. Almost in unison, they began firing their M16s into the huts. The rounds lit up the jungle, and after several minutes, the shooting stopped. The Tigers started inching toward the clearing, not sure if the snipers were hit or were setting up another ambush.

Ybarra was the first to walk into the hamlet, followed by Green and others. They passed by two dead bodies as they entered the first hut, looked inside, and then moved to the next. Kerrigan and Miller followed, searching each hut for weapons and more bodies. The only living things they found were some newborn puppies in a small woven basket. No American had been killed, but this much was clear: Quang Tin was a dangerous place. Unlike the Song Ve, where the Tigers could call a chopper and be whisked away, this was no-man's-land.

An hour after the ambush, the Tigers were still trying to figure out where to go next. They didn't know for sure if the hamlet was an NVA encampment or simply an outpost. Team leaders surmised the NVA didn't know how many American soldiers were in the area; otherwise they would have stood their ground. They certainly had the advantage, since they knew the terrain.

The Tigers gathered for a moment on the edge of the clearing and waited for a radio transmission from Chu Lai about whether to continue looking for the encampment.

From his seat in the command-and-control chopper, Gerald Morse could see the clearing where the Tigers had landed just before their firefight. "Take it down here," he told his pilot. The lean, muscular lieutenant colonel was the new battalion commander, taking over for Harold Austin. Most of the Tigers had never set eyes upon Morse. He had been monitoring their radio activity during the skirmish and had impulsively decided now was the perfect time to introduce himself to the platoon members.

After touching down, Morse emerged from the chopper — crew cut, starched shirt, and all. He walked over to the Tigers who were standing near the huts and asked why no one had answered his call on the radio. Doyle jumped up. He was supposed to monitor the transmissions but had missed the signal. "Who the hell are you?" Doyle asked.

"Your new commander," Morse responded.

The Tigers were surprised. They had rarely, if ever, seen a battalion commander in the field. But unlike his predecessor, Morse was not going to lead his troops from the rear. At thirty-eight, he had been a career soldier, and a brave one, earning a Silver Star for pulling seventeen men from a minefield at T-Bone Hill in Korea. In the same war, he was awarded two Purple

Hearts for action at Triangle Hill and Pork Chop Hill. For most battalion commanders, a battlefield assignment was a sure way to get a promotion, and Morse was on the fast track.

A physical education major at the University of Maine, Morse was fit, trim, and energetic — a prototypical combat leader — who understood military definitions of success in the Vietnam War. Before taking command on August 9, he had been told by Army brass about the importance of the Central Highlands campaign. It was his first major assignment in the war, and he didn't waste any time. Within twenty-four hours of taking over, he was already in the air. As his command-and-control chopper soared over a rice paddy, the gunners spotted four suspected Vietcong running and shot two dead. In the command log, it was noted that Morse's first mission was a way to show the "battalion was deadly at any echelon of the command."

While talking to Doyle, the new commander could see several Tigers about twenty-five meters away, standing in a shallow stream. As he approached the men, he saw them dunking puppies underwater. "Why are you drowning the dogs?" he asked.

Doyle immediately responded, "Because they're making too much noise."

Morse frowned but wheeled around and walked away. He knew about the Tigers, and what he knew, he liked. They were going to be an indispensable unit in the new campaign. He supposed that how they treated dogs didn't matter. Heck, they were probably right to kill them.

Morse nodded to Hawkins and then walked back to his chopper and ordered the pilot to take off. Other choppers were called to pick up the platoon. As Morse's helicopter disappeared over the trees, several Tigers looked at one another. "We knew," recalled Carpenter, "this guy was different." Just how different, they would learn.

CHAPTER 15

Terrence Kerrigan used to be predictable. He would ride the saddle on patrol — walking the middle — never venturing far from the pack. At camp, he would get stoned on pot instead of getting drunk with the others. He would joke that he was going AWOL and surfing. "The guy was always smiling," recalled Kerney.

But two weeks into the new campaign, he was changing. At first it was subtle: he was quiet but every now and then would blurt out a jagged, sarcastic remark. His once clean-shaven face was covered with a rough beard. He wasn't bathing, and he was losing weight, sporting dark circles under his eyes.

Kerrigan was sitting within earshot of the men but wasn't listening. He was rocking back and forth on the ground. Ever since the end of the Song Ve campaign, he had started this habit. His old team from the valley knew why, but no one really talked about it.

While venturing into a burned-out hamlet in the Song Ve, the soldiers had discovered a Vietnamese man curled up behind a tree, trying to hide. When they frisked him and didn't find any weapons, Trout had ordered Kerrigan to shoot the detainee.

Surprised, Kerrigan had asked about a chopper.

Trout snapped, "We ain't gonna give our position away. Shoot him."

Kerrigan was on the spot. Trout was testing him. Slowly, he raised his M16, clutching the rifle to keep from twitching. He could see the man shaking uncontrollably as he kneeled on the ground. Kerrigan had used his gun before but had never killed anyone.

He detested the order but knew in his heart he had to obey. Trout was keeping Kerrigan alive. He had taught him how to pack lightly and only the things he needed, and how to creep low under fire. He had taught him how to recognize an ambush and avoid trip wires that could trigger explosions. Kerrigan believed he had a better chance of surviving with the team sergeant than without him.

Kerrigan had squeezed the trigger.

In slow motion, he had watched as the man's head exploded, his body jerking into the air and falling backward. Kerrigan had quickly turned around. He felt like vomiting but didn't want anyone to see him. So he walked into the brush. After a few minutes, he caught up with the team as they were leaving. Strangely, he felt better. He had crossed a line, and for some reason, it wasn't so unseemly.

Now, here he was, three weeks later, clutching his M16 and waiting. As the chopper landed, he ran with the others and hopped aboard, sitting down next to Ybarra and Green. The Tigers had been deployed to a new area around the base every day, but this time, they were going to a place where American soldiers had rarely ventured: the mountains of the Que Son. Lately, Kerrigan had been hanging out with the two friends and recently discovered he had gone to grade school with Ybarra's cousin Linda at Denker Avenue Elementary School in Gardena, California. No one would have guessed the two shared anything in common.

From the air, the Tigers could see the Que Son Valley in the distance. Intelligence reports gathered from prisoners warned that a battalion of NVA soldiers was boldly setting up encampments in the valley and the river that runs through the basin. General Rosson's staff was concerned the NVA would soon control a chunk of the province from the Que Son to the South China Sea — a fifteen-kilometer stretch that included Highway One. The Tigers needed to find the camps and engage the enemy, if need be.

For the Tigers, it was a difficult assignment. Other U.S. units had skirted the Que Son but had not been deployed there for any extended periods. The terrain was dense and the trails were heavily mined. Maps showed some cities but did not reflect the scores of hamlets deep in the mountains.

Barry Bowman dreaded the thought of going into another unknown area. The villages around Chu Lai were difficult enough because of the underground tunnels and bunkers. But at least in their initial patrols, the Tigers had run into only one ambush — that first day. Now they were being sent twenty kilometers northwest of Chu Lai for a recon mission that could last several weeks. Everything about it spelled trouble.

As a Tiger Force medic since May, Bowman had patrolled the Song Ve as well as the new province and was coming to a realization that the war was not changing. The Army could call in dozens of air strikes and destroy dozens of encampments, but nothing seemed to deter the enemy. As he sat in the chopper, Bowman checked his supplies of bandages, medicine, and syringes.

The Tigers didn't have to search for long. Just before landing south of the valley, they located huts with people milling around. The Tigers gathered near Hawkins, who pointed in the direction of the hamlet. The people in this area had long been told to leave. Rather than divide the group into teams, he had the platoon walk single file through a thicket of elephant grass, hacking their way through the tall, sharp stalks until they reached a narrow trail. Before long, no one knew for sure where the village was located. The maps were useless. Not knowing what else to do, with Ybarra and Green at the point, the men followed the trail as it led eastward.

After walking for several minutes, the Tigers were startled by gunshots. At first, the men in the rear thought the shots were from the point men, but as bullets began flying around them, platoon members realized they were under attack. Barnett and other team leaders yelled for the men to hit the ground. Before Private James Messer could move, he was hit by an onslaught that seemed to come from snipers in the trees. An eighteen-year-old newcomer from Springfield, Massachusetts, Messer was one of the new paratroopers to join the Tigers at Chu Lai. It was Messer's first day in the jungle. Bowman ran to the injured soldier, who wasn't moving.

The Tigers began blasting into the brush, using their M16s and grenade launchers. They didn't know how many enemy soldiers were in the trees, nor did they stop to care. Ybarra watched as one sniper dropped from a tree, followed by two more. After several minutes, the soldiers stopped firing. Ybarra rushed to the first body lying on the ground. He then went to the second and to the third. They were all dead NVA soldiers.

For the Tigers, this wasn't a good sign. For the enemy to be in trees meant that they were entrenched — and waiting. How many more were out there?

Even though the Tigers had been in the field for a while, this was spooky terrain: dark, jungle, and a long way from the line companies. There were no clear trails, and the vines were so thick they knotted the trees, shutting out the light but trapping the heat. Every now and then, the silence was shattered by an elephant screaming in the distance or, even closer, the shriek of a wild monkey. The South Vietnamese translators warned the Tigers to look out for bamboo vipers, a green snake so venomous, one bite would attack the nervous system, causing convulsions and, soon, death. The Tigers were also told about black jungle leeches, inch-long insects that dropped from trees, attached to the flesh, and left painful welts.

The Song Ve Valley had also been dangerous, but at least it was a picture-postcard of natural beauty compared to this place. The green mountains rising above the spectacular expanse had resembled Hawaii — with the rushing blue waters of the Song Ve River winding through the basin, palm trees and banana groves everywhere. This place was a hellhole.

Bowman could feel his body tense. How many more were hiding? He didn't want to die, not here. As he looked around, he could see everyone was just as vulnerable as he was. His job was to care for the wounded, but he couldn't even take care of himself. He had kept everything bottled inside, but now he was going to explode. His heart was pounding and he gasped for breath. "Gotta get out, gotta get out," he kept saying to himself.

His fellow medic Douglas Teeters had just a few weeks left before shipping out. This was no place to die, and yet, it was: triple canopy, where the vines from the mangroves wrapped like snakes around the trees, creating a virtual wall blocking the sunlight. It was so dark. How would the Tigers even know if an entire battalion was coming toward them? "Stay close to the others," he said to himself.

After regrouping, the platoon members decided to look for a village they had passed over in the choppers just before being dropped off. It was possible the village was actually serving as the enemy camp. If not, they could set up a perimeter around the village and call in a medevac.

The Tigers moved single file down a trail with the medics carrying Messer's body. Within minutes, they spotted a circle of huts, wondering if this was the hamlet they saw from the air. The men broke into teams and started looking into the huts. After searching a dozen hooches, the Tigers came up empty, though it appeared people had been there earlier. After several soldiers surrounded the hamlet, a team leader called for a chopper to land in the same spot where the Tigers had originally been dropped off.

While waiting, some of the Tigers began talking about Messer. They didn't know much about him. Most of the men didn't even know his name. "He was just a kid. He never had a chance," Bowman recalled.

"He joined the unit in the morning," Carpenter said, "and by the end of the day, he was dead."

Barnett seized on the moment. "You see what I mean?" he asked angrily, grabbing everyone's attention. "That could have been any one of us."

No one said a word. They knew what he meant. The Tigers were still divided over how the leaders were treating the Vietnamese, and many remembered the words of Wood and Sanchez: *Not everyone is the enemy. Good soldiers stay in control.* But now Barnett had the stage and was making a point. Some of the soldiers stared at Messer's body, covered with blood. No one wanted to go home like that — not in a body bag. In the distance, they could hear the blades of the approaching chopper.

For soldiers, such moments can be powerful, forcing them to question their own conceptions of behavior in battle — whether they should exercise discretion or discard it altogether. Kill or be killed. If you're angry or scared enough, you can shoot anything that moves.

Ybarra and Green began talking about their own mortality. Green brought up the fact that a bullet had struck a tree inches above his head during the firefight. Ybarra said he noticed the same marks but didn't want to say anything to Green at the time.

Green looked over at his friend. "You gotta wonder, Sam, who's going to be the first to get hit," he said. Ybarra didn't respond. He didn't like to talk about death — his or Green's. Of all the places they had been, this was by far the easiest place to die. The enemy owned this province. They were in control.

As the soldiers loaded Messer's body onto the chopper, the Tigers were ordered to move from the area and continue to look for the encampment. If they weren't ready to engage the enemy when they landed, they were now. The Tigers gripped their rifles and looked side to side as they walked single file, moving along the trail until they came to the edge of another clearing, where huts blended into the shadows.

With Ybarra at the point, the platoon members stopped and squatted down, peering through the brush to see if there was any activity. To the surprise of the soldiers, young children and women began running from the huts. Ybarra and Green quickly followed and found the villagers were scurrying into three sloped entranceways leading into the ground. Women and children jumped one by one into the openings, which were designed like storm cellars, with the entrances raised aboveground and covered by leaves and brush.

The Tigers waited until all the people were inside. Ybarra began to creep toward the bunkers, with Green and six others following, while the rest waited with rifles raised.

Sergeant James Haugh reached one of the entrances and began yelling inside, *"Didi Mau,"* a command ordering the villagers to exit.

He waited for a minute, but no one came out.

"Do we go in there?" asked one of the soldiers.

Haugh was annoyed at the question. "Bomb 'em," he said, breaking the silence.

The soldiers looked at one another and hesitated for a moment. Haugh ordered them again: "Drop your grenades into the holes." He was in no mood to deal with these people.

Most of the underground shelters used by the Vietnamese in the Central Highlands were supported by bamboo and brick and were dug about fifteen feet deep to hold at least a dozen people. Slowly, two Tigers unclipped their grenades and, after looking at each other, dropped them into the holes before stepping away from the entrances. Explosions shook the ground. After a moment, the soldiers could hear moans and cries coming from the entranceways. One more time, the soldiers unclipped grenades and dropped them into the holes, and again they felt the earth tremble under their feet.

The Tigers knew no one could survive the blasts, not unless there were tunnels leading away from the bunkers. While Haugh and others waited near the entrances, other soldiers carefully walked across the clearing to the huts, rifles raised. But no one was inside. Whoever had been in the hooches had fled to the bunkers.

No one knew how many villagers were in the shelters. For now, Tigers set up camp at the edge of the village.

As darkness set in hours later, Sergeant Charles Fulton recalled the cries coming from the bunkers. Two Tigers asked whether they should go into the shelters, but team leaders said no. "We kept hearing human sounds," recalled Fulton. "They were the sounds of people that had been hurt and trying to get someone's attention to get help. Although faint, they were clear." Throughout the night, other Tigers heard the same cries, but as the hours dragged into dawn, the sounds grew faint. By morning, the bunkers were quiet.

As the men began to rise for the day, they received another radio transmission from Chu Lai: There was enemy-troop movement near another village south of the Que Son. Get ready for pickup by choppers.

As the soldiers packed their belongings, a team of Tigers was sent into the bunkers. One by one, they began pulling bloodied and mangled bodies out of the entranceways and lining them up along the trail to the village. All of the villagers were dead, including young children. It was difficult to tell how many were inside, because part of the structures had collapsed from the blasts. In any case, no one bothered to count.

Barnett asked if any weapons were found, but the Tigers shook their heads. They had searched the floors and walls with flashlights but found none, or even a shred of evidence that the dead were enemy sympathizers. "There was nothing there," recalled Kerney. "Nothing."

After dropping from the choppers, the Tigers expected a firefight. But as they approached the village, which turned out to be nothing but a cluster of huts, the only inhabitants were their fellow soldiers from C Company. A skirmish had already taken place between C Company and the NVA, and the enemy had fled. Before the Tigers could even get the scoop about what had happened, the platoon received another radio transmission: return to the village where the bunkers were bombed — a chopper pilot had just spotted people darting in and out of the huts.

The Tigers were more than frustrated. They had been ordered to leave the village and now they were being told to go back. If there were NVA soldiers in the area, they would be waiting.

"We're going to get killed," groused Hawkins.

And even if the village was serving as the enemy encampment they were sent to find, what did it really matter? It was probably one of hundreds scattered from the Que Son to the sea. It seemed as if every radio transmission the Tigers overheard was about various U.S. elements in the southeast portion of the province stumbling on North Vietnamese soldiers. A U.S. Marine platoon had encountered the enemy soldiers, and so had the 502nd, and the 2nd Battalion/327th Infantry. For days over the radio, the Tigers had listened to accounts of U.S. Air Force planes bombing the area, but it didn't seem to be having any effect whatsoever on the enemy.

But of course, as the Tigers noted, their complaints didn't matter. They had to follow orders. Three choppers returned to pick up the men, and within minutes, they were being taken to a clearing a few kilometers away from the village. Commanders did not want the enemy to know where the Tigers were heading.

The Tigers were dropped on a hillside that featured trails leading to the village. With Ybarra at the point, the platoon moved on a well-worn path along the Son Ly River. Eventually, the soldiers found another trail that led up an incline, with the village at the top. Haugh, who was behind Ybarra, motioned for the point man to step aside. Haugh wanted to lead the Tigers into the village clearing. As he moved closer to a row of huts, an elderly Vietnamese man jumped from the doorway and started to run. Without warning, Haugh opened up and peppered the old man with bullets. As quickly as Haugh fired his gun, Ybarra followed up with his M16, and seconds later other Tigers formed a line and began spraying the huts.

The firing continued unabated until some huts, with so many rounds ripping into the thatch and bamboo support poles, collapsed.

And then, as quickly as the firing started, it stopped. As the soldiers moved toward the entrances, they could see bodies on the ground, some moving, others still. Bowman walked over to the elderly man who had been shot by Haugh. Moaning on the ground, the man was wearing a long gray robe with tassels. A pot used for burning incense was on the ground next to him.

Bowman didn't know if the villager was a holy man, but it appeared he was at least an elder. The man was not carrying any weapons. Standing over him, Bowman could see the villager's intestines were exposed through the torn flesh. The man's moans were growing louder and more pained. There was a time Bowman would have reached into his medic kit for bandages and morphine. It didn't matter whether the wounded man was a Vietnamese or American soldier; that was Bowman's job. But the moaning was too much. It was actually making Bowman angry — angry at everything: the war, the Army, the Vietnamese. It was all a horrible nightmare, a wail and a screech and a caterwaul and all of it just getting louder and louder and louder.

He lifted his M16, pointed it at the man's head, and, to the surprise of other Tigers, pulled the trigger.

He had never killed an unarmed villager before. He had been tempted but had refused. Just a month earlier, Trout had ordered him to kill a wounded prisoner in the Song Ve and Bowman had said no.

He turned around and walked away. Six other bloodied villagers were pulled from huts. As Bowman moved around the wounded, he felt better. He reached down and wrapped gauze around a young girl's leg, and then one by one helped the others. He then walked to the edge of the clearing. For him, the war had changed; his entire reason for fighting altered. It was no longer about winning. It was now about surviving. And all he wanted to do was go home.

Hawkins wanted to keep moving. It didn't matter that the sun would set in an hour over the Que Son Valley, and the men would be hard-pressed to walk the trails in the dark. "Saddle up," he said. "We're riding."

Carpenter looked at Hawkins in disbelief. So did Barnett. "We can't go back out there now," Barnett protested. "It's going to be night. It's the worst time to move." With the assistance of the Vietcong, the NVA knew the terrain and the Tigers didn't. Any movements by the platoon at night could draw the enemy's attention in an area already inundated with snipers and booby traps. But Hawkins insisted.

"This guy is going to get us killed," Carpenter complained.

Carpenter argued they were safer setting up camp and a security perimeter at night, and moving during the day when they could at least call in air support and reinforcements. "I'm telling you these gooks already know where we are," he said. But the commander didn't want to hear it. "You move when I tell you to move!" Hawkins shouted back. It was his belief that the soldiers needed to keep moving to stay alive. The longer they were in one place, the longer they became targets.

For the Tigers, the pace was maddening. They were going from one dizzying skirmish to another. At least in the Song Ve Valley, they had a goal: clear the land and get the people out. The Tigers were part of a larger operation — one designed to win the war. Here, it was the opposite: they were bouncing around like pinballs. The jungle terrain was stifling, and snipers were everywhere. Find the enemy base camp? Which one? To the commanders back at Chu Lai, everything was on a wall map, with pins and flags showing suspected enemy positions. But in the field, the entire operations area seemed to be one big enemy encampment — with the Tigers in the crosshairs.

Sooner or later, the stress was going to take its toll unless the Tigers took a break and returned to Chu Lai for stand-down. No one was sleeping, or even eating for that matter. Their stomachs were in knots.

For now, the Tigers were fighting in a vacuum — and just trying to survive. Something happens to soldiers when they are forced into a survival mode. They take no chances. They are more apt to fire without discretion, sometimes out of sheer desperation. That's what was happening to the Tigers.

With flickers of daylight still streaming through the trees, the Tigers began walking back to the trail that followed the Son Ly River. Their maps showed nothing but jungle for at least a mile, but when they reached the top of a hill, the Tigers came in sight of a village about twenty-five meters away. In the little daylight that was left, Ybarra spotted several villagers bolting from their huts and running into the nearby brush. He immediately stopped and passed the word that people were in the hamlet.

With rifles raised, the Tigers walked quickly into the clearing but now didn't see anyone. They broke into teams and began going hut to hut. *"Didi Mau,"* the soldiers said at each entranceway, ordering the occupants to get out. But each hut was empty.

Some Tigers began circling the hamlet, looking for the villagers who had run for cover, but they couldn't find anyone. Angry, Hawkins announced, "Saddle up. We're leaving." Once more, Carpenter asked his commander if the Tigers could set up camp for the night. Hawkins ignored him.

Just as they were leaving, the Tigers spotted a Vietnamese man carrying a rucksack, running between the huts. Without hesitation, several Tigers opened fire and shot him. Trout ordered the men to search the rucksack. Inside were papers in Vietnamese, but no one knew for sure what they represented. The Tigers began searching the huts again, and behind a table in one of the larger hooches they were surprised to find an elderly man who looked to be in his seventies wearing a white conical hat. As he was led out of the hut, the old man looked over at the body on the ground and began shaking. Several Tigers guessed the man was related to the dead Vietnamese.

As Trout rushed over to the old man, the other Tigers turned away. They knew what was coming, and this time, no one was going to say anything. No one was going to call a chopper or even protest. They were tired and just wanted to go back to the base.

Trout turned to Private James Cogan, a nineteen-year-old combat engineer, and shouted, "Grease him!" Cogan looked around but didn't know what to do.

"Just get it over with," said Kerrigan.

Cogan waited for someone else to say something. The other platoon members turned and walked away.

Cogan was all alone. Slowly, he led the old man behind a hut.

He had only been with the Tigers less than a month and knew what he was doing was wrong. The line companies didn't do this — they wouldn't get away with it. But who was going to say anything out here? He pulled out a .45-caliber handgun from his waistband, stuck the barrel in the old man's mouth, and fired. The man fell backward to the ground.

Some of the Tigers came from around the hut and gathered around the villager, noticing he was gurgling, his hands and feet shaking. Cogan leaned over and tensed up, but now he couldn't pull the trigger.

Carpenter cringed. He watched from ten meters away, listening to the man choking on blood. He could tell Cogan wasn't going to shoot. Carpenter abruptly walked over and, pointing the barrel of his gun at the man's throat, squeezed the trigger.

Cogan and another Tiger watched the shooting, and no one said anything. They were surprised that Carpenter would finish the job; it wasn't like him. He was "good-time Bill," as some of the soldiers called him, a country boy from Ohio who liked to get drunk and laid and would reminisce about barhopping on High Street in Columbus and heading to the Horseshoe to watch the Buckeyes. He could be goofy and at the same time dependable — a guy who would break the tension with a joke, but also scurry to the front of the line if need be. He was one of the few souls trusted by Wood. In fact, he was Wood's confidant — a fellow midwesterner who wasn't like the crackers: Barnett, Trout, and most of all Hawkins. What he had just done could be construed as a mercy killing. But it also could be seen as cold-blooded murder. The medics noted that Carpenter, Cogan, and Bowman were suddenly shooting unarmed Vietnamese — acts they once condemned. The dominoes were falling. One by one, the men were breaking down, many through fear and intimidation. This didn't happen in just one night. It was a gradual erosion. No one could have predicted when Carpenter or Cogan or Bowman was going to break. It just happened.

In every war, soldiers carry their own unique moral code and tolerance to outside pressures. Much of this code is formed by several factors, including background and upbringing. What kind of family raised this soldier? Did the soldier have a strong, supportive father or mother? Was he deeply influenced by religion? Ultimately, all of these traits provide the fiber a soldier needs to resist crossing the line. At the same time, everyone has a breaking point when it comes to survival. If a soldier watches his fellow soldiers being killed and he fears for his life, he may look to his team leader to stay alive. If the team leader is killing civilians, the soldier will feel pressured to follow suit. He may even begin justifying his actions. *If this team leader is keeping me alive, he must be doing the right thing.* Soon, the soldier is joining in the slaughters.

The platoon members gathered in the clearing, fell into line, and began slowly walking away from the hamlet. It was now dark, and the Tigers had no idea where Hawkins was leading them. Several Tigers began complaining it was difficult to see the trail. "This is crazy," said Barnett. "We can't see a thing." Carpenter angrily shook his head. "I'm going to kill that son of a bitch." It was clear Hawkins wasn't listening to them, whatever they said. In the past, that hadn't mattered. But here, in a place that was so concentrated with enemy soldiers, to ask the Tigers to move in the dark, without knowing precisely where they were, surrounded by NVA, was suicide.

Carpenter recalled he and others came up with a grim solution: if they were going to stop the night maneuvers, they needed to kill Hawkins.

CHAPTER 16

I f not for the river, the Tigers would have been lost. In the darkness, everything looked the same, but the sounds of the current kept the soldiers on track, and since their trail followed the waterway, the Tigers knew they were walking in the right direction. For now, all they could do was keep moving and hope the enemy was somewhere else.

As the platoon rounded a bend of the river, Ybarra spotted some sort of illumination through the brush. He turned and relayed a message to Green for the line to stop. It looked like the light was coming from campfires burning in what was an enemy encampment or another village. Ybarra relayed another message to Green: he was going to crawl through the brush to get a closer look.

After moving about twenty meters into the trees, he could see six grass-and-wood huts, with fires burning at the entrances. The people appeared to be peasants, but he wasn't sure.

After Ybarra returned, the Tiger team leaders agreed to wait until dawn before going into the hamlet. This time Hawkins concurred and the Tigers backtracked about twenty-five meters before coming to a halt and resting on the trail. They would pause until sunrise.

The hours dragged on as the Tigers waited. They were tired, but no one wanted to sleep. Some were nervous and others were wired from popping Black Beauties. A few sat in the darkness, full of dread, among them Ken Kerney. He was worried about how the Tigers were changing, especially the ones who joined in June. Bowman was growing more sullen and angry. Kerrigan was so jacked up he was now constantly rocking back and forth, clenching his teeth, and cradling his rifle. Trout was turning into a mean, surly team leader who would berate soldiers for showing any hint of weakness or humanity. The other veteran Tigers, such as Ervin Lee, had seemed to give up, surrendering to the whirlpool. When Cogan had looked to them for help, they ignored him. The Tigers were becoming as dark and foreboding as the jungle around them.

Kerney was fighting the forces himself. There were times he was tempted to shoot anything that walked. He was trapped in a Tiger Force in which there was no way out. The Tigers used to be a volunteer unit in which the soldiers could move in and out. But those days were over.

The commanders had told those soldiers joining the platoon at Chu Lai not to expect to rotate out anytime soon. The top brass intended for the Tigers to be in the field for as long as it took to win the province. But it was increasingly clear that the province would never be won.

In the darkness, the Tigers could hear low, hushed sounds coming from the front of the line. At first, no one knew what it was. But slowly, they could hear Ybarra. He was chanting in his native tongue. Green had heard the chants before, when they used to hunt for game.

Before sunrise, Ybarra crawled to the area where the fires had been burning the previous night. An hour later, he returned to the Tigers and passed the message down the line: it was definitely a village. He didn't know the number of people there, but they were up and out of their huts. The Tigers moved down the trail until they found the opening to the hamlet. As Ybarra and Green entered the clearing, the people began to run. Ybarra and Green opened fire, and soon Kerrigan and others joined the attack.

Villagers started dropping to the ground as they were hit, but the Tigers didn't let up. They continued firing in a frenzy that seemed to go on for several minutes — Doyle, Barnett, and Hawkins — firing into the huts until the soldiers yelled to one another to stop. Team leaders ordered the Tigers to check the huts. One by one, the soldiers looked through the round, thatch-covered entranceways. Some of the villagers were bloodied and crawling. Others were sprawled motionless on the ground. Team leaders agreed that they would leave the hamlet without calling for a medevac. They didn't want to give their position away, and most of the villagers looked as if they would die anyway.

As the soldiers began walking away from the village, Hawkins received a call on the radio from battalion headquarters: the 2nd NVA Division was inching closer to the city of Tam Ky, and the Tigers — just twenty-five kilometers away — were to find the base and call in air strikes, no excuses. The officer on the other end of the radio reminded the Tigers that two weeks had passed, and they still had not found the specific enemy encampment they were sent to find.

Hawkins called for team leaders to gather around him and began ranting about the officers at Chu Lai. "They're not out here in the damn field," he said. He told team leaders a chopper would be landing momentarily with reinforcements, including a combat veteran sergeant, and then the platoon would leave the village.

As the rest of the platoon gathered around the commander, the helicopter arrived and set down in the clearing. Three soldiers — all replacements — and a South Vietnamese interpreter jumped out and ran to where the platoon was waiting. One of the newcomers passed the message that Green and

Ybarra were to board the chopper for the ride back to Chu Lai. They looked at each other with surprise. They had no idea their month leave was starting.

Green couldn't hide his excitement. He pulled Ybarra to the side, their words drowned out by the noise of the chopper. After a moment, the pilot signaled for the two to hop aboard. They were going home to family members who would barely recognize them.

Once the Tigers were positioned around the village, Hawkins allowed the platoon to rest. It was barely noon, and several Tigers were cramping up with diarrhea. The jungle covered the sun's rays, but it didn't protect men from the steamy 100-degree temperatures and heat exhaustion.

After gathering in a circle, some began to doze off when suddenly they were startled awake by loud voices. A couple of Tigers on the perimeter had captured two unarmed men and were dragging them into camp.

The men, who appeared to be middle-aged and malnourished, were led to a clearing. Hawkins walked over and stared at the men and then motioned for his demolitions specialist, Private Floyd Sawyer, to "take care of them."

Sawyer, who was personally recruited by Hawkins three weeks earlier, decided to scare the two Vietnamese. Reaching into an ammunition bag, he pulled out a roll of detonating cord and began tying them up. He pulled out another cord and connected it to a claymore mine that he wrapped around a small tree. As the Tigers watched from a distance, Sawyer exploded the mine, blowing up the tree. The men began whimpering, their hands trembling. Bowman turned his head and couldn't watch. "I hated what I was seeing," he recalled. "It was just going too far."

Two Tigers walked over to the detainees and, one by one, began punching and kicking them, while another Tiger beat them over the tops of their heads with a shovel.

The interpreter was brought over to the men, and he asked the prisoners the whereabouts of the NVA camp. The men shook their heads and insisted they didn't know. Again, two Tigers took turns kicking and punching the men in the face until one fell unconscious in the dirt, dying. The other, covered in blood, was untied and told he could run away. The man tried to flee but stumbled to the ground. He rose again and began to run. From a distance, Sawyer, unaware the man had been ordered to run, looked up and noticed the prisoner was staggering away. *"Dung Lai!"* Sawyer yelled, meaning "halt." When the man didn't stop, Sawyer pointed his M16 and fired a shot, the bullet piercing the man's neck. Now both were dead.

Bowman, who turned around long enough to watch the shooting, covered his face. He had seen too much. To him, it was murder. "I couldn't take it," he recalled. He had enough. He had made up his mind to tell someone about what was happening to the Tigers.

After sunrise, Hawkins was called to the radio to talk to Captain Carl James, liaison between the battalion and the Tigers. Battalion officers were anxious to know if the Tigers found the NVA base camp. Hawkins was at a loss for words. Daily, he had been getting the same call and the same question. And each time, Hawkins had been unable to provide the desired answer. All the killing and all the destruction his men had accomplished was, in so many ways, extracurricular. The base had been the target, and it had been elusive.

"Where is the base camp, Lieutenant?" asked the voice on the other end.

There was no response.

Then the officer asked about the Tigers' body count — the number of enemy soldiers killed in the past day. Hawkins responded they had just killed a prisoner who tried to escape, but never mentioned the other murder. He gave no other details and snapped the discussion to a close. "We're still looking for

Charlie," he said before tossing down the handset. He wanted a promotion, but fuck 'em. He didn't need this kind of treatment. If the commanders were trying to force him out, he wasn't going without a fight. What was war? War was killing the enemy, anywhere and everywhere. And that's exactly what he was doing and was going to keep doing.

After pacing around the campsite, Hawkins ordered team leaders to gather around him. He wanted them to break into small units. Using an antiquated map, he jabbed a finger at the paper, showing how he wanted each team to move in a different direction. Look for every possible tunnel and search every hut, he instructed. Every villager was the enemy. "This is a free-fire zone," he reminded his men. "Anyone out there is fair game." The enemy base camp was, Hawkins declared, near. "I can smell them," he said. "They're so close I can smell them."

Doyle's team was the first to move out. He was one of the few Tigers who genuinely liked the platoon commander. When other soldiers criticized Hawkins, Doyle never joined in. After all, it was Hawkins who had encouraged Doyle to join the platoon when they were both recovering from injuries in a hospital in June. And it was Hawkins who had liberated Doyle to do what was needed. "He lets me fight the war the way I want to fight it," he told other Tigers.

Doyle wasn't going to disappoint his commander. If the enemy was in the area, Doyle was going to find him. And then he was going to destroy. "We'll get the bastards," he said. And then he set out.

The village was near the top of a hill, and below were terraced rice paddies, each one cascading into the next in what looked like a giant green waterfall. The soldiers could tell that at one time, this was a thriving community. There were the remains of a pagoda, a school, a barbershop, and even small wooden storefronts. The team was relieved to just get out of the jungle and see open space. No one was working in the rice fields that morning, but the stalks were healthy and close to being cut.

Doyle told his men to get ready. Judging from the rice in the fields, the village was probably not abandoned. "You got gooks here," he growled as he approached the huts.

The South Vietnamese interpreter, known as Hanh, said he knew the area, and to the best of his knowledge, the people were not VC sympathizers. In fact, the VC had been extorting rice from the peasants for years.

As they approached the first hut, a man emerged from the entranceway, smiling and waving papers. "Chieu Hoi," referring to the leaflets dropped by the Americans. "Chieu Hoi." Standing behind him was a pregnant woman and two small children. The interpreter quickly walked over to the man.

After a brief conversation, Hanh turned to Doyle. "This man is here with his wife and children. They want to go to a relocation camp. He says the VC are all around, stealing his rice. But he's afraid of them. He says his younger brother is hiding in the bunker near the hut." Gerald Bruner, one of the replacements who just joined the Tigers, volunteered with two other Tigers to get the brother in the bunker just twenty-five meters away.

Bruner, a talkative sergeant with broad shoulders, muscular biceps, and a bushy mustache, wasn't sure about the Tigers. He had witnessed the beatings of the prisoner the day before and didn't like it. His compassion for the people was rooted in his own background. When he was three, his father had abandoned their home outside Evansville, Indiana. His mother had loaded her three children in a car and headed to Los Angeles. At times, they lived in roach-infested apartments. From kindergarten through twelfth grade, Bruner and his brothers bounced around to seventeen different public schools. But his mother, Dorothy, who "was strong-willed and religious," he recalled, was determined to improve their lives. At times, she worked three jobs, all the while encouraging them to stay in school.

The brothers would often go to the truck-stop diner where she worked as a waitress, waiting to walk her home after her second shift ended. They once arrived home to find her being beaten by a drunken boyfriend and chased him out of the apartment before cornering him in an empty lot. Bruner smashed the end of an empty bottle and held the jagged piece to the man's throat, warning him to stay away from his mother.

For Bruner, life on the streets was unavoidable, but he developed a reputation for protecting younger kids in the neighborhood, one brother recalled. He was fast with his fists and agile, said Jack Bruner, now a plastic surgeon. "He wasn't one to mess with."

Gerald joined the Army in the late 1950s and arrived in South Vietnam in 1965. While training, he lived with a Vietnamese family — an experience that opened his eyes to the Vietnamese people and a culture far removed from the mean streets of south-central Los Angeles. "I had found a sense of peace that eluded me in my childhood," he later told his family. "These were strangers, and yet, they made me feel like family."

As Bruner walked toward the bunker, Doyle told Hanh to find out if the man knew the whereabouts of the enemy camp. Hanh turned to the man and asked. "He knows," Hanh told Doyle. "But he's afraid. He wants his family to be taken to the relocation camp first. He knows the VC will hurt him for telling."

But Doyle wasn't about to budge; he wanted the information now. "You tell him that I'm not making any deals," he said, his face turning red. Hanh talked to the man, trying to explain the team leader's position, but the peasant shook his head. He did not want any harm to come to his family.

Without waiting, Doyle swung his rifle around and struck the man in the head. The man fell to his knees, blood running down his forehead.

The man's wife and children ran to him but were held back by the soldiers. The wife looked at Doyle and began begging him to leave her husband alone. Doyle ignored her. He wheeled around, raised his rifle, and fired a round, the bullet striking the man's forearm. Doyle tried to fire again but his gun jammed.

The man, holding his arm, began crying and pleading tearfully for the soldiers to leave him and his family alone. But Doyle was undeterred. He turned to his men and said, "Shoot him." Three Tigers raised their rifles and fired numerous rounds into the man. From the bunker, Bruner was startled by the sounds of the shots. He quickly motioned for the brother to follow him.

When he reached Doyle, he saw the team leader standing over the peasant's body. Nearby, the man's wife and children were crying.

"What happened?" Bruner asked.

"What do you think? I shot him," Doyle responded.

"Why?" Bruner asked incredulously.

"He's VC." Doyle sneered. "They're all VC."

Suddenly, two soldiers grabbed the teenager and threw him to the ground next to his dead brother. One of the Tigers held a .45-caliber handgun to the young man's head.

Bruner quickly turned around and shoved the barrel of his M16 in the soldier's face. "If you fire up the kid, I'll do the same to you, damn it."

For a moment, no one moved. No one had ever raised a rifle against another Tiger to save a Vietnamese. Doyle ordered Bruner to lower his rifle, but the sergeant refused. "I'll shoot your ass. You get your man off this kid now!" Bruner screamed.

The two sergeants locked eyes, neither man knowing the other. Both came from broken families and had grown up on the streets. In any war, there are many wars, and now another had begun.

The Tiger clutching the handgun stepped back and put the gun in his waistband.

Trout, who had been standing nearby, ran over to Bruner and told him to back down. "Leave it alone," Trout said. With his rifle still raised, Bruner turned to the radio operator and ordered a chopper to evacuate the family. There was no way he was going to let the Tigers harm these people.

That night, Bruner didn't sleep. He stayed up with his M16 at his side, guarding the surviving family members until a Huey could whisk them away in the morning.

The call the next morning came from headquarters: the Tigers were being jerked around again, pulled back to Chu Lai. No reason was given. They had expected to stay in the field for another week but were now told to clear a landing zone and wait for the helicopters. One would pick up the Vietnamese family; the others would pick up the Tigers.

As they waited for the choppers, no one spoke to Bruner.

CHAPTER 17

After arriving at Chu Lai, the Tigers trudged back to their camp and anxiously waited to be briefed about why they were yanked from the field. Some of the Tigers wondered aloud whether word had reached the battalion about the execution of the farmer in the Que Son Valley.

But by the end of the day, nothing had happened. Then another day passed, and still nothing. No warrant officers showed up to pester the soldiers. Even the MPs seemed oblivious to the Tigers' presence at the base.

The third day after returning to Chu Lai, the Tigers were summoned to the mess area, but only to be told they were free to roam the base, including the bars. For the Tigers, it was the first time in weeks they had a chance to drink and unwind. As they broke into groups and ventured into Chu Lai, they began to talk to chopper pilots. The word was that there was a big operation brewing — the biggest since the Army began Task Force Oregon. It was no secret that the Army was losing ground in the Central Highlands. It didn't matter that the Army and Air Force flew hundreds of sorties that had dropped more than fifty thousand bombs since late February. The enemy kept coming. Thousands of soldiers from the 21st and 3rd Regiments of the 2nd NVA Division were now entrenched — some in miles of underground tunnels.

Even if the Tigers had found the enemy camp they had been sent to find, there were dozens of others. While the Army controlled key cities such as Tam Ky, Da Nang, and Quang Ngai City, it was failing in the other areas. The vast mountainous region along the Laotian border was under enemy control, but no one was saying so publicly.

It didn't take the Tigers long to figure out they hadn't been brought back to Chu Lai for disciplinary reasons. The Army had much bigger plans, and somehow they were going to be a part of it.

New troops were arriving on base every day to replenish the units losing soldiers in the Central Highlands. One of the newcomers to the Tigers was Daniel Clint.

The nineteen-year-old private was already in the field with the battalion's A Company and remembered seeing the Tigers at Carentan in their striped fatigues and jungle caps. "I always saw those guys together — a real bond," he recalled. "And I wanted to be a part of that."

For Clint, joining the Tigers was his way of jumping into the war feetfirst. He didn't like the way the line companies operated in the jungle. When he had arrived in South Vietnam in May 1967, he had been sent to the line company with 150 other soldiers. "It just seemed like we were too big and made too much noise. We could be seen from a mile away," he recalled. "I wanted to get into jungle warfare."

That was a big step for a young man who was raised as a Mormon and had never fired a gun before joining the military. He broke his mother's heart when he enlisted in the 101st Airborne at the end of 1965. Junuetta Clint never got over losing her first husband in World War II when she was pregnant and married only four months. Now she was worried she was going to lose her son.

But for Clint, he didn't see any other future. He grew up in a home with two brothers and a sister, and knew what it was to be poor. When he was five, his father, David Clint, died in a train accident, leaving his twice-widowed mother to raise the kids mostly by herself. Though she had a master's degree in psychology from Brigham Young University, she rarely worked because of complications from polio. "I remember going to bed hungry more than once," he recalled. After graduating from high school in 1965, he waited tables at the Old Faithful Inn at Yellowstone Park but realized it was a dead-end job. The Army offered adventure and a steady paycheck.

As Clint was arriving, Teeters was leaving.

Uptight and surly, the twenty-year-old medic was close to the edge and everyone knew it. It was better for him to get out. He couldn't get through the day without popping amphetamines and smoking pot. He was losing weight and sleep — his nerves frayed from the speed and gunfire. He had once dreamed about going to medical school; now he wasn't dreaming at all.

"By the time I left," he recalled, "there was an anger and a frustration with the soldiers who were left, and it was getting worse by the day. Everything was becoming so crazy and so damned demeaning and so damned sick." Emaciated and strung out on drugs, Teeters headed home.

Since returning to Chu Lai, Bruner had spent his days alone. He had noticed something about the Tigers that bothered him, and it wasn't just the dustup in the village.

To Bruner, there was something deeply rotten about this unit. What bothered him was that after the prisoners were beaten and killed, he heard one of the Tigers laughing. And then he saw Doyle and the others smirking as they walked away from the village after the killing. In some of the Tigers, such as Kerrigan and Barnett, he noticed a vacant, hollow look in their eyes, he later told his family. "It's like they're dead," he said.

Within the unit, Hawkins and Doyle were already putting

their own spin on the confrontation in the village: Bruner was a coward who didn't belong in the Tigers, they said. If he couldn't kill, then he should be in the rear. "Bruner should be a civilian affairs officer," Doyle told his men.

Two days after returning to Chu Lai, Trout walked into the tent area and informed Bruner he was to report to Carl James's office. Bruner assumed right away why he was being summoned. Hawkins had written a letter to James condemning Bruner's actions in the village.

As soon as Bruner arrived at the captain's office, James lit into the sergeant. "Don't you ever threaten another soldier with a gun! What's wrong with you? You need to see a psychiatrist?"

Before Bruner could respond, there was a knock on the door. It was a sergeant from A Company who needed to see James. He said he heard about the complaint against Bruner and wanted to vouch for him. "He's a good soldier," the sergeant said. "We never had a problem with him."

James took a breath and then looked over at Bruner. "What happened?" he asked. Bruner hadn't wanted the episode to come up, but now he was upset. They were trying to hang his ass and treat him as a criminal. He recounted the day's events and how he was justified in using his rifle. And while he was willing to forget the event if that's what the brass wanted, he wouldn't agree to do so without a transfer. He had been with the Tigers less than a week, but he wanted out.

James shook his head. "We need every soldier," he said. Bruner was going back in.

CHAPTER 18

I n the darkness of his parents' Arizona living room, Kenneth Green shifted restlessly on the sofa, his head throbbing. He swallowed four aspirin, shut the curtains, turned out the lights, but nothing seemed to ease his headache.

Kathleen Green watched from the kitchen as her youngest son turned to one side, then another, unable to shake the pain that had been nagging him since coming home on leave. She had noticed the day he arrived he was uneasy and tense, and when he laid down, he complained about the pain shooting through his head. He was skinny and seemed to walk slower. When she asked him questions about Vietnam, he didn't answer.

Kathleen had been looking forward to seeing Ken but had been disturbed by the way her son had acted. For the first three days, he slept on the sofa, once waking up screaming. "It's not about you, Mom," he told her after one of his long naps. "It's about everything over there and I can't take myself out of it. It's like I'm still there, but I'm not. I don't know how else to explain it."

She asked him why he was going back; he had served his year in the war. "I don't understand why you're doing this," she said.

Ken looked at her. "I gotta be back there with Sam and the others," he said.

Kathleen Green shook her head. It was the last thing she wanted to hear. She never liked her son hanging out with Ybarra. It's not that she didn't like the boy. She actually felt sorry for him. But he wasn't a good influence on her Ken. Every time she saw Ybarra, he was angry, and that was the last thing her son needed. Ken already had a bad temper, a trait he picked up from his father. And he always seemed to get angrier when Sam was around.

After four days in the house, Green decided to leave in the morning before anyone was up. He jumped in his '64 SS Chevelle and began driving. He knew coming home was a mistake. He should have gone to Bangkok or Hong Kong; instead, he was back in Roosevelt, and he didn't want people to see him like this, especially not his mother or father or siblings. He wasn't the same person, and he knew it. Too much had happened. And the only people who could begin to understand were a world away in South Vietnam.

Green drove by the rusted and faded San Carlos Indian Reservation sign and turned onto the dirt driveway of the home where Ybarra was staying with his mother and stepfather. Ybarra was already standing near the front steps, a beer in hand and a six-pack at his side.

Ybarra grabbed the beers and jumped into the car. He said they should head into Globe so they could catch up with some of their old friends, but Green gripped the wheel and didn't say anything. He didn't want to see anyone. If he wasn't with Sam, he would just as soon be alone. He didn't want to talk about the war, and he didn't want to answer any questions. He just wanted to get on the open road and keep driving forever, never having to stop for anything. He knew he couldn't tell Ybarra about not wanting to return to Vietnam or his premonition about dying. But maybe they could just drive and get drunk and pretend it was like it once had been.

They pulled into an open lot where several cars were parked, and immediately a dozen people bounded out of their cars and ran to Green's familiar blue Chevelle. Ybarra jumped out and began shaking hands, while Green stayed in the car, barely nodding to the friends who pressed around the driver's window.

Ybarra motioned for Green to get out and join the friends, who were cracking open bottles of Coors. Green took his time walking over to the crowd.

The group was waiting for others to arrive before heading to an old drinking spot in the hills along Sugar Creek overlooking Globe. Some of Green's high school buddies began peppering him with questions about the war, but he tensed up and just nodded. "Aw, man, it's a war, what else can I say," he said.

In much of America, it was the Summer of Love, 1967, the emergence of hippies, Haight Ashbury, psychedelic rock, and the beginning of a cultural revolution that would sweep the nation. But it was clear the movement hadn't reached here, in the hills of central Arizona, where teenagers wore crew cuts and military families were still moving into 1950s-style subdivisions. This is where Democrats turned out en masse to elect Republican Senator Barry Goldwater — a conservative icon who pushed the military to bomb Hanoi into dirt and rubble. In these parts, there were no antiwar protests.

One by one, the cars pulled out of the lot and headed up the winding roads to Sugar Creek. Once they reached the spot, they parked, grabbed their beers, and headed to a thicket of cottonwood trees along the creek that would shroud their private party.

For hours, they stretched along the grassy banks and guzzled beers, laughing. Some of the friends talked about enlisting in the service before they were drafted. "It's just a matter of time," one said. Ybarra piped in. "You should join the 101st," he said, nudging Green. "Right, man?" Green didn't say anything.

Ybarra stood up. "You should see what we do over there," he said. "We're the Tigers, man. We're killing more gooks than the other units in our battalion."

For the next few minutes, he bragged about the Tigers sweeping into villages and "firing everyone up," he said. "They'd run when they saw us."

Some of the friends looked at Green for his reaction, but he was stone-faced. "You could see he was really uncomfortable," recalled Roger Askins, who went to high school with Green. "Everyone could see Ken wasn't happy with what Sam was saying."

By nightfall, Green was sitting on a large boulder and staring into space. "He wasn't joking. He wasn't talking about girls," said Askins. "He wasn't the same guy."

That became clearer just before the party broke up. As Ybarra continued raving about the war, Green suddenly rose and crept up on a stray cat near the creek. With everyone now fixed on Green, he bent over and grabbed the animal, holding it tightly in his hands.

"You want to see what we do in Vietnam?" he asked, his eyes bulging. Before anyone could respond, Green bit down on the back of the cat's head — and then in one motion, snapped the animal's neck.

With his friends staring up, he tossed the limp cat to the ground and casually walked back to the rock. "Man, Ken," one friend said incredulously.

For the rest of the night, no one bothered Ken Green.

Two nights before his leave ended, Green dressed in his uniform and joined his family for dinner. For days, he had been avoiding everyone, but he realized it was almost time to return to Vietnam.

His younger sister Sherry had been asking him to go bowling, but he kept putting it off. After dinner, he finally told her he would go. Still in his dress uniform, Green and his sister drove to the bowling alley but said very little on the way. Green and Sherry had always been close, but he couldn't bring himself to open up. He couldn't share his secrets, because they were his nightmares — too deep, too diabolical, too incriminating.

From the moment he walked into the bowling alley, Ken felt as if everyone was looking at him. No one came over — they just stared. He immediately grew uncomfortable but didn't want to lose it, not in front of his sister. Deep down, he wanted to make her proud, even if he wasn't so. It was better not to say anything.

After hanging out for a couple of hours, he and his sister left. Green was depressed, and out of place. He didn't belong in the bowling alley. He didn't belong in the bars. He didn't belong in the restaurants. After a year in Vietnam, nothing felt right.

He was resigned to return to the Tigers but didn't like the way the war was playing out and was even less certain about surviving another tour. He had told Ybarra and others about his grim premonition. There was no disputing the fact that returning was dangerous. With more than 100,000 North Vietnamese coming into draft age each year, NVA leaders such as General Vo Nguyen Giap were prepared to fight for another generation, or longer. Besides the endless stream of trained NVA soldiers, thousands of North Vietnamese civilians had already joined the cause: grandmothers digging tunnels and children dragging bags of rice to NVA soldiers. Families were willing to bear sacrifices — even the deaths of loved ones. The people were swept up by a nationalistic fervor not lost on American soldiers, who witnessed how quickly the North Vietnamese would rebuild after U.S. bombs were dropped on their camps and bases.

As major trails were blown up and bridges incinerated, civilians from the North would quickly clear the routes and rebuild the spans over waterways so that their soldiers could keep moving southward. It was amazing how quickly the people could reconstruct a bamboo bridge. As with the war with the French the previous decade, the strategy was to remain strong while enduring losses.

Despite the setbacks against a powerful American military, NVA leaders believed the war could be won, though it might take twenty years. That's how long they were willing to fight. The Americans were formidable, but the strength of the enemy only made Giap and other military leaders more determined.

No matter how many bombs were being dropped on the Quang Ngai and Quang Tin provinces, "they keep coming," Green told Ybarra. Vietnam was a sinister loop.

In fact, unknown to the two Tigers, a debate over the air campaign was heating up in Washington that same week. Several generals told a Senate subcommittee they were handcuffed by the Johnson administration's policy of selective bombing. The answer, they claimed, was an all-out bombing assault: open season on the North. The hawkish chair of the subcommittee, John Stennis of Mississippi, agreed, and took the administration to task on national television. He ripped into Secretary of Defense McNamara, saying his reluctance to bomb key targets in the North was a sign of weakness. After the panel debate, Senator Strom Thurmond of South Carolina added salt to the wound. "Your words," he told McNamara, "are the words of a Communist appeaser. It's a no-win policy."

No one was home when Green packed his duffel bag. He looked around the house, the photos on the walls of him and his family members. He thumbed through his high school yearbook and placed it back in his room.

His mother was waiting outside.

They talked briefly about writing. Kathleen told him to be careful and hugged him before he left. She worried not just about her son's surviving combat but also about his future return. "I was afraid that with everything he was going through — and with his temper — there was no telling what he would have done when he got home for good." But Ken Green would not be coming home ever again.

Several Tigers stood on the edge of the airstrip, waiting for Ybarra and Green to get off the C-130. They had thought about throwing a welcome-back party for them but didn't have time; they were gearing up to go into the field on the mission they had been hearing about for weeks.

As the two Arizonans exited the plane, Kerrigan ran up to greet them. He had been fretting for days about whether Ybarra and Green would make it back for the new operation. For someone who used to be scared of Ybarra, the once free-spirited surfer now craved the company and approval of the most ruthless Tiger.

After returning to the campsite, the Tigers began telling Green and Ybarra about the new campaign, a "balls to the wall" search-and-destroy effort to win Quang Tin. Nothing was sacred: No more villages. No more NVA base camps. Erase everything. The official name of this new campaign was Operation Wheeler, named after General Earle Wheeler, chairman of the Joint Chiefs of Staff. The Tigers would be turned loose with very little restraints. Morse and others were clear about their objective: "Find, fix, and destroy all VC and NVA forces and neutralize VC and NVA base camps," according to the command log. They were to find all outposts of the 2nd NVA Division, and if the Tigers ran into anything, they were to wipe it off the map.

"You're the Tigers," Morse told Hawkins and team leaders. "I expect you to be the Tigers." In preparation for Operation Wheeler, to begin on September 11, Morse changed the names of the battalion's line units from A, B, and C Companies to Assassins, Barbarians, and Cutthroats. A sign bearing the names of the new companies was posted over the base headquarters.

During the first week of Operation Wheeler, the platoon saw little action. Most days were spent looking for camouflaged enemy bunkers fifteen kilometers northwest of Chu Lai, but as the Tigers walked the trails they were unable to find any underground hiding places. (They didn't see any NVA either, though six soldiers in other companies were killed in the first few days of the campaign.) Every morning and every night, the Tigers would hear the radio crackle and Morse, under his name "Ghost Rider," firing the same questions: What's the body count? How many enemy soldiers were killed? The Tigers didn't have a lot to report.

On September 20, the ninth day of Operation Wheeler, things began to pick up. The Tigers were instructed to go to the top of a hill to check on the condition of an American adviser who had been out of radio contact twelve hours. The South Vietnamese camp he had been staying in had been hit by mortar fire the night before, and no one knew if anyone was still alive.

After hiking two kilometers, hacking part of the way through thick mangroves, the Tigers stopped at the edge of a rice paddy. On the other side of the field was a thicket of trees at the base of the hill. The soldiers began moving single file across the rice field when shots were fired. With bullets flying, the Tigers retreated quickly into the jungle.

Using the trees for cover, the Tigers lined up and opened up on the hill, where — judging from the rising smoke — the enemy was positioned. For several minutes, the two sides exchanged fire, and suddenly the enemy stopped shooting. The Tigers waited and then began firing again, but no one fired back. They agreed to take a chance and walk back toward the hill. As they crept to the trees just in front of the hill, they discovered empty platforms and spent shells where the NVA had been positioned.

Ervin Lee, acting as a team leader, grabbed the radio and told commanders about the firefight. "I think we're clear," he said. But he was ordered to wait before scaling the hill; a couple of new replacements were on the way.

Lee and the others took a break in the shade of the trees. It had been their first firefight in several days, and their adrenaline was pumping.

Sergeant Terry Lee Oakden, who just joined the Tigers, held up his jungle cap and put his finger through a bullet hole. "Look," he said, "they almost got me."

The Tigers laughed. Oakden turned to Robin Varney, who had been showing the new sergeant the ropes. "They ain't gonna get us," Oakden said, smiling.

A base camp mail clerk just a few weeks ago, Oakden had been in South Vietnam since July 18 but hadn't seen any action. "I didn't join the Army to hand out mail," he would say. When Oakden ran across the Tigers at the base, he would pester them about hitching up. Varney took a liking to the eager twenty-year-old upstate New York native and helped him get in. As they waited for the reinforcements, some of the men began unbuttoning their shirts. It was incredibly hot, even in the shade, with a slight wind. The ground was dry and dusty, and the dirt blew into their eyes.

Varney, who had been in South Vietnam ten months, announced that he had decided to sign up for another tour. Several Tigers immediately looked up. "Are you crazy?" asked Dan Clint. "Why would you do that?"

Varney just shrugged. The Seattle native with thick horn-rims was confident he would survive. After all, he had already lived through so much.

By late afternoon, a chopper swooped over the jungle and landed in the rice paddy. Clint recognized one of the newcomers jumping off. He couldn't believe his eyes: it was Private Harold Fischer III. They had been best friends at Fort Campbell. Clint ran over and greeted his old buddy.

Fischer, a new medic, fit the mold: he didn't respect authority and had already faced a disciplinary hearing for laughing at a drill sergeant during an inspection at Fort Campbell. Harold had grown up on Army bases. His father, Harold Fischer Jr., was a jet ace in Korea who shot down ten MiGs during the war in 1953 and spent two years in a Chinese military prison. After the war, Fischer's parents split up, and his mother, Dorothy, married another military man, Earl Harrell, a sergeant. Harrell turned out to be an abusive drunk who took out his frustrations on his stepson. Fischer dropped out of high school on his seventeenth birthday and enlisted in the Army.

The night before he hopped on the chopper to join the Tigers at the hill, Fischer, barely eighteen, got stoned for the first time — and loved it.

With the new arrivals, the Tigers were ready to climb the hill. As they neared the slope, Hawkins ordered them to stop. He was told over the radio that mines had been planted on the hillsides by the South Vietnamese, and the Tigers were to wait until someone from headquarters could bring the platoon maps of where explosives were buried.

Lee, Carpenter, and others set up a security perimeter around the hill while the rest of the platoon waited. Clint removed his shirt to cool down and broke out a can of pound cake as he monitored the radio. For nearly a half hour, Carpenter stared at the trees and brush on the hill for any signs of movement. "We didn't want to be caught off guard," he recalled.

Suddenly there was an explosion up the hill. The men on the security detail froze before looking up. "I could see a wall of dirt moving toward me, and I hit the ground," Clint remembered. He could feel his back sting like "someone had taken a baseball bat with nails sticking out and hit me."

Carpenter and others were stunned to see four American soldiers sprawled on the hillside, one of the men screaming in pain.

Hawkins ordered the remaining Tigers not to move.

From a distance, Carpenter yelled to his commander, "Why do we have people up there?"

Hawkins said he had ordered the men to climb the hill to see if they could spot anything. Carpenter had enough. He began to rush toward his commander but was restrained by other soldiers. "You fucking idiot!" he yelled at Hawkins. "Why do you think we're waiting for the maps? What the fuck is wrong with you? I'm going to kill you! How could you do that? You sent those guys into a minefield."

Hawkins stood in silence as the soldiers continued to restrain Carpenter. "Take it easy," said Leo Heaney, trying to hold back the specialist. "We got hurt people up there." But the

Tigers were unable to help the soldiers because doing so risked tripping more mines. A radio operator called for a medevac while Carpenter and the others waited.

The Tigers could see that one of the men lying motionless on the hill was Oakden. Three others were moving, but barely: Charles Fulton, Dan Clint, and Robert Diaz. Carpenter was sickened at the sight. He had tried to talk Oakden out of joining the Tigers. "I told him that he was going to make the same money being a mail clerk as being a Tiger. You're not going to get a bonus for being in the Tigers." But Oakden had kept pressing battalion officers to let him join. Now Carpenter waited for the chopper to arrive and remove Oakden's body.

A few minutes later, a South Vietnamese courier arrived with a map of the hill showing where the mines were planted. There appeared to be an open pathway close to where the soldiers tripped the explosives. Several Tigers volunteered to walk the path to reach the injured men.

One by one, the Tigers inched closer to the bodies. Fischer rushed over to Clint, who was in pain on the ground from shrapnel wounds to his leg and back. Fulton had a large bulge in his thigh from where the shrapnel had passed through. The bottom of Diaz's leg was nearly blown off. The medics quickly shot up the wounded with morphine and albumin to stop the bleeding before loading them onto a chopper for the long trip to a field hospital.

Since the area now appeared to be secure, the Tigers set up camp. Carpenter and others had long wanted to eliminate Hawkins or get him shipped back to the States. They had hoped he had learned something from his earlier mistakes, but they now agreed that nothing had changed. "If you guys didn't hold me back at the bottom of the hill," said Carpenter, "I would have killed him."

That night, none of the grunts talked to Hawkins. In their minds, his mistakes were finally catching up with them. They could survive in the Song Ve with someone like Hawkins, but not here. There was no room for error in this godforsaken province. He was going to get them killed.

Hawkins seemed oblivious to what happened. Early the next morning, he and the unit's forward artillery observer, Lieutenant Edward Sanders, headed off in the distance and began firing their rifles. Bruner, who thought the Tigers were being ambushed, grabbed his M16 and sprinted to the officers. When he reached them, he saw the two men laughing. He looked over and could see a farmer running for cover in a rice paddy, leaving two water buffalo in the middle of the field. Bruner turned around angrily and asked Hawkins what he was doing.

"Test firing into the rice paddy." He smirked.

Bruner lowered his rifle and clenched his teeth. If he had been back on the streets of Los Angeles, he would have pounded on Hawkins without hesitation. It was enough that a field commander allowed the killing of civilians and even placed his own men at risk. But now the commander was using a villager for target practice. He looked Hawkins in the eye. "I want out of here," he said. "I want to go to a line company."

Hawkins stepped back. He didn't like Bruner telling him what to do. "The only thing I'm going to do is send you to the battalion commander," he said. "You can be court-martialed."

Disgusted, Bruner turned around and walked away. There was nothing he could do, not now. But he made up his mind that this would be his last assignment with the Tigers, no matter what, do or die.

Varney was already up monitoring the radio when he heard the message: the Tigers needed to set up a blocking position. Thirty minutes earlier, B Company had run into a snake pit: NVA soldiers armed with grenade launchers. The Americans had opened fire, forcing what appeared to be a platoon-size element to retreat along the river. The Tigers were now ordered to cut off the escape.

Varney and Haugh — whose team was closest to the river — rousted the others and ordered them to follow. Within a few minutes, they were rushing to a ridge overlooking the waterway. It wasn't a smart move. The team members had no idea how many NVA soldiers were fleeing. To mobilize five soldiers as a blocking unit — a role normally reserved for at least a platoon — was crazy.

But Varney wasn't the sort to wait around. He could be cocky — a trait that came with surviving almost a year of ambushes, jungle rot, booby traps, and heat exhaustion. And he, like other Tigers, was past the point of no return. He had come to the grim conclusion that the secret to surviving was to kill all Vietnamese, no matter whose side they were on — the sooner, the better; the more, the merrier.

Varney turned to Jerry Ingram, an eighteen-year-old private from North Florida who had been with the Tigers since the Song Ve Valley campaign. Ingram earned the respect of the veterans, partly because of Varney. The older Tiger had taken the time to show him how to survive, and Ingram had shown the others that he was bold and loyal.

"Look," Varney whispered, "down there."

The Tigers watched as a line of NVA soldiers began wading into the river, guns held high. It appeared as if the Vietnamese were crossing to the other side. The Tigers waited, and as the last soldier entered the water, they opened fire.

Some soldiers dropped below the surface, and at least two scurried to the other side and began running. Varney spotted the fleeing NVA and took off. Right behind him was Ingram.

The two jumped to the riverbank and, with their rifles pointing toward the escaping Vietnamese, crossed the shallow water. As soon as Varney pushed through a thicket of trees, he was hit once in the chest by enemy fire, falling to the ground. He jumped up and began running toward the fire before he was hit three more times, his glasses flying in the air.

Ingram took off in the direction of the shots and, as he broke through the same thicket, was shot in the head. Across the river, Carpenter and others heard the gunfire, but waited. They didn't know how many NVA were waiting in the brush, or whether they had fled. Nor did they know what had happened to Varney and Ingram.

After several minutes, Carpenter and his men waded across the river and began searching for the men. Before long, they came upon the bodies.

Carpenter took one look at Varney on the ground and turned away. To see a veteran Tiger, one who had survived so many firefights, lying motionless in the dirt was too much. This wasn't supposed to happen. Varney was the one who killed — not the other way around. Other Tigers began huddling around Carpenter and looking at the two bodies in disbelief.

By the next day, platoon members were listening to radio calls from the line companies reporting casualties every hour.

The evidence that Operation Wheeler was a disaster was becoming clear with each reported fatality. They had walked into a giant ambush.

The Tigers decided to regroup and stalk together as a unit.

Bowman wasn't usually in the front of the line. His job was to stay behind to treat injured soldiers. But by late afternoon, he moved ahead of the others. His days of being cautious were over. He didn't care. He again recalled how, after one of the Tiger Force murders, he had spoken to a chaplain in Chu Lai, and the response had been, *Don't stir things up. Let it go.* So that's what he would do. And if he was going to die, he would die, and it didn't matter where he was walking.

Carpenter noticed his friend's position and warned him to get back. But Bowman ignored him — he wasn't going to be told what to do. Carpenter had noticed the medic changing, like so many other Tigers. In the beginning, he would have listened, even jumped when he was ordered. Now — emotionally drained — he was cadaverous and exhausted, his eyes and demeanor making it clear it was going to end here, one way or another.

Soldiers are trained to be brave and kill, but they also need to be rational to survive. To exercise proper thought processes. Bowman, like other Tigers, was shutting down. He had been through so much trauma, he was unconsciously cutting himself off from everything that was important, including staying alive. "I just wanted to die," he recalled. He had simply seen too much — and done too much. He wasn't even thinking about the war anymore — not the war he came to fight. Not the war against Communism — good versus evil. That was light-years ago. This was an entirely different excursion, one about taking lives, not saving them. For days, he had been trying to reconcile with what he and others were doing to civilians, and with his own moral code, but it was impossible. So he came to a grim conclusion: continue to kill or get out — even in a body bag.

As the team came to the top of a steep hill, shots were fired from the trees. Someone had been waiting for them. The soldiers dropped to the ground and fired back. Hit, Bowman fell and grabbed his right bicep. Carpenter and others jumped to his side. Bowman was in terrible pain. "Stay calm, stay calm," Carpenter said. "You know what this means? You're going home."

After Bowman was whisked away to safety, the Tigers found a winding trail leading to the high ground and began walking. No sooner did they reach the top than they spotted an NVA soldier, who saw them and began running. Several Tigers lifted their M16s and fired, catching the soldier in the back. It was a Pyrrhic killing: they knew that by shooting, they had given their position away, and it would be a matter of time before others — many others — would be coming. "There were a lot more of them," recalled Kerney, "and we knew it."

The Tigers decided to stay on the trail and stay close to one another. After hiking for another thirty minutes, they saw two more NVA soldiers. Again, the Tigers opened up, killing one and confiscating several AK-47s, 120 rounds of ammunition, and a pistol belt.

With the sun now slowly sinking below the trees, the Tigers would soon have to call Morse with the body count, and also report they had still not found any enemy complexes. As they began to look for a place to clear for a camp, gunfire ripped through the foliage. The Tigers dived for cover, pinned down by a steady round of fire from what appeared to be AK-47 assault rifles. Team leaders agreed to break into three teams. Judging from the gunshots, there were more than a dozen enemy soldiers. "It sounded like an entire platoon," recalled Fischer, who lay flat on his stomach as the bullets whizzed by.

Not far away was Lee. Without flinching, he ordered Ken Green and Ed Beck to move forward to scout the enemy's position. Because of the seven-foot elephant grass, thornbushes, and mangroves, it was difficult to see where the enemy was nesting.

Green and Beck didn't hesitate. They rolled over and cut through a patch of the high grass until they came to a clearing. It was a terribly exposed place to be, and they immediately paid a price. Within seconds, Lee and the other Tigers heard Green's voice: "Shit, I'm hit."

Ybarra and the others wanted to run to him, but Lee ordered them to stay put. They then heard Beck cry out, "We need a doc!"

Though Lee ordered the Tigers to wait, Fischer jumped up and sprinted toward the wounded men. He may have been scared, but once he heard the voices calling for help, he felt he had to respond. When he reached Green, he could see a bullet had ripped through the soldier's upper thigh. But other than the leg wound, it looked like he could be saved.

Green was even smart enough to play dead so that the snipers would let up. Beck, who had watched Fischer rush to Green's side, began firing into the trees to provide cover. Fischer grabbed Green's ankle to drag him back into the brush, and as he pulled the body, shots ripped into the ground around them. One of the bullets tore into Green's head, pieces of skull and flesh exploding all over Fischer's uniform. The medic looked down and knew right away: Green was dead.

Just a few seconds later, Beck fell to the ground, his shirt covered in blood. "Doc," he said, "you gotta help me." He had been shot four times in the stomach and upper torso. Fischer didn't want to make the same mistake of dragging Beck and exposing him to fire, so he dropped to his knees and reached into his bag for bandages. But he knew it was too late. Beck was gasping and shaking, and within seconds, he stopped moving.

Fischer turned around and ran toward the other team members who were waiting. "Where's Ken?" shouted Ybarra. Fischer was shaking, unable to answer.

Again, Ybarra shouted, "What's going on, man?"

But Ybarra didn't have to ask. He already knew. As he wheeled around and began to run toward the bodies, several Tigers pounced on him. "Sam was freaking out," Carpenter recalled. "He had to be held back." Lee ordered his point man to stay calm and then walked over to Fischer to find out what happened to Green and Beck. But the medic, shaking and sobbing, was in no condition to explain. "They're dead," he mumbled.

With tears rolling down his cheeks, Ybarra turned to Lee. "Can I get his body?" he asked. But again, Lee said no. "Sam, they're waiting for us, and I can't afford to lose you or anyone else."

Sam abruptly turned around and walked over to Fischer. "You killed him," he said, pointing his finger at the young medic. Several Tigers immediately ran over to subdue Ybarra.

Fischer didn't know why Ybarra was blaming him. He was trying to save Green — not get him killed. But he hadn't known that the NVA routinely waited for other Americans to come to rescue the fallen soldiers, only to then pounce. The other Tigers knew to stay put because they had combat experience. Fischer had only been in South Vietnam less than two weeks.

Ybarra finally walked away from the others and curled up on the ground, sobbing. "Let him go," said Lee. "Don't go near him." Throughout the night, as the soldiers waited for the next attack, they could hear Ybarra in the distance wailing in a deep, mournful voice — a chant taught to him by his elders. "He was in pain," recalled Carpenter. "We all felt bad." But the chanting grew louder. "It was getting to the point that he was going to give our position away, and we couldn't afford for him to get louder. He was going to get us all killed, so we started talking about ways to shut him up. I mean, it got to the point that we were even talking about taking Sam out if we had to." As the hours passed, however, the chanting stopped. The first stage of Ybarra's period of mourning was over. Something else was next.

The NVA always waited. They always waited because the Americans never left their dead in the field. For the Tigers, it was better to camp until morning, when the reinforcements came. Meanwhile, platoon members gathered silently in the Vietnamese darkness.

In his own world, Ybarra plunged his knife into the ground, sobbing. His best friend — one of the few people in the world who really knew him — was dead. He had talked Ken into joining the Tigers, had told him they would help win the war together. And not only had he convinced Green to join but he had also talked Beck into volunteering for the platoon.

Ybarra turned to Barnett. "I'm going to kill every gook I can find," he said, loud enough for everyone to hear.

Kerrigan looked up. "I am, too."

Other Tigers nodded in agreement. "You know what I say," Doyle sneered. "You kill anything — anything that moves, even if it's not moving. Just kill it."

Sitting on the edge of the campsite, Fischer could hear the Tigers talking, and it scared him. He wasn't the cocky soldier who came to Vietnam for adventure — the military brat who thought he knew it all. He was now a part of this unit and there was no way out. He was more alone than at any other time in his life.

On the other side of the camp, Bruner sat by himself. When his team had returned and found out Green and Beck

were killed, he knew their deaths would set off an uncontrollable rage. The volcano was going to blow and he didn't want
to be there when it did. There was not much time.

Two Hueys arrived, but instead of landing in a space cleared by
the Tigers, the airships swerved over the area where the platoon
was ambushed. The gunners wasted no time, firing into the trees.

Within seconds, the snipers fired back, and for several minutes, the two sides exchanged rounds, with the choppers circling the trees to avoid being hit. The Tigers' instincts were
right: the NVA soldiers had never left. For several minutes, the
choppers blasted away at the sniper posts until finally the firing
stopped.

Ybarra, who was watching the exchange, waited. Then,
without asking team leaders for permission, he sprinted to the
two bodies still lying in the brush. When he reached his friend's
body, he quickly stopped. He knew Green was killed, but actually seeing him was too much to bear. He fell to his knees. Kerrigan and others surrounded Ybarra and the bodies. "Sam, we
need to get out of here," he said. "Those snipers may still be
around."

For at least a minute, Ybarra refused. He didn't hear anyone. He began rocking back and forth, and started chanting
again.

No one knew what to do about Ybarra, but they knew
they needed to evacuate the bodies. Team leaders motioned for
one of the choppers to land, while the other Huey circled to
provide cover.

Shortly after the helicopter landed, the medics discovered
the pilot didn't have body bags. Grabbing ponchos, the medics
ran over to the bodies, where Ybarra was still grieving. Without saying a word, they carefully wrapped the two corpses in
the ponchos and carried them to the chopper. Ybarra stared in
silence at the medics as they loaded his friend's body through
the hatch.

Just then, one of the medics ran over to Bruner. "You're heading back to Chu Lai," he said. The pilot, he explained, was instructed to bring Bruner back. Surprised at the order, Bruner didn't have time to ask questions. He grabbed his rucksack and M16 and jumped on board.

As the chopper took off, Bruner looked down on the Tigers who were gathered in a circle and shook his head. On the way back to Chu Lai, the chopper had one last stop: a small fire base twelve kilometers northwest of Chu Lai, where the pilot was instructed to drop off boxes of coffee.

The rain was coming down, and one of the soldiers on the base volunteered to help unload the boxes. As he neared the entranceway, he spotted the two bodies wrapped in ponchos. As the rain pounded the chopper, one of the ponchos blew open, exposing the body inside.

The soldier looked over and felt his heart sink. Leon Fletcher backed up momentarily to catch his breath. It was his friend Ken Green. This was the friend he had tried to talk out of joining Tiger Force in the bar that night with Ybarra. This was the friend who had taken Fletcher under his wing when he joined the mortar patrol.

The coffee delivered, the chopper rose and headed to Chu Lai.

CHAPTER 19

When the Huey landed at Chu Lai, Bruner was instructed to report directly to battalion headquarters, where Captain James was waiting for him.

At first, he hesitated. It had been two weeks since Bruner was in the captain's office, and he was still seething over the way he was treated. It was James who ignored the sergeant's request for transfer, James who didn't give a damn about the way Doyle and Hawkins were treating civilians.

Without saluting, Bruner stepped into the office and sat down. James looked up from his desk and barely acknowledged the sergeant. "Report to B Company," he said. "You're out of the Tigers."

Bruner was tempted to say something about the way the Tigers were acting in the field, but he caught himself, stood up, and walked out the door. Finally, it was over. He would never forget the likes of Doyle, Hawkins, and Ybarra. In his own mind, they were fighting their own sick kind of war — and now pulling in the others, even against their will. He could see the anxiety in the young kids and knew they weren't strong

enough to keep their own bearings. It was simply too scary out
there for them not to go along.

With four Tigers dead in just a few days, the hatred and
fury would only act as a wicked undertow, sucking younger
soldiers further into the darkness. There was no one there to
stop it. This wasn't about Communism or freedom or politics.
This was about pure hatred. "It was just murder," he later told
his family. "It was plain, flat-out murder."

Bruner had joined the Tigers after they had been well into
their campaign and had always been an outsider. But coming
into the platoon late had given him a clearer picture of the unit.
He firmly believed the Tigers should have been pulled from the
field a long time ago. They were beyond burned out. They
were beyond combat fatigue.

As he walked by an airstrip on his way to his new headquarters, he bid farewell to the chopper pilot who brought him
back to the base. "Where you heading?" he asked. The pilot
pointed to several soldiers waiting to board the helicopter. "I'm
taking them into the field. Some are going to be new Tigers."

Bruner shook his head. He wished he could have warned
them before they volunteered, but they were going to learn on
their own.

When he hopped off the chopper, Rion Causey was anxious,
his stomach in knots. The skinny, blond-haired twenty-year-
old was a Tiger by chance. He and another medic had flipped a
coin to see who would be replacing Bowman, and Causey won.

Getting into the Tigers was, he felt, better than some other
options. "I just thought it was safer to be with them than with
a line company," the South Carolina native recalled. It was October 1, and he had been in country for only a week.

For Causey, joining the Army was part escape, part adventure. He didn't have to enlist. He was already enrolled at the
University of North Carolina at Chapel Hill, a dorm room

waiting for him, when he decided to pull the plug on campus living. Watching the news reports about Vietnam had been stimulating at a time when he was restless. College seemed like the right thing to do for his father, a schoolteacher, but not for Causey. He didn't care about a deferment. Going to Vietnam was an invitation to another world.

Looking around the camp, Causey noticed most of the platoon members were brooding. Ybarra was by himself in a corner, talking aloud, and Barnett was mumbling about how the Tigers were going to "even the score" and "get them back."

Causey just listened. He knew before he joined the platoon that the Tigers had lost several soldiers but didn't know the depth of their despair and bitterness. "What I remembered," he said, "was they were bloodthirsty. There was no other way to describe it."

The bonding among combat soldiers is deep and pervasive — and the Tigers were no exception. They saw themselves in those ponchos and body bags, and were now going to get even. For civilians, it's difficult to understand the ties among soldiers, but it's deep and visceral. When a fellow soldier is killed, anger and a sense of revenge take over. Four comrades went down in two days: Green, Beck, Varney, and Ingram. Soldiers believe revenge can lead to some cathartic release, but it doesn't work that way. The lust can never be satisfied, no matter how many Vietnamese the soldier blows away. Like a drug addict, he must kill more and more. For some soldiers, the situation gets worse because they're overwhelmed by a sense of guilt — they survived, but not their comrades — so, to purge those feelings, they must kill more.

It wasn't until noon before the platoon received its assignment — a vague call about a village eighteen kilometers due west of Chu Lai. Several Tigers ran over to the radio to listen to the voice breaking up on the other end. The order was unmistakable: clear the village. Twenty of the forty-five Tigers would be going. The assignment had nothing to do with re-connaissance, with searching for a hidden enemy camp. It was strictly destroy. This time, the enemy was in the open.

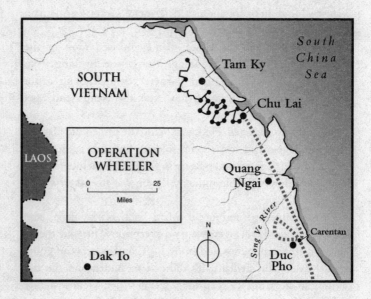

From the air, the village was easy to see: two trails crisscrossing the center of a collection of huts, peasants scattered about, carrying bundles on their backs. Nevertheless, because of the thick foliage, the choppers were forced to find a clearing a kilometer away. Once the soldiers jumped off the Hueys, there was little time to lose.

Ybarra led the way. He found a trail and began walking in the direction of the village, occasionally moving so far ahead he would have to be reined in by a team leader. Ybarra wasn't the only soldier anxious to get there. The whole group was supposed to have been joined by C Company soldiers, but they had decided not to wait. Their stopwatch was their heartbeat.

After walking for nearly a half hour, they began to see a

Private Sam Ybarra, one of the most notorious killers in the Tiger Force platoon, was known for severing ears and scalps of villagers to keep as souvenirs. Investigators were unable to charge the Arizona native because he left the military before the investigation was complete. He died in 1982 of complications from cirrhosis of the liver at age thirty-six, after years of struggling with alcoholism and drug abuse. **Courtesy of NARA**

Kenneth "Boots" Green joined the 101st Airborne in 1966 with Sam Ybarra, his high school buddy. Ybarra persuaded Green to join Tiger Force and later encouraged him to take part in atrocities. Green was killed in action on September 29, 1967, in Quang Tin province. **Courtesy of NARA**

Rion Causey, a former Tiger Force medic and now a nuclear engineer in California, watched as scores of villagers were slaughtered during the platoon's rampage through the Central Highlands. He counted 120 unarmed civilians killed during a thirty-day period in October and November 1967. **Ron Lewis, reprinted with permission of the Blade, Toledo, Ohio, 2003**

Lieutenant Colonel Gerald Morse, known as Ghost Rider, was the battalion commander who oversaw Tiger Force during the platoon's maneuvers in the Central Highlands from August to November 1967. He was under investigation by the Army for dereliction of duty in connection with the platoon's atrocities, but he denied ever knowing that the unit was steeped in war crimes. The Army dropped the investigation in November 1975. He retired in 1979 as a colonel and now lives in Arizona. **Courtesy of NARA**

Bill Carpenter recalled more than a dozen incidents of Tiger Force soldiers killing unarmed villagers and severing their ears for souvenirs. He later became one of the most important witnesses during the Army's investigation of Tiger Force. **Courtesy of NARA**

Sergeant William Doyle is awarded combat medals during a ceremony at Phan Rang in November 1967 at the end of Operation Wheeler, a campaign to win control of the Central Highlands. Doyle, who was considered one of the most ruthless Tiger Force team leaders, later bragged about killing unarmed men, women, and children, saying, "I only wish I killed more." **Courtesy of NARA**

Lieutenant Donald Wood was one of the few platoon members who tried to stop the killing of unarmed villagers, saying it was "out of control." His clashes with Lieutenant James Hawkins over the shooting of civilians are still remembered by surviving Tiger Force soldiers. After leaving the military, Wood became an Ohio lawyer. Married with two children, he died of a brain aneurysm in 1983 at age thirty-six. **Courtesy of Joyce Wood**

Sergeant Gerald Bruner tried to stop the killing of civilians by Tiger Force soldiers but was later transferred from the unit. Before he died, he tape-recorded his recollections in 1988 of his experiences in Tiger Force. **Courtesy of Karen Bruner**

This is a rare snapshot of Tiger Force soldiers descending into the Song Ve Valley in the summer of 1967. **Courtesy of Bill Carpenter**

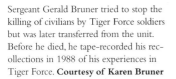

Sergeant Harold Trout, a veteran team leader for Tiger Force, was accused of forcing younger soldiers to kill unarmed villagers. Army investigators recommended that Trout be charged with the murder of a wounded villager, but the investigation was later dropped and the records buried in the archives of the Army. A career soldier, Trout retired from the Army in 1985 as a sergeant major. **Courtesy of NARA**

Sergeant James Robert Barnett confessed to killing an unarmed mother during a rampage on a village near Chu Lai in 1967. His tearful interview with lead investigator Gustav Apsey in November 1974 was one of the most revealing discussions during the Army investigation of the Tiger Force atrocities. Barnett died of cancer in 2001 at the age of fifty-seven. **Courtesy of NARA**

Secretary of the Army Howard "Bo" Callaway was kept abreast of war-crimes investigations, including the Tiger Force case, between 1972 and 1974. Years later, he told reporters he couldn't specifically recall the Tiger Force investigation. **Courtesy of NARA**

The official Tiger Force patch issued to paratroopers who served in the platoon in Vietnam. **Courtesy of NARA**

James Hawkins was the controversial platoon leader of Tiger Force between July and November 1967. Years later, he admitted to executing unarmed villagers, saying they should have been in relocation camps instead of in the fields. Investigators recommended murder charges be filed against him in June 1975, but the entire case was later dropped by the military. Hawkins retired as a major in 1978 but later served as a civilian helicopter instructor at Fort Rucker, Alabama. **Courtesy of the Orange County, Florida, sheriff's office**

Lieutenant Colonel Harold Austin (left) was aware of discipline problems in the unit but claims he didn't know about atrocities in the summer of 1967. Captain Carl James (right) was a liaison between the troubled platoon and the battalion commander. James was later investigated for failing to report war crimes. The entire case was ended by the Pentagon in 1975 with no court-martial hearings held. **Courtesy of NARA**

Private Ken Kerney said he was under constant pressure to kill villagers during his stint with the Tigers in 1967, but he refused to cross the line. A suburban Chicago native, Kerney told investigators in 1974 that the Tigers had been turned into an "assassination squad" for commanders. **Courtesy of NARA**

A map of the operations area of the Central Highlands that was carried by Lieutenant Donald Wood, a forward artillery observer, during his maneuvers with Tiger Force. **Courtesy of Joyce Wood**

Gustav Apsey and his wife, Luise, stand in front of the Army's Criminal Investigation Command office in San Pedro, California, where the veteran investigator led what became the longest war-crimes case of the Vietnam conflict: the Coy Allegation, otherwise known as the Tiger Force case. A veteran of over one hundred criminal investigations, Apsey directed the probe for more than three years from the Fort MacArthur office. **Courtesy of Gustav Apsey**

Kieu Trak walks through a Song Ve Valley rice paddy in June 2003, where his sixty-year-old father, Kieu Cong, and other farmers were killed by Tiger Force soldiers more than three decades earlier. **Andy Morrison, reprinted with permission of the** *Blade,* **Toledo, Ohio, 2003**

Nyugen Dam, sixty-eight, recalls running from Tiger Force soldiers as they attacked farmers in July 1967. He later returned to the Song Ve Valley to bury many of his fellow villagers. **Andy Morrison, reprinted with permission of the** *Blade,* **Toledo, Ohio, 2003**

Tam Hau, seventy, says a prayer in June 2003 at the grave of her uncle Dao Hue, who was killed by Tiger Force lieutenant James Hawkins while pleading for mercy in July 1967 in the Song Ve Valley. Tam and another family member buried the body not far from where they found it along the Song Ve River in 1967. **Andy Morrison, reprinted with permission of the *Blade*, Toledo, Ohio, 2003**

Therlene Ramos visits the grave of her son, Sam Ybarra, at a cemetery on the San Carlos Indian Reservation in August 2003. She said that after her son returned from Vietnam, he drank for days at a time. "He was alive, but dead," she recalled. **Andy Morrison, reprinted with permission of the *Blade*, Toledo, Ohio, 2003**

few scattered Chieu Hoi leaflets on the trail and knew they were close to the village. Ybarra was supposed to stop and wait when he reached the perimeter; instead, he kept walking straight ahead, oblivious to the potential dangers from snipers. Some of the soldiers behind him yelled for him to stop, but he kept moving forward.

Suddenly, Fischer and others heard the firing of an M16. As they ran toward the front of the line, they saw Ybarra, rifle raised, firing and screaming as peasants ran in all directions. Other Tigers joined in the attack, shooting into the huts. One soldier unclipped grenades and dropped them into a well, and then took his gun and began shooting water buffalo in a pen. A mother cradled a baby nearby, and an old man huddled against the well. Team leaders began screaming for the soldiers to cease firing, but the men didn't stop. Fischer watched in disbelief. No warnings were given. None of the villagers had raised a rifle. There were no weapons. He remembered turning his head away, unable to watch.

Barnett, who had spent three clips firing into every hut, finally ran out of ammunition. So did Ybarra. The soldiers stood with their rifles raised. The firing stopped. There was no sign of movement. Without delay, Ybarra and others ran over to the huts and began flicking their lighters. In the past, they would have waited, first conducting a detailed search. No longer.

Barnett ran up to Hawkins. "We better try to find some weapons," he said. "We got a lot of bodies, but we're not finding any weapons." Hawkins turned to him and snapped, "Don't worry about the weapons. We can get them later."

As the Tigers gathered near the trail to leave, Fischer fought his way through the thick black smoke, turning over bodies to see if there were any survivors. Just as he reached the center of the village, he could see the Tigers leaving. They weren't going to wait for him to treat the wounded.

Not all of the Tigers were ready to leave, though: Ybarra, Kerrigan, and two other Tigers told the others they would catch up. They ran over to where bodies were on the ground. Each soldier leaned over a body and, after removing knives from their belts, began frantically cutting off ears.

The Tigers waiting near the trail looked back and saw Ybarra and the others standing over the bodies. The newcomers wondered what the men were doing, but the veterans knew.

Like clockwork, Morse was on the radio, demanding to know what happened in the village. The answer: the village has been cleared, numerous VC dead. Morse was elated, praising his recon unit. "That's why you're the Tigers," he said before signing off.

By evening, the Tigers regrouped and set up camp. Causey hadn't accompanied the unit that cleared the village but was told that tomorrow he would be assigned to Barnett's squad. He didn't know much about Barnett but could tell by his accent that he was a southerner and, by his demeanor, that he was edgy. He was snapping at everyone over nothing and was constantly pacing. No one could talk to him.

By the time the morning radio transmission came from headquarters, Barnett was already geared up. There really was no specific plan; Morse wanted the Tigers to set up patrols — once again, with destruction as the objective. No village should be standing. If you find enemy positions, call in an air strike and move on. It was that simple.

Barnett and Causey broke away with two other Tigers and headed on an eastward trail leading to the town of Diem Pho, and they were expected to pass through dozens of hamlets along the way, though none of them were supposed to be inhabited, Hawkins reminded the team.

They walked for what seemed to be hours, passing several burned-out huts but no villagers. After checking in with Hawkins by radio, Barnett led the men down a slope until they reached a stream with a cluster of huts on the other side. From the distance, Barnett could see there were people in one hut and motioned for his men to follow and stay quiet.

Quickly, Barnett crossed the stream, jumped up on the bank, and ran to the hut. With his rifle pointed inside, he shouted in Vietnamese, *"Dua Tay Len, Dua Tay Len,"* ordering them to raise their hands. Seven males exited the hut with arms in the air — some teenagers, some elderly. Causey could see the terrified look in their eyes. One Tiger checked the hut for more people and weapons but came up empty; another called on the radio to a team leader. "What do we do?" he asked. "We have seven people, no weapons."

The response was swift. "They're not supposed to be there." Barnett didn't need to hear anything else. He ordered the Tigers to line up the Vietnamese against the hut and then yelled, "Fire!" Barnett and the two Tigers opened up, but Causey couldn't shoot. Though he was a newcomer, he knew the difference between combatants and noncombatants. What he was witnessing ran counter to everything he learned as a soldier and as a human being.

Barnett called battalion headquarters on the radio with his report: seven VC killed after a "brief engagement" with the enemy. His team was headed back to regroup with the rest of the element.

The Tiger teams returned to camp and tossed off their rucksacks. For the first hour, no one spoke, most of the soldiers simply too tense. Eventually, team leaders walked off by themselves and began talking out of earshot of the other men. Minutes later, Barnett headed back to the center of the campsite and told his team it was a "kill day" for everyone. The newcomers didn't know what that meant, but Ken Kerney did. Kerney had been on patrol with his own team when they had entered a hamlet and surprised the people by opening fire. He hadn't been able to pull the trigger on his M16, not on unarmed civilians, not on women and children, but others had. Just like Barnett's team, the soldiers left the bodies and burned the huts.

Kerney didn't know how long he could stay restrained. It

was easy to hate the Vietnamese for what happened to the
Tigers over the past two weeks. It was easier to hate them for
everything that happened since he joined the Tigers in May.
And it was even easier to assume every Vietnamese was the enemy. They looked different. They talked different. Easier to assume they were less civilized, maybe even uncivilized, and their
lives were less valuable.

In the past, he could talk to other Tigers about these inner
conflicts and find that others felt the same way, and those discussions had been a way to keep sane, to purge the bad feelings.
Now, Kerney wasn't so sure. He didn't know whom he could
trust anymore. He knew that if he complained about the killing, he might get a bullet from another Tiger.

That was the dilemma for many Tigers who disagreed with
the leaders. They could stand back and helplessly watch the
slaughters, or they could go along.

As the men sat around the campsite, Kerney looked over at
Ybarra, who had retrieved several bloodied, severed ears from a
ration bag and, holding up a shoelace, was trying to string the
first ear onto the lace. "Shit," Ybarra said as he tried to poke a
hole in the flesh. Not far away, Kerrigan was trying to make his
own necklace.

Ybarra looked up, his eyes growing dark, and stared at Kerney so long that Kerney had to look away.

The radio call came early in the morning: intelligence reports
indicated that a Vietcong leader organizing ambushes on American troops was living with his wife in a village fifteen kilometers southwest of Chu Lai. The orders were to surround the hut
and capture him. There was a sense of urgency in the commander's voice. The VC operative was being blamed for setting
up scores of ambushes on line companies and may have been
responsible for dozens of casualties. "You find him," said a
voice over the radio.

The Tigers didn't need prompting. Trout and Barnett agreed

to lead a team — the first time in quite a while they found themselves on the same squad. The village wasn't on any map, but the soldiers were given the grid coordinates. They were also told a South Vietnamese intelligence officer was being sent to the village to meet them at the entrance. Within a half hour of getting the call, the six-man team left the camp and headed east on a trail that would take them to the general area.

Trout and Barnett didn't talk much on the way. Trout considered Barnett a coward who went out of his way to keep from walking the point and who, in firefights, tended to move to the rear. Barnett, on the other hand, thought Trout was a loud-mouth who was quick to criticize soldiers he didn't like.

Despite poor directions, the team managed to find an inhabited village near a slope that matched the description given by headquarters. Just as promised, a translator was waiting at the end of the trail.

After walking a short distance, the translator pointed to the hut where the VC was believed to be living. The Tigers went to the doorway and found a woman inside cradling an infant. The translator asked when her husband would return, but she said she hadn't seen him in days.

Trout was angry but decided to wait. He ordered the team to camp at the edge of the village, hoping to spot the man coming home. The soldiers watched the hut all night and saw nothing.

At dawn, the team walked toward the hut again, and this time, they saw a man running from the rear of the structure. The translator shouted for him to stop, but he escaped into the brush. Two of the Tigers ran after him but lost him beyond the trail. Trout was furious. He turned to his men and ordered them to burn down the hooch. After dragging the woman and her baby outside, the soldiers lit the thatch and watched as it went up in flames. Holding her baby, the woman began screaming for the soldiers to stop. The more she screamed, the more Trout grew annoyed. He turned to a medic and ordered him to give her a sedative. As two soldiers pulled her to the side, an elderly woman peering out of her hut ran over to the woman and carefully took the baby out of her arms. By now, two soldiers were jamming pills (the sedative Darvon) into the woman's mouth and forcing her to swallow. Within minutes, she was stumbling as she unsuccessfully tried to walk away.

Trout grabbed the woman by the hand and ordered the men to stand by. He then dragged her into a hut, and for several minutes the men waited. Other villagers came out of their huts, confused and angry at the soldiers. After ten minutes, Trout emerged again, dragging the woman by the arm. He told the men to gear up and then turned to Barnett. "Grease her," Trout said.

Barnett looked at Trout. He had no problem killing unarmed teenagers and men. But for some reason, he cringed about carrying out the order. This was a young mother. Even in his anger, this was going to take some strength. As the men were leaving the village, Barnett raised his rifle and aimed his M16 at her chest from five meters away. She looked confused, her eyes glazed, seemingly unable to comprehend what was about to happen. Barnett pointed at her chest and squeezed the trigger.

Hawkins was irrelevant. No one respected him. No one listened to his orders. But for the first time in weeks, the soldiers had been so busy on search-and-destroy missions that they didn't have time to dwell on the commander or his mistakes. The Tigers were operating in small squads, answering mostly to their team leaders, and they preferred it that way.

One morning, Hawkins called for a platoon meeting, but only Doyle and a couple of others were listening. The commander lashed out, "I'm still in charge here." But no one gave a damn. There were no real rules and regulations anymore. Half the unit had grown long, scraggly beards and had cut the sleeves off their uniforms. Kerrigan, Ybarra, and several others were openly wearing necklaces of ears, and others were carrying severed ears in pouches. Whenever the smell of rotting flesh was too strong, Ybarra would toss away his current necklace and make a new one from ears he carried in a ration bag filled with vinegar.

For the Tigers, the severing of ears wasn't only for souvenirs — a practice by other soldiers in the war. Now, they were mutilating bodies to deal with the rage and, in many cases, simply discarding the ears and scalps. Corpses were being repeatedly stabbed in a frenzy. Noses and fingers were being cut off. "Going berserk" is a phrase used to describe soldiers who fly into an incredible rage after long periods of trauma and combat. The soldier believes that somehow, by carrying out his anger in a bloody, dehumanizing way, "the gook" can never hurt him or his comrades again. This kind of savagery — a form of overkill — goes beyond taking body parts for souvenirs.

Most of the men had lost a great deal of weight, their faces gaunt, ribs protruding when they peeled off their shirts. At least a dozen were hooked on amphetamines and constantly pestered the medics for daily allowances.

During a sweep south of the Que Son in late October, the sight of the Tigers approaching a hamlet one day startled several soldiers from the 196th Light Infantry Brigade on patrol. To the men in the 196th, the Tigers not only looked like hell — they looked like they had come from some horrid circle of the underworld itself. The 196th stayed away as the Tigers passed. The brigade had passed numerous units in the province but none like this. "They didn't want anything to do with us," recalled Causey.

One morning, Hawkins received a call from battalion headquarters. On most days, it was a routine request for a body count, but this call was different: a helicopter was on its way to pick him up and bring him back to Chu Lai. The rest of the Tigers would stay in the field and wait for orders.

After arriving at Chu Lai, Hawkins jumped off the Huey and headed directly to battalion headquarters. One of the first officers to greet Hawkins was James. There was little love between the men. James had been hearing rumors of Hawkins's incompetence in the field and had been talking to others about relieving Hawkins of his command. But the operation was in full swing, and it was too late to break in a new leader.

James explained the reason for Hawkins's visit. Officers from the MACV were scheduled to arrive the next day, and Hawkins was expected to join the commanders at the briefing.

After meeting with James, Hawkins went to the officers' club. He had been in the field for weeks and wanted to unwind. For the rest of the afternoon and into the evening, he sat at a table drinking. When the battalion command officers arrived, hours later, Hawkins was still there. James and other officers sat down and began talking, when an alcohol-fortified Hawkins interrupted. To their surprise, he began ranting about the "command structure" and its lack of knowledge in the field. He told the men that they didn't know what it was like to be in the field under constant enemy surveillance, never knowing whether you were going to make it out, that they knew nothing about what the war was really like.

At first, the officers didn't say anything, allowing him to vent — but he didn't stop. "He kept cussing and acting obnoxious," James said. "I had to get him out of there." James jumped up from the table and told Hawkins "he was out of line." As Hawkins continued his tirade, James lifted the lieutenant out of his chair and led him out the door. "If he had stayed there any longer, he would have been court-martialed," he said.

The two went to the officers' barracks, where Hawkins plopped down on James's cot and passed out. The next morning James was awakened by loud screams, and when he jumped up, he saw Hawkins thrashing in the cot. "I can't see!" Hawkins yelled, furiously rubbing his eyes. James ran over to him and could see that during the night Hawkins had thrown up, and the vomit had hardened over his face and eyes. James splashed water on Hawkins's face to help open his eyes. By the time they went to breakfast, James realized that Hawkins had to go.

★ ★ ★

Harold McGaha was a captain who acted like a grunt. While he could rub shoulders with other officers, he was more comfortable with line soldiers. When the infantrymen returned from patrols, he was always questioning them about the VC — their movements and habits. He particularly liked talking to the Tigers. For a small unit, they seemed to have a high kill rate — and to the commanders, that spelled success.

Since arriving in Vietnam on June 7, the tall, muscular captain from the mountains of southwestern North Carolina had wanted to lead a combat unit, and it didn't matter whether it was a platoon or line company — anything was better than sitting behind a desk. McGaha would spend his mornings outside his barracks doing push-ups, sit-ups, and performing kata — a system of karate kicks and punches designed to develop quickness and agility. He preferred shooting his M16 at the range to the daily battalion briefings, but for an S-2 intelligence officer, the meetings were mandatory. He absolutely hated paperwork.

When McGaha learned that commanders were getting ready to ax Hawkins, the twenty-seven-year-old captain quietly lobbied for the job. He had been in the Army since October 13, 1958, and had been steadily moving up the ranks. He wanted someday to command his own battalion. A successful command could mean a promotion. And that would make his wife, Fannie, proud, as well as the rest of his family in Franklin. He was already becoming a hero of sorts in the small town in the Smokies, from which he was receiving a steady stream of cards from schoolkids.

When McGaha mentioned to other officers that he was going to put in for the Tigers, he was warned by several of them to think long and hard about the move. The Tigers were a tough bunch and had been on their own too long.

McGaha shrugged at the notion that he couldn't handle the job. He was cocky enough to believe he could lead this platoon. And besides, he wasn't going to be the Tigers' commander for

MICHAEL SALLAH AND MITCH WEISS

the duration of the war. "I just need to put in my time," he told other officers. "Just put in my time."

McGaha knew this wasn't going to be an easy assignment, but he was well aware of the priority the Army was placing on Operation Wheeler. And he had a chance to be a part of it. Most of all, he didn't want to disappoint Morse. He looked up to the battalion leader as a mentor — a commander who wasn't afraid.

On November 1, he was sent into the field to take over the platoon. Meanwhile, Hawkins was reassigned to the rear. He would never again lead the Tigers.

After landing in the operations area, McGaha trotted to the command post where the Tigers were waiting. As he neared the soldiers, McGaha was taken aback. They were gaunt and skinny, with beards and dark circles under their eyes. He immediately thought they had been in the field too long. Several were pacing, oblivious to the new leader. Others were staring him down.

He didn't flinch, even after he noticed that several were wearing what he recognized as human ears. It wasn't a secret at the base that some soldiers were mutilating bodies, but he wasn't going to make a big deal about it. He heard rumors the Tigers were "taking ears," but so what? That meant they were killing Vietnamese. He locked eyes with everyone who was looking at him. "I'm Captain McGaha!" he yelled to the group. "We got a lot of ground to cover, don't we?" He didn't wait for an answer. "Let's go."

McGaha already had a plan. From a map he studied just minutes before taking off, he knew there were several hamlets in a row, just a kilometer from the landing zone. From the daily reports and grid coordinates, he could see the Tigers had not swept through the hamlets.

To show he was in control, McGaha took the lead. Slowly, the Tigers rose and followed, mumbling about the new commander and where he was taking them. Clutching his map, McGaha found a trail, eager to impress the Tigers that he knew how to get around. He was going to set up camp a couple of kilometers away and then get ready for the morning orders.

Before sunset, he found a small clearing and told the men to set up camp. After they removed their gear, McGaha pulled team leaders aside to talk. They immediately saw that he was different from Hawkins. He was gung ho but not convinced he was in a Howard Hawks Western. He was sober and could even read maps. Those were good signs.

One of the first problems the team leaders brought up was Ybarra. The point man had been openly threatening to kill Fischer, blaming him for the death of Green. Several soldiers had tried to reason with Ybarra, but he ignored them.

McGaha listened intently and then made it clear: they were to keep their eyes on Ybarra, but they should not hold him back. "We need him," he said, adding, "but just don't let him go off crazy."

That wasn't easy. That night, Ybarra disappeared. When the other soldiers looked for him to stand guard for his four-hour stint, he was gone.

Furious, McGaha wanted to send a team to look for the point man, but team leaders assured him Ybarra would return. Ever since Green's death, he would sometimes leave at night, only to return at dawn. On this night, it was no different, except when he returned, he was carrying an object on the end of his rifle — a human scalp. Team leaders just looked the other way, but McGaha was still seething. He walked over to Ybarra and pointed a finger. "I don't care about what you're carrying," he said. "I don't give a shit who you kill. But don't ever leave camp without telling me. You do it again, I'll ship you back to Chu Lai."

Ybarra stared back, and for a moment, it looked like the two soldiers would start swinging. But to everyone's surprise, Ybarra turned away. At least for now, McGaha was the leader.

Even before sunrise, the Tigers were up and walking. McGaha wanted his first mission to be successful, and that meant creating the element of surprise. Unlike Hawkins, this platoon leader wanted to lead the column, walking just inches behind Ybarra. The soldiers stopped at the edge of the clearing before reaching the huts. McGaha was ready. So were the other Tigers. Barnett aimed his M60 machine gun at the first hut. Ybarra, Kerrigan, and others carefully raised their M16s, waiting for the order. McGaha raised his right hand and motioned to fire.

The Tigers opened up and, for the next minute, blasted away at the thatch, and suddenly, the soldiers could hear the screams of people. Some tried to run out of the openings of the huts but dropped in the fusillade. A mother carrying a baby tried to crawl from a hatch in the rear of a hut but was immediately gunned down, the infant falling from her arms. It was a slaughter.

McGaha quickly ordered the men to stop, but they didn't. Instead, they continued moving closer to the huts, firing. Unable to watch anymore, some of the medics turned away. Short of stepping in front of their bullets, there was nothing McGaha could do. It wasn't until every hut had been blown apart that the firing finally stopped.

The platoon leader peered through the smoke and could see more than a dozen bodies lying in the dirt: babies, women, and children. Some of the adults were on top of the children in what looked like desperate attempts to shield them from the assault. While team leaders bent over the bodies looking for any signs of weapons or enemy maps — anything to show this was a VC village — McGaha watched. After several minutes, Barnett reached for the radio and called headquarters. "We got sixteen dead VC," he said. After hanging up the receiver, Barnett approached the platoon leader. "No weapons," he confessed.

At the other end of the hamlet, Kerrigan, Ybarra, and others were leaning over bodies, knives in their hands. McGaha watched as Ybarra reached down, grabbed the lower portion of an ear, and, holding a knife, began cutting the flesh, bit by bit, until he was able to yank the rest of the ear from the head.

McGaha wasn't going to say anything. His job was to keep moving, to sweep through the next hamlet. "Let's go," he said. As the Tigers began forming a line, Ybarra had moved on to a new body and started kicking the face of a villager on the ground. At first, McGaha thought the Vietnamese was alive and the soldier was trying to finish the job. But as the platoon leader approached the point man, he noticed the man on the ground wasn't moving. "Ybarra," said McGaha, "what are you doing?"

Ybarra didn't answer.

Later, the platoon commander learned his point man wasn't trying to kill the Vietnamese. Ybarra was trying to kick out the teeth of the dead villager for gold fillings.

Carpenter perked up at the command over the radio: "You're the 327th Infantry," said the voice. "We want 327 kills." The early-morning message was meant for the entire battalion. Seven weeks into Operation Wheeler, command wanted the soldiers to keep the body count spiraling upward on the charts.

"Do you want them before or after breakfast?" said a Tiger who overheard the report.

After talking to team leaders, McGaha agreed to break up the platoon into smaller teams — two to three members — with Doyle, Trout, Barnett, McGaha, and Haugh each leading his own squad into an area around Thang Binh, roughly ten kilometers from the coast. McGaha told the Tigers to kill as many enemy soldiers as possible, and if they saw any hamlets, they were to burn the hooches. Leave nothing standing.

Not far from the campsite, Doyle and his team followed a trail running just east of Than Moi, where they found three elderly peasants outside a hut. No words were exchanged, nor did the soldiers give the villagers time to react. They simply lifted their rifles and began shooting. Seconds later, the three old men lay shredded on the ground.

Another team consisting of Barnett and Causey entered a hamlet just west of Than Moi, where Barnett surprised a man outside a hut who was believed to be a bona fide Vietcong. The man had no weapon. "You motherfucker, we caught you!" Barnett screamed. Before the Vietnamese could move, Barnett opened fire from just a few feet away.

The other teams were within a kilometer of each other and could occasionally hear the gunshots of the other teams. Over the radio, Causey and Fischer heard a familiar phrase repeated again and again: "VC running from hut," followed by a specific number of VC killed in each encounter. There were at least eight transmissions that day carrying the same message. But no one knew whether the dead were VC. And no team was offering an account of actual combat between VC or NVA and the Tigers.

Before sunset, the soldiers began filing back into their makeshift command post. Causey's nerves were shot. Each day, he had to psych himself up to go on patrol. Sometimes he played mind games when unarmed Vietnamese were killed while fleeing for their lives. *Just tell yourself, It doesn't mean anything. It doesn't mean anything.* But he knew, deep down, it did. This wasn't war. It was murder. He realized others were playing the same mind games with themselves, especially the ones who didn't want to go along.

Kerney had watched the total breakdown of a unit. He remembered in June when there was a camaraderie and sense of goodwill. Back then, the Tigers were badasses, but they weren't murderers. There were too many good guys in the unit, checks and balances. But a dark force had taken over the platoon in the last few months, impossible to describe, and to watch people collectively descend into mayhem and murder was too much for any person to witness. For Kerney, the guilt was overwhelming. He was watching the killing but did nothing to stop it. If he tried, he would have risked his own life. "So we watched it and didn't say anything," he recalled. "Out in the jungle, there were no police officers, no judges, no law and order. Whenever someone felt like doing something, they did it." What scared him was that there was no one to stop these assaults, that the leaders were actually encouraging it.

The Tigers were in a rage mode and were shutting down.

When this happens, the soldier undergoes a unique set of physiological changes that few people understand outside combat. The midbrain — that part of the brain responsible for breathing, heart rate, and blood pressure — takes over for the forebrain, the part that processes information. The survival instinct takes over, and the soldier relies more on reflex than reasoning. In combat, this is good, because soldiers kick into a survival mode, and they kill. That's what they're supposed to do. But they're also supposed to have strong leaders to set limits. Good soldiers use discretion. Good soldiers stay in control.

Harold Fischer and Dan Clint (who had just returned to the Tigers) volunteered to go on guard detail so they wouldn't have to join the rest of the men. Clint, who had been gone since September, noticed how much his friend had changed. Fischer was deeply depressed. He didn't want to be with the Tigers, whose uniforms, Clint noticed, were covered with black, dried blood. Fischer was hiding his surgical blades because the Tigers were stealing them to cut off ears. By now, just about everyone was carrying shriveled lumps of flesh in ration bags, openly and proudly. And Ybarra had increased his stash of teeth with gold fillings.

Fischer was clearly losing it. Clint had to keep his friend calm. Neither soldier was going to be leaving the unit anytime soon. Instead of allowing his friend to dwell on the insanity, Clint started talking about something they loved: music. Clint reminisced about their days at Fort Campbell when they drove to Nashville to see the Monkees in concert. At the base, they would spend hours listening to Beatles albums.

"What are the Beatles doing now?" he asked Fischer.

For a moment, Fischer thought about the question, then piped up, "Yeah, *Sergeant Pepper*. It's their newest album."

Clint shook his head. He had arrived in South Vietnam in May — a month before the album was released. He hadn't heard anything about it. "Is it any good?" he asked.

"Yeah," said Fischer, "it's different than anything they've ever done."

Fischer began humming the first song on the album, "Sgt. Pepper's Lonely Hearts Club Band," and then slowly broke into the lyrics, the words fresh in his mind: *"It was twenty years ago today, Sergeant Pepper taught the band to play . . ."*

Fischer began singing other songs from the album, just like he did in the days before leaving for South Vietnam. Clint smiled as he listened. For a short time, the madness went away.

For eleven consecutive nights, the Tigers called in their body counts. "What I best remember about that time," Causey recalled, "was that no one who was killed had any weapons. I don't remember any enemy soldiers." Fischer said the Tigers didn't know how many they were killing but were only reporting estimates. "They didn't want to report every death," he said, because the lack of weapons seized would raise too many suspicions. "We'll never know how many were killed," he said. By this point, Causey said he came up with his own count of 120 murdered — all unarmed, and mostly males between the ages of sixteen and seventy — but that was just his own count. "Who knows how many others?" he mused.

Kerney said the Tigers had a sick joke for anyone who questioned the lack of weapons: "We would just say they were carrying getaway sticks."

The magic number of 327 kills was reached on November 19 when a Tiger shot a villager "running from a hut," according to the records. No weapon was found. Their goal achieved, the Tigers remained in the field, hoping to add to it. Their chance came quickly when they received an urgent radio message that part of the line company known as the Cutthroats was under fire. The Cutthroats hadn't taken any precautions when coming upon four huts on the side of a mountain and were ambushed.

A seven-man team of Tigers checked the coordinates. They were within a half mile. With Ybarra leading the way, the team found the trail heading west. As they moved closer to the area, they could hear gunfire. Stalking on their own, the Tigers hadn't run into a line company for weeks.

When they came within twenty meters of the tiny hamlet, the soldiers could see the other Army unit soldiers on the ground, spread around the perimeter and firing into the huts. The Tigers hit the ground and began firing their M16s and an M79 grenade launcher into the huts.

It didn't take long before the enemy fire ceased. The Tigers moved closer and, with some of the line company soldiers, began searching the huts. Kerrigan stood outside the doorway of one hooch while Ybarra bolted inside. In the corner was the lifeless body of a young mother shredded by bullets. Next to her was an infant, still alive and crying. Shortly after Ybarra ran into the hut, the crying stopped.

Kerrigan inched closer to the doorway, then peeked inside. Ybarra was kneeling over the infant's body, a knife in his hand and the baby's severed head on the ground. Kerrigan watched as Ybarra placed a bloodied band on his wrist. Kerrigan quickly turned around and walked away.

He hurriedly passed by Fischer and, with trembling voice, recounted what he had just seen. "Sam just cut a baby's head off." Fischer walked to the hut and, as he reached the doorway, brushed by Ybarra, noticing the point man was wearing a bloodied bracelet. When Fischer went inside, he saw the baby's headless body.

Sickened, he turned around and left.

Cutthroat line company soldier John Ahern had been in Vietnam since July 7 but had never heard of anything so vicious. He watched as Ybarra passed by wearing the bracelet, a Buddha band placed on children to bring good luck.

Ahern had heard stories about the Tigers but hadn't believed them. Soldiers from his company had killed civilians caught in the cross fire, but never like this. It was an unwritten rule to turn the other way, but he couldn't keep it to himself. Two nights later, while gathered with other company soldiers, he pulled aside his close friend and fellow line soldier Gary Coy.

"I've seen rotten shit during this war. Bad shit. But I've never seen anything like this," he said, his voice quivering. He then recounted the story and the blood on Ybarra's hand.

Coy shook his head. He had never heard anything like this. They spent most of the night talking about the brutality of the war and how people were caught between both sides. Before they dozed off, they made a pact: Whoever survived the war would tell the people back home about the innocent civilians who were killed. They would tell the people back home about how a soldier beheaded a baby.

What they didn't know was whether anyone would believe them.

CHAPTER 20

1972

G us Apsey was shuffling through a stack of files on his desk when he heard a knock on the door. He assumed it was his secretary, coming to retrieve his weekly report, but when he looked up, he was surprised to see Colonel Kenneth Weinstein in the doorway. It wasn't a routine visit. Ken Weinstein never made routine visits.

Weinstein was one of the Army's top officers in the Criminal Investigation Command (known as the CID, despite the 1971 upgrade from "division" to "command"), and when he came to an agent's office at Fort MacArthur on the Los Angeles Harbor, some four hundred miles from his own office in San Francisco, it was usually about a pending case that had snared the attention of the upper echelon. A small, wiry officer whose moralistic approach to his job set him apart from other CID commanders, Weinstein was known for inspiring believers and pissing off career agents who had long been passed over for promotions.

As Apsey rose to greet the commander, Weinstein motioned

for the investigator to stay seated. "I need you to look at this, Gus," the colonel said as he tossed a file on Apsey's desk.

The two men had known each other through other cases, including a homicide just two months earlier involving a soldier who was about to be promoted. Weinstein liked and respected Apsey, and would periodically steer difficult situations to him. Unlike other agents who left their jobs at 5:00 P.M., Apsey worked long days, often staying late to type reports or drive to remote locations to question suspects. And Weinstein knew he could trust his warrant officer — Apsey shared information on a need-to-know basis, often to the chagrin of other agents.

Apsey opened the file and began reading the cover sheet. At first glance, it looked like just another war-crimes case from Vietnam. This one was stamped NO. 221, the COY ALLEGATION.

The Army had been trying to clear up these cases ever since revelations of the My Lai Massacre. In a small cluster of hamlets known as My Lai in Quang Ngai province, more than five hundred Vietnamese had been slaughtered just after dawn on March 16, 1968, by an angry Army brigade led by Lieutenant William Calley. Details of the massacre were exposed by journalist Seymour Hersh the following year, sparking a media frenzy and bitter protests.

My Lai had been too much for an Army investigations command untrained in applying the rules of engagement and Uniform Code of Military Justice to war crimes. Three years later, there was still a backlog of additional cases to be cleared and decidedly mixed feelings in the military about bothering to investigate.

As a regional commander of the CID, with more than one hundred agents under his command, the forty-one-year-old Weinstein could have picked anyone for the Coy Allegation. Apsey had spent a year in Vietnam as a CID agent, and by the time he returned to the United States in 1970, he was far more experienced in recognizing atrocities than the average CID investigator. That experience, along with his tenacity, was enough for Weinstein to assign Apsey to the case.

To some agents, Apsey was the Army's version of Columbo, a plodding detective whose inane questions and mannerisms were often mistaken for incompetence. He even looked the part, with baggy pants and shirts that always seemed to be several sizes too big. After a childhood in Austria, he spoke with an obvious accent and at times fumbled to find the right word. But Weinstein knew Apsey was anything but incompetent. His cases were so thoroughly investigated that the vast majority led to military convictions — far better than the average 50 percent conviction rate for CID agents. Part of his success was due to the fact that suspects were lured into a sense of security by Apsey's harmless demeanor and sincerity. But he was also relentless.

Apsey had become a CID agent at the age of twenty-three. While stationed in Germany as a military policeman, he watched as an Oldsmobile barreling down the road struck and killed a woman, before the driver sped away. Apsey jumped into his car with a German policeman and gave chase. He followed the car for twenty kilometers, passing along narrow roads and over bridges that cut through villages. "I lost contact with my post," he said — a violation of Army regulations. "But I said the hell with it. I was going to catch that guy."

After an hour, he rounded a corner and spotted the Oldsmobile parked outside a bar. He stopped and went inside, where he saw the suspect downing a beer. Irate that someone could be so casual after running over another human being, Apsey immediately slapped the cuffs on him before he could take another drink. "You're coming with me," he snapped to the surprised driver.

When he returned to his base, his company commander jumped all over him, saying he violated regulations. But one commander was impressed: CID senior agent Frank Sugar. He said he was looking for the kind of agent who would take those types of risks to follow a case. Over the next year, he took Apsey under his wing and taught the young agent the intricacies of detective work.

Sugar was meticulous. He wore suits, carried a white hand-kerchief, and always stressed that his agents behave like professionals — not hacks. CID agents used to be derisively described as hapless gumshoes who couldn't make it as soldiers. Sugar was aware of that reputation, but also saw how crucial the agents were to maintaining a well-disciplined Army. He wanted to elevate his staff to be like FBI agents, personally helping them write reports, conduct interviews, and follow leads — all leads. And Sugar was never intimidated by rank, questioning generals just as easily and aggressively as privates.

Apsey tried to be like Sugar in every way, and in turn, the elder CID supervisor looked out for Apsey. Sugar knew that his underling had not always been treated fairly by the military. Apsey had spent four years in the Marines prior to joining the Army. The Marine Corps had promised him admission to Officer Candidate School, but in the end, Apsey was passed over and quit in disgust. He finally rejoined the military — the Army this time — after beating around the streets for three months and longing to return to the structured service life.

Sitting there on his desk, the Coy file looked like dozens of others Apsey had investigated in the last few years. But once he turned the first page and read the actual description of the allegation, he stopped short. "The baby's throat had been cut," said the report, "and there was a lot of blood on its throat and front." The report listed only the first name of the suspect: Sam.

Apsey looked up from the report and shook his head. Weinstein nodded. "I'm giving you the case because it has been sitting around for a year," he said. "We've had an agent working this, but he hasn't gotten anywhere." He told Apsey to put all his other cases on hold. This was a priority one investigation — the highest category for a CID case.

The date was March 8, 1972.

Apsey quickly determined why the previous agent had struggled to close the case: the initial complaint contained only a few pages and an imprecise description of where the alleged incident took place. The military was full of soldiers with the first name of Sam — thousands, probably.

But the real problem was the timing of the case. It had been a year since a sergeant, Gary Coy, tipped off Army investigators that a soldier somewhere in the mountains near Chu Lai had severed the head of a baby. But while Coy had first talked to investigators on February 3, 1971, the atrocity had taken place back in November 1967.

"Five years old," said Apsey. So much had happened since 1967. Even the war was different. Americans were trying to win in 1967, and now the military was just trying to get out of South Vietnam without things getting even worse.

By now, most of the soldiers who could have witnessed the alleged crime were probably out of the Army, scattered all over the country. No doubt, some were dead.

Apsey decided to take the case home that night, knowing he would need extensive records of Coy's unit, the 1st Battalion/327th Infantry, and that he would have to track down Coy for an interview. Probably more than three thousand soldiers had rotated in and out of the battalion during the period in question. Where would he start? Where should he start?

Sitting at his desk, Apsey thought about some additional obstacles. Most immediately, this would probably not be a popular investigation with other agents at Fort MacArthur, since they would have to pick up the rest of his caseload. This was a busy CID office, with eight agents juggling up to twenty-five cases at any given time.

The fact that it would be a war-crimes case didn't make things any better. These days, few agents at the CID office liked these investigations. Scores of soldiers were stepping forward with allegations, sometimes after their military discharges a year or two later, and often for infractions that could never be proven. Potential witnesses were scared to talk, and in the end, hundreds of investigations went nowhere fast. Furthermore, these investigations were often seen by the troops as unpatriotic, attacking soldiers who had to carry out impossible orders. But to the commanders, war-crimes cases were a political priority since My Lai. All agents were now on notice that such allegations had to be investigated swiftly.

Apsey took his job seriously — maybe too seriously. He was married without children, and the CID had become his life. He would often carry his files home, spreading them out on the kitchen table in the small apartment he shared with his wife, Luise, in San Pedro, an old port city on the Los Angeles Harbor.

It was at night in the quiet of his home, his wife asleep in the next room, when cases would come together in his mind — a shred of evidence, a single word or phrase from an interview, connections between moments that had seemed distant. They were lonely nights, full of darkness and the ghosts of hamlets, rice paddies, and jungles many miles away.

There were also the demons in his own past: a young boy growing up in Innsbruck, Austria, and a father — a Nazi in the German Army — killed by the Yugoslavian resistance in 1944. For years, young Gus and his mother were left to fend for themselves. And for years, the young boy was left wondering what had happened to his father and why he had sworn his allegiance to a demon like Adolf Hitler.

As he opened the file Weinstein had given him, Apsey's eyes were again drawn to the words on the typewritten sheet. "The baby's throat had been cut, and there was a lot of blood on its throat and front." He had investigated atrocities in Vietnam — rapes, murders, assaults. He was well aware of the frustrations of soldiers fighting a war with civilians caught in the middle. But the act of cutting off the head of a baby went beyond anything he had ever encountered. He knew then he was not just looking for a soldier who had used poor judgment or panicked under fire. He was looking for someone completely different.

By the next day, Apsey had dissected the report, searching for clues that would lead him to possible suspects. He had already placed a call to Fort Campbell, Kentucky, where CID investigators had initially taken the statement from Gary Coy. The commander's office at the fort — the home of the 101st Airborne Division — called back: Coy was no longer based at Campbell. They would try to locate him.

In reading the report, Apsey noticed that Coy told investigators about another witness, Private John Ahern, who was killed in action in March 1968. Otherwise, there was nothing.

While Apsey waited for someone to call back, he decided to phone the Army records center at Suitland, Maryland, a massive repository with some files dating back to the Civil War. He knew that all battalions kept morning reports — a daily roster of all people serving in the units at a specific time. If he could get these records, he could find out who was in the battalion in November 1967. But he would also have to be lucky. Many of these reports from Vietnam no longer existed. Some had been deliberately destroyed; others were still overseas. He put in his request, knowing it could take weeks to get the relevant records — if they existed.

He noticed on the bottom of the first page of the report was the name "Tiger Force" — the unit to which the suspect was assigned. The report said Tiger Force was "similar to a ranger unit," but nothing else. Apsey grabbed a directory of combat units in Vietnam from 1965 through the present but found no listing for Tiger Force. He began asking other agents in the office about a unit known as Tiger Force but drew blanks. Apsey assumed it was a platoon, since so many of the ranger units were broken into such smaller groups, and that perhaps the name "Tiger Force" had been an unofficial designation. The report indicated that Coy was not part of the unit but assigned to Company C of the same battalion to which Tiger Force belonged. Apsey decided to call the military historian at Fort Campbell, but even after reaching him, Apsey was unable to get an answer. There was, apparently, no such record of a unit known as Tiger Force, at least after a cursory search of the archives. The historian promised to do a more thorough search and call back.

Now Apsey was in a quandary. How could he investigate a unit that didn't exist on paper? And if it did exist, what was it? By the end of the day, he briefed his immediate supervisor, Captain Earl Perdue, who was just as perplexed.

The call several days later from the Army's records center provided some hope: the morning reports of the 1st Battalion/327th Infantry had been located and would be shipped to Fort MacArthur.

But the call from Fort Campbell wasn't as promising: Coy was stationed at Camp Sukiran in Okinawa, and any questions that Apsey had for him would have to be typed at Fort MacArthur and then sent via mail to a CID agent at the Okinawa camp. The answers would be sent — again via mail — to Apsey. It wasn't a great way to conduct an investigation, but Apsey didn't have a choice. In the meantime, he would continue to try to find someone who knew something about Tiger Force.

Every week, Colonel Henry Tufts, the commander of the CID, reviewed all active war-crimes cases in the event someone from the White House got wind of an investigation. Tufts had promised the White House there would be no more surprises like My Lai. A tough, cigar-chomping fifty-four-year-old lawyer who worked from a command center in the old Navy building in Washington DC, he demanded his agents jump quickly. Ever since congressional hearings in a Detroit motel in November 1971, the American public and U.S. House members such as Morris "Mo" Udall and John Conyers had pressed the government to look into stories of soldiers brutalizing Vietnamese people. During those hearings, dozens of soldiers, including a former Navy officer named John Kerry, had testified before a congressional panel that some soldiers were taking out their frustrations on civilians, torturing and killing them, sometimes mutilating their bodies. Investigators were ordered to look into every accusation raised during the hearings, no matter how frivolous and vague. When the Coy case was thrown in Tufts's lap, there were sixteen active war-crimes cases.

By April, Captain Perdue received the first phone call from CID headquarters asking about the Coy Allegation. That was unusual for the CID; normally status reports were enough. Unsure why CID command was pestering him, Perdue began pressing Apsey for an update. But there was nothing new for Apsey to report. He was still looking for the soldier named Sam.

After two weeks, the morning reports arrived from Suitland. Usually the records of a battalion show the various units that make up the overall structure, starting with companies and then the smaller platoons. Apsey found reference to three companies — A, B, and C — but nothing about Tiger Force.

Apsey called military historians at other bases and placed calls to CID headquarters at Fort Belvoir. No one knew anything about the platoon.

It wasn't until May that Apsey received another box of records from Suitland that shed some light on the unit. Enclosed were pages of another war-crimes investigation. Unlike most allegations of atrocities, these hadn't begun with a formal complaint but with a news conference staged in downtown Phoenix in December 1969. Under the glare of television lights, former military journalist Dennis Stout had appeared before the cameras, hands trembling, with his lawyer, Gerald Pollock, standing close by. Stout said he had been keeping a deep secret but wanted the truth to come out before it was too late. He said he was in South Vietnam two years ago and was still haunted by the gang rape and murder of a woman and the shooting of two villagers who were seeking refuge in the Song Ve Valley by American soldiers who were part of the 1st Battalion/327th Infantry (he never mentioned that some of the soldiers belonged to a platoon in the battalion known as Tiger Force). He said he was just trying to find positive stories about the grunts in 1967 when he had watched the atrocities. He went on to talk about other war crimes. After hearing about the press conference, Congressman Udall had ordered the Army to investigate. Within days, CID agents started looking into the allegations, focusing on two line companies in the battalion.

Apsey began sorting through the witness statements. Most of the soldiers refused to talk, and others said they couldn't remember anything. But as Apsey sifted through the papers, he saw that Gary Coy had been one of the 112 soldiers interviewed in the case. Though Coy said he didn't know anything about Stout's allegations, he had told CID agents about the beheaded baby. Sam, he said, belonged to a platoon known as Tiger Force, a unit of paratroopers from the 101st Airborne who were selected for special operations. Apsey had something to grab on to.

The Stout investigation had been closed on February 9, 1972, because the agency could not "prove or disprove" the allegations. But because of Coy's mention of the baby, the CID had opened a separate case file — the Coy Allegation file that now sat on his desk. Apsey went back to the records to find the agent who first interviewed Coy in 1971 and learned that Frank Toledo was still at Fort Campbell. The veteran investigator had long moved on from the case but agreed to go over his own records of his interview. He vaguely recalled the story of the baby but said he would need some time to organize his thoughts.

Within a few days, Toledo got back in touch. The only name he had in his records was Sam — no last name — but he said he would check interviews he had conducted with other soldiers.

When Toledo called back, he had the answer. He had interrogated an officer, James Robert Barnett, on March 10, 1971. As part of the interview, Barnett said the only Sam he knew was Sam Ybarra, who had served with Tiger Force from April 1967 to January 1968. Barnett, who was a member of Tiger Force for most of 1967, said he didn't recall Ybarra murdering a baby.

Toledo had another tip for Apsey. The name of the sergeant who supervised Ybarra was a veteran by the name of Harold Trout. And Toledo passed on one more interesting development in the case before hanging up: Barnett had surprised his commanders at Fort Campbell by abruptly resigning a month after the CID interview, telling fellow soldiers that he feared "going to jail" for something as big as My Lai and that he wasn't going to stick around to take the fall. "I'm getting out," he had told them. He had been acting strange during his final days at Fort Campbell, saying he wasn't going to be a scapegoat, fellow soldiers had said.

Apsey began to wonder if maybe the baby was just the beginning.

Shortly thereafter, Apsey received word that CID agents had finally tracked down Coy. But the news wasn't good. Not only did Coy fail to add anything to the story but he changed his account. The twenty-four-year-old sergeant now said he didn't actually see the soldier kill the baby but heard about it from his friend. That changed everything.

Apsey was angry. He had already invested several weeks into this case, and now a witness was flip-flopping. He decided he would get back to Coy, but first he wanted to turn his attention to Sam Ybarra, whose last known base was Fort Bragg, North Carolina. Apsey sent a message to the fort, requesting Ybarra's records and an immediate interview, and within a few days received his answer: Ybarra was no longer in the Army. He had been dishonorably discharged in April 1969 after a spate of disciplinary problems, including marijuana possession and insubordination, and was now living on an Indian reservation in San Carlos, Arizona. There was no mention of war crimes in his file.

For all intents and purposes, Ybarra didn't have to talk to investigators — particularly not for war crimes. That was the advantage of being out of the military, and most soldiers knew it. In the My Lai case, the Army had held up the discharge of the main suspect, Lieutenant Calley, specifically so that he could be tried in a military court. But maybe, Apsey mused, this case wasn't just about Ybarra. There was some bigger mystery here — he could feel it in his bones. There was James Barnett's sudden resignation a month after questioning by CID agents. And then there was the truly exceptional difficulty of even tracing the history of the unit. He was investigating a ghost platoon that nobody knew. A soldier changing his story. A soldier quitting under ominous skies. "I had a gut hunch about this case," Apsey recalled. "I couldn't put it down." Gus Apsey had never learned how to coast. His work habits were rooted in his background. Several years after his father was killed, his mother — to the young boy's surprise — married an American GI who moved his new wife and stepson to the United States in 1952. Young Gus, who couldn't speak any English, was lost. His mother enrolled him in a public school in northern Virginia, but he fell behind. He pleaded with his mother to send him back to Austria, and eventually she relented and allowed him to live with his grandparents in Innsbruck. There, he went to Jesuit schools, which were known for instilling discipline and a strong sense of social justice that would stay with him the rest of his life. It was in these schools that he found a sense of peace and purpose. "I guess more than anything, they taught us to do the right thing," he recalled. At eighteen, he returned to the States to live with his mother and stepfather.

Gus Apsey's sense of justice was soon to be sorely tested.

Sam Ybarra was startled by the knock on his door. No one visited his dilapidated home in the San Carlos Indian Reservation, especially this early in the morning. Ybarra told his wife to see who was there.

Janice Little cracked open the door and was greeted by two men on the front steps, one flashing an Army badge and introducing himself as a CID agent from a field office in Arizona. "We'd like to see Sam Ybarra," he said.

Little returned to the bedroom to tell her husband, but he had overheard the conversation and wanted nothing to do with the CID. He told his wife to tell the agents to go away.

Since returning to the reservation in 1969, Ybarra had just wanted to be left alone. He had tried to work jobs, but somehow he would always find a way of showing up late — or not showing at all.

Ybarra had not told anyone on the reservation about his dishonorable discharge. No one was going to know what happened. Like other family members, Little was oblivious to her husband's military record, but not his drinking and drugging. "At first, it really wasn't so bad," she recalled. "But then, it got worse. The more I got to know him, the more I realized that he had serious problems." At first he didn't drink until late afternoon, but now he was downing beers in the morning and constantly smoking marijuana, often until he passed out.

When the agents drove away, Janice asked her husband why they were at the door, but he just shrugged. "I don't know," he said. She wasn't going to press him.

She had known him for a few months and was still learning things about him. They met in a diner at the reservation in 1972. She was a waitress when she noticed him walk through the door in his Army uniform. He sat down in a booth and asked for her to wait his table.

For weeks, he came in every afternoon, placing the same order: cheeseburger, fries, and a strawberry shake. Soon after they began living together, she noticed his heavy drinking. "What I learned," she said years later, "was that he was drinking to forget."

In May, Apsey was sorting through the mail when he noticed an envelope with the return address for the CID offices in Arizona. Without wasting any time, he ripped open the envelope. He knew it contained the results of an interview with Sam Ybarra and couldn't wait to read the statement.

What he found was a terse response: Ybarra had refused to talk — no further information. Apsey was disappointed. He had hoped the interview would have cleared up questions about the case.

As he continued sifting through the mail, Apsey came upon an envelope from Fort Bragg, stamped CONFIDENTIAL and bearing his name. When he opened the contents, he saw the papers also pertained to Ybarra. It was a psychological profile, and it wasn't a pretty picture.

The report had been written in 1969 by an Army psychiatrist who evaluated Ybarra after he refused to go into a bunker during a mortar attack in South Vietnam a year after leaving Tiger Force. He was described as a volatile and bitter soldier who threatened officers with bodily harm. He could be vicious and unpredictable, and was in no condition to go into battle. In short, he was trouble.

Apsey was intrigued. For some reason, Sam Ybarra had been considered a leader in Tiger Force — this much Apsey had already discovered. So why did Ybarra fall apart when he was transferred in 1968? Why did he fit into the Tigers but not other units? What was it about the Tigers that allowed a soldier like Ybarra to thrive?

Apsey was seasoned enough to know that if the Army had zealously worked this case a year ago, agents might have been more easily able to find witnesses to shed light on Ybarra and Tiger Force. Now he would have to play catch-up.

Apsey found that Harold Trout was still in the military, stationed in Europe at Camp Wildflecken, a former German military training base taken over by the U.S. Army at the end of World War II. That meant Apsey would have to depend on CID agents in Germany. He followed the same routine he had for Coy by typing out questions designed to gauge how much Trout really knew. Within ten days, the agents found Trout, interviewed him, and then sent his responses back. Trout said he recalled Ybarra but nothing about the murder of a baby. In fact, he insisted no war crimes occurred under his watch. That wasn't surprising to Apsey: no soldier in his right mind would confess to war crimes occurring under his supervision, since by doing so he would open himself up to prosecution. But what did surprise Apsey was that Trout had actually kept his own detailed notebook of every soldier who served in Tiger Force in 1967 and that copies were turned over to CID agents. The notebook represented the only record of the platoon's members — and a big break in the investigation. Apsey now had names.

Using Trout's notebook, Apsey took the names of the soldiers from Tiger Force and matched them to the military serial numbers in the morning reports. He then sent the numbers to the Pentagon to find where the men were currently based. Over the next few weeks, Apsey sent dozens of additional requests to Army personnel, demanding locations of soldiers and immediate interviews by the local CID offices. In some cases, the soldiers were at bases as far away as Korea and Taiwan. In others, the Army had no data and would have to do several weeks' worth of tedious hand searches through thousands of records just coming back from Vietnam.

Nevertheless, one by one, the names and locations of former Tiger Force platoon members were sent to Fort MacArthur. One of the first soldiers to be found was Forrest Miller, the former Tiger Force medic, now at Fort Bragg. When agents pulled him aside and began to ask him about Ybarra, he threw up his arms and said he didn't want to talk. Tiger Force was a long time ago, Miller declared, and he just wanted to get on with his military career. Why not, he suggested, talk to the former commanders? "I didn't see anything, and I don't know anything," Miller told agents Joseph Reiner and Frederick Lepfien. Before the discussion was over he even went a step further, claiming he didn't even know Ybarra.

Agents also located Ken Kerney, who was then out of the Army and renting an apartment in Chicago. He was uneasy, even nervous about talking.

Kerney's mother had told the agents where he was renting. Only she knew where her son was living, which is how he desired it. Kerney didn't want anyone to know, especially the Army. Right after his discharge in 1969, he had burned his uniform. When he had returned to his home in suburban Chicago, he tried to settle down for the sake of his mother. He had hooked up with a high school sweetheart, gotten married, and begun working at a computer company. On the outside, everything had seemed right. But inside, his stomach had been in knots and he couldn't control his thoughts. He had to be by himself. No one else understood — not his wife, not his mother, no one. "Get the hell out," he said to himself, and that's what Kerney did. He left his wife and began hitchhiking across the country, getting drunk and getting stoned. When he finally returned to Chicago, he found a small apartment and picked up a job tending bar at a rock club.

When CID agents came to his door, Kerney froze up. All they did was bring back bad thoughts, and he had tried so hard to forget. Surely there must be others they could talk to, he suggested. But after several minutes of questioning, Kerney admitted he knew Ybarra, though nothing about a baby being killed. "I just don't know anything," he said.

In the ensuing weeks, more soldiers were found, each one a near and useless carbon copy of the other: they were clearly distressed and edgy but drew a blank when it came to war crimes. "These guys are nervous. Something's up," one agent wrote Apsey. But one couldn't base a case on shadows and nervous tics.

In November, Apsey decided to fly to New Orleans to interview Harold Fischer. Like so many other veterans, Fischer was clearly traumatized by the war. He had trouble sleeping and keeping jobs after his discharge, but had kept much of his troubles to himself. Shortly after he rotated out of Tiger Force, he had been shipped to a line company to finish his tour, but he was clearly distressed from his days with the platoon. When a lieutenant ordered him to skip a stand-down — a brief period of rest and relaxation — and return to the field, Fischer refused. When the officer insisted, he had picked up his M16 and fired at the lieutenant's feet. Fischer was court-martialed for insubordination and spent sixty-one days in the military jail known as Camp LBJ. After returning to the United States, he began dropping acid and drinking. "I had to dull the pain," he recalled. "I had nothing in common with the average person."

Fischer was sent to Fort Sam Houston in San Antonio to finish his last few months in service, when an antiwar protest sent him into a tizzy. "I just couldn't take it," he said. "It just triggered everything from the war." He went on a long binge, drinking and smoking marijuana for days. After his discharge, he moved with a girlfriend to New Orleans, where he got a job selling used cars.

Fischer knew the CID agents would keep hounding him, so he agreed to meet Apsey on the tenth floor of the federal building on Loyola Avenue. First, Apsey showed the former private some photos of Tiger Force members, asking him to identify the ones he recognized. Fischer picked out McGaha and a few others. Apsey could see Fischer was nervous and didn't want to talk, so he tried his usual approach of backing into the interview, starting with questions about Fischer's military background.

Fischer twitched in his seat. He didn't know what to say, or how much he could say.

Apsey realized he had to act quickly, before Fischer closed up entirely, so he directly asked the question: "Do you know anything about Ybarra cutting off the head of a baby?"

Fischer sat straight up in his chair. He had never expected *this* to come up. Never. Why now?

He told Apsey he had nothing to say. Apsey dived back in without pause: "Do you have knowledge of such an incident?"

After several tense seconds, Fischer looked down. He

couldn't even deal with the war on his own. Why would he want to talk to the CID about it? How was this going to help him at this stage in his life?

But Fischer was also pragmatic, and he could tell that Apsey wasn't going to go away. He would be back.

So, slowly, Fischer began to recount what had happened five years earlier. After a sweep of a village, Fischer explained, he had passed by Terrence Kerrigan, who had appeared flustered. Fischer had asked him what was wrong, and Kerrigan had responded by saying, "Sam just cut a baby's head off." Fischer could see that Kerrigan was upset and had never forgotten the expression on his fellow soldier's face.

Apsey interrupted Fischer by asking him if he saw Ybarra cut off the baby's head. Fischer shook his head no. All he would say was that Ybarra was capable of such an act. In fact, though he kept his fear to himself, Fischer was afraid about telling the whole story because he believed Ybarra would hunt him down and cut his throat for saying anything. Ybarra, he imagined, still blamed him for Green's death, and five years later, Fischer still had nightmares about the Indian with the pockmarked face and black, angry eyes. He had to be careful. Fischer had seen Ybarra leaving the hut. He had immediately looked inside and seen the baby's headless body. There was no question Ybarra carried out the despicable act. But he wasn't going to tell Apsey. He had said enough, maybe even too much.

Apsey asked if there were problems with this unit. Was there anything wrong with Tiger Force, or anything Fischer was trying to hide?

Fischer was quiet. He had been thinking about what he had said. He took a deep breath. "There were the ears," he said, "the ears." He added that other things happened, but he couldn't talk about it.

Apsey tried to press Fischer for more details. "What else can you remember?" he asked, stressing the importance of telling the truth. But by now, Fischer was starting to shut down. He was through with the interview, whether Apsey liked it or not.

Fischer rose from his chair, left the room, and walked to the elevator. Apsey gathered his stuff and walked out into the balmy New Orleans afternoon.

When Apsey returned to Fort MacArthur, he immediately pressed the Pentagon for any information on the whereabouts of Terrence Kerrigan. Within days, he received his answer: his witness was living a half hour away, out of the Army in Pasadena. After several phone calls, Apsey reached Kerrigan and coaxed him into coming to the base for an interview on December 12.

Kerrigan didn't want to go to the base. He was living with his mother and spent most of his days smoking joints and drinking. He now walked with a limp — the result of injuries he had suffered after being struck by a car near Fort Bragg in 1970. He had spent nearly a year in the hospital and was now addicted to painkillers.

Kerrigan had originally joined the Army to get the benefits to go to college, but now everything was on hold. He tried going to UCLA but dropped out after a semester. He tried to study but couldn't concentrate. He would open his books and stare at the pages. One night, he tossed a textbook to the floor and quit. He left his home and went to a bar, where he immediately got into a fight.

The good-natured, clean-cut guy who loved to surf had died. People were stunned just by the difference in the way Kerrigan looked: deep-set eyes, long, stringy hair and mustache. "He wasn't the same boy who went to Vietnam," said his mother, Joan Kerrigan. He shared one story with his mother: the death of a baby in a hut. And every time he heard a baby cry, he would turn to her and say he didn't want children.

Kerrigan hesitated to shake Apsey's hand. He was scared and, at the same time, defiant. Right away, he said he didn't feel comfortable talking about his former platoon and wanted to leave.

Apsey didn't beat around the bush.

"I'm not going to go away," he said.

Kerrigan looked up. Apsey then leaned over the table, confronting the former private directly: Did Sam Ybarra murder a baby after a sweep of a village in Quang Tin?

Kerrigan stared at Apsey with surprise and then turned away. "I don't remember," he said. The former point man kept him alive and showed him how to turn his fear into hate. There was no way he would turn on Sam.

Apsey reached over and grabbed a piece of paper from his desk. It was Fischer's statement. Kerrigan looked at the document and then tossed it back on the desk. His face flushed with anger, he snapped, "I can't close out the possibility that this incident happened."

Apsey asked him what he knew about the incident, but Kerrigan jumped up, announcing, "I'm not saying anything more." As Kerrigan left the room, Apsey asked him if he would be available for one more interview. Kerrigan angrily pointed his finger at the agent. "This is all bullshit!" he screamed. "I'm not going to tell you anything about Tiger Force. Nothing. Do you hear me?"

Apsey sat there wondering what it was that these men were so scared of. Or who.

CHAPTER 21

When Apsey arrived at his office on January 12, 1973, there were already two phone messages on his desk. Both were from Special Agent Donald Needles, who worked out of an Army office in Columbus, Ohio. Both were marked "urgent."

Apsey was aware that Needles was interviewing a former Tiger Force specialist who lived in Ohio and that the interview was supposed to take place in the morning. Apsey tried to reach Needles twice but was told both times the agent was still interrogating the same witness. That was a good sign. Most interviews in this investigation had lasted less than thirty minutes.

By noon, Apsey tried again. This time Needles picked up the phone. "I think you may want to come out here," Needles said. "This guy's talking. You're not going to believe what he's saying."

It wasn't like Bill Carpenter to slump into his seat and stare into space. Usually, he was quick to crack jokes with his young wife, Deb, or toss his baby into the air before going off to his sales job for Brown & Williamson Tobacco. But as he sat across from Deb and their six-month-old son on a cold January morning, he couldn't stop thinking of the phone call he had just received a few hours earlier. He looked out the window at the snow now falling, at the gray leaden skies of southeast Ohio, and knew he better leave soon before the roads were impassable. The forecast called for three to six inches, and on the narrow country roads of Jefferson County, that could be treacherous if he waited too long.

He didn't have to tell his wife why he was bothered or where he was going. She knew he had received a call from the Army CID that morning. He had risen from the table, kissed her and the baby, grabbed his coat, and headed out the door. As he had driven north through the rolling hills, Carpenter had tightly gripped the wheel of his car. The images were returning: Jungles. Tiger Force. Death.

Carpenter had spent the last six years trying to forget the year he spent in Vietnam. But the past had a way of creeping up, even startling you. He was young when he went to war, and it had been hard enough to learn how to kill, and then to watch as things got so crazy, so merciless.

The faces — that was the hard part. Remembering the faces of the dead. He wanted to just pretend it was all a bad dream. A phone call like this morning's reminded him that it had been a nightmare made flesh.

As an Army reservist, he couldn't ignore the request to talk to an investigator about Tiger Force. He had blown off the first call several months earlier by telling the agent he didn't want to talk. But Carpenter knew that if a second request was made, he would have to comply or risk being called back into active service, something he most certainly did not want. He had a family and a three-bedroom home in the small rural town of Brilliant. He held down two jobs, one with the tobacco company and the other with the Brilliant police department as a second-shift patrolman. Carpenter didn't want anything to jeopardize his new life.

A week ago, he agreed to talk to Special Agent Needles, and it had just started coming out, everything. Now he was on his way to tell the story again — this time, to Gus Apsey.

A cold wind whipped across the tarmac of Port Columbus International Airport as Apsey stepped off the plane. He knew the Midwest could be cold, but he didn't realize how numbing the air could be in the middle of January. When he reached the terminal, he was greeted by Needles, who had arranged the meeting with Carpenter at a Holiday Inn in Steubenville, ten miles from Carpenter's house. The drive to the coal-mining town — 120 miles of boring flat farmland that eventually rolls into the hills of southeastern Ohio — went quicker than expected.

By the time they walked into the lobby, Carpenter was already waiting. Unlike some of the other veterans who grew their hair long, Carpenter was clean shaven and had a crew cut. He was slightly nervous but polite. The three checked into a room and plopped down in chairs as Apsey took out his pen and notepad and turned on a tape recorder. Apsey looked at Needles and then turned back to Carpenter.

"What made you want to talk to us?" Apsey asked.

Carpenter took a breath. "You know, the Tigers killed a lot of people while I was with them," he said. "And I may have shot one or two myself that would not be considered justified killings."

Though Needles had told Apsey that Carpenter was willing to talk, the lead agent was nevertheless surprised at the veteran's candor. Apsey asked Carpenter about Ybarra. Was it true he murdered a baby during a mission in Quang Tin? Carpenter responded that he didn't witness any such act but heard about it. Everyone knew that Ybarra was crazy and seemed to enjoy killing.

Apsey waited for Carpenter to say more, but for a moment, there was silence. It wasn't easy for Carpenter. He had buried so much after the war — countless stories that he didn't even tell his wife, his parents, his closest friends.

Apsey sensed that Carpenter was hesitating, but then, to his surprise, the former Tiger Force soldier began talking as if he had been rehearsing this moment for years. "One thing you need to know," Carpenter said, taking another deep breath. "I was scared."

He looked around the room as he collected his thoughts and then began. It was morning in the Song Ve Valley, and the platoon had just received fire from snipers but didn't see where they were perched. Moments later, the unit came upon a rice paddy where ten unarmed farmers were in the field. Word was passed down the line to go ahead and fire.

Apsey interrupted. "Who gave the order?" he asked. Carpenter looked at Apsey. "It was our commander, Lieutenant Hawkins."

For the next several minutes, Carpenter gave a detailed account of the men lifting their rifles, without any provocation, and firing at the farmers as they began to run for cover. "We killed about ten," he said slowly, "and then stopped firing." He went on to explain that the soldiers "knew the farmers weren't armed to begin with, but shot them anyway because Hawkins ordered it."

Apsey interrupted again. "Who was there during this incident?" he asked.

Carpenter responded, "The whole Tiger Force platoon." Carpenter insisted he never fired on the farmers, knowing "it was unjustified. I just couldn't do it."

Next, Carpenter brought up the execution of an old man as he pleaded for his life near the banks of the Song Ve River. The man had just crossed the river carrying a crossbar with buckets at each end and geese inside. At the time, some of the Tigers were intoxicated. They had been drinking beer and shouldn't have even been on night maneuvers. They were drunk. Carpenter said the old man, who was unarmed, was brought to Lieutenant Hawkins, who began "shaking the old man, yelling at him, telling him he was a son of a bitch, and generally cussing at him." He said while the commander was screaming at the man, Sergeant Harold Trout walked up and clubbed the man on the head with the barrel of his M16. "I saw this old man fall to the ground, and at that time, his head was covered with his blood."

Carpenter said he tried to reason with Hawkins to stop the beating, "but Hawkins pushed me away with his left hand, saying, 'You chicken shit son of a bitch. If you don't shut up, I'll shoot you.'" At that point, Carpenter said Hawkins aimed his rifle at the man's face and fired twice. "I knew the old man was dead, as half of his head was blown off," Carpenter said quietly.

As he talked, Apsey put down his pen. As long as the tape recorder was running, he would transcribe the words later. For now, the investigator just wanted to listen. This is what he had been waiting for — to finally get a member of this unit to talk — and he wasn't going to stop him now.

Carpenter began describing the afternoon he was walking with Sam Ybarra when the point man spotted a teenager running. Without hesitation, Ybarra lifted his M16 and shot the boy. He then walked over to the body and took off the boy's tennis shoes. "That's why he shot him," Carpenter said to Apsey. "For his shoes." And he recalled that when the shoes didn't fit, Ybarra tossed them away and then sliced off the teenager's ears.

And there was more. The execution of a prisoner west of Duc Pho. The shooting death of a wounded detainee by a team leader in the Song Ve Valley in July. The stabbing death and scalping of a prisoner by Ybarra in the same month. The bayoneting of a prisoner.

Carpenter grew quiet, and for a minute, no one said anything. Finally, Apsey broke in. "Did your commanders know?" he asked. "Did you ever think of telling them?" How, Apsey wondered, could a platoon carry out such actions without the knowledge of the top element?

Carpenter then said something that would stay with Apsey for the duration of the investigation. "We were told to kill everything that moves," he explained. "It was standard practice for the Tiger Force to kill everything that moved when we were out on an operation."

Apsey stopped him. "Are you telling me that all of the members of the Tiger Force killed everything that moved when they went out on a mission?"

"With a few exceptions, that is correct," Carpenter said.

He said he still recalled the rallying cry that crackled over the radio from battalion headquarters: "You're the 327th Infantry," the voice said. "We want 327 kills!"

Apsey interrupted. "Who gave that order?"

Carpenter thought for a moment, then responded, "It came from Ghost Rider." The same name used by the battalion commander, Lieutenant Colonel Gerald Morse.

There was plenty of time to think about Carpenter's statement during the four-hour flight to Los Angeles. Apsey was an experienced agent who had investigated atrocities but was startled by what he heard. Either Carpenter was lying or this unit was so egregious, no one wanted to tell the truth.

Carpenter had given him more than twenty names of suspects and witnesses. Apsey now knew who to talk to and what to ask. He would go back and contact the people who had already been interviewed and he would make sure agents knew what Carpenter said.

In addition, Apsey had to learn more about Carpenter and whether he was credible. The former specialist had described war crimes between May and November 1967. But alone, Carpenter's statement didn't mean anything. Under military law, accusations have to be substantiated — the equivalent of probable cause that a crime occurred. That means talking to other witnesses to corroborate the story. The suspect is then required to appear in what is known as an Article 32 hearing to determine if a court-martial is held.

Apsey was struck by the amount of work still to be done.

He had already spent ten months on the case. The irony was that the investigation was revving up at a time the war was coming to an end. On the seat next to the tired agent was a copy of the *Columbus Dispatch,* dated January 28, 1973, proclaiming a peace treaty had been signed the day before in Paris. The war was over. But Gus Apsey's battle had just begun.

When Apsey returned to Fort MacArthur, he turned over the notes of his interview with Carpenter to the office secretary to be transcribed. He was now going to take the investigation solely into his own hands. He had learned a long time ago not to rely on other agents. You have to look your own subject in the eyes. You have to know everything.

As Apsey briefed Colonel Weinstein over the phone that morning, the commander asked where the case was going. The truth was, Apsey didn't know. "I need some time," he said. But how much? It was clear the investigation needed to be expanded, and that could take several weeks, or months. Normally, Weinstein wouldn't have minded. He always pushed his agents to be thorough, not sloppy. But with the peace accords, most of the troops would be out of the country by March. The Pentagon was trying to wrap up the war — not prolong it.

Worse, because the war was ending, huge numbers of soldiers and officers would be leaving the Army. That meant they would no longer be under the jurisdiction of the military. Even if there were probable cause to charge them, they would escape the reach of Army prosecutors.

Weinstein and Apsey agreed the investigation needed to move forward without interruptions. That meant Apsey had to set priorities. He had learned years ago that the person most responsible for the actions of a fighting unit is the officer in charge. The first thing Apsey needed to find out was whether James Hawkins was still in the military. That question was answered almost right away when Apsey checked the roster sent to him by the Pentagon and saw that Hawkins was listed as a lieutenant in the 1st Battalion/327th Infantry. He had been promoted to captain and was now assigned to a student detachment at the University of Tampa in Florida.

While reading his notes, Apsey spotted the name Ervin Lee and found that the former soldier was now living in Bell Gardens, California — just twenty miles north of Fort MacArthur. Lee had been identified by Carpenter as one of the soldiers who watched as Hawkins shot the old man at the edge of the river. Since Lee was living so close, Apsey decided to call the former sergeant before traveling for any more interviews. Apsey was able to reach him and coax him into coming into Fort MacArthur several days later.

The onetime team leader quietly made it obvious he didn't want to be interviewed. He had been living in the streets and just recently found himself an apartment. It was a long way from his hometown of Anniston, Alabama, but Lee had hoped living in California would help clear his head. It was just the opposite. He couldn't sleep and would often walk the streets aimlessly. Though he had served in the Tigers for more than a year, he hesitated to talk about former soldiers whom he said answered the call when no one else did.

"What do you guys want with us now?" he asked, dropping down in a chair.

Apsey immediately slid Carpenter's typewritten statement across the table, with Lee's name underlined in bright red ink on the pages as a witness. Lee glanced at the documents and then turned away. Apsey then asked him, "Did you see the old man killed?"

Lee had two choices: he could leave or talk. If he left the office, there was no guarantee he wouldn't be called again. He knew some of these CID guys were relentless. Maybe it was better to get it over with now.

Lee thought for a moment and then began to speak. He was one of the soldiers who escorted the old man to Hawkins, he told Apsey. Before walking away, Lee watched as Trout whacked the man on the head, and then a few minutes later, he heard gunfire. "Later, I heard that Hawkins had shot the prisoner."

Lee said he didn't know anything else about war crimes. Apsey suspected that wasn't quite true, but rather than press Lee, he decided to wait until later. For now, he had reason to believe that Carpenter was telling the truth — at least about Hawkins killing the old man.

Apsey would interview one more witness before going to Florida. Leo Heaney was now a second lieutenant at Fort Jackson, South Carolina. He was yet another name that Carpenter had disclosed, and the next day, after interviewing Lee, Apsey contacted Heaney. Two weeks later, Apsey met the officer at the fort's CID office.

Armed with Carpenter's and Lee's statements, Apsey went into the interview loaded. Unlike previous interviews when he felt like he was fishing, he was now more confident. He said he knew about the murder of the old man and that two other soldiers identified Heaney as a witness.

Heaney was surprised. He knew that when Apsey contacted him by phone, the purpose was Tiger Force and war crimes. But he hadn't actually expected something like this to surface six years later.

Apsey insisted the interview wouldn't take long. Still, Heaney didn't want to talk. Finally, Apsey pulled out a copy of Carpenter's statement and handed it to Heaney. The veteran carefully began reading the pages and slowly slumped in his chair.

When he finished reading the typewritten pages, he returned the documents before folding his arms. Yes, he said, he knew all about the shooting. He said he had tried to reason with Hawkins to leave the victim alone. "I mentioned the fact that he was a harmless old man, and Hawkins said something to the effect, 'If I want your opinion, I'll ask for it.'" He had turned his back just before Hawkins pulled the trigger. "There was no justifiable reason the old man had to be killed," Heaney told Apsey.

★ ★ ★

From the fifth floor of the Holiday Inn, Apsey had an excellent view of downtown Tampa. Outside his window, guests were lounging around the pool below, and spring breakers were making noise down the hall. All of it was wasted on him. Apsey had spent most of the morning writing the questions he would ask the former Tiger Force commander.

When Apsey heard a knock on the door, he covered the papers on a table, thinking it was Hawkins. But it turned out to be another agent, Donald Weaver, who had driven from the CID office at McCoy Air Force Base near Orlando to join Apsey in the interview.

Before the men could discuss the case, there was another knock. This time, it was Hawkins. Almost right away, the agents noticed he was fidgety. After sitting down at the table in the cramped room, Apsey immediately informed Hawkins he was suspected in a war-crimes case of murder, dereliction of duty, and conduct unbecoming an officer, and had the right to a military lawyer.

Hawkins pushed away from the table and looked at the two men in disbelief. He told them he didn't know what to say. He agreed to come to the motel because he thought he was assisting the CID in a case. He had no idea he was a suspect.

"Look," he said, "I don't like this."

"Do you want a lawyer?" Apsey asked.

Hawkins looked at Apsey and shook his head. "I've got nothing to hide," he said.

Apsey quietly reviewed his list of questions and then looked up at Hawkins. "Did you shoot an old man in the Song Ve Valley in 1967 after you had been drinking?"

"No," Hawkins responded matter-of-factly. "No, I did not."

Apsey then slowly read aloud the statements of Carpenter, Lee, and Heaney. They said it was Hawkins who shook the old man mercilessly, and Hawkins who rebuffed attempts by soldiers to stop, and Hawkins who ultimately pulled the trigger.

When Apsey finished reading the witness statements, he placed the papers down on the table and stared at Hawkins.

It was apparent that Hawkins was uncomfortable, shifting in his chair, looking confused, almost dazed. He began babbling that to the best of his knowledge, he never killed anyone needlessly and certainly didn't remember killing an old man.

Hawkins asked about a lawyer.

Apsey responded, "You have a right to one. That's your decision."

Hawkins stood up and took a few steps toward the window, but then stopped. "I'm going to need time to decide," he said. "At this point, I don't know what I'm going to do."

After Hawkins left the room, Weaver turned to Apsey. "How much do you bet he doesn't come back?" he asked. Apsey thought about the question for a moment and then responded. "How much do you bet he comes back," he said, "but with a lawyer."

The next morning, Hawkins knocked on the door of Room 501. He wasn't alone. At his side was Captain Guyton Terry Jr., a judge advocate general (JAG). The two came inside.

Immediately, Apsey followed protocol by informing Hawkins he was a war-crimes suspect.

Before sitting down, Hawkins made it clear his lawyer wasn't going to allow him to answer incriminating questions. He wasn't going to be blindsided this time, he said.

Apsey asked Hawkins if he was going to cooperate by answering any questions.

"You can ask," he responded.

Apsey looked at his list again and asked the question, "Did you shoot an unarmed older Vietnamese man in the Song Ve Valley in 1967?"

Terry whispered something to Hawkins, who then shook his head. "On the advice of my lawyer," he said, "I'm not going to talk about that."

Apsey then went on to ask him if he ordered the shooting of unarmed farmers in a rice paddy in the same valley in 1967.

Again, Terry whispered something to Hawkins, who said he was not going to answer.

Apsey then asked Hawkins a litany of questions about the routine torturing and killing of prisoners, the practice of cutting off ears and threatening to kill soldiers if they complained. After each question, Hawkins refused to say anything.

Apsey could see the interview wasn't going anywhere. Finally, he asked if Hawkins's superiors knew about war crimes carried out by the platoon. This time, Hawkins abruptly stood up and moved away from the table. He had enough, he said. He motioned to his lawyer. They were ending the interview, and without saying anything more, they walked out of the room. There was nothing Apsey could do to stop them.

Apsey filed his weekly report after returning to Fort MacArthur, and for the first time, the Coy Allegation, No. 221, was formally fleshed out. The report now included the names of Sam Ybarra, James Hawkins, and Harold Trout, and the phrase "other unidentified members of Tiger Force" who were under investigation for crimes ranging from murder to body mutilation. In short, the investigation was expanding to the entire unit.

In keeping with the routing system, the report was typed at Fort MacArthur and then sent to five places: Weinstein at the Presidio, CID headquarters, the offices of the defense secretary and Army secretary, and, finally, the White House.

The first call to Weinstein's office after the report was filed was from CID headquarters. Tufts was going to keep a separate file on the case. He did not want any surprises, nor did he want details of the case to reach the media. In most CID investigations, the agents were often the last to know what was happening at the top. Under Tufts, that was certainly the procedure. He didn't want his agents fettered by the politics that sometimes seeped into these cases, especially now. Tufts was painfully aware that the Nixon White House was paranoid about war-crimes cases breaking in the news. Nixon had been forced to perform damage control in the wake of the My Lai revelations by calling the atrocity an "isolated incident" on December 8, 1969. Tufts had been told time and again to keep the president's office abreast of all potentially embarrassing cases. His two key contacts in the administration were John Dean, legal counsel to the president, and Charles Colson, special assistant to the president.

To keep track of the case, Apsey made a copy of the report about the farmers being killed and taped it to his office wall. Then he made a copy of a report on the killing of the old man crossing the river. He taped it next to the first report. One by one, he taped more reports to the wall, along with the names of the suspects.

Based on a blueprint of what he now knew, starting with Carpenter's allegations and subsequent interviews supporting those accusations, Apsey would need to interview every Tiger Force member who served in the period of May through November 1967. That included going back and reinterviewing former and active soldiers who had already been interrogated.

Apsey went over the list. At least sixty-one had to be reinterviewed, and at least another thirty had yet to be located. Apsey would be assigned help, but not full-time. He was on his own.

The key would be getting soldiers to talk. Without a dead body, a war crime is tough to substantiate, especially when the events took place six years earlier. It takes credible witnesses to corroborate a crime. In My Lai, there at least had been graphic photographs of the victims. But even with the horrifying images, only one soldier was ever convicted, Lieutenant Calley.

What was frustrating to Apsey and his superiors was that this case, in many ways, had the potential to get much bigger. How big they didn't yet know.

★ ★ ★

As he stared at the names on his office wall, Apsey's eyes kept returning to the same one: James Robert Barnett. Why had he abruptly resigned after being interviewed about the case in 1971? What did he know? Apsey went into Earl Perdue's office and closed the door.

"Look," he said, "I got a funny feeling about this one."

Puzzled, Perdue looked at his agent.

Apsey explained that Barnett's sudden resignation was one of the first clues that the case involved more than just one soldier killing a baby. "I need to fly out there."

Perdue waved his hand and agreed. He was already under orders to make this case a priority, and if his lead agent believed he suddenly needed to fly somewhere for a key interview, Perdue wasn't going to stand in the way.

The next day, Apsey boarded a flight to Tennessee and, for most of the trip, pored over Barnett's personnel file and other records. After serving in the Tigers, Barnett went on to put in three more tours, including a stint in Special Forces. He brought back a Silver Star, a Purple Heart, and a bad attitude.

Apsey arrived and called Barnett's home. To his surprise, the former officer answered. Apsey said he had some important things to talk about.

There was silence on the other line. "I thought I dealt with you people already," he said in a deep drawl. The CID had already come to his base at Fort Campbell and asked him questions.

"I'll make this quick," said Apsey.

Barnett wasn't happy.

"I don't have much to say," he told Apsey when the investigator appeared at the door. Back in his hometown, like so many other veterans, Barnett couldn't get a good job — at least not right away. He had been driving a bulldozer and a truck to make ends meet. He was married, with a month-old son and more bills than ever.

Apsey had come to understand Vietnam vets and had learned

not to push too hard (the surest way of ending an interview). "This won't take long," he said.

The two moved from the front steps to the living room. Apsey broke the ice by first saying that other Tiger Force members had spoken candidly about war crimes. Did those events, if true, have anything to do with Barnett resigning as a second lieutenant while stationed at Fort Campbell?

Barnett tensed up. He didn't know what to say. More importantly, what were others saying? He slumped down in his chair.

"What's this about?" he asked, his hands slightly trembling.

Again, in a reassuring voice, Apsey said he was trying to get to the truth. Barnett was no longer in the service and probably couldn't be prosecuted anyway, though that wasn't Apsey's decision. Apsey went on to describe the attack on the rice farmers and the shooting death of the old man in the Song Ve Valley.

Barnett responded that he didn't know anything about the farmers, and yes, he recalled the shooting of the old man but didn't see it.

Apsey asked him about Ybarra and the baby. Barnett again said he didn't see it but heard about it. Barnett turned away, his face red, and looked down. Apsey could tell Barnett wanted to say something, so he let the man take his time while he watched the strapping, six-foot, four-inch former soldier for any clues in body language. He could hear the big man breathing harder now.

"Okay," said Barnett. "Okay. I want to say something, just for now, but I'm not going to repeat it under any circumstances. When we were out there, on patrol, it was generally understood that we would — well — kill anything that moved."

Apsey immediately stopped writing. He wanted to hear this again.

"Anything?" he asked incredulously.

"Yes, as far as we knew, the civilians had been moved out, and what was left in our areas of operations were strictly enemy or enemy sympathizers." On nearly every mission, he explained, the platoon's orders were to kill anything that moves. Men, women, anything.

Apsey asked Barnett if the platoon soldiers knew for sure the people they were killing were truly enemy soldiers. Barnett shook his head no.

Apsey returned to California with more information than he ever expected. Before he had a chance to type his report, he received a call: agents had located Barry Bowman, a former Tiger Force medic who was mentioned by Carpenter as a witness. Though he was no longer in the Army, the CID had traced Bowman to the small college town of Macomb, Illinois, where he was operating a bar.

When Apsey called, Bowman said he didn't want to be bothered, especially by the CID. Nothing good could come out of talking to agents, he said. But Apsey insisted.

In less than two days, Apsey was knocking on Bowman's door. At first, Bowman didn't answer; he knew it was the CID and began having second thoughts about an interview. After several knocks, however, he walked to the door and let Apsey in.

"This won't take long," the investigator promised.

Bowman escorted the agent into the kitchen but again said he was reluctant to say anything. "What are you guys looking for?" he asked.

Turning on his tape recorder, Apsey said he would get right to the point. He knew that the events in question took place six years earlier. But it was important that Bowman remember. Apsey then described an incident in which Tiger Force soldiers shot and wounded an unarmed Vietnamese man at dusk in the Song Ve Valley. Witnesses said that Sergeant Trout ordered Bowman to execute the man, but the medic refused. So Trout ended up doing the honors.

Bowman was angry. He didn't need the intrusion, he said, nor did he need to relive the war. Apsey said he wasn't blaming

Bowman but just wanted the truth. "Did this happen?" Apsey asked.

Clenching his teeth, Bowman repeated that it didn't do any good to talk about this all these years later. "It was a long time ago," he said.

Apsey listened, then said he wasn't going to go away. "I've put a lot of time into this case."

Bowman looked at Apsey across the kitchen table and could tell the agent was intent on finding out what happened. Bowman could either refuse to talk, hoping the agent would move on to others, or open up.

"I'll talk to you," said Bowman, "and then this is over."

Slowly, Bowman went on to describe how someone shouted for a medic after several shots were fired. Bowman said he walked over and found the man on the ground, seriously wounded. "Trout was there and he said to me something like, 'C'mon, Doc, break your cherry,' which meant I should kill him because I hadn't done this sort of thing because I was rather new in the outfit. I declined this and then Trout took my .45-caliber pistol and shot and killed the Vietnamese." It was "a mercy killing," said Bowman. But to Apsey, there was no such thing as a mercy killing. Ending the life of a wounded civilian was a violation of Army regulations and the Geneva conventions.

Before the interview ended, Bowman confirmed three other incidents: the old man being killed by Hawkins near the river; a prisoner being beaten and shot by Private Floyd Sawyer after the man was ordered to run; and an old man being shot twice in the head by Private James Cogan after being pulled from a hut. Carpenter had told Apsey about the killings, and now Bowman was reluctantly corroborating them.

After nearly two hours of questioning, Bowman ended the interview. He was through talking and made it clear to Apsey that he didn't want agents ever coming to his home again.

By now, Apsey was starting to see a pattern in the former Tigers. They were troubled and, in some cases, nervous wrecks. What he didn't know was that Bowman and others were suffering from post-traumatic stress disorder, or PTSD — a condition afflicting thousands of Vietnam veterans but years away from being identified by mental health experts. By 2000, nearly one in every six veterans of the war was afflicted by the disorder, according to the U.S. Department of Veterans Affairs. The trauma of what they experienced was so painful, they shoved it down deep inside, but the psychological symptoms — flashbacks, nightmares, and depression — reminded them almost daily of what they left behind. Many turned to drugs and alcohol to ease the pain. They didn't want to talk about the war, especially to a CID agent investigating war crimes.

When he returned to Fort MacArthur, Apsey was concerned about getting to former platoon members before they had a chance to talk to one another. His fear was that once they talked, the case would shut down.

He immediately tried to get to Cogan. The combat engineer had been with Tiger Force during much of the Song Ve campaign. But after checking with the Pentagon, Apsey found out Cogan resigned from the Army a year earlier. If Apsey had known earlier that Cogan was a suspect, he could have "flagged" the soldier, the legal tool that the Army had used in the case of My Lai to halt a soldier's discharge. Now it was too late. Apsey tried to reach the former platoon member but never got beyond his mother. "Leave him alone," she told Apsey. She said her son was undergoing "medical treatment for a mental problem" brought about by the war and had experienced difficulty trying to adjust to a normal life.

Again, this was the reason the Army should have aggressively pursued this case when they received the initial complaint in 1971, Apsey concluded. Barnett had resigned and so had Cogan. How many others were out there who had also dropped out? Apsey immediately notified the commanders overseeing Trout and Hawkins to hold up their discharges if they tried to leave the Army. He didn't want anyone else to get away.

Without wasting any more time, he turned his attention to Floyd Sawyer, who was accused by Carpenter and Bowman of beating and shooting a prisoner. Sawyer was still in the Army and assigned to Fort Lewis, the sprawling base near Puget Sound.

Shortly thereafter, Sawyer was pulled into a base office, where Apsey was waiting for him. Though the interview was long, it didn't break any ground. Sawyer corroborated the shooting of the villager by Cogan, saying the men even joked about it because it took two shots to finish off the elderly Vietnamese. But he became defensive when they asked him about his own case. He insisted he never beat the prisoner and only shot him because he was trying to escape.

Apsey informed Sawyer that two other former Tigers said the opposite: Sawyer senselessly beat the prisoner and even tied him up with a detonating cord, threatening to blow him up before shooting him. When Apsey pressed further, Sawyer clammed up. No more questions, he insisted.

Days later, Apsey decided to reinterview Kerrigan, but the former Tiger had refused to take the investigator's call. Kerrigan knew what Apsey wanted — and it wasn't good. There were already enough demons in Kerrigan's life. He couldn't stop them. The noises. The voices. Memories of the jungle and the faces of the dead. Those horrible faces.

"What happened to me?" he would ask his friends. But no one knew — least of all Kerrigan.

He bolted from his mother's house after getting Apsey's message and started walking. Just when he had forgotten the images, they were coming back. His heart began to beat harder and he picked up his pace. As a surfer, he remembered the power of the riptide — the currents pulling him out to sea, no matter how hard he swam against the waves. He was now being pulled into the same vortex.

There was no way he could talk to Apsey. He didn't want to go into that world again — the one where he had killed so many Vietnamese, spraying the hooches with his M16 and screaming like a madman. "What happened?" he would mumble to himself.

Kerrigan, like so many other Tigers, was starting to see himself as he really was in Vietnam. That he sank into a level of anger and brutality that now made him feel so ugly and alone. So many times, he thought he was the only one who felt this way. That somehow it was just him. What he didn't know was that so many others were feeling the same.

No one knew as much about the Tigers as did Harold Trout. He had trained the grunts, especially after so many Tigers were lost in the Mother's Day Massacre. And while Hawkins held the rank, it was Trout who had spent an entire year with the platoon. It was Trout who had kept records of the platoon's missions and personnel, noting when they were killed or wounded. If anyone could shed light on what went wrong, it was he.

In October, Apsey received information that Trout was no longer in Germany but was at Fort Benning, Georgia. Apsey had been anxiously waiting for him to return to the States. Now he had his chance to meet the former platoon sergeant he had been hearing about for months.

Before contacting the CID office at Fort Benning, Apsey prepared a list of questions for the thirty-six-year-old sergeant. He wanted to give Trout a chance to respond to the accusations, now being made by five soldiers.

On October 17, 1973, Apsey flew to the base in western Georgia and met Trout. A stocky soldier with a crew cut and an iron-grip handshake, Trout showed little emotion as Apsey began the interview by informing his subject he was under investigation for murder, aggravated assault, dereliction of duty, and conduct unbecoming a soldier.

Trout listened and then waved a hand, signaling the interview was over. He had been through this before in Germany, but the CID agents asked only about war crimes in general and

Ybarra and the baby. Now Trout could see that he, too, was a target. He wasn't going to say anything until he spoke to a lawyer.

Trout was escorted to the fort's judge advocate general's office, where he was met by Army lawyer Captain Robert Taylor. After a brief conversation, Taylor said he was representing Trout and his client wasn't going to cooperate. From now on, he was off-limits.

Frustrated, Apsey decided to shake out witnesses by trying a "shotgun" approach. Instead of sending requests to field agents one at a time, he mailed separate copies of case summaries — including revealing information from Carpenter, Barnett, and Bowman — to two dozen field CID offices. That way, the witnesses would know the local agents sent to interview them weren't just fishing. And it would be more difficult for former Tigers in the military to plead ignorance if faced with specific, corroborated allegations, especially with the threat of being charged with obstruction.

Within a week, the reports started coming back from field agents — this time, with results. One of the first to cross Apsey's desk was a statement from Forrest Miller, the former medic, now based at Frankfurt, Germany. When first interviewed in November 1972, Miller had said he didn't see any atrocities. Now, after agents rattled off a laundry list of war crimes, Miller broke down. Sure, he remembered Ybarra. Who couldn't? And yes, he collected ears, but he wasn't the only one; many did. They wore them as necklaces and carried them around like keepsakes.

As far as Hawkins, Miller had vivid memories of the Tiger commander passing down the order to shoot the ten farmers in the field and, days later, the smell of the rotting corpses and water buffalo.

But Hawkins wasn't the only one who ordered Tigers to kill civilians, Miller said. Sergeant William Doyle was another one. The team leader was a "sadist" and a "killer" who was quick to order the executions of unarmed villagers. He once told a Vietnamese teenager to leave the area and, as the teen walked away, fired a fatal bullet into the boy's back. "He was even grinning about the killing," Miller said.

To the best of his memory, most of the atrocities took place in the Song Ve Valley, where there was very little oversight by superiors. He recalled a moment when Tiger Force members ran across two brothers who appeared to be blind being led by a young boy. The brothers were led to a field and shot to death.

Another report was sent back from a CID agent who tracked down former Tiger medic Ralph Mayhew in Oregon. Though reluctant to be interviewed, Mayhew described one event that would stay with him the rest of his life. After entering a village, he said, he watched helplessly as Doyle confronted a Vietnamese farmer who was not hurting anyone. Doyle began striking the man with a rifle. "As Doyle was beating him," he said, "the Vietnamese fell to his knees in a praying position and spoke tearfully in his language. I didn't like the sight of it, so I turned away." Moments later, Doyle ordered his men to open fire on the man. "It was," said Mayhew, "cold-blooded murder."

With her husband hunkered down at the kitchen table for another night of studying, Joyce Wood quickly grabbed the phone so he wouldn't be disturbed. Monday night was usually a good time for Donald Wood to catch up on his required reading for law school, but this was a call that he had to take.

On the phone was CID agent Christopher Olson from Cleveland with an urgent request. He needed to see Wood as soon as possible. "We can be there tomorrow," the agent said. Since Wood lived in Findlay, Ohio, just ninety miles southwest of Cleveland, the agents could arrive at Wood's apartment on Main Street before noon.

Wood asked why CID investigators were coming, but Olson was vague. "It's an investigation that goes back to Vietnam," he said. "Do you recall a unit known as Tiger Force?"

Wood was caught off guard by the question. "Why are you asking?" he replied. The agent said he would explain everything tomorrow in person.

Wood hung up the phone. His wife asked him what the call was about, but he just shrugged. "They just want to talk to me about Vietnam," he said.

He went back to the kitchen table but could only stare blankly at the words of his textbook. *Tiger Force*. He had tried so hard to forget his time in Vietnam. When the years didn't erase the memories, the alcohol would, at least temporarily, ease the pain. He had gone to Ohio Northern University law school in hopes of moving on in his life. But how could he forget? The screams, the gunfire. His incessant battles with a platoon commander who was hell-bent on wiping out everything: villages, huts, people.

After returning from the war, Wood would sometimes hop into his car, press the pedal to the floor, and drive one hundred miles per hour on country roads. His wife and friends would tell him to be careful: he was going to kill himself. People thought he was a daredevil, but what they didn't know was that the adrenaline rush helped him forget — even if just for a moment.

The last time Wood had talked with anyone about the Tigers was in 1968, when he had made good on a promise to unload to someone at Fort Bragg about the unit's actions in the Song Ve Valley. Haunted by the memories, he had walked into the inspector general's office and opened up to a JAG. Nothing had happened, nor did he expect it. But he wanted someone to know, as if somehow, once he said something, the nightmares and night sweats would stop. That he would be able to forget.

Now it was January 22, 1974, and the Army was coming to his home. What had changed? All night long he wondered.

The next morning, he opened the door of his apartment

for the CID agents, Olson and Gary Kaddatz. The two had told Apsey the day before that they were meeting with Wood, but no one had expected anything significant from this interview. Apsey simply didn't want to leave any stones unturned, and that meant talking to everyone who rotated in and out of the unit between May and November 1967.

Wood was anxious to know what the CID wanted and wasn't surprised when they told him it involved war crimes, specifically those carried out by the Tigers. "Why is this coming out now?" he asked. The agents responded that they were carrying out orders, and this was an active investigation.

Wood was undeterred. "Did you know about my complaint?" he asked.

The agents looked at each other. "We are here to ask you some questions," said one of the agents. Did he know about the killing of the old man near the river?

Wood responded that not only did he remember but he had tried to stop Hawkins from carrying out the field operation because the Tigers were drunk. "I argued with Hawkins about the order," he recalled, "protesting that this is dangerous." But it didn't matter to Hawkins, Wood explained. The two didn't get along — never did. Wood told them about an instance when he tried to stop several Tigers from firing on two elderly women walking toward their position. Hawkins told the men to shoot, but Wood tried to counter the order. Because Hawkins was the commander, they fired, injuring one and just missing the other.

Wood said that he went to Lieutenant Stephen Naughton, then a battalion officer, to complain about Hawkins's actions in the field, but nothing was done. Wood said he also complained to an executive officer at battalion headquarters, but again, nothing happened. Not only did he raise these concerns in the field, he said, but after returning to the United States, he complained to the inspector general's office of the 18th Airborne Corps at Fort Bragg. "What you need to know," he insisted, "is that I tried to get people to listen."

★ ★ ★

Apsey was startled at the report from Ohio. For two years, Wood had been just another name on the Tiger Force roster. Suddenly he was a key witness. It wasn't so much that he recalled atrocities that made him crucial to the case. And it wasn't so much that he had challenged Hawkins. Far more than those actions, Wood had broken the platoon's code of silence and gone to commanders to complain. If that was true, it was a significant development. It was the first time since taking over the case that Apsey had learned of an effort to bring this to a higher command. And worse, the pleas were ignored. If top officers knew a platoon was systematically killing unarmed civilians and looked the other way, those commanders could also be charged with war crimes, specifically dereliction of duty.

"My God," Apsey said as he looked over the Wood interview. He would have to tread lightly. But Apsey couldn't ignore Wood's story. To do so would be derelict on his part. And it would go against everything he believed in.

Gerald Bruner walked into the CID office at Fort Bragg on the morning of February 12, opened up a metal chair, and sat down. The career soldier knew all about the Tiger Force investigation and didn't want any part of it. He had been through this before — two years earlier — and told an agent then what he was going to tell agents now: he had nothing to say.

The day before, a CID agent visited Bruner at the base to request the sergeant come into the office to answer questions about Tiger Force. Bruner was puzzled, because he had been interviewed in September 1972 and had never heard back from the CID. He assumed the investigation had ended with the war.

Now married with a daughter, Bruner had become disillusioned with life in the Army. He was stuck in a desk job that he hated and was drinking every night, partly to forget Vietnam. He had served four tours in nearly a dozen jobs, including a year as a sniper.

"I already talked to you guys," he groused as he sat across from Special Agents Alan Boehme and James Davis.

But Boehme was determined to follow through on the orders he received from Apsey. Boehme explained that it didn't matter if soldiers had been previously interviewed — they were being called in again.

Bruner declared that was fine, but he didn't like being interviewed — period, and didn't like the CID. He said they weren't around when he needed them years ago, and he didn't need them now.

Boehme assured Bruner that the agents were not trying to get him into trouble but that they had reason to believe Bruner served with another sergeant who was a war-crimes suspect. "Do you know an individual by the name of Doyle?" the agent asked. Bruner replied that he remembered the name but not much else. "I served with a lot of people over there," he said.

Immediately, the agent set three photos on the desk for Bruner to see and asked which was Doyle.

Bruner looked down at the desk, staring at each photo, and then pointed to the one on the far right. "That's him, the one with the bald head," he said.

Boehme then pulled out a document and began reading a description from medic Ralph Mayhew's statement of Doyle shooting and then ordering the execution of a wounded farmer who cried for his life. Bruner shifted uneasily in his chair.

Before the interview, he had made up his mind he wasn't going to say anything. But now it was all coming back: the Tigers walking into a friendly village and Doyle, undeterred by a farmer's pleas for safety from the Vietcong, raising his rifle and shooting the man. The bullet struck only the man's arm, and Doyle tried shooting the man again, but this time his gun jammed. So he ordered his men to finish the job, and they obeyed.

Bruner could see it all as if it were yesterday. The same men had turned their guns on the farmer's younger brother, but Bruner had lifted his own rifle and threatened to shoot any soldier who shot the boy.

If there was one soldier he could never forget, it was Doyle. If there was one soldier he despised, it was Doyle. William Doyle stood for everything that was wrong with the war.

"Yes," said Bruner, "I was there."

For the next hour, he opened up and talked about Doyle and the village — spelling out details.

"You know, I've been trained by the U.S. Army to be a professional killer," Bruner told the agents. "That's what I'm trained to do. Now I don't know what you're trained to do, but that's what I'm trained to do. And the difference is: I know who to kill. These people forgot."

The Bruner interview confirmed Apsey's suspicions that battalion commanders knew what was happening in the field. He now needed a new roster — this time, with the names of all battalion officers in 1967.

But before the spotlight could turn on the commanders, Apsey still needed to complete the basic investigation of the war-crimes allegations. How many more atrocities took place? Who was involved? Apsey needed to get to dozens more former platoon members and, in the process, keep this second phase of the investigation quiet. He didn't know how far up the food chain this went, and if word got out, the entire case could be jeopardized. And Apsey needed to speed up all interviews. It was early 1974 — one year since U.S. combat troops left Vietnam — and Apsey no longer had the luxury of time.

On March 1, 1974, Henry Tufts returned to his office to find a file on his desk marked "Coy Allegation." Once consisting of two pages, the file was now thick with weekly reports dating back to February 1971 — a period of three years and a month.

Tufts had been reading the reports all along, watching the case expand from a routine complaint to a full-blown investigation. But in the last year, he had been sidetracked. He was still trying to wrap up a massive reorganization of the CID that began in 1971 and was now steeped in drug cases exploding at Army bases in Europe and Asia. By the time the file once again reached his desk in late June, the Tiger Force case was the last major war-crimes investigation from Vietnam. It thus marked the end of a spate of investigations that had consumed the CID for years — a total of 242 investigations ranging from body mutilations to murder.

Tufts read through the file and then picked up the phone to call the Presidio. This wasn't the same case he reviewed a year ago. What happened? The Tiger Force investigation had grown considerably, and these weren't just allegations anymore. They were real, provable war crimes — bad ones, among the worst he had seen. It was one thing for soldiers to lose control after a firefight and take out their frustrations on a civilian. Even then, a commander would put his foot down and the men would be brought to justice. But this was a small unit — a special force — that carried out crimes as a matter of routine, without any commander giving a damn.

Beyond his own concerns, the Tiger Force case had the potential to be a major news story — one that could be embarrassing to a White House already reeling from an unfolding scandal known as Watergate. Though 1600 Pennsylvania Avenue was preoccupied, CID headquarters was still obligated to keep the Pentagon in the loop on a case that was powerful enough to explode. Tufts immediately ordered a spreadsheet — an $8^1/_2$ by 14–inch report listing the allegations, a summary of statements by witnesses, and the investigators' remarks. He asked for the personnel files of the battalion commanders. Lastly, he instructed his secretary to send a summary of the ongoing investigation to the offices of Howard "Bo" Callaway, secretary of the Army, and James Schlesinger, secretary of defense — a procedure set up by the Nixon White House.

With the arrival of that summary, the final cover-up of Tiger Force began.

CHAPTER 22

O f two dozen requests for interviews, eighteen were on Apsey's desk by the end of February 1974. And in those interviews, half supported the earlier confessions. Though it was a pain, Apsey's persistence at asking agents to reinterview ex-Tigers was paying off.

Two former Tigers at Fort Bragg, Cecil Peden and Manuel Sanchez, had changed their stories from the first time they were contacted. Peden, now a sergeant, didn't remember any war crimes in November 1972. But he now swore under oath that he recalled standing by as Sergeant Robin Varney pushed the head of a prisoner into a bayonet held by Sergeant Ernest Moreland. Sanchez, who had professed to not know anything when interviewed in July 1972, now said he watched as the Tigers executed two prisoners he was trying to guard.

Sanchez didn't want to be a snitch. The military was his career. It allowed him to support his wife and three young children. Besides, the Army could be a cruel place, and he fretted about commanders retaliating against him for exposing the sins. He hadn't even told his buddies at Fort Bragg he served in a

unit known as Tiger Force. He wasn't proud of his time with
the unit. His wife, Mary, whom he married after returning
home in 1968, knew not to ask him. When CID agents first
went to him in 1972, he said he didn't know anything about
war crimes. He had locked that secret deep inside and tossed
away the key. But doing so came at a price. "He would sit in his
chair with this faraway look," his wife recalled, "and just tell me
he couldn't talk about it."

Sanchez was showing the classic signs of PTSD. He rarely
told family members about his nightmares, but he was constantly waking up, slipping from the bedroom to the living
room, waiting in the darkness for the images to go away. With
counseling, some veterans recovering from post-traumatic stress
can openly recall terrible events without feeling the trauma.
The frequency of nightmares decreases while the veterans seem
to gain more control over their lives. Sanchez wasn't ready to
talk to a counselor — not now — but when CID agents visited
him at Fort Bragg, he decided he couldn't keep hold of his secrets anymore. He told the agents he would see them the next
day, and that night he prayed for strength. "I have to meet with
the agents in the morning," he told Mary. "But I can't tell you
any more than that."

During the interview, he told them about the time he tried
to keep two Vietnamese detainees alive, but the Tigers later
shot them. "I'll never forget," he said angrily. "It was so wrong.
I think about it all the time. And I can't tell anybody. I can't talk
about it. I don't even feel good telling you about it. I'm a soldier and I'm loyal to the Army. But I hate what they did. They
did other stuff, but they knew better not to do it in front of me.
I don't murder people, man."

Other witnesses, some contacted for the first time, also
opened up. Michael Allums, a former medic now living in
Tampa, swore that Ybarra bragged about cutting off the infant's
head and showed him the bloody necklace worn by the baby. "I
remember being repulsed by the whole thing," he stated. He
said he watched as Ybarra's friend Ken Green repeatedly jabbed

a prisoner in the neck with a knife before plunging the blade into the man's throat.

Benjamin Edge, a sergeant at Fort Hood, Texas, swore that Ybarra and Green beat and killed a prisoner with Hawkins and Trout present, and that Hawkins radioed headquarters to report the death as an enemy kill.

With a list in front of him, Apsey began numbering the allegations, locations, and approximate dates, and then checking off suspects and witnesses connected to each war crime. It was the only way to keep track. Every detail in every allegation was noted. The time had come to count the crimes.

With most of the agents gone for the day, Apsey sat at his desk and began to feel faint. He had been working long hours in late March, and the grind was slowly wearing on him. He had trouble sleeping and was smoking two packs of cigarettes a day.

Luise pleaded with him the night before to take some time off, but he just shook his head and stared across the kitchen table. He couldn't put the case down. Not now. He was obsessed. He would think about the case in the morning while driving to the base and at night while heading home. Sometimes, he would fixate on the slightest difference in a story: Carpenter recalled that the shooting of the farmers was after sunrise; Miller thought it was a couple of hours later. He would agonize over the discrepancies at home, mulling over what he needed to do the next day to resolve the differences.

Worse, he was ignoring his wife, a woman he deeply loved. They did everything together, planning their weekends around each other: trips to the beach and the movies, walks in the park. They met by chance in 1961 when Apsey saw Luise on a train in Frankfurt, Germany, and began talking to her. He mustered the courage to ask for her number, but she declined. In the past, he would have walked away, but not this time. On a whim, he scribbled down his number and handed it to her, and to his surprise, she called him a few days later. What began was a courtship that lasted three years until they finally married shortly before Apsey was transferred to the United States.

The only time they had ever been separated in their ten years of marriage was when Apsey was in Vietnam — a painful period for both. Just before Apsey departed, Luise had undergone surgery for a tubal pregnancy that threatened her life. She was in a hospital for fourteen days and nearly died. After she returned home, the couple learned she would never be able to have children.

Now, sitting at his desk in the longest CID investigation of his career, Apsey felt guilty. He had been coming home late, not touching the special meals she would prepare for him. She would talk to him, but he wasn't listening. Yet he could not let go of his search for the truth.

His fellow agents would kid Apsey about wrapping up the case, saying he had already surpassed the length of time it took to investigate My Lai. But lately, the ribbing had been getting to him. He didn't need to be reminded about the case taking so long. Just trying to keep up with the suspects, witnesses, and war-crime allegations was trying enough. And the truth was, Apsey was harder on himself than anyone else.

A group of other agents had gone out that night without inviting him. It's not that they didn't like or trust Apsey. But to the younger agents, he was boring. When they got off work, they wanted to get drunk and laid. The bars around San Pedro were hopping with officers and young secretaries looking for fun. It was the 1970s in Southern California: the birthplace of the sexual revolution. But Apsey was just too straitlaced. Though he was only thirty-five, he seemed like he was thirty years older. And these days, he was moving even slower.

Perdue noticed his agent was working long hours. Before heading home that night, Perdue glanced down the hall and saw the lights still on in his agent's office. He stuck his head inside the door. "Gus," he said, "go home. It's late. What are you going to do now that you can't do tomorrow?"

Apsey looked up but just shook his head. "Pretty soon," he

said. But Perdue knew it would be hours before the agent headed wearily home.

CID agent Robert DiMario had spent years investigating soldiers for crimes against other soldiers — thefts, burglaries, even murder. But the veteran agent had no desire to probe into grunts accused of war crimes. To him, it was dirty work — holding another soldier responsible for killing Vietnamese. It was war, and that happens.

So when he received an order to interview former platoon member Dan Clint, DiMario was angry. He had already interviewed the private twice before and sent Apsey the results: the former Tiger didn't have much to say, other than that he disliked Ybarra. But Apsey wanted the agent to probe deeper with the same witness. Clint had spent at least six months with the Tigers and had to have seen *some* of the same atrocities as the others.

DiMario knew he had to follow orders, so he left his office in Denver and drove 155 miles to see Clint at a motel in Oak Creek, Colorado, where he was staying.

Instead of following normal procedures, DiMario said he wanted to get the interview over with. "Just do me a favor," said the agent, looking directly into Clint's eyes. "Just say you don't remember anything."

Clint was puzzled but didn't object. DiMario then went through a series of questions sent to him by Apsey, and Clint said he didn't know anything.

The former Tiger was just as glad to get the interview over with. Now a carpenter, he was building a town house in Oak Creek, Colorado, and just wanted to pour himself into his work. "It's all I wanted to do — work and stay outdoors," he recalled. The only person he kept in contact with was Harold Fischer, who had visited Clint in Colorado.

But even when they talked, they never discussed Tiger Force.

For Apsey, it meant yet another blank report. For every five statements with information to use in the case, there was another from a former soldier who claimed he didn't see anything. On its face, that was puzzling, because these soldiers all served side by side. But on a deeper level, it made sense. Apsey and even his supervisors had noticed that a growing faction of CID agents was complaining about atrocity cases. Too much was being made of these investigations, and it was all because of My Lai and the antiwar protesters, they said. They couldn't refuse to find witnesses, but that didn't mean they had to press them for answers.

Forrest Miller had just returned from the mess hall on April 5 when someone in a suit and tie barged into the barracks, calling his name. Miller could tell the man was CID just from his dress. "Don't tell me: Tiger Force, right?" he said.

Agent Gary West nodded his head. He had several questions for the sergeant and needed to get the responses back to Fort MacArthur before the next mail plane left the base.

Miller knew the drill. He had been pulled into CID offices twice in late 1972 at Fort Bragg, and again just three months ago. At this point, he wasn't going to hold back anything. It was clear the Army had already uncovered these shootings. Miller tried to fill in the blanks as much as he could: the farmers were huddled in a rice paddy and were about three hundred meters away. Satisfied by his answers, West went on to ask about another subject: the villagers who died in the bunkers outside Chu Lai. What happened to the women and children?

Miller paused for a moment. He didn't mind talking about the farmers, but this one bothered him. In his last interview, he had mentioned without great detail the Tigers stumbling upon bunkers, and children scampering inside. Now, the Army wanted more.

Miller moved uneasily in his chair. There were a lot of bad things that happened in South Vietnam, and he was able to live with most of them. But this one tore at him. West asked, "Did you see grenades being thrown into the bunkers?"

"Yes," Miller responded. "I was there." They never bothered to count the dead, he added, and in the end never found any weapons. In fact, they never turned up any evidence whatsoever that the people were Vietcong.

Five days later, Miller's interview and sworn statement — marked "urgent" — arrived at Fort MacArthur. Apsey had been bothered by several atrocities, but this one had nagged at him for one particularly grim reason: there were bunkers all over the province where Tiger Force patrolled. He knew the Tigers broke into small teams, often with one team oblivious to the actions of another. No doubt, other teams were coming across other bunkers. If Miller's team could casually blow children and women apart in a bunker, what were the other teams doing?

Ybarra jumped up from the couch, cursing at the television. He had just watched a news report of the North Vietnamese openly violating the peace accord by building roads in the South, with soldiers from the opposing countries exchanging gunfire. He usually ignored the news, except when it came to this; it didn't matter if he was drunk or stoned on marijuana, he would turn up the sound on the television or radio for any news on Vietnam.

The war, in fact, had been fading from the airwaves — eclipsed by the latest Watergate developments. With every newscast, a once confident president now appeared old and haggard, fighting to hold on to an office that was slipping away. The House Judiciary Committee was weeks away from voting on three articles of impeachment. Ybarra ignored all that, instead obsessed with a war that never ended, at least in his mind. The most recent reports of the North Vietnamese transgressions only reinforced his views. "You can't trust those bastards!" he screamed, standing in front of the television like it was an enemy soldier.

In early June, reservation police tipped off Ybarra that the Army CID had called them to find out if he was still living there — sending Sam into a rage. He had last heard from the Army in 1972 and thought whatever investigation they were conducting was over. Now, he was spooked again. Why were agents calling the reservation? "I got nothing to say to them," he mumbled when his wife asked him what they wanted.

By now, Janice Little was tired of his outbursts. Every time he blew up, she became scared, and a few times she bolted from their home with their two young daughters. She just wanted it all to end — the tension, the arguments. She loved her husband, but their marriage was failing. He had ballooned to three hundred pounds and rarely left their home. His drinking was out of control, and he was constantly smoking pot. Most days, he ranted about the peace treaty, the loss of lives, the way the Americans just gave up. He would always bring up Ken Green. He had been carrying the guilt of his friend's death for seven years and couldn't seem to shake it. "It's my fault," he would say. "He shouldn't have died."

One day in June, he decided he was going to visit Green's mother in Roosevelt, something he had talked about doing since returning from the war. Ybarra drove the thirty miles to the Green home, rehearsing a speech to break the ice. But by the time he arrived and met Kathleen Green at the door, he didn't know what to say, and neither did Green's mother. She was never fond of Ybarra and had told her son so. But this wasn't the time to bring up the past. She invited Ybarra inside, and after several minutes, he took over the conversation. He was sorry for what happened to her son and, in his own way, accepted personal responsibility for the death. He didn't go into detail but told her that her son "didn't suffer. He died a hero."

Ybarra slowly reached into his pocket, hesitated for a moment, and then pulled out Green's wallet. "Here," he said. "This was Kenny's. I had been keeping this for you for a long time."

She thanked him but couldn't help noticing Ybarra was pained. She asked him if everything was all right, but he just nodded. He didn't want to tell her that his world was falling apart. First his dishonorable discharge, then his return to a reservation that he longed to escape, and now the CID agents coming for him. Though he told his wife and others that he was unfazed by the Army investigation, it was just the opposite. He was deeply afraid of what they wanted.

When he showed up at his mother's home that night, he had already been drinking. He went inside and began to talk about the war. Therlene had heard it all before: the killing of villagers, the children, the look in their eyes before he killed them.

But now she was scared for him. Her son had struggled after he returned to the reservation, but it was getting worse. "Please, Sam, please," she said. "You need to get help."

She had never been able to predict her son's behavior. At times, he would be enraged, screaming about how the gooks were all the same and how he should have killed more; other times he was contrite, deeply sorry about opening up on unarmed men, women, and children. Like others with PTSD, Sam would vacillate between justifying his actions and condemning what he did. He was on a seesaw, and so was everyone around him.

It was easy to understand why he drank himself to sleep every night. What he and other soldiers in the field had never seemed to realize was that their minds were constantly taking snapshots of what they did. The images of the people shot or scalped were never lost but were stored like a computer program in the brain. Years later, these images would come back, and the soldiers — in the comfort of their homes and with their families — would be forced to stare at the snapshots in all their gore.

For the past several days, Henry Tufts had been at his desk, his glasses at the end of his nose, poring over the soldiers' statements and the personnel files. Even to a hardened commander who saw every war-crimes case from Vietnam, the words on the pages were disturbing.

He was satisfied that the Tiger Force case was being investigated thoroughly. There were enough substantiated allegations to take this to an Article 32. But that wasn't the issue. To Tufts, it was not about what happened in the Central Highlands of South Vietnam, but *why*.

He had reviewed 242 war-crimes allegations investigated by the Army CID beginning in 1965 with the first arrival of the troops. There were more than a dozen rapes, twenty-one assaults, a dozen murders, and several cases of body mutilations, including the case of an officer who was prosecuted for fastening human ears to his Jeep antenna. But most of the cases involved one or two people and a single crime. And in nearly a third of the allegations, enough evidence was gathered to take the cases to military court. When soldiers were convicted, they were forced to serve time or, in many cases, docked pay for the lesser offenses. Some were busted down to lower ranks.

A few allegations were against entire combat units, but none involved platoons that carried out war crimes for so long without anyone stopping the carnage. "Seven months," Tufts told his staff. How many people were killed in those bunkers when the Tigers lobbed in the grenades? How many children were killed? What happened to these soldiers to make them lose control for so long? Tufts knew that many atrocities occurred during the war that were never reported. But this case was documented, and that separated it from others.

Tufts may have looked the curmudgeon, but he was fully capable of exploring the deepest recesses of human behavior — particularly in combat soldiers. Indeed he had spent his life studying the psychology of men in war. He once told his agents that he saw every different type of soldier when he commanded his own battery in the 868th Field Artillery Battalion in Europe in World War II. And had seen them run, seen them fight, seen them cower and cry, seen them kill, and seen them die.

In his earlier years in the CID, Tufts hadn't cared much about the deeper philosophical reasons for soldiers committing war crimes. His job was the nuts and bolts, to make sure soldiers weren't committing crimes and, if they did, to dig up the evidence against them. It was police work. But after Vietnam, that changed. It wasn't just about throwing the book at soldiers. It was about trying to understand what went wrong in the war. What went wrong with some of the troops. He had spent months overseeing My Lai, the worst case his office had ever investigated. But even My Lai was just one horrific day — not seven months.

Tufts began to go beyond Apsey's reports. He was able to get background information on more than a dozen suspects, including Ybarra and Doyle. He saw that some soldiers, such as Doyle, had long juvenile police records. Ybarra had been arrested numerous times before enlisting. In addition to the personnel records, Tufts got his hands on documents that showed that Tiger Force was created as a special unit with minimal oversight. Few commanders were supposed to know what the platoon was doing.

After thirty-two years in the military, he was now seriously looking at retirement. He had just endured a long, brutal struggle to centralize CID operations — a three-year intramilitary battle that he clearly despised. But he made up his mind he wasn't going to step down until the last war-crimes investigation was complete.

Most CID agents at Fort MacArthur had checked out for the long Fourth of July weekend, but Apsey still had a stack of statements to read from ex-Tigers and was anxious to see if any missing witnesses had been found. In an age before the Internet and fax machines, he was at the mercy of the post office and a military mail system that was often a week behind.

As he thumbed through the stack of names, he was disappointed. Apsey had hoped the agents had found William Doyle, whose name popped up innumerable times. Besides Ybarra, no one had been accused of more cold-blooded killings of civilians. And yet, little was known about the team leader. Another person missing was Rion Causey, the medic whose trail disappeared after his discharge.

But the mail brought some good news. Two former Tigers helped answer a question that had been nagging Apsey for weeks: did the Tigers bomb bunkers without warning civilians?

At first, Ken Kerney hadn't wanted to talk, telling agents in 1972 to leave him alone. Now, two years later, he had agreed to shed some light on Apsey's question: yes, it happened. He told agents that during a sweep of a hamlet, no interpreter had been available to lure the people from the underground shelters, or even to warn them about what was to take place. "The Tiger Force knew what to do," he said.

Charles Fulton was even more revealing, because he not only admitted to tossing grenades into a bunker but later heard the cries of the people underground. No one, he said, bothered to help the wounded Vietnamese. He freely admitted there were no weapons or signs of Vietcong.

Apsey wondered, Could this have been a routine practice? It violated the Army's policies and procedures and the Geneva conventions. Worse, because there were so many bunkers, no one would ever know how many in the province were turned into mass underground graves.

He wondered with a growing sense of dread how far up the chain of command this case went.

On August 8, everyone in the CID office at Fort MacArthur took a break from his or her work to tune in to one of the most historic events of the American presidency. Some gathered around a television while others listened to radios as Nixon addressed the nation from the Oval Office, saying that he had "never been a quitter" and that leaving office before his term ended was "abhorrent to every instinct in my body. But as president, I must put the interest of America first."

Apsey, who had been holed up in his office most of the day, walked out to catch a few minutes of the lonely figure on the screen. Like most of the other agents, he wasn't surprised by Nixon's resignation. Just two weeks earlier, the House Judiciary Committee approved one of three articles of impeachment. But while Watergate had been front-page news for nearly two years, Apsey had not been paying close attention to most of the developments — he had been so steeped in his investigation, he often didn't have time to read the newspaper or watch television. His head was in 1967, his heart in the Central Highlands of South Vietnam. When he came home at night, he would spread out the sworn statements on his kitchen table and scribble down new questions on a notebook for agents. If he was lucky, he caught a few minutes of the *Tonight Show* with Johnny Carson — but only a few minutes. Indeed, the only moment Apsey had dwelled on Nixon in recent years was when he heard rumors that the president had been told about the Tiger Force investigation and was concerned about the case being leaked to the media. But Apsey never knew for sure, and to him, it didn't really matter. He was going to continue to do his job.

Three thousand miles away, Henry Tufts was at his home in suburban Washington DC, watching the same drama unfold on television. With deep contacts in the Pentagon and Congress, he had predicted this was going to happen. There were enough votes for impeachment, and the truth was there was simply too much evidence against the president.

For weeks, Tufts had been keeping one eye on the Watergate events and the other on the Tiger Force case. He was now reviewing daily reports about the CID investigation. He wanted to know about every interview. He wanted to know about which ex-Tigers were still at large. He wanted to know about any new allegations.

Tufts had the power to bury the case and simply chalk it up to a war that was fading from the nation's attention. Or he could press ahead and resurrect war crimes that rivaled My Lai.

He called the Presidio and made it clear: the president's resignation would have no effect on the last war-crimes investigation of the Vietnam War.

After several weeks of sorting through the case, Tufts had seen enough. Tiger Force was a military experiment that failed — failed miserably. This was a group of men — some abused and abandoned — who had finally belonged to something special. They were allowed to carry their own sidearms, grow beards, dress in their own distinctive uniforms.

They were special.

With little supervision, they were to creep into the jungle in small teams, find enemy positions, and call in air strikes. This was a new kind of war, with a nearly invisible enemy hiding in jungle and underground tunnels. The Army needed a new kind of soldier and a new kind of unit. If they needed to kill, then they could do so without telling anyone. The less they talked on the radio, the better. They were a spy squad.

But then things changed. The Army was desperate to win the war quickly in 1967 and had a problem: the farmers in the Central Highlands weren't leaving their homes. As long as they were growing rice, the VC had food. This had to end. That's when Tiger Forced turned from a spy squad to a kill squad.

In a perversion of warfare, the Tigers were sent into the Central Highlands with their anger, pain, and resentments — with none of the supervision that existed in larger units — and allowed to run riot among civilians.

Tufts was painfully aware that the Vietnam War — with its frustrations and politics — spawned units that targeted civilians. But typically, the atrocities stopped after someone got wind of an out-of-control squad. Soldiers were disciplined. There was an end to the madness. Even at the massacre at My Lai, the carnage eventually stopped after helicopter pilot Hugh Thompson Jr. threatened to turn his chopper guns on the 11th Brigade soldiers who were carrying out the slaughter on the morning of March 16, 1968.

In Tiger Force, there was no end, no commanders to slam on the brakes. The Army *wanted* Tiger Force to terrorize the Vietnamese. The Army created a Frankenstein, and then turned it loose. The rampage ended only when the Army decided to end Operation Wheeler on November 25, 1967.

Tufts was disgusted. Tiger Force was the battalion's execution squad. What had happened to his Army? What had happened to the Army that saved the world from Nazi Germany during World War II? The Army of his generation was made up of commanders who did not routinely target civilians. There was a code of honor. Tufts was an old-school soldier. Despite the exigencies of battle, he believed commanders and soldiers should never abandon what's right. They do not need to target civilians.

To see young kids deteriorate into such a monstrous unit was an indictment of the Army itself. It was the Army that created Tiger Force. Now, it was up to Tufts to clean up the mess.

But what Tufts didn't know was that he was about to be ousted from his job. The longtime CID director had been under pressure to step down himself by Army Chief of Staff Creighton Abrams, who years earlier had taken Westmoreland's place as chief commander of forces in Vietnam. Tufts was trying to hang on to his office long enough to see the Tiger Force case through. With Nixon's resignation, however, it was impossible. The new choice for the CID was Colonel Al Escola, a younger officer who was handpicked by Abrams. Escola liked Tufts but realized the old colonel's days were numbered. "They wanted him out," recalled Escola. "There was a decision: a change had to be made."

Before departing on a warm summer afternoon, Tufts packed up numerous mementos of his years in the CID, including letters and commendations and copies of the regulations he wrote that defined the agency. But he also took a batch of classified documents regarding one case — a rare move for someone who prided himself on following the rules. The files would stay in his basement for the rest of his life: Tiger Force.

While Apsey waited for the last of the interviews to be sent to his office, he began examining the Army radio logs. Each entry — complete with grid numbers, dates, and times — showed where the unit was moving on a particular day. Using an old Army map of the Central Highlands, he began plotting Tiger Force's movements across the Quang Ngai and into the Quang Tin provinces. Along with each entry was a brief description of what the unit was doing that day. For hours, he leaned over his desk, connecting the dots from hamlet to hamlet.

His suspicions were raised when he began reading the daily radio logs for November 1967. Going over each day, he noticed the same phrase: "VC running from hut, resulting in VC killed." Apsey counted forty-nine killed in a period of eleven days. For the same period of time, no weapons were found.

What bothered Apsey even more was that the radio logs were routinely reviewed by the battalion commanders as well as monitored over the airwaves. Not only did the soldiers report enemy kills but they also reported the number of weapons seized. Somebody in the chain of command had to know the soldiers were shooting people who weren't carrying any guns.

In looking over the logs, he noticed something else out of place. The records showed that on November 19, 1967, the Tigers logged the 327th kill of the ongoing military campaign. He recalled that a command had been broadcast over the airwaves weeks earlier with a goal for the battalion: "We want 327 kills," the same number as the battalion's infantry designation. Suddenly, Apsey had a terrible revelation: Tiger Force hadn't been killing scores of innocents. It had been killing hundreds.

★ ★ ★

James Barnett rummaged through his dresser until he found his medals from Vietnam, including his Silver Star for gallantry, before slapping the drawers shut. Cursing, he stuffed the medals in a package, sealed it with tape, and then drove to the post office.

Barnett had been angry ever since hearing the news on the radio that the newly sworn-in president, Gerald Ford, was offering amnesty to deserters and draft dodgers who fled the country to escape service during the Vietnam War. Ford had been in the White House only five weeks when he announced the amnesty as a way to "heal the deep national divisions the war had caused." To most political observers, his announcement on September 16 was the first real indication that the new president was serious about moving the country away from divisions created by the war. But to the former Tiger Force team leader, it was a cold slap in the face. It took Barnett several minutes to compose himself before addressing the envelope to the White House. It wasn't so much the issue of patriotism that angered him. It was the fact that he had gone through so much hell when others were allowed to skate free.

At twenty-nine, Barnett was suffering from the symptoms of post-traumatic stress disorder: sleeplessness, nightmares, and an anger that had been welling inside of him ever since the war. The last time he was this upset was when a CID agent — for the fifth time — showed up at his home on June 21. A furious Barnett had refused to be interviewed. He was tired of the military and tired of the government. He had already taken part in a war that was eating away at him every day, and didn't think the Army had a right to intrude in his life.

What the military should have been doing was arresting draft dodgers, not mollycoddling them. For the president to wipe away their crimes was shameless. "No one had a right to do that," he told reporters after shipping the package to the president. Barnett's comments were carried in the Tennessee newspapers, and by the time they were picked up by the news wires, Apsey received a call from an agent at Fort Campbell.

Apsey was immediately alarmed. If Barnett was willing to go public about sending his medals to the White House, he could just as easily spill his guts about Tiger Force. No one wanted the case to blow up in the media — especially now. For starters, the Ford administration would not react well to the news. Members of the administration, including Defense Secretary James Schlesinger and Chief of Staff Donald Rumsfeld, were trying to move the country in a different direction. Schlesinger, who had continued in his cabinet post from the Nixon administration, was trying to set an agenda that called for the rebuilding of the military to meet a growing Soviet threat. Vietnam had taken a toll on the American psyche, with most of the world now believing the United States was essentially defeated in the war. Rumsfeld, who was in Brussels during much of the Watergate crisis as an ambassador to NATO, was a leading proponent of not only moving beyond Vietnam but reforming the military. Rumsfeld believed public opinion turned against the war because of high casualties, not because of the war itself. To avoid the kind of casualties that came with ground troops, he and others pushed for a modern military that depended on technology and surprise — meaning massive airpower. Under his watch, the MX intercontinental ballistic missile was developed along with the B-1 Bomber and the Mark 12A nuclear warhead.

Apsey phoned the Presidio to talk to Weinstein. After all, it was the colonel who had dropped the file on Apsey's desk. But when he reached Weinstein, nothing had changed. He was told to continue working the case.

It was already November, and agents were still searching for Doyle. They had visited the Philippines, South Vietnam, and even his home state of Missouri. But Doyle always seemed to be one step ahead. Ever since his discharge on June 10, 1971, he had disappeared.

Apsey needed the former team leader. He knew Trout and

Hawkins wouldn't talk. They were both in the Army and had too much to lose. But Doyle was out and free to talk without fear of prosecution. So where was he?

In mid-November, Apsey received a call. The CID office in Guam received a tip that a thin, balding American covered with tattoos was living on the island. At long last, Doyle had been tracked down.

While Apsey waited for the agents to investigate, he rechecked where Hawkins and Trout were stationed. He was leaning toward recommending murder charges against both men, and if they transferred, he didn't want to spend time locating them again. He called officials in Florida and learned that Hawkins was now at Fort Rucker, Alabama.

He wasn't so worried about Trout's whereabouts since he had already requested the sergeant be flagged — but unknown to Apsey at the time, the flag had been removed. Trout, now stationed at Fort Benning, had asked the warning be lifted from his record, and on November 19, the fort staff judge advocate agreed. Under CID procedures, Apsey should have been notified, but for some reason, no one bothered to call him until several weeks later. Trout was essentially free to walk.

The removal of the flag felt like a punch in the gut. While Apsey waited for word on the status of Doyle, he received an urgent call from the Presidio on November 21 with an odd message: Barnett had called the CID office at Fort Campbell. He desperately wanted to talk about Tiger Force.

Ever since interviewing Barnett two years ago, Apsey sensed the veteran was ready to explode. During the last two visits by CID agents, he was evasive and antsy. And of course, most recently, he had angrily returned his combat medals. But after reaching Barnett by phone, Apsey could tell the man at the other end wasn't the same tough-talking vet from their interview nearly two years ago. His voice was strained, and he began rambling about Tiger Force and Vietnam. He said he wanted to talk, but not over the phone; he wanted to see Apsey in person.

"There are things I need to say," Barnett said in his deep drawl. "I'm going to talk to you about Trout and Hawkins, and I'm going to tell you about myself."

Apsey said he could meet with Barnett in a few days at the earliest.

For Apsey, the timing couldn't have been better. He had been dealt a setback by the flag being lifted on Trout, and worse, the Army knew it. Why would anyone allow this, knowing the time and resources the CID devoted to this case? Depending on what Barnett had to say, Apsey might be able to make a case to reinstate the flag.

Six days later, he arrived by plane in Memphis, checked into a motel, and phoned Barnett. But now, Apsey sensed Barnett was hesitant to meet. Something must have happened in the last six days. Barnett stammered on the phone and then blurted out a demand for immunity. Apsey was taken aback. He traveled all the way to Tennessee in hopes of another break-through interview — one that could put the investigation over the top. But he didn't have the authority to promise anything — that had to come from a JAG.

"I can't do that for you," he said.

There was silence on the phone. "Let me think about it," Barnett said, asking for Apsey's phone number.

The next morning, Barnett reached Apsey in his motel room. He said he talked to a close friend who advised him to keep quiet, but Barnett said it was too late. He was going to talk — with or without immunity.

Barnett hung up the phone without giving directions, but since Apsey had been to the house eighteen months earlier, he figured he could find Barnett's home. Unfortunately, when Apsey drove into Loretto, he couldn't find the street. He drove around in circles before he stopped into a small post office and asked for directions. The clerk shook his head. "We don't like Army cops around here," he said. "You find it yourself."

Apsey got back into his car and drove until he finally found the street. By the time he knocked on the door, Barnett was already waiting. Apsey almost forgot how imposing a figure Barnett could be, at nearly six and a half feet and a much heavier 260 pounds. He led his visitor to the kitchen table but didn't sit down.

"I got to keep moving," Barnett said, pulling a chair out for Apsey.

As Barnett paced the kitchen floor, Apsey removed a notepad and a small, portable typewriter from a case and placed it on the table, looking curiously at the man in blue jeans.

Before saying anything, Barnett excused himself and walked back into the bathroom.

Moments later, he was back in the kitchen, clutching a .20-gauge shotgun over his shoulder. Apsey immediately put his hands up.

"Whoa," he said. "What are you doing?"

Barnett, breathing heavy, his face red, plopped down in the other chair, putting the gun on the table with the barrel pointing directly at Apsey.

Apsey had conducted dozens of interviews, and no one had ever pulled a gun on him. For a moment, he froze, unable to say anything. This was his worst fear — an unstable veteran shooting him. His heart pounding, Apsey kept telling himself to stay calm, stay in control. He had a .38 handgun under his sport coat, but he could never draw it in time. He had to try to talk to him, to reason with him.

"Look," Apsey said, staring into Barnett's bloodshot eyes, "all I got is a .38. It's peanuts compared to what you got there. Put it down. Don't do this."

Barnett turned his head and, for a moment, was quiet. His eyes dropped to the floor, and then slowly he breached open the double-barrel and removed two shells — one at a time — laying them on the table. He then leaned the gun against the nearby wall.

"I'm tired," he said.

For the last three years, he hadn't been able to stop the nightmares, the sweats. He hadn't been able to forget the killing. "Most of those incidents," he said slowly, "could be classified as war crimes today."

Everything the CID was investigating, from the assault on the farmers to the systematic executions of unarmed men and women, was real, Barnett said. He was willing to accept responsibility for what he did to villagers but wasn't about to point the finger at the other grunts. "It wasn't just them," he said. The Tigers' descent into brutality was caused by a breakdown in leadership — and more than just a breakdown, the crimes were actually encouraged from the top, he said. Hawkins and Trout led the way, setting the tone for the unit and "giving the orders." But he said their superiors knew what was happening and did nothing to stop it.

Barnett could still see the face of the young mother he shot point-blank in the chest on the orders of Trout.

The worst part, he said, was how easy it was to squeeze the trigger. "I didn't think about whether it was right or wrong," he said. "To me, it was just another day in Vietnam."

Apsey interrupted to ask whether anyone could corroborate the shooting. Barnett answered that he couldn't recall who was around, but "I would have to be crazy as hell to tell you that I shot that woman, if I didn't do it."

Apsey stopped writing and paused for a moment.

He noticed that Barnett was fighting to hold back tears. The once defiant veteran from two years ago was now a broken figure, hunched over the table, his hands trembling.

Without saying a word, Barnett stood up slowly and walked over to the door, staring outside. "You know," he said, "I gotta make sure no one is watching me." He said he left the Army in 1971 because he was afraid he would be charged in the investigation. He had wanted to stay in the military, to make it his career. He pushed aside the drapes over his living room window and peered outside. "There are people," he said, "who would kill me for this."

He stepped back from the window and turned to Apsey, who was beginning to understand that Barnett — like so many other Tigers — carried deep emotional problems into the war.

Barnett was too young to comprehend the psychological damage that had been inflicted on him by his father. Too young to understand that he, like his father, had become an abuser. Too young to control the rage and fury he had against a people whom he didn't understand. As if all the bad feelings would go away. As if he would be able to purge himself of the anger and resentment and pain of a boy who wanted only his father's love. The tragedy was that his actions against the Vietnamese had only made him angrier, had only made him kill more.

Apsey rose and began putting away his notepad, watching warily from the corner of his eye to make sure Barnett didn't make any moves.

Trying to stay calm, Apsey walked over to the veteran and held out his hand. Barnett looked at Apsey and hesitated, wondering what Apsey was going to do next. "Is this it?" he asked. "Is the CID going to come around again?"

Apsey shook his head. "Not right away," he said. "I'll let you know."

Apsey walked out and stepped quickly to his car. He placed the key into the ignition, turned on the engine, and after looking one last time at the house, backed out the driveway and drove off. As he reached the main highway, he stepped on the gas. He didn't even know how fast he was driving. He just wanted to get away. Apsey couldn't stop thinking about the close encounter in the kitchen. He pulled by the side of the road, stopped the car, opened the driver's door, and walked to the grassy embankment. He began to take deep breaths to calm himself down but couldn't control himself any longer. His heart racing, he leaned over the guardrail, steadied himself against the cold steel, and threw up.

★ ★ ★

Flying back to California, Apsey peered out the window. After the long drive to the airport and a glass of water, he was finally feeling better. Not since his interview with Carpenter nearly two years ago had he reeled in such damning information. This was someone who actually confessed to murder, and who said that other Tigers were encouraged by commanders to kill civilians.

Apsey had long thought about focusing on the brass but had been understandably reluctant. To go up the food chain, you needed solid, irrefutable evidence. Otherwise, it could be a career-shattering move. The Army had frowned on targeting high-ranking officers during the Vietnam War. In the wake of My Lai, it had brought too much bad publicity. But after spending a day with Barnett, Apsey was now convinced it was the only way to find out why this platoon was able to carry out war crimes unabated for seven months. Commanders had to be held accountable. It was up to them to ensure that the soldiers weren't killing unarmed villagers. It was up to them to make sure their men weren't torturing noncombatants. It was up to them to make sure their unit wasn't mutilating bodies. Anything less was dereliction of duty. And it didn't matter whether you were a colonel or a major, a captain or a lieutenant.

Apsey had sat with dozens of veterans in this investigation, some angry, others depressed. But he had never interviewed anyone like Barnett. No one had ever broken down so completely, confessing to murder and random, unjustified shootings. No one had cried or pulled out a gun. But he had heard this before. Donald Wood had said he tried to stop the killing by going to commanders. So had Gerald Bruner. Carpenter, Miller, and Bowman were among the ex-Tigers who had said superiors knew what was happening in the field.

As soon as Apsey returned to Fort MacArthur, he began getting the names of the commanders — captains, majors, and colonels — who served in the battalion that oversaw Tiger

Force in 1967. No one was sacred. For the first time since the investigation of the My Lai Massacre, high-ranking officers were being sought for questioning in a war-crimes case. Apsey knew it was risky, but he didn't care. He had dug too deep to stop now. And he knew that if he didn't follow this case to wherever it took him, he would be failing not only his country but himself.

Apsey was convinced he made the right decision after receiving a special report on a CID interview with a former battalion captain, Carl James. Apsey had wanted to track down the former battalion officer ever since learning that James was the liaison between the Tigers and the battalion leadership from June to November 1967. A CID agent was finally able to reach James at Fort Benjamin Harrison, Indiana. During the interview, James nervously told the agent he recalled talking to a soldier named Bruner about war crimes, but never bothered to report the allegations to superiors. When the agent asked James to elaborate, James stopped the interview. He wanted a lawyer. Apsey was getting closer.

CHAPTER 23

Going after commanders in a war-crimes case was rare during Vietnam. To do so after the war was unheard-of. Not only did the passing of time make it more difficult to present testimony and evidence but the political will to press such a case was questionable. The war had ended two years earlier. Despite the peace treaty, by January 1975, NVA troops were pouring over the borders in a blatant violation of the agreements signed in Paris. The South Vietnamese government had been pleading for money and arms, but U.S. lawmakers were reluctant to even touch the subject. Though President Ford was willing to provide some assistance, Congress had refused every funding request.

Despite the changing climate, Apsey was prepared to challenge any effort to shut down the case. He had come too far. If anyone tried to tell him to end the investigation, he would ask for the order in writing.

In early December 1974, he called the Pentagon and requested immediate locators on all officers in the battalion between May and November 1967 to see who was still in the service. He couldn't personally interview all the commanders; some undoubtedly would be stationed overseas. He also knew that officers had a tendency to talk to one another and compare answers. So again, Apsey was forced to employ the "shotgun approach," just as he had done with the grunts: the CID would question all the officers at once.

He had been a part of more than one hundred investigations but never one that would reach so high. He knew he would receive support from Weinstein and Perdue, but still, Apsey was a career serviceman, and he was now focusing on people who wore more stripes than anyone he knew.

He remembered what his mentor Frank Sugar once told him: "It doesn't matter how many stripes they're wearing. You apply the law. No one is above that. Do you hear me? No one."

After six frustrating weeks of checking the mail, Apsey received locators on eighteen officers in mid-January 1975. The only one missing was Harold Austin, the former executive officer who later became battalion commander. Agents told Apsey that Austin was out of the military and believed to be somewhere in Thailand. They would keep looking for him.

There was one name on the list that Apsey circled: Gerald Morse. The former battalion commander known as Ghost Rider was now stationed as a full colonel in Heidelberg, Germany. No doubt, his time as a battalion commander had helped lead to his promotion. Apsey would save that interview for last.

There were many questions Apsey needed to ask, but perhaps the most important one involved a definition. A free-fire zone was based on the premise that the United States was in a friendly country and needed permission from the South Vietnamese government before opening fire or ordering an air strike on a specific village. The targets had to be military.

What Apsey found was that in numerous incidents, the Tigers were taking the phrase literally — freely firing on civilians. Apsey suspected battalion commanders knew that the free-fire zones were being abused and looked the other way.

And there were other questions, too. Did the commanders know about body mutilations? Did they ever question why the Tigers never brought in prisoners? Did any soldiers ever bring war crimes to their attention? He knew that some commanders would not have had any supervision over the Tigers. But he also knew the command structure over a battalion was small enough that the officers often knew what was going on throughout the unit. All the officers had to attend daily mandatory briefings, including the battalion surgeon, executive officer — and chaplain.

Within weeks, the responses from commanders came back. And they were just as Apsey predicted: the officers expressed ignorance about civilian deaths — the routine execution of prisoners and unarmed villagers. But in their responses to free-fire zones, the officers offered a snapshot of a battalion obsessed with body count — and of officers who rarely ventured into the field. Again and again, Apsey read similar accounts. Major James McElroy, who served under the battalion's executive officer, told agents that "if movement was seen in a free-fire zone, whether identified as armed or not, it could be fired upon." Another officer, Captain Jerry White, said that in a free-fire zone, the soldiers "could fire at will." And Captain Joseph Westbrook told agents that if a Vietnamese was killed in a free-fire zone, "he was considered a combatant."

One key interview was with the former battalion surgeon. Dr. Bradford Mutchler was asked whether he ever heard rumors about the Tigers collecting ears, gold teeth, and scalps. "Yes," he answered. "It was something that no one really talked about in the open. It was something that you just kept trying to sweep under the rug and forget because you really didn't want to know if it was true or not."

As far as free-fire zones, he said, battalion leaders routinely declared large areas as free-fire zones, especially in the Song Ve Valley. The order "to kill everything that moved" was given all the time. "As the battalion surgeon, I attended all of the mission briefings. I heard that order, or similar orders, given at every briefing." Mutchler was then asked what the order meant. "In my opinion, it meant kill whatever was in the area," he said. "If it moves, kill it."

Stephen Naughton had been tracked down in Harker Heights, Texas, on February 5. The former platoon leader, now a civilian, admitted that Donald Wood came to him twice — once at Carentan and later at Fort Bragg — to talk about atrocities carried out by Hawkins and others. Naughton said he, in turn, contacted a colonel in the inspector general's office at Fort Bragg to pass on Wood's complaints. But he said he was told "to forget it. That I would just be stirring things up."

A man was sitting in his apartment kitchen in Saint Petersburg, Florida, when the phone rang. He picked up the receiver, and the voice on the other end asked if William Doyle was home. The caller then identified himself as Bonnie Sapp, a CID agent. Doyle wanted to slam the phone down but knew it was now too late. It was February 1975, and the Army had been looking for him for three years.

He had picked up their trail back in Guam when agents began snooping around a fishing village where he was living, but he had managed to stay one step ahead. He assumed they wanted to know about his participation in a secret operation known as the Phoenix Program. (Hatched by the CIA, the covert operation was set up to assassinate Vietcong supporters, after Doyle left the Tigers.) But whatever they wanted, Doyle knew it probably wasn't good news for him, so he had ducked into the shadows.

He was angry. He had always prided himself on his ability to outsmart his adversaries. Sapp wouldn't say how he had found him, but it didn't take long before Doyle figured it out. Just weeks earlier, he had checked himself in to a mental ward at the Bay Pines Veterans' Administration Medical Center in Saint Petersburg. He admittedly had been close to a breakdown, partly from years in Vietnam, partly from the unresolved issues of a troubled childhood. Because his name was in the system, his admittance in the facility had tipped off the military to his whereabouts.

Doyle asked Sapp why he wanted to question him. Sapp would say only that allegations were made against Doyle from his time in Tiger Force.

"Tiger Force?" Doyle asked incredulously. "What do you want to know?"

Again, the agent said it was better to meet in person. Doyle agreed but gave the investigator a warning. "I'll tell you now," Doyle said, "I don't discuss things that happened during the war. The only thing I'll say is that while I was in Vietnam, I did everything I could, and killed anybody it was necessary to kill to keep Americans alive."

The following day, Sapp and another agent showed up at Doyle's apartment. Before asking any questions, they read Doyle his rights under military law, which meant he was under investigation but not under arrest. The suspected crimes: murder and aggravated assault. He had the right to remain silent and to call a lawyer.

Doyle sneered at the agents, saying he had nothing to offer. Each time they asked him a question, he answered with a "no comment."

At one point the CID agents brought up the name of the man who fingered Doyle during the investigation: Bruner. Doyle immediately jumped to his feet, his face red, and began spewing obscenities. "Bruner was a wiseass!" he shouted. "He couldn't be depended on! He was always trying to make peace, instead of making war."

Most of the people accusing the Tigers didn't even know what it was to fight a war, he sneered, including the CID.

"Tiger Force was my kind of unit, I can tell you that," he said. "We fought the war the way we thought it should have been fought."

After three hours of additional "no comments" and obscenities, the agents finally gave up. They turned off their recorder and rose to leave. Doyle was quick to stand. "I can tell you this," he said. "Don't ever bother me again. I'm finished."

Several hours later, he received another call from a man who identified himself as a CID agent who knew about the case. The agent told him investigators would probably be returning but that Doyle should keep his mouth shut. The agent didn't want to tell Doyle much, other than to say there was "a faction of CID agents who were against the investigation. They're trying to protect you guys." Doyle was surprised and told the agent he appreciated the heads-up.

"Are you guys going after Hawkins?" he asked.

The agent then spelled out the whole case, based mostly on the fact sheet and summaries prepared by Apsey. Doyle listened. When the agent finished, Doyle asked for Hawkins's phone number. The agent didn't hesitate and, against Army regulations, passed on the number and even Hawkins's address at Fort Rucker.

No sooner did Doyle hang up the phone than he called Hawkins. The two had not talked since Vietnam. Doyle was one of the few soldiers who had stuck up for Hawkins in the field, and Hawkins knew it.

Doyle told him everything. Hawkins said he was well aware of the investigation, because his own career was on the rocks. He had been informed it could be years before he was promoted — if at all. He could even go to jail.

By the end of the conversation, Doyle was seething. In his mind, he and Hawkins never did anything wrong in Tiger Force. Doyle announced he "wasn't going to take any shit from anyone."

He had taken shit from people his entire life. Beneath the tough exterior, Doyle was a wounded man. Pounded by a drunken, enraged father, he was protected by his mother, who would step in between the young boy and his abuser while she was alive. She was his protector, his savior. She died in a car accident when he was in grade school, and he lost anything decent in his life. The hurt and, later, the rage was uncontrollable, so much so that he turned it inward. For years, he blamed himself and, later, blamed the world. Dropped into South Vietnam, he found the perfect place and the perfect people to take out his wrath.

The day after CID agents visited his home, he began making a barrage of calls to the Pentagon. He demanded to talk to Defense Secretary James Schlesinger and didn't give a damn how long it took to reach him. After the calls bounced around the labyrinth bureaucracy, he managed to reach a secretary who worked in Schlesinger's office. Doyle began ranting about the Tiger Force investigation, saying the Army was trying to railroad "good soldiers who answered the call" and that he was one of them. He said the Tigers did nothing different than what the soldiers did during the Phoenix Program. Doyle knew that Schlesinger had at one time been director of the CIA in 1973, taking the place of Richard Helms, who oversaw the program. "I want to know why all of a sudden these are war crimes," he said to the secretary. "I was in the Phoenix Program, and I know damn well you all knew what the hell we were doing the whole time."

He demanded to speak to Schlesinger, but the secretary said she would make no promises. She would take Doyle's name and number.

Doyle was still angry after he hung up the phone. He wasn't sure whether he would ever get a response, but at this point, it didn't matter. He wasn't going to stay in the country. He needed to get the hell out again, this time to the Philippines. He had spent time there during R & R sessions and liked it. Americans were left alone. He could disappear.

★ ★ ★

In a military career that spanned twenty-four years, Gerald Morse had done everything right. He had successfully attended the command general's college, served in Korea, where he earned two Purple Hearts, and led a battalion in one of the most contested regions of Vietnam. Two years after the war, he had been sent to Heidelberg as part of a contingent to the Army's 7th Army. From all indications, he was on a track to become a general.

On the afternoon of March 17, 1975, Morse was returning from a training exercise when two CID agents approached him. They said they needed to talk to him about Tiger Force.

Morse agreed to chat but wasn't pleased. He reminded the agents that he had already been interviewed by the CID about this case in 1972 and didn't know anything then. What made them think he knew anything now?

But the agents, Gary Lawrence and Ellis Collins, reminded him that the interview he was referring to was three years ago and that a lot had changed. One of the agents pulled out a card and began reading Morse his rights. Morse hadn't expected this. He had always been a gung ho officer who excelled under fire without a hint of scandal. "You are under investigation for dereliction of duty," said the agent. "You have the right to a lawyer." Morse didn't flinch. He said he would waive his rights to a lawyer and told the agents to fire away.

The first question: "What was your radio call sign?"

"Ghost Rider," he said, "everywhere I went. Whether in a helicopter, vehicle, or stationary."

"Did you ever say you wanted a body count of 327?"

"I don't recall anything about that," he responded. "That was so long ago."

"Did you offer a promise and award or any other type of recognition to the person or the unit which made or surpassed the 327th kill during Operation Wheeler?"

He fired back, "Absolutely not."

Asked why Morse changed the names of the companies from A, B, and C to Assassins, Barbarians, and Cutthroats,

Morse responded, "This was done as a means of bringing to-
getherness and esprit within the units." He explained that he
needed to breathe life into the battalion to fight the enemy. He
defended the use of free-fire zones but said the idea was not to
kill unarmed civilians. There were times when villagers would
be discovered in such areas, but he insisted the troops weren't
ordered to kill them.

"Was it justified to shoot and kill any Vietnamese who was
unarmed and running from your troops in free-fire zones?" an
agent asked.

"That's a hard question," Morse replied. If there was a
triple-canopy jungle and visibility was limited, he said, he
could understand a soldier would be "justified in shooting."
But again, he insisted that it would "not be justified to shoot
and kill an unarmed fleeing person."

There was one last question: "There have been reports of
many atrocities, body mutilations, murders, mistreatment of
prisoners and civilians committed by members of your battalion and particularly by the Tiger Force. Can you explain why
none of these reports came to your attention while you were
the commander?"

Morse turned directly to the agent. "I believe that if such
things had happened, the personnel involved would have been
less than stupid to inform me, knowing that I would have took
action to court-martial them. . . . I find it hard to believe that
any such war crimes occurred in my battalion."

On a warm, late April afternoon, Apsey hiked along a trail in
San Pedro Valley Park until he came to a grassy hill overlooking
a meadow blanketed by wildflowers. He removed a Canon
from his bag and crouched to capture an image of the rolling
landscape.

It was one of his favorite places for nature photography and
one of the few spots where he could escape an investigation
that had dominated his life. Usually he was able to focus on his

hobby, looking for the best angles and lighting. But even amid the flowers and sunshine, he was unable to relax.

For months, he had been trying to find time to visit here to shoot some photos but had been too busy. He was already feeling alone. Fellow agents weren't asking him about the investigation anymore, and agents in CID offices elsewhere didn't want to get involved. He wasn't exactly an outcast, but he knew he wasn't popular among some agents just by their reactions when he called for routine assistance.

At times, the stress was overwhelming, and he was slowly showing symptoms of diabetes: shortness of breath, lightheadedness, fatigue. He wasn't helping his condition by smoking more and spending the balance of his time at work and not at home. It was impossible to separate himself from the case. He had returned last month from Arizona and couldn't shake the image of an emaciated Ybarra, sunken eyes, staring up from a couch in the darkness of a filthy shack. The faces of the others — Barnett, Bowman, Carpenter, Kerrigan, Fischer — as they spoke of what had happened those years ago were images too pitiful to forget.

Unlike the rest of the country, they didn't have the luxury of putting the war behind them. Just a week earlier, on April 23, President Ford announced America would not help the South Vietnamese in their efforts to fight back the North Vietnamese who were on the outskirts of Saigon. He was not about to send troops to refight "a war that is finished as far as America is concerned." It was time, he said, "to bind up the nation's wounds."

Of course for Apsey, it was one thing to forget the war but another to dismiss the crimes — no matter how he felt personally about the soldiers. After spending three years on the case, he was convinced that despite a brutal conflict in which things went awry and innocent people were killed, this was a nightmare unit that had again and again and again lashed out at defenseless people, many of whom were caught in a war they never wanted. In the end, there was no excuse for what Tiger

Force did. And there was no excuse for the commanders who knew things were spinning out of control but did nothing to stop the killing. These were not fog-of-war killings, Apsey told his superiors. These were premeditated murders by members of a unit who were on a brutal rampage. If you can look the other way on these actions, then anything goes. You won't even need rules of engagement. You won't need a military code. You won't even need CID agents spending years on war crimes.

God knows, he knew the consequences of his work — and the explosive information that was about to be written in his final report. He knew people could be charged and careers could be ruined. Worse, if this ever reached the American public, it would be a national disgrace. American soldiers killing women and children, scalping villagers, kicking out the teeth of the dead, and wearing necklaces of human ears? It was understandable for a unit to lose control once, maybe even twice. These were eighteen-, nineteen-, twenty-year-olds in a confusing war. But this was different. "This is my job," he would tell his wife when he brought his work home. "I'm getting tired of it, too, but I can't just take the easy way out."

Apsey knew the North Vietnamese and Vietcong were far worse than Americans in the treatment of their own people. More than six thousand civilians were executed at Hue during the Tet Offensive in 1968 in one of the worst spates of war atrocities.

But Americans should have a higher standard, the highest. We were supposed to be humane, to be tough, brave soldiers — not killers. Ultimately, it wasn't up to Apsey to enforce standards. That would be carried out by the Army's justice system. But he at least had to do his job by pointing out the breaches. Otherwise, he was no better than the officers who chose to look the other way.

Apsey never forgot the Jesuits who taught him about the power of a higher good — the grace of God interceding in the lives of people. He tried to stay away from applying his own morality to cases. But with Tiger Force, that was difficult. Beyond the mechanics of the investigation, he saw evidence of a deep, underlying struggle between good and evil. It wasn't so much a fight for power. That was too easy. It was a battle over whether platoon commanders and soldiers would succumb to their own dark instincts. They needed to be held accountable. Otherwise, the crimes would happen again and again.

Through their own words, the former Tigers had told Apsey everything he needed to write his final report. But what they never gave up was the reason for their fall from grace. At times, they gave clues through the tension and tears, but nothing more. They never confessed that somewhere between the ambushes and booby traps and humping in the glaring sun, they lost hope. Somewhere in the blackness of the night, they lost faith. And in the end, there was nothing to separate them from the devil.

Apsey peeked over the stacks of records, photos, and military maps covering his desk as Woodrow Eno entered his office. They had been collaborating by phone and now were finally meeting to talk over the progress of the final report. Apsey turned off his tape recorder and stood up to greet the twenty-eight-year-old Army lawyer who was assigned by the Presidio to review the investigation. Eno appeared fresh in his crisp uniform, in contrast to Apsey, who looked tired and haggard, the ashtray on his desk filled with cigarette butts and the floor covered with crumpled paper.

He rarely left his office these days, instead spending endless hours examining records — allegation by allegation — searching for the strongest testimony in each case. For each allegation, there was a separate stack of records, including sworn statements, maps, and suspect photos. The stacks carpeted his desk, his floor, and the tops of his cabinets. He now struggled to find a way to charge soldiers for the shooting of the farmers.

Based on interviews with Carpenter, Miller, and Allums, he was convinced that the assaults took place and that Hawkins had overseen them. But he wasn't sure which members of Tiger Force fired their weapons.

Eno sat down and picked up the spreadsheet. He made it very clear that unless people were proved dead, there would be no murder charges. That seemed so obvious it was unclear why Eno had said it. But he explained that he was hesitant to press assault charges in the case of the farmers because no one had bothered to check on them after the shootings. Sure, Apsey had assumed they were dead; so had some of the soldiers. But were they?

"We need strong, unequivocal evidence, as much testimony as possible," Eno announced. That meant many of the allegations Apsey had spent time investigating were "probably not going to be actionable." He would review everything after Apsey finished writing the report. But, he reminded Apsey, the case was eight years old. The South Vietnamese government had collapsed on April 30 with the fall of Saigon, and the last thing the American public wanted was more Vietnam.

"How can we just walk away?" he asked. But he had a terrible feeling as he looked at Eno, a sense that things were suddenly not as he had believed, not as he assumed, that someone had hold of a rug and was about to yank it.

The killing of the prisoner on May 8 near Duc Pho had always bothered Apsey, mostly because the man, nicknamed the Big Gook, was tortured for days before he was shot to death after being ordered to run. It was one horrible thing to shoot a civilian without warning, but it was another to spend days beating and taunting him first. Since each witness — Barnett, Carpenter, and Heaney — agreed to the details, it could be reported as a war crime. The problem was that no one could recall who shot the prisoner. So the murder could really only be used to show a pattern.

Continuing his dictation, Apsey turned to the torture and stabbing death of a prisoner in July near Duc Pho. Speaking as clearly as he could, Apsey recounted the details: several Tigers placed bets that Robin Varney couldn't knock out the prisoner with one punch. When he failed, Varney pushed the prisoner into a bayonet held by another soldier, the blade plunging into the prisoner's neck. Apsey couldn't recommend charges, since Varney was dead, but again, it was part of a larger pattern.

Apsey turned to the summary executions of two brothers in the Song Ve Valley in July. As he dictated details of the shootings without a hint of emotion, he remembered how Manuel Sanchez — a decorated career soldier — expressed sorrow over his failure to protect the prisoners. Apsey noted that Sanchez couldn't identify the Tigers who killed the brothers, but said "this execution was ordered by the officer in charge: Hawkins."

After reporting on the treatment of prisoners, Apsey moved on to the Tigers' practice of bombing bunkers. But even after reviewing several written statements, Apsey was hard-pressed to recommend charges. The basic problem was there were so many attacks on bunkers, it was difficult to pinpoint just one. Some occurred during the day, others at night. The one case in which every witness seemed to agree — bunkers in a hamlet near Chu Lai in August — involved two former soldiers who were out of the Army and couldn't be charged.

By including some of these statements, Apsey was hoping to establish the unit's culture — at least among the leaders — and, in so doing, make a stronger case against those who may be charged. Body mutilations were another way of showing the platoon's brutality. Though these were not the most serious offenses, Apsey was determined to use the evidence to support his overall case. He noted that numerous Tiger Force members "were observed in possession of human-ear, scalp, and gold-teeth collections," basing his findings on twenty-seven separate witness statements.

Of all the soldiers, Ybarra was the prolific offender, Apsey wrote in his report. "Ybarra on numerous occasions cut ears from dead Vietnamese bodies, possessed a set of human ears and a jar containing two ears, possessed a string of human ears, which he wore on several occasions around his neck, and a bag with about fifteen to twenty gold teeth, suspected to have been removed from dead bodies." Apsey couldn't charge Ybarra, since he was no longer in the Army, but that wasn't the reason the information was written into the report. Apsey wanted to show that someone such as Ybarra could garishly display his souvenirs without even drawing a blink, that these were dark crimes committed in the brightest sunshine.

Apsey then moved into Operation Wheeler, the mission launched by the military on September 11, 1967, to take over the Central Highlands. Drawing on the platoon's radio logs, he went into detail, showing that the Tigers reported forty-eight Vietcong killed between November 11 and 21, without a single knife or rifle seized. He noted that battalion commanders, who were actively monitoring the radio logs, should have questioned the discrepancies, but they had not said a word.

Though Apsey was careful about drawing conclusions, he hinted that one of the reasons the Tigers were killing so many people was to reach a goal of 327 deaths. Apsey stated the platoon was acting under the orders of Morse to reach the magic number — an accusation, he noted, that was denied by the former commander. Apsey also accused Carl James of knowing about, but not reporting, the killing of an unarmed farmer near Chu Lai.

Apsey noted that "several of the 1/327 officers that were interviewed related they heard rumors that mutilations had occurred," and included the testimony of battalion surgeon Bradford Mutchler: "The subject of mutilations was swept under the rug and not openly talked about because no one wanted to find out if the rumors were true." Lastly, Apsey wrote that neither Morse nor Austin "put into effect an affirmative plan for the discovery or prevention of war crimes."

Apsey had always said the investigation was like a cold case, except he didn't have bodies or weapons. All he had was the words and memories of former Tigers. Despite the passing of time, he would try to prove that twenty, or two-thirds of the allegations, took place. There was no doubt in his mind they occurred. But time had passed. Four of the suspects were killed in combat, seven had left the military, and two could not be found. It was now June 1975, some eight years after the killings.

As a child in Austria, the son of a Nazi, Apsey had heard about the Nuremberg trials — and the importance the world placed on prosecuting war criminals. Such prosecutions were the only way to hold people accountable for their actions and prevent future atrocities. How, he wondered, was the American military going to prevent future Tiger Forces from happening if it didn't address the problems now? Lives had been lost, but lives could be saved, too.

Apsey's final report was fifty-five pages long, signaling the end of his "three years of hell," he later recalled.

No one in Apsey's office really understood the pressure he endured. But then, no one had ever investigated a war-crimes case for such a long period of time. When he inherited the Coy Allegation file, there were 133,000 American ground troops in South Vietnam, and the war was still on the front pages. When he completed it, the war was over and Saigon had fallen, as had an American president.

Under the Army's justice system, it was up to the suspects' commanders to decide whether to convene an Article 32 hearing. In most cases, commanders would read the final reports and supporting evidence and consult with military lawyers assigned to their base before making a decision. Apsey and other agents in his office thought he would be stationed at Fort MacArthur at least until the case reached a hearing, at which point he might be required to testify or provide additional reports. He was certainly ready. There was a sense of relief after he finished the paperwork. In the ensuing days, he began to take down the maps and statements on his wall, and to go out for lunch. Even Perdue noticed his agent was moving a bit quicker around the office. "It was like a weight had lifted off him," he recalled.

In the back of his mind, Apsey expected a promotion, perhaps even a crack at running his own CID office in the years to come. No one could doubt his work ethic and expertise. For the next two weeks, Apsey waited.

When he received the call from the Presidio in late July, he was stunned. It had nothing to do with the Tiger Force case. He was told to pack his bags and be ready in two weeks to ship out. He was heading to South Korea to work in a CID office north of Seoul.

The two Army officers walked side by side down a long corridor of the Pentagon, their footsteps growing louder as they reached a marble conference room at the end of the hall.

The taller officer with a shock of silver hair, General William Maddox, turned to the other, James Hawkins, and motioned for him to wait outside the room where a team of Army lawyers was meeting.

Hawkins had known this day was coming for a long time. It was November 1975 — three years since Hawkins was first confronted about the case — a case he had been trying to forget. He was now married and stationed at Fort Rucker, Alabama, with only three years to go before retirement.

Hawkins had been nervous ever since boarding the plane with Maddox, his commander, for the flight to Washington — his career and even the specter of a jail sentence riding on this trip. He feared becoming another Calley. The last thing he wanted to do was stand trial with the world watching.

In his mind, every killing was justified, and he would say so if he had to testify. But he knew the American public wouldn't understand. They would treat him just the way he was being treated now — like a common criminal. If not for this damn investigation, he could have been a major by now. He had served when others had run. This was the thanks he was getting.

Hawkins shifted uneasily in his chair until he finally saw his general emerge from the room, followed by an Army lawyer.

He rose to his feet as the two men approached him. The lawyer handed Hawkins an eight-page brief.

Hands slightly trembling, he began reading the pages with descriptions of murders and assaults by Tiger Force members. By the last page, he came to his own name and the murder of the old man by the Song Ve River.

There it was — the word "murder." This could be his career, or even his life.

But when he reached the final paragraph, he took a breath. Despite ample testimony against him, Hawkins would not be charged. No one would. The Pentagon had decided that it was better to cover up what had happened. Let the country move on.

Hell, it was only some Vietnamese.

The Army brief concluded that despite the evidence, "nothing beneficial or constructive could result for prosecution at this time." Four commanders were asked to read the final report of the Tiger Force case, but no action was to be taken in those cases. The investigation would now be closed, the documents shipped to a storage room at CID headquarters. The longest war-crimes case of the Vietnam War was over. There would be no charges. There would be no press conferences. There would be nothing at all. It would be as if nothing had ever happened.

And so it was.

EPILOGUE

As he neared the doorway, Rion Causey hesitated for a moment — not quite sure whether he wanted to walk inside even after traveling across the country for his first Tiger Force reunion. Inside the brightly lit banquet room near Fort Campbell, Kentucky, people were laughing and talking.

Causey spotted a few faces — barely recognizable from another time, another place. He remembered some of them but not their names. Too much time had lapsed since his last day with the Tigers, when he was being airlifted to a hospital after being sprayed by shrapnel in March 1968.

He could feel his own heart racing as he walked into the room and approached an open bar where several men from the Tigers and the 1st Battalion/327th Infantry were holding drinks, smiling. It was the kind of nervous anticipation that comes with any reunion.

Across the room, he spotted a man in the corner, someone vaguely familiar. He noticed that one by one, the other men began forming a circle around him. Causey inched closer and peered through the bald and graying heads to get a better look.

All at once, he remembered: Harold Trout, his sergeant. Trout was no longer the stocky, athletic, tough-talking team leader who could strike fear in the hearts of young soldiers with a glance. He was now round and pudgy with an affable grin — nearly all of his hair thinned by time.

Causey waited for the others to clear out before he walked across and introduced himself. They shook hands, but Causey could tell Trout barely recognized the former medic.

That wasn't a big surprise. To Trout, Causey was just another skinny, sandy-haired kid who was coming into the war with no real combat under his belt. Now he was older, graying, with a doctorate in nuclear engineering and nothing in common with the former sergeant who spent his career in the military.

After making small talk, Causey waited for a moment, then turned to Trout with a serious look. "I need to ask you something," he said, staring into Trout's eyes.

For a moment, Causey wasn't sure this was the right time. It was a reunion and people were supposed to be enjoying themselves. But after all these years, he didn't have a choice. It was now or never. For years, he had been keeping the pain inside, something he didn't even share with his family, secrets so deep he would wake up at night, sweating, scared to close his eyes. Middle-aged and divorced with a son, Causey was tired of carrying the guilt, the anxiety.

Trout politely stood and waited.

Causey took a breath. "I need to know: What happened at Chu Lai? Why did we kill so many people?" Causey wasn't asking about killing enemy soldiers. That was expected. This was about the civilians — unarmed boys and men — systematically gunned down, in many cases without any resistance.

Trout knew what Causey was talking about. So did the others in the room that day. But for so long, they had avoided talking about it. For so long, they had avoided one another. This was a reunion, and no one wanted to discuss a topic so disturbing. The slaughters, or the CID investigation? How could they forget? It forced them to scatter all over the country, forced some to hide. Reunions? Forget it. They didn't want to see one another. Not until the Vietnam veterans began to feel welcome by the rest of the country in the 1990s with the Welcome Home Parade in New York and other events did the former Tigers even begin to reach out to one another. With the Internet, it became easier to find people from their platoon. And finally, it seemed the time had come to reunite.

Some of the men turned around and walked away. They knew what Causey was talking about. Everyone did. It was their secret — hidden from everyone.

On a cold, windswept morning in December 2002, several boxes arrived in the mail at the University of Michigan's Harlan Hatcher Graduate Library.

The packages were the latest additions to a repository famous for housing papers from radical groups in American history. So it came as some surprise to librarians that this latest delivery consisted of the records of Army commander Henry Tufts. Most of the researchers had never heard the name.

For years, the boxes collected dust in the Tuftses' basement — remnants of the years he spent as the Army's top cop. The former head of the Army's Criminal Investigation Command once talked about writing a book but never found the time. He knew his records were valuable — a snapshot of the inner workings of the Army — but he wasn't sure what to do with the boxes filled with twenty-five thousand papers.

Though Tufts detested reporters, he developed a fondness for Michael Woods, who happened to be a veteran science and technology writer for the *Toledo Blade*'s Washington bureau. Woods never bugged Tufts for story information, respecting his friend's privacy.

When Tufts died on July 24, 2002, he left his papers to his friend with one condition: that Woods make an effort to get the documents into the public domain.

Woods intended to honor his friend's request but also

wanted his hometown paper to have the first crack at doing so. So Woods worked out a plan: he would find a university close to Toledo and allow reporters from the paper to dig through the documents. After six months, the records would be open to public inspection.

He contacted a colleague, the newspaper's national affairs writer, to take a look at the shipment that was already on the way to Ann Arbor, just fifty-five miles away. That correspondent — Michael Sallah — is one of the two authors of the book you now hold in your hands. In time, the documents would spark one of the most comprehensive war-crimes investigations ever undertaken by an American newspaper.

Sallah and fellow reporter Mitch Weiss (the other author of this book) would uncover one of the darkest secrets of the Vietnam War — the longest series of atrocities carried out by a U.S. fighting unit in the conflict and, later, a massive Army investigation that was eventually covered up.

Sallah had researched the background of Tufts but had no idea that a small file tucked away in one of the commander's boxes would be the key to unlocking the story. In fact, for the first month of research, the reporter was unable to find anything new in the collection. All the investigative cases saved by Tufts — including the My Lai Massacre of 1968 — had been splashed in the media over the years.

By early February, there was one last box to inspect. Sallah began sifting through the papers when he found the thin manila file with the words "Coy Allegation" on the label and the twenty-two documents labeled "Confidential" or "For Official Use Only" inside. Just to make sure this information had never been published, the reporters spent several days combing the *New York Times,* the *Washington Post,* and other papers on microfiche, searching for any references to Tiger Force. Nothing. The reporters began reading every book they could find at local libraries about the war. Again, nothing about Tiger Force. Weiss began faxing requests to the Army under the Freedom of Information Act, asking for records about a war-crimes case known as the Coy Allegation. Sallah turned to another source: the National Archives in College Park, Maryland, the largest government repository of military records open to the public.

The archivist promised he would look and, two weeks later, called back with good news. "I found the case," said the researcher. "But it's probably seven hundred pages. You're going to have to wait." The archivist promised it would be ready in two weeks. It was the first time a reporter had ever asked for it.

By the time Sallah and Weiss arrived at the large glass-and-steel center in suburban Washington in March, the papers were ready. For three days, the journalists copied the reports, stopping occasionally to read the typed pages. Most of the statements were from former Tigers, describing the disturbing events. Sallah and Weiss were struck by one fact: there was no record of a military hearing. They took the time to look at other cases on file at the center and found that many had led to hearings — but not this one. It was clear from the reports there were atrocities — lots of them. Even more startling, the war crimes were corroborated by the soldiers who were interviewed in the Army's investigation. The details they recounted were so specific that it was hard to believe the soldiers were making them up — especially since they were admitting to them. What happened to the case? The Army wasn't going to tell them. The Pentagon had processed the earlier request by the newspaper but sent only one hundred pages of the investigation before stopping. No more reports would be sent, and the records were sealed from the public.

Sallah and Weiss quickly discovered the lead investigator in the case was living in Washington state, his name appearing on the bottom of nearly every important document. Gustav Apsey was surprised by the call. Reluctantly, he agreed to talk about the investigation, a case he said was troubling and "the hardest investigation of my career." Sallah asked whether there was ever a court-martial. Apsey said he couldn't talk about it. "I'm retired, but technically, I can still be recalled to active duty. I can't say anything else about this case." He did admit he didn't recall any hearing.

Over the next few months, the reporters began tracking down scores of former Tigers who served between May and November 1967 — the period in question. Some of the names came from the Tiger Force Web site. Others were found in the records. The interview that opened the first door to understanding the soldiers' actions took place in late February 2003, when Sallah and Weiss tracked down a former medic. Rion Causey would offer the first real hint that what was reported in the records was painfully true. Slightly balding and thin, Causey had a pleasant face and a gentle demeanor. On the surface, it looked like he was unaffected by the war. He said the Tigers were a brave unit with a high casualty rate. "They were great soldiers." But when he agreed to an interview in the backyard of his home in Livermore, California, the afternoon sun streaming through the trees, Causey revealed another side. "We did things," he said, "that still bother me to this day." Several Tigers had just been killed when he joined the unit in late September, "and everybody was bloodthirsty at the same time, saying, 'We're going to get them back. We're going to go back there. We're going to even the score.'" For just the short time he was with the Tigers, he described a trail of atrocities in the Central Highlands. One hundred twenty people — Vietnamese — killed, unarmed, with no one knowing if they were the enemy, shot over a period of thirty-three days. "I counted them," he said. "It was all about body count. Our commanders just wanted body count." He described men who were out of control — and leaders who looked the other way. And then he said the words that resonated throughout the reporting process: "I still wonder how some people can sleep thirty years later."

While Sallah was interviewing Causey, Weiss was uncovering more secrets — this time, from the dead. The reporter reached

family members of Sam Ybarra and Ken "Boots" Green —
two Tigers whose names appeared prominently in the records
for war crimes but who were long deceased.

Ybarra's mother, Therlene Ramos, confirmed everything
the reporters needed to know about her son and the allegations
against him. After returning from the war, Ybarra openly talked
to her about killing women and children.

"He was alive," she said, "but he was dead."

He held one wish before he died, she said: to return to
Vietnam and help the people whose lives he had torn apart.
"Something happened to Sam, and he was trying, trying to
make good on what he had done," said Ramos. "He wanted to
help the people. To say he was sorry. But he never made it. He
died before he could do anything." In his last years, Ybarra was
a drug addict and alcoholic who was always ranting about Vietnam. The cops were constantly warning him about public
drinking and disorderly conduct. He tried to spend time with
his two daughters, but in the end was too weak to leave the
house. When he died in 1982 of complications from cirrhosis
of the liver, he weighed ninety-five pounds. He was thirty-six.

In all, Sallah and Weiss reached more than sixty-five Tigers,
some by phone, others by finding where they lived and knocking at their doors. At times, it was frustrating, with many hanging up. Others were taken by surprise but reluctantly talked.
Many had never told these stories to even their closest family
members. Some, such as Douglas Teeters, then fifty-five, had
battled drug and alcohol addiction. A few, such as Floyd
Sawyer, fifty-six, had spent time in prison. Married four times,
former sergeant Ernest Moreland in 1999 had placed the barrel
of a .45 handgun in his mouth and threatened to kill himself.
Knowing he needed help, he walked into a Veterans' Administration hospital in Jacksonville. "My nervous system is overwhelmed by everything," said the fifty-six-year-old veteran. He
suffered flashbacks and insomnia, but he would not talk about
any specific war crimes. "I could still be charged," he said. In
the course of these interviews, Sallah and Weiss began con-

firming what was in the records, and how the atrocities — three decades later — affected the men. Over the course of five telephone interviews, Barry Bowman said he was still haunted by one of the central war crimes in the Tiger Force case: the killing of an elderly man by unit leader James Hawkins. "I was sprayed by pieces of his skull," he said in a telephone interview from his home in Warwick, Rhode Island. Bowman wasn't innocent, either, he confessed. He shot a wounded villager.

When Sallah and Weiss reached Harold Fischer, fifty-four, he was collecting disability after selling used cars for twenty years. Divorced and living in San Antonio, Texas, he still regretted not doing enough to stop the atrocities. "I knew the slaughter of civilians was morally wrong," he said, but he feared retribution from platoon leaders for speaking out. He spent years battling drug and alcohol abuse. "It was my only escape."

All of the Tigers interviewed said they recalled the CID investigation — many worrying they would be dragged into a court-martial. Now living in Salem, Oregon, Teeters said the investigation ruined his life. He said he lost his job after Army agents showed up and flashed their badges at an alarm company where he was a supervisor in Seattle in 1972. "My supervisor was really security minded," he said; his boss was scared about any publicity that would come out. "My life kind of spiraled down after that. I went the other way," he said. "It was the last time I really held a steady, good job."

He still struggles with the memories of soldiers slaughtering unarmed civilians. "I wake up with those sweats, soaking wet, man," he said. "It's not as bad nowadays because I got these pills. I take Zoloft and Triazoline. It knocks me out. That's the only way I'm able to get through this." Sawyer, who performed odd jobs most of his life, spent seven years in prison for beating a man in a barroom fight. "I beat him half to death," said the former combat engineer who currently lives in Washington state. "I got drunk, got into an argument, and went back to Vietnam." Married three times, he said he "drinks a case of beer a night just to sleep. I've tried very hard not to think about Vietnam."

Sallah and Weiss found Bill Carpenter, a former sheriff's deputy, living in Jefferson County, Ohio. Alone and divorced, he has become the self-appointed historian for Tiger Force. He didn't always pay this close attention to his former unit. In fact, during the CID investigation, he and other former platoon members stopped talking to one another. "People were scared," he explained. "Everyone just kind of lost touch for years." During reunions the men began to reconnect, swapping stories about their families, jobs, and war-related disabilities, but there were still two subjects they tried to avoid: the CID probe and their former platoon commander James Hawkins. Even today, that's something not lost on Hawkins. When he was reached by phone at his home near Orlando before the newspaper series was published, he admitted to not being invited to the gatherings. "I know there are some of them who got differences with me," he said.

He even went on to confirm some of the atrocities documented in the records. "Look," he said, "I killed people I had to kill. If they were in a free-fire zone, they were fair game."

Hawkins had volunteered for one more tour in Vietnam after leaving the Tigers, serving as a helicopter pilot and eventually retiring as a major in 1978. He then spent the next two decades as a civilian flight instructor at Fort Rucker, Alabama. Twice, he ran into trouble with the law after retiring to Central Florida: once for shoplifting twenty dollars in goods from a Wal-Mart, another for soliciting an undercover female officer for sex. Neither offense resulted in any jail time.

Bald with a slight paunch, William Doyle still bears a tattoo on his trigger finger — the ace of spades — and lives in a dilapidated farmhouse in Missouri. He criticized the CID investigation, saying no one understood what it was like to fight in Vietnam. "No one had any business looking into Tiger Force," he snarled. Married with five daughters, Doyle said he only did what he had to do to survive while ordering the executions of dozens of unarmed civilians. "If I walked into a village and everyone wasn't lying prostrate on the ground, I shot those standing up," he told Weiss in a series of long, rambling telephone interviews. "If they didn't understand fear, I taught it to them. We were living day to day. We didn't expect to live. No one out there with any brains expected to live. We were surprised to be alive next week. So you did any goddamn thing you felt like doing — especially to stay alive. I'm not saying you give up and die. You struggle to live. But the way to live is to kill, because you don't have to worry about anybody who is dead."

For all those Tigers who bothered to talk to the CID and who now feel guilty about not doing enough to stop the atrocities, he offered his thoughts: "Those sorry sons of bitches. What's the matter with them?"

Doyle admitted to everything, adding that he only had one regret: he didn't kill more Vietnamese.

Sallah and Weiss were anxious to reach the two Tigers who tried to stop the killing, Donald Wood and Gerald Bruner, but were disappointed when they learned the men were deceased. Wood was thirty-six when he suffered a brain aneurysm during his son's soccer game in Findlay, Ohio, and died in 1983. Bruner died of throat cancer in 1997. He was fifty-nine. From conversations with Wood's relatives, including his wife, son, and brother, it became clear that the onetime lieutenant avoided talking about the war. "There were things he saw that clearly bothered him," said his son, John, thirty-two, a bank officer in South Bend, Indiana. "The killing of civilians. But he didn't like to talk about it." Wood only discussed the war after drinking — something he did often — and usually only to fellow vets. One was Henry Benz, a onetime neighbor and now a Pittsburgh public schools administrator. He said Wood mentioned Tiger Force but didn't elaborate. "From what I could tell, he looked at the Vietnamese as people — not stereotypes. He tried to understand them." In the Hancock County Courthouse, Wood was known as a lawyer who took on tough criminal defense cases that many lawyers in the conservative Findlay area wouldn't touch. "He didn't give a damn about what those people thought," said his brother, Jim Wood. "He always told his kids to stick up for the underdog. I always knew there was something driving that, and it may have been his time in Vietnam."

Bruner didn't try to hide his disdain for the way the Tiger leaders treated civilians, relatives recalled. After receiving an honorable discharge from the Army in 1975 as a sergeant, he lived most of his life in Colon, Michigan, spending many years assisting veterans suffering from post-traumatic stress disorder. Before he died, he recorded a tape in 1988 about his tours in Vietnam, recalling the shooting of the farmer by Doyle. In the tape, he condemned the killing. "He wanted it known what happened," said his wife, Karen Bruner. "He could never accept what they did. That's just not the way he was." She said her husband always felt he was forced from the Army for talking in the Tiger Force case. "They were writing him up all the time for being late and really small stuff. He finally gave up and got out."

Of the 120 soldiers who rotated in and out of the forty-five-member platoon during the seven months in question, less than a dozen were killed in combat, records showed. Two were killed in action in 1968: Captain Harold McGaha was killed on January 21, 1968, and Sergeant James Haugh died on March 27, 1968. Sallah and Weiss tried to reach James Barnett, but they found out he died of cancer on August 27, 2001, at the age of fifty-seven. They also learned that Terrence Kerrigan succumbed to cancer and related complications on December 15, 2000, at age fifty-two. Former Tiger team leader Sergeant Manuel Sanchez suffered a heart attack and died on July 15, 1992. He was forty-six. Other Tigers had passed away: James Cogan on July 26, 1993, at forty-five; Ervin Lee in 1977 at thirty; Forrest Miller in 1979 at forty-five; and Benjamin Edge in 1990 at fifty-three.

The key interview would be getting to the top commander: Gerald Morse, the man known as Ghost Rider. His name was all over the records. The reporters tracked him down in Arizona, where he is a well-known senior racquetball player. Morse, seventy-four, who retired from the Army as a colonel in 1979, agreed to a brief interview by phone, insisting he did not know the Tigers committed war crimes. "Not under my watch," he snapped. But when Sallah and Weiss called him several times later to answer more questions, he refused to return the calls. When a *Blade* photographer showed up at his door, his wife peered through the curtains, asking the photojournalist to go away. "He wants to be left alone," she said.

Harold Austin, seventy-three, who retired from the military in 1971, preceded Morse as battalion commander and is now living in Duncanville, Texas. Like Morse, he said he was unaware of serious problems in the unit. "If I knew what was going on, I would have cracked down," he said. "But I don't know if that would have stopped it. When you're not in the field, you have no control over what's going on."

Carl James, sixty-two, the former captain and designated liaison between the Tigers and battalion headquarters, blamed the Tigers for the end of his military career. During a battalion reunion several years ago, he began railing about the investigation into the Tigers. "I told them they held up my promotion for years because of that damn investigation," said James, who lives in suburban Los Angeles. "I got so sick and tired of the Army, by the time I was finally promoted I was ready to get out." He retired from the military in 1980.

In all, Sallah and Weiss successfully interviewed forty-three veterans during the newspaper's investigation, but just talking to the ex-soldiers wasn't going to tell the whole story. Part of the investigation required going to Vietnam. The radio logs of the platoon from the period in question, showing the platoon's movements from day to day, were still on file at the National Archives. Using Army grid maps from 1967, Sallah and Weiss were able to trace the trail of the Tigers.

With the assistance of a translator, the reporters spent sixteen days in the Quang Ngai and Quang Nam (formerly known as Quang Tin) provinces, visiting Quang Ngai City, Duc Pho, and later Tam Ky and the Que Son. They heard plenty about atrocities, but none could be connected to Tiger Force. But when Sallah and Weiss went to the Song Ve Valley, everything changed. Within three days of interviewing elders, the reporters found people who had witnessed three war crimes by the Tigers. Tam Hau, a frail, gray-haired seventy-year-old who was barely able to walk alone, described finding the bloodied body of her uncle, Dao Hue, who was carrying a shoulder bar with buckets at both ends stuffed with geese. Everything she described matched the soldiers' statements. Then there was Nyugen Dam, sixty-six, a rice farmer who watched as the two blind brothers were executed by the Tigers in a rice paddy. The last war crime was recounted by Kieu Trak, seventy-two, who described the assault on the ten elderly farmers — including his father.

With the soldiers on one side of the world and the victims on the other, Sallah and Weiss were now prepared to ask the Pentagon, What happened to this case? During a sweep of records at the National Archives, the reporters discovered that summaries of the Tiger Force investigation were sent in 1973 to the offices of Defense Secretary James Schlesinger and Army Secretary Howard "Bo" Callaway.

Sallah and Weiss called Schlesinger, Callaway, and others who served during that period. Schlesinger refused to return phone messages. Callaway said he didn't remember the case. Through his secretary, President Ford declined to comment on atrocities during the Vietnam War. Schlesinger's successor, Donald Rumsfeld, who was now serving his second stint as defense secretary, this time under President George W. Bush, would not talk about the case, either.

Stumped, the reporters went back to Apsey, who led the investigation, and in a moment of reflection, he broke his silence. "There was no political will," he said. "They didn't want to prosecute." No one had directly told him the case was dead, but when they had shipped him to the CID office north of Seoul a few weeks after filing the final report, he knew why. "They were really concerned about the press finding out. It was a bucket of worms. So it was better that they be done with it. To just end it." Apsey added that after all these years, he felt vindicated. "I can tell you that I have been waiting for this for thirty years," he said. "I always understood that someday this may come up. I am just relieved that it has."

After six months of research, interviews, and a dozen trips to Washington DC and other cities, as well as sixteen days in the Central Highlands of Vietnam, the reporters wrote a four-part series in October 2003 that would eventually prod the Pentagon to reexamine the case. The story would reemerge in the middle of the 2004 presidential campaign as a debate surfaced over whether atrocities occurred in the war — with both candidates forced to revisit their own actions during the conflict. That same year, Sallah, Weiss, and a third reporter who joined the team later, Joe Mahr, were awarded the Pulitzer Prize for Investigative Reporting in recognition of their series on Tiger Force, "Buried Secrets, Brutal Truths."

On the first day of publication of the series, the *Blade* had been flooded with e-mails, letters, and phone calls. At first, most of the messages were negative — critical of the newspaper running such a dark story at a time when the United States was engaged in Iraq. "You are the reason we lost the Vietnam War," read one message. "The *Blade* is the reason why there are 58,000 names on the wall at the Vietnam Veterans Memorial," declared a caller. But by the end of the series, with the former Tigers and the people of the Song Ve Valley interviewed about the impact of the war crimes on their lives, the feedback began to change. "Thank you for telling the truth," wrote one Marine veteran who served in the war. "This is a story that needed to be told." Another said Tiger Force soldiers should be prosecuted. "We were in Vietnam," said one veteran. "We wouldn't have tolerated that."

At first, the Army refused to comment on the series. But eight days later, on October 30, the Army announced that it was reviewing the case because of pressure from the media and calls to the U.S. Embassy in Hanoi. In February 2004, military lawyers began interviewing veterans, including Rion Causey and Dennis Stout, as part of an expanding investigation. Army officials also started poring over the records of the Tiger Force investigation from the 1970s, comparing the information to what was published in the newspaper series. On September 5, 2004, the *Blade* published a story that a military lawyer reviewing the case for the Army recommended that Hawkins be brought back to active service for an Article 32 hearing — the equivalent of a military grand jury — for his actions during the Tiger Force rampage. As of the publication of this book, the Army has still not acted on the recommendation.

Whether the military should press for a hearing nearly four decades later is open to debate, a question better answered by legal scholars and military historians. Perhaps the more critical question with far greater consequences is whether the Army has learned anything from the rampage so many years ago. Whether the Army acknowledges the longest series of atrocities by a U.S. fighting unit in the Vietnam War or continues to bury its past. To do the latter would come at an enormous price. Part of the culture of any military institution is what it has learned and failed to learn from prior mistakes, providing an institutional memory with clear-cut rules and guidance. Covering up war-crime cases such as those of Tiger Force may save the institution from being embarrassed but does little to prevent such cases in the future.

What institutions fail to recognize is that the real consequences are not in the publicity but in the human costs. The tragedy of Tiger Force extends beyond the Vietnamese whose lives were shattered. The soldiers themselves have paid an incredibly deep price — day after day, year after year. "It's in the middle of the night, when the demons come, that you remember, that you can't forget," says Bill Carpenter.

Driven by zealous commanders, many of the Tiger Force soldiers ignored the rules of war. They went berserk. Instead of abiding by what was right, they opened up on unarmed men, women, and children, and almost forty years later, they are still suffering emotionally and spiritually. In the words of Tiger Force sergeant Ernest Moreland, "The things you did, you think back and say, 'I can't believe I did that.' At the time, it seemed right. But now you know what you did was wrong. The killing gets to you. The nightmares get to you. You just can't escape it. You can't escape the past." He said he tries to reconcile his past deeds with his morality today, but in that struggle, he rarely — if ever — finds peace.

So many of the Tiger Force soldiers have been diagnosed with post-traumatic stress disorder. The symptoms include flashbacks and nightmares. But for those who committed atrocities or failed to stop such actions, the condition can be worse. In addition to the trauma, they are often saddled with a strong sense of guilt that can complicate the deeper feelings of fear and isolation. "It's another layer that needs to be addressed," said Dr. Dewleen Baker, director of a PTSD research clinic in Cincinnati. "It's not that easy. How do you reconcile killing civilians? It's hard, especially when you have a core set of values."

In the Tiger Force case, the burden of responsibility has fallen on the soldiers — for now. Their names have been linked to one of the biggest war-crimes cases of the Vietnam War. But so far, the Army has not accepted responsibility and continues to conceal the records.

After the *Blade* broke the story of Tiger Force, the reporters said they hoped the Army would assume responsibility for what happened in the Central Highlands in 1967 so that someday some other newspaper — five, ten, twenty years from now — didn't turn up hidden records from some other series of atrocities committed in Iraq, Afghanistan, or another country. Until the military does so, the dangers of another Tiger Force will always be there.

ACKNOWLEDGMENTS

This book grew out of an investigative newspaper series, "Buried Secrets, Brutal Truths," published in the *Blade* of Toledo, Ohio, and its sister paper, the *Pittsburgh Post-Gazette*, from October 19 through October 22, 2003. As lead reporters on the project, we were granted a nine-month leave of absence to turn the stories into a book just days before the Pulitzer Prize Board recognized our work in the category of investigative reporting. Also sharing in the prize was reporter Joe Mahr, whose effort was invaluable in the stretch.

We want to thank a number of people at the *Blade*, especially publisher John Robinson Block, for allowing us the time to work on this book, and also *Blade* correspondent Michael Woods, whose friendship with Henry Tufts led to the *Blade* acquiring more than twenty-five thousand documents of the Army commander's personal papers — important records that made the newspaper series and book possible.

Much of our work for the *Blade* became the foundation for this book, and to that extent, we would like to thank Mahr, a close friend and colleague who helped track down several former

Tigers for the series. *Blade* editors also supported the newspaper investigation, including executive editor Ron Royhab, managing editor Kurt Franck, assistant managing editor Luann Sharp, state editor Dave Murray, copyeditors Ann Weber and Todd Wetzler, and librarians Mary Mackzum and Vesna Radivojevic.

Special thanks to Doug Koerner and Wes Booher for their insightful graphics, maps, headlines, and first-rate contest presentation of the newspaper series to the Pulitzer Prize Board and jurors. When the pressure was mounting, Doug and Wes stood by us. The same measure of thanks goes to *Blade* legal counsel Fritz Byers.

Kudos to the *Blade*'s photo department, including photographer Andy Morrison, who accompanied us to Vietnam and whose compelling photos of the Tiger Force survivors added a powerful dimension to the series and to this book. Also thanks to *Blade* photo editor Dave Cantor.

We'd also like to express our gratitude to former Army captain Billy Kelly, a Vietnam veteran, for his technical expertise during the writing of this book, and to the numerous Tiger Force members who agreed to be interviewed — however painful the memories. A special debt of gratitude to the families of deceased platoon members Donald Wood and Gerald Bruner — soldiers who risked their lives to stop the atrocities.

We would like to recognize the University of Toledo's College of Arts and Sciences and Department of Communication for granting us office space while we wrote this book, especially the college's former dean, David Stern; communication professors Richard Knecht, Jacqueline Layng, and Paulette Kilmer; and secretary Pat Damschroder.

Undertaking a book project of this magnitude can be frustrating and challenging, but along the way, several colleagues helped boost our morale and inspire us, including *Blade* reporter Larry Vellequette, *Chicago Tribune* reporter Sam Roe, Bowling Green State University journalism professor Melissa Spirek, *Miami Herald* assistant managing editor Manny Garcia, and attorney Gerardo Rollison.

In Vietnam, we were assisted by interpreter Nyugen Minh Nguyet, who joined us for sixteen days in the Central Highlands, and whose precise translations were crucial to understanding the events that transpired nearly four decades ago. A special thanks to the people of the Song Ve Valley for allowing us into their homes and sharing their painful recollections.

We'd like to thank the Collins McCormick Literary Agency, especially PJ Mark, for recognizing the value of the newspaper series just days after publication, and we would also like to express our gratitude to the people at Little, Brown and Company for their editorial support, including Junie Dahn and Karen Landry, and especially Geoff Shandler, our book editor, who truly understood the historical significance of the story and who pushed us to greater heights.

Additionally, a number of journalists deserve mention for seeing the importance of the Tiger Force story and sharing it with the rest of the country, including Seymour Hersh, who penned an article in *The New Yorker;* the late Peter Jennings, Ted Koppel, and veteran producer Jill Rackmill of ABC, who devoted generous segments to the series; and Terence Smith, media correspondent and senior producer for the Public Broadcasting Service's *NewsHour with Jim Lehrer.*

In the end, this work would not have been possible without the dogged persistence of the lead Army investigator who refused to be undermined. Gus Apsey reluctantly talked to us about the case, his loyalty torn at times between the Army he loved and telling the truth about a case that dominated his life for more than three years. He refused to cast aspersions on the Army, even though he was deeply disappointed about the way the case was dismissed without a hearing.

Finally, to our wives, Judi Sallah and Suzyn Weiss, and our children, who were often left on weekends while we wrote the manuscript. Without their love and support, this work would not have been possible.

Michael Sallah and Mitch Weiss
October 2005

NOTES

INTRODUCTION

Main Sources

We talked at length with Gustav Apsey, a Criminal Investigation Command warrant officer and lead investigator in the Tiger Force case. We also interviewed Sam Ybarra's mother, Therlene Ramos; his wife, Janice Little; former reservation police officers; and numerous friends and family members.

For biographical information on Ybarra, we drew on extensive interviews with family members and friends. We also drew on interviews with Tiger Force soldiers and Army documents related to the Tiger Force investigation, known as the Coy Allegation.

Our account of Apsey's visit to Ybarra's home was based on interviews with Apsey, CID agents, and former reservation police officers familiar with the case. We also relied on CID documents about the meeting.

For information about pressure facing the Army in the wake of My Lai, we drew on numerous sources, including newspaper articles, books, and interviews with historians. In addition, we utilized records from the National Archives in College Park, Maryland, and documents from the Colonel Henry Tufts Archive at the University of Michigan in Ann Arbor, Michigan.

Army Records

Sam Ybarra's military personnel record. The file contained a history of Ybarra's military service, including details about his court-martial.

Army psychiatrist Irwin H. Noparstak evaluated Ybarra on March 13, 1969. The evaluation was included in Ybarra's court-martial. The document was Exhibit 456 of the Coy Allegation. It contained the following:

Patient claims he knows exactly what he wants from the Army, and he came to RVN to be in an active Airborne unit. To him he neither wants nor can tolerate the type of unit he is in and the type of work he is doing. Patient feels he is an asset to the Army and is suitable if he is placed where he wants to be placed.

This man makes it very clear that he can be an asset and suitable when put in his niche. He is limited, inflexible, lacking in tact, and with a low frustration tolerance. He seemingly must have what he wants now and cannot procrastinate so as to utilize the means to get to an end. Everything is now. His present unit certainly does not fit his demands or talents. I suspect that if his niche was found, if he were transferred to a more appropriate unit for him, that he could become suitable for the Army. As he stands now in HHB Div Arty, he is not suitable.

The sworn witness statement of Sergeant Buford F. McClure. The document was Exhibit 454 of the Coy Allegation. It included the following:

McCLURE: Since I have known Pvt. Ybarra, approximately two months, he has been a constant problem to not only myself but to the officers and NCOs of this battery. He has also been a bad influence and example to the other men in this unit.

The sworn witness statement of Captain Billy Stafford, who recommended Ybarra's dishonorable discharge. The document was Exhibit 455 of the Coy Allegation. It contained the following:

STAFFORD: He is a very volatile individual and is resentful of any authority. He constantly threatened various noncommissioned officers with bodily harm. The military did not foster such hatred and resentment toward authority. It is my opinion that Pvt. Ybarra should be discharged as an undesirable immediately following his confinement.

The sworn witness statement of Gustav Apsey, who attempted to interview Ybarra on March 20, 1975, and March 21, 1975. The document was Exhibit 22 of the Coy Allegation. It included the following:

APSEY: At 15:30 hours, 20 March 75, the undersigned was advised by Detective Everett Little-Whiteman at the Indian Police Station, San Carlos Apache Indian Reservation, San Carlos, Az., that Ybarra could not be interviewed because he was drunk and passed out in his residence. It was learned that he is drunk beyond his capacity just about every day and is suffering from diabetes and acute cirrhosis of the liver. At 09:30, 21 March 1975, Detective Robert E. Youngdeer related that Ybarra would have to be interviewed at his residence because he refused to come to the police station.

Books
Beattie, Keith. *The Scar That Binds.* New York: New York University Press, 2000.

Bilton, Michael, and Kevin Sim. *Four Hours in My Lai*. New York: Penguin Books, 1992.

Herring, George. *America's Longest War: The United States and Vietnam*. New York: Knopf, 1996.

Karnow, Stanley. *Vietnam: A History*. New York: Viking Press, 1983.

Kimball, Jeffrey. *Nixon's Vietnam War*. Lawrence: University Press of Kansas, 1997.

Kissinger, Henry. *Ending the Vietnam War*. New York: Simon & Schuster, 2003.

Langguth, A. J. *Our Vietnam: The War 1954–1975*. New York: Touchstone, 2000.

Periodicals

Stars and Stripes story in November 1967 about Ybarra killing the one thousandth enemy soldier of Operation Wheeler

CHAPTER 1

Main Sources

We interviewed numerous Tiger Force members, including William Carpenter, Lieutenant Gary Forbes, Ernest Moreland, Joseph Evans, and Douglas Teeters. We talked at length with childhood friends and family members of Sam Ybarra and Ken Green, including Ybarra's mother, Therlene Ramos; Brad Daniels; and Green's Army buddy Leon Fletcher.

For the section about Ybarra's and Green's adolescence in Arizona, we drew on information from numerous friends and family members as well as Tiger Force soldiers. During their tour in Vietnam, Ybarra and Green often talked to others about their "hell-raising days" in Globe and Roosevelt.

For the part about the Mother's Day Massacre, we drew on dozens of interviews with Tiger Force soldiers who fought in the battle, including Forbes and Carpenter. We also relied on information from a duty officer log, the unit history of the 1st Battalion/327th Infantry, maps, and combat records.

Our account of Ybarra convincing Green and Edward Beck to join Tiger Force was based on an interview with Leon Fletcher, who was sitting at the table with the men when they decided to transfer to the platoon.

For the section on the history of Tiger Force, we relied on 1st Battalion/327th Infantry records and documents from the National Archives in College Park, Maryland. For the part about how Tiger Force members were chosen before the Mother's Day Massacre, we drew on extensive interviews with soldiers and officers.

Army Records

The unit history of the 1st Battalion/327th Infantry between January and December 1967. It contained the following information about the Mother's Day Massacre:

On 15 May, the elements of the "Above the Rest" battalion initiated 12 separate contacts. It was the elite Tiger Force that came in contact with the largest size enemy force to date, an estimated VC battalion. The Tiger Force, consisting of 40 men, was enroute to relieve enemy pressure on one of its engaged sub elements at BS702418. At 11:00H, they came under intense enemy fire. The Tigers were in a valley with the enemy in well-constructed fighting positions on the high ground. A tremendous firefight ensued. This elite small group of dedicated young warriors gave no thought to the over-whelming odds and plunged headlong into the battle.

The unit history of the 1st Battalion / 327th Infantry shows commanders cre-ated Tiger Force in November 1965.

Exhibit 63 of the Coy Allegation, which included CID interviews with 1st Battalion / 327th Infantry officers about Tiger Force: "The Tiger Force has killed a substantially larger number of armed insurgents than could be expected from a force its size." "The unit could be counted on to tackle a mission and deliver out-standing results." "The Tiger Force is a fighting unit that is light, highly mobile, and extremely effective against the VC and Main Force units."

Books

Hackworth, David. *About Face: The Odyssey of an American Warrior.* New York: Touchstone, 1990.

Just, Ward. *To What End.* Boston: Houghton Mifflin, 1968.

Karnow, Stanley. *Vietnam: A History.* New York: Viking Press, 1983.

Langguth, A. J. *Our Vietnam: The War 1954–1975.* New York: Touchstone, 2000.

CHAPTER 2

Main Sources

We interviewed numerous Tiger Force soldiers and commanders, including William Carpenter, Douglas Teeters, Harold Trout, William Doyle, Joseph Evans, Ken Kerney, Barry Bowman, Captain Bradford Mutchler, and Lieutenant Colonel Harold Austin. In addition, we interviewed friends and family members of Ter-rence Kerrigan, Manuel Sanchez Jr., and James Barnett.

For information about the unit's chemistry in May and June 1967, we drew on extensive interviews conducted in connection with the *Blade*'s four-day series "Buried Secrets, Brutal Truths." The series ran October 19–22, 2003. We also relied on subsequent interviews in connection with the book. In addition, we drew on statements Tiger Force soldiers made to CID agents during the Army's four-and-a-half-year investigation of the platoon.

For the section on the Central Highlands campaign and the Vietnam War in June 1967, we relied on historical records at the National Archives in College Park, Maryland. We also drew on information from newspaper articles, books, and memos from the MACV.

Our account of General William Westmoreland's visit to the battalion's base camp was based, in part, on interviews with Tiger Force soldiers.

NOTES

Army Records

A unit history of the 1st Battalion/327th Infantry in Quang Ngai. It described the dangers facing soldiers after the battalion arrived in Quang Ngai province in May 1967. It contained the following:

> The area around Duc Pho had been an old Marine stronghold, but very little had been done to conduct operations in the area. The terrain consisted of gentle rolling beaches with prominent hill masses overlooking partially destroyed hamlets. Trails and villages were well fortified with spider holes and prepared positions. Mines and booby traps were frequently encountered, especially along trails, at village entrances, and in hedgerows. The enemy sniper was effectively employed and could disappear quickly without leaving a trace.
>
> The Marines had practically no pacification program, leaving the civilian populace at the mercy of the VC in the area. The few inhabitants that were in the area were VC dominated and lived in constant fear of both VC and friendly units. The area had long been a known enemy infiltration route for supplies and equipment.

The sworn witness statement of battalion surgeon Captain Bradford Mutchler on January 21, 1975. The document was Exhibit 323 of the Coy Allegation. It included the following:

QUESTION: Was the Tiger Force a volunteer force?

MUTCHLER: Yes, for the most part, unless they were hit unusually hard and needed replacements badly. They were also all seasoned combat veterans, both enlisted and officer personnel. The Tiger Force was considered an elite unit within the elite and as such wore a special uniform. They wore soft hats and camouflaged jungle fatigues. There was a great deal of pride within the unit and when an outsider wore their uniform he was told to change it by a member of the Tiger Force.

QUESTION: What was the mission of the TF in comparison with the other line companies in the battalion?

MUTCHLER: They were mainly a recon platoon with search-and-destroy missions. They were given greater leeway while they were on their missions, which was different from the other line companies.

Books

Bilton, Michael, and Kevin Sim. *Four Hours in My Lai.* New York: Penguin Books, 1992.

Fall, Bernard. *Street Without Joy.* Rev. ed. Mechanicsburg: Stackpole, 1994.

Herring, George. *America's Longest War: The United States and Vietnam.* New York: Knopf, 1996.

Karnow, Stanley. *Vietnam: A History.* New York: Viking Press, 1983.

Langguth, A. J. *Our Vietnam: The War 1954–1975.* New York: Touchstone, 2000.

The Pentagon Papers. New York: Bantam Books, 1971.

Schell, Jonathan. *The Military Half.* New York: Knopf, 1968.
Westmoreland, William C. *A Soldier Reports.* New York: Doubleday, 1976.

CHAPTER 3

Main Sources

We interviewed numerous Tiger Force soldiers, including William Carpenter, William Doyle, Joseph Evans, Ken Kerney, and Barry Bowman. We talked at length to Sam Ybarra's mother, Therlene Ramos. We also interviewed friends and family members of Donald Wood, including his wife, Joyce, and brother, Jim. In addition, we talked to Lu Thuan and dozens of Vietnamese villagers who lived in the Song Ve Valley in the summer of 1967.

For information about Tiger Force's first two months in Quang Ngai province, we drew on numerous interviews with platoon soldiers. We also drew on sworn statements that the soldiers gave to CID agents during the Coy Allegation. In addition, we examined the duty officer log and unit history of the 1st Battalion/ 327th Infantry.

For biographical information about Donald Wood, we drew on information from his friends and family. Our account of Tiger Force members killing a mother and child during a firefight was based, in part, on interviews with Carpenter, who was on Wood's team.

For the section about the Struggle Movement and the South Vietnamese pacification programs, we relied on books, newspaper articles, and interviews with historians.

Our account of the evacuation of the Song Ve Valley was based on interviews with soldiers and Vietnamese civilians. In addition, we drew on Army documents from the National Archives in College Park, Maryland, and the unit history of the 1st Battalion/327th Infantry.

Army Records

"The Nine Rules of War," a card handed to U.S. soldiers on the importance of treating civilians with respect.

U.S. military instruction cards on how to properly handle prisoners of war and civilian detainees.

Directives from the U.S. military defining eighteen war crimes mirroring the prohibitions of the Geneva conventions. All soldiers were required to immediately report war crimes to a commander.

Books

Bilton, Michael, and Kevin Sim. *Four Hours in My Lai.* New York: Penguin Books, 1992.
Fall, Bernard. *Street Without Joy.* Rev. ed. Mechanicsburg: Stackpole, 1994.
Karnow, Stanley. *Vietnam: A History.* New York: Viking Press, 1983.

Schell, Jonathan. *The Military Half*. New York: Knopf, 1968.
Topmiller, Robert J. *The Lotus Unleashed: The Buddhist Peace Movement in South Vietnam 1964–1966*. Lexington: University Press of Kentucky, 2002.

CHAPTER 4

Main Sources

We interviewed numerous Tiger Force members, including William Carpenter. We also talked to the friends and family members of Donald Wood, including his wife, Joyce, and brother, Jim. In addition, we talked at length with Lu Thuan and numerous Vietnamese villagers.

For information about relocation camps, particularly Nghia Hanh, we drew on extensive interviews with villagers who lived in Quang Ngai province in the 1960s. These included interviews with villagers forced to move to Nghia Hanh.

Our account about the Army moving civilians from the Song Ve Valley to Nghia Hanh was based on interviews with Tiger Force soldiers and historians, books, newspaper articles, and military records, including the unit history of the 1st Battalion/327th Infantry.

For the section about Lieutenant Colonel Harold Austin's relationship with Tiger Force, we drew on interviews with platoon members, Austin, and documents related to the CID's investigation of the platoon.

Army Records

A June 1967 news release from the 101st Airborne about the cattle drive.

The unit history of the 1st Battalion/327th Infantry, which included the following:

> At 1150H, 21 June, the battalion entered into Operation Rawhide. The Cobra Cowboys received 2 herds (BS612559), one from the 2nd Battalion (Airborne)/502nd Infantry and one from the 2nd Battalion (Airborne)/327th Infantry. The herds totaled 846 cattle and 125 water buffalo. The Cobra Cowboys drove the herd northeast toward a point where it would be picked up by the Nghia Hanh District Chief the following morning. Everything went smoothly and all precautions were taken to protect the herd from VC rustlers.

Books

Bilton, Michael, and Kevin Sim. *Four Hours in My Lai*. New York: Penguin Books, 1992.
Karnow, Stanley. *Vietnam: A History*. New York: Viking Press, 1983.
The Pentagon Papers. New York: Bantam Books, 1971.
Schell, Jonathan. *The Military Half*. New York: Knopf, 1968.
Topmiller, Robert J. *The Lotus Unleashed: The Buddhist Peace Movement in South Vietnam 1964–1966*. Lexington: University Press of Kentucky, 2002.

CHAPTER 5

Main Sources

We interviewed numerous Tiger Force soldiers, including William Carpenter, Ken Kerney, and Barry Bowman. In addition, we talked to family members of Manuel Sanchez Jr. and James Barnett. We also talked to dozens of Vietnamese who lived in the Song Ve Valley in 1967.

Our account of Ybarra killing the teenager and severing his ears was based on interviews with Carpenter as well as CID records related to the Tiger Force investigation. Many platoon members said Tiger Force wasn't the only fighting unit in Vietnam severing ears from dead enemy soldiers. But former medic Barry Bowman said, "Cutting off ears was a rite of passage in Tiger Force. When I was a cherry medic, they actually took little plastic bags out and showed me the ears. Those were like notches cut on your six-gun in the era of the Old Wild West. Cutting off ears was a way of showing you belonged in the unit." As Tiger Force medic Larry Cottingham told CID investigators in 1973, "There was a period when just about everyone had a necklace of ears."

We based the section about Barnett's altercation with Sanchez on interviews with soldiers and CID records.

Army Records

The sworn witness statement of Sergeant Benjamin Edge on January 18, 1974. The document was Exhibit 69 of the Coy Allegation. It included the following information about Ybarra killing the teenager:

QUESTION: Was the man shot by Ybarra armed with any type of weapon?

EDGE: After making a check of the immediate area around where he had run from and where he laid, we could not find a weapon.

The duty officer log and unit history of the 1st Battalion/327th Infantry.

The sworn witness statement of William Carpenter on January 18, 1973. The document was Exhibit 23 of the Coy Allegation. It included the following information:

CARPENTER: We were nearing a hillside in the Song Ve Valley while walking on a foot trail when Ybarra fired his M16 twice. As soon as we heard the shots we took defensive positions, then Sgt. Edge and I went over to Ybarra, who was kneeling over a Vietnamese boy. The body had blood all over its head and a large portion of the head was missing as a result of being shot twice by Ybarra. As I got to Ybarra, he was holding a hunting knife in one hand and a human ear in his other hand. While I was watching, I saw Ybarra cut the remaining ear from the dead body. Ybarra put both of these ears into a ration bag that he had taken from his jacket pocket. While he opened his ration bag, I could see that there were several human ears in it also. Ybarra replaced the bag of ears into his pocket just as calmly as he removed it.

QUESTION: Why was Ybarra permitted to cut this boy's ears off?
CARPENTER: Cutting the ears off of the dead was an accepted practice
within the Tiger Force. By accepted practice, I mean it was accepted by the
men in the field that were actually doing the fighting.

Books

Bilton, Michael, and Kevin Sim. *Four Hours in My Lai.* New York: Penguin Books,
1992.
Karnow, Stanley. *Vietnam: A History.* New York: Viking Press, 1983.
Langguth, A. J. *Our Vietnam: The War 1954–1975.* New York: Touchstone, 2000.
The Pentagon Papers. New York: Bantam Books, 1971.
Schell, Jonathan. *The Military Half.* New York: Knopf, 1968.
The Winter Soldier Investigation: An Inquiry into American War Crimes. Boston: Beacon
Press, 1972.

CHAPTER 6

Main Sources

We interviewed Dennis Stout — a military journalist who witnessed atrocities
committed by Tiger Force soldiers — and other troops from the 1st Battalion/
327th Infantry. We also talked at length with numerous Tiger Force soldiers, including those who served in Quang Ngai province in May and June 1967. In
addition, we interviewed friends and family members of Donald Wood, Sam
Ybarra, Kenneth Green, and James Barnett.

For information about Quang Ngai province and conditions at relocation
camps, we drew on military records at the National Archives in College Park,
Maryland. We also drew on numerous interviews with villagers who lived in the
province in the 1960s, including Nyugen Dam, Lu Thuan, Tam Hau, and Vo
Thanh Tien. It's interesting to note that when Vo Thanh Tien escaped from Nghia
Hanh in 1971, he joined the Vietcong: "The mistreatment of civilians — the lack
of food, poor conditions, and beatings from soldiers forced many people to flee.
We were treated so poorly we had no choice but to join the other side."

For the section on the history of Tiger Force, we drew on historical and military documents and interviews, including interviews with soldiers and officers who
served in the unit in 1965 and 1966.

For the section about Ybarra and Green killing the NVA solider, we drew on
interviews with soldiers. Some Tiger Force members told us that they saw the scalp
braided on the end of Ybarra's M16. They also said they heard Ybarra and Green
brag about the killing.

Army Records

Duty officer log of November 23, 1965. It contained the first reference of Tiger
Force's whereabouts in the field: "Tiger Force (relay): 300 meters north of the
objective recon area by sight. Neg contact."

The unit history of the 1st Battalion/327th Infantry in 1965. It included one of the first references of Tiger Force in combat. The following appeared on page 28:

Phase I commenced at 121155H December 1965. TF 1/327 conducted a helimobile assault on LZ Sierra. The assault consisted of two lifts of 40 UH-1D helicopters and Companies A and B (1st lift) securing of the LZ at 121217H meeting no resistance. The second lift consisting of Company C and Tiger Force (a composite unit made up of elements of the Recon, AT, and Mortar Platoons of HHC) touched down at 1215H and received small arms fire from the wooded western portion of the LZ.

The sworn witness statement of William Carpenter on January 18, 1973. The document was Exhibit 23 of the Coy Allegation. It included the following:

CARPENTER: This LTC came to the field in his chopper. I know his call sign was Night Rider. He called us a bunch of barbarians and just chewed us out for stealing money from the Vietnamese. To my knowledge this LTC didn't know anything about the mutilations going on in the Tiger Force. The day he came down he had the Vietnamese woman with him and she pointed out the man that took her money and the LTC made him return it to her. I'm almost sure it was Barnett who took the money.

CARPENTER: The next morning my team left the village for a patrol mission, for some reason Ybarra did not accompany the team on that particular patrol. When we returned to the village, I found a dead North Vietnamese soldier in my position in the village. This North Vietnamese had its throat cut from ear to ear. Ybarra and SP4 Kenneth Green were standing near me at the time and were laughing. Ybarra explained to me that he and Green had found this North Vietnamese hiding after my patrol left. Ybarra said he and Green brought the North Vietnamese into the village and killed him by cutting his throat. Ybarra specifically said, "I cut his throat."

CARPENTER: There was another incident involving a very large prisoner, he was about six feet tall, a Chinese, I think. This was in May 1967, around the time when Hatten was killed (6 May 67). We had taken the guy prisoner and he had some explosives with him, either tied to his body or in a bag that he was carrying. The guys took the explosives and were going to blow the guy up, but someone said we'd get into trouble if the guy was mutilated, the guys there then started beating the prisoner and told him to *Didi,* when the guy ran away, he hollered something that the interpreter said was "Long Live Ho Chi Minh" and the guys shot him. I saw the dead body just after that, also, I had seen the man alive too.

Books

Fall, Bernard. *Street Without Joy.* Rev. ed. Mechanicsburg: Stackpole, 1994.

Hackworth, David. *About Face: The Odyssey of an American Warrior.* New York: Touchstone, 1990.

Herring, George. *America's Longest War: The United States and Vietnam.* New York: Knopf, 1996.

Just, Ward. *To What End*. Boston: Houghton Mifflin, 1968.

Karnow, Stanley. *Vietnam: A History*. New York: Viking Press, 1983.

Langguth, A. J. *Our Vietnam: The War 1954–1975*. New York: Touchstone, 2000.

The Pentagon Papers. New York: Bantam Books, 1971.

Schell, Jonathan. *The Military Half*. New York: Knopf, 1968.

Topmiller, Robert J. *The Lotus Unleashed: The Buddhist Peace Movement in South Vietnam 1964–1966*. Lexington: University Press of Kentucky, 2002.

Periodicals

Several editions of *Stars and Stripes* and *Diplomat & Warrior* published in 1967

CHAPTER 7

Main Sources

We interviewed Dennis Stout, a military journalist who watched Tiger Force soldiers kill unarmed civilians in the Song Ve Valley. We talked at length with numerous Tiger Force members who served with the fighting unit in 1967. In addition, we interviewed dozens of Vietnamese villagers who lived in Quang Ngai province and the Song Ve Valley in the summer of 1967.

For information about civilians fleeing to the foothills encircling the Song Ve Valley, we drew on dozens of interviews with Vietnamese villagers, including Lu Thuan. They provided us with extensive details about how they survived. They talked about how they moved along the rough terrain — mountains, ridges, and jungles — without being detected by U.S. troops, Vietcong, or North Vietnamese Army regulars.

For the section about U.S. policy in Vietnam, and the Central Highlands in particular, we relied on numerous historical and Army records from the National Archives in College Park, Maryland.

Our account of the execution of two men holding the Chieu Hoi leaflets was based, in part, on interviews with Dennis Stout, who accompanied Tiger Force soldiers on several missions in June and July 1967.

For the section on free-fire zones, we drew on Army documents. In addition, we interviewed numerous military experts and historians about free-fire zones.

Army Records

Documents from an investigation known as the Stout Allegation. It contained the following information: "Stout alleged witnessing and being informed of numerous atrocities perpetrated by members of his unit in RVN," including "rape, mutilation, and torture of the enemy, murder, and other indiscriminate acts."

Maps of Tiger Force's operational movements in Quang Ngai province in late June 1967. They included Exhibit 447 of the Coy Allegation.

Radio logs with grid coordinates showing Tiger Force's daily combat activities in the province. The documents included Exhibit 438 of the Coy Allegation.

NOTES

Books

Bilton, Michael, and Kevin Sim. *Four Hours in My Lai.* New York: Penguin Books, 1992.

Fall, Bernard. *Street Without Joy.* Rev. ed. Mechanicsburg: Stackpole, 1994.

Karnow, Stanley. *Vietnam: A History.* New York: Viking Press, 1983.

Schell, Jonathan. *The Military Half.* New York: Knopf, 1968.

Topmiller, Robert J. *The Lotus Unleashed: The Buddhist Peace Movement in South Vietnam 1964–1966.* Lexington: University Press of Kentucky, 2002.

The Winter Soldier Investigation: An Inquiry into American War Crimes. Boston: Beacon Press, 1972.

CHAPTER 8

Main Sources

Interviews with numerous Tiger Force members who participated in the Song Ve Valley campaign, including William Carpenter, Barry Bowman, and Ken Kerney. We also interviewed friends and family members of Donald Wood. We talked at length with Vietnamese villagers, including Tam Hau and Bui Quang Truong.

For information about James Hawkins, we drew on an interview with the former Tiger Force platoon leader, as well as with childhood friends. We also interviewed Tiger Force soldiers who served with Hawkins during his stint as platoon commander. In addition, we examined Hawkins's military personnel records. Other information about Hawkins came from CID records related to the Tiger Force investigation.

For information about the Tiger Force mission in the Song Ve Valley, we depended on extensive Army records and numerous interviews with soldiers. Some of the information was included in the unit history of the 1st Battalion/327th Infantry — documents detailing the battalion's operations in Quang Ngai province.

For the section about the death of Dao Hue, we drew on numerous conversations with Tiger Force members and witness statements from the Coy Allegation. We also used Army grid maps to track the platoon's daily movements through the Song Ve Valley.

Army Records

The sworn witness statement of Stephen Naughton on January 17, 1974. The document was Exhibit 123 of the Coy Allegation. It contained the following:

QUESTION: Did you accompany Hawkins on any Tiger Force missions either prior or after his assuming the position of commander?
NAUGHTON: No, I did not. I only gave him a briefing and then I departed on 2 July 67, when Hawkins assumed duties as the commander of the Tiger Force platoon.

The sworn witness statement of Leo Heaney on February 13, 1973. The docu-

3333

ment was Exhibit 25 of the Coy Allegation. It contained the following about the death of Dao Hue:

HEANEY: Prior to this incident, we had occupied a small village along the west bank of the Song Ve River. On the evening of the night move, we received a supply of beer and soda in two duffel bags. The beer and soda was consumed by and I recall Hawkins, SSG Trout, the platoon sergeant, and an SSG Miller, who was a medic, getting loud and I believe boisterous, as a result of the beer consumption.

After Tiger Force crossed the river on the night patrol:

HEANEY: About that time, an old Vietnamese male carrying a pole with two baskets over his shoulder bumped into me. He had come down the trail from the direction the firing had come from. I grabbed hold of him. He was terrified and folded his hands and started what appeared to me as praying for mercy in a loud, high-pitched tone of voice. About this time, we also detected movement on the trail further down from the direction this old man came from. I then released the old man to the CP element further up the trail. There the old man continued his screaming, and Trout struck him on the head with the barrel of his M16 rifle. I left him with Trout and returned to my position because I was concerned about the movement we had heard behind the old man. About two minutes later, I heard a couple of rounds fired from the CP location where I had left the old man with Trout. I assumed that the prisoner had been shot because he stopped screaming. I walked back to the CP element and asked somebody there what had happened and someone answered that the old man had tried to escape. I saw the body on the ground and figured that he was dead. I mentioned the fact that he was a harmless old man and Hawkins said something to the effect "If I want your opinion, I'll ask for it."

The sworn witness statement of Barry Bowman on May 31, 1973. The document was Exhibit 41 of the Coy Allegation. It contained the following exchange:
QUESTION: Did Hawkins have any justification to kill that old man?
BOWMAN: No.

The sworn witness statement of Bill Carpenter on January 18, 1973. The document was Exhibit 23 of the Coy Allegation. It contained the following about the events leading up to the death of Dao Hue:

CARPENTER: Just after we crossed (waded) the river we came upon a footpath, very near the river. As soon as we got to this path, there was an old Vietnamese farmer about 60 years old. I believe he was carrying two chickens in a wire cage. Lt. Hawkins confronted this Vietnamese and started shaking the old man, yelling at him, telling him he was a son-of-a-bitch and generally cussing him. While Hawkins was talking to this Vietnamese farmer, SSG Trout struck him over the head with the barrel of his M16. I saw the old man fall to the ground and at that time his head was covered with blood. I was standing on Hawkins's left side by that time. I told

Hawkins that the old man was just a farmer and was unarmed, right then Hawkins pushed me away with his left hand saying, "You chicken-shit son-of-a-bitch, if you don't shut up I'll shoot you." With that statement, Hawkins pulled the old man up from where he was kneeling and shot him in the face with a CAR-15 that he (Hawkins) was carrying. The old man fell backwards onto the ground, then Hawkins shot him again.

The sworn witness statement of Tiger Force Sergeant Ervin Lee on January 31, 1973. The document was Exhibit 40 of the Coy Allegation.

The sworn witness statement of Forrest Lee Miller on January 18, 1974. The document was Exhibit 54 of the Coy Allegation. It included the following about the night of Dao Hue's death:

MILLER: I was at the rear of the element, and as I came up over a small bank, I observed an elderly Vietnamese who was dead and appeared, by the way he was lying, to have been thrown into the bushes.

Earlier that night:

MILLER: We had faced resistance prior to this night in this same area and everyone, including myself, were pretty well uptight. As we moved along the trail, we stopped about 100 meters from where the Vietnamese was, and as I remember, there was a disagreement between Trout and Hawkins, and words were spoken about the dead Vietnamese on the trail. I don't remember what it was about, but as I remember, there was an unpleasant atmosphere in the air. As I think back, Hawkins was pretty high at the time, we had received beer on the afternoon, and Hawkins got a few beers in him and decided to make a night move.

QUESTION: You mentioned earlier that you felt that Hawkins was high on this patrol. Can you tell me more about this, and why you feel that he was high?

MILLER: This was our first night move. We had never made a night move before. He was acting funny, more brave than he actually was, and we had received beer on that afternoon. We learned later that Hawkins could not hold his beer.

The sworn witness statement of Manuel Sanchez Jr. on January 28, 1974. The document was Exhibit 57 of the Coy Allegation. It included the following about Dao Hue's execution:

SANCHEZ: As far as I could see he had no weapons and offered no resistance. I looked back, after I passed him back, and I saw a group cluster around him. The old man was making quite a bit of noise at this time. It was dark, so I couldn't see who was doing what, but about five minutes later, I saw a rifle come up, point at the man's body, fired, then drop from sight again. Then the old man fell to the ground.

The sworn witness statement of Donald Wood on January 22, 1974. The document was Exhibit 45 of the Coy Allegation.

NOTES

Books

Schell, Jonathan. *The Military Half.* New York: Knopf, 1968.

Topmiller, Robert J. *The Lotus Unleashed: The Buddhist Peace Movement in South Vietnam 1964–1966.* Lexington: University Press of Kentucky, 2002.

CHAPTER 9

Main Sources

We talked at length with numerous Tiger Force soldiers, including Barry Bowman, William Carpenter, William Doyle, Ken Kerney, and Douglas Teeters. We interviewed Donald Wood's friends and family members.

For the section about Tiger Force shooting two elderly women as they approached a perimeter, we drew on interviews with platoon members and CID documents related to the Tiger Force investigation.

For the section about Tiger Force members rounding up and executing villagers, we drew on extensive interviews with Dennis Stout, an Army journalist, and others. In an interview, William Doyle refused to comment about Stout's allegations. "I'm not going to say whether it happened. I'd be an idiot," Doyle told us. "But if I gave the order to kill those people, it was to keep my men alive. You don't have to worry about the dead. You know what I mean. Those damn people were farmers by day and VC at night."

Our account of Sergeant Harold Trout executing a wounded Vietnamese male was based on interviews with Barry Bowman and William Carpenter, along with CID documents related to the Tiger Force case.

Army Records

The sworn witness statement of Donald Wood on January 22, 1974. The document was Exhibit 45 of the Coy Allegation. It contained the following about two Vietnamese women shot by Tiger Force soldiers:

> WOOD: About two weeks after the first incident, we were in a perimeter on the edge of the same small village west of Duc Pho. A perimeter guard whom I cannot identify saw two persons approaching the village from our front. As I arrived at the edge of the perimeter, Hawkins arrived at the same time and ordered the perimeter guards to open fire. I countered Hawkins's order, stating that the two individuals were approaching our location directly. Hawkins overruled my order and opened fire himself and was then joined by the guards on that side of the perimeter. Both of the individuals fired on were old women. One was wounded and they were both evacuated to battalion.

The sworn witness statement of Barry Bowman on May 31, 1973. The document was Exhibit 41 of the Coy Allegation.

The sworn witness statement of William Carpenter on January 18, 1973. The document was Exhibit 23 of the Coy Allegation. It included the following:

CARPENTER: I had just fallen asleep when I heard several shots. I woke up and could hear someone calling for a medic, a Vietnamese civilian male had approached the village where we were and some of the positions fired at him. The man was wounded in the leg and needed help. Just after someone yelled for a medic, Sgt. Trout hollered that he would administer first aid. Trout took Bowman's .45 pistol and walked about 50 feet to the wounded Vietnamese and shot him twice in the chest and once in the head. Trout then drug [*sic*] the dead man to a fairly large hole in the ground a few feet away and rolled the dead Vietnamese into it.

Books

Bilton, Michael, and Kevin Sim. *Four Hours in My Lai*. New York: Penguin Books, 1992.

Schell, Jonathan. *The Military Half*. New York: Knopf, 1968.

The Winter Soldier Investigation: An Inquiry into American War Crimes. Boston: Beacon Press, 1972.

CHAPTER 10

Main Sources

We talked at length with numerous Vietnamese who refused to go to Nghia Hanh. We conducted extensive interviews with Tiger Force members, including William Carpenter, Barry Bowman, and Ken Kerney, about the Song Ve campaign in late July 1967. We interviewed friends and family members of both Manuel Sanchez Jr. and Donald Wood. We also obtained maps Wood saved from his tour of duty.

For the section about the attacks on Tiger Force in the Song Ve Valley, including the death of Sergeant Domingo Munoz, we relied on extensive interviews with platoon members. We also drew on Army documents, including the unit history of the 1st Battalion/327th Infantry and radio logs — documents showing Tiger Force's daily movements in the Song Ve.

For the section about Lieutenant James Hawkins's leadership, we drew on extensive interviews with Tiger Force members. Most of the soldiers claimed Hawkins constantly led them into dangerous situations because of his inability to read Army grid maps.

Our account of the death of the two visually impaired men in the Song Ve and the execution of two brothers by unknown Tiger Force members was based on lengthy interviews with platoon members and CID documents related to the Tiger Force investigation.

For the section on Tiger Force members discussing atrocities, we drew on numerous interviews with platoon members who served in the Song Ve. Many told us there was a point where soldiers openly began talking — and even joking — about killing prisoners and civilians. During the CID investigation — which took place between 1971 and 1975 — agents substantiated several of the war crimes mentioned in the chapter. They included Terrence Kerrigan following Trout's order to execute a prisoner, Green torturing and stabbing a prisoner with a knife, and Sergeant Robin Varney killing a detainee after he lost a bet with a fellow Tiger about knocking the man out with one punch.

Army Records

First Battalion/327th Infantry radio logs, which show Tiger Force's daily movements in the Song Ve Valley. The unit had to radio battalion headquarters after contact with enemy soldiers. The logs also showed the platoon's location — known as "grid coordinates" — at the time of contact. The radio log on the day Sergeant Domingo Munoz died contained the following: "At BS704568 Tiger Force was probed by 5 VC resulting in 4 VC KIA, fired M-79 rounds, resulting in US KIA and 2 US WIA."

The unit history of the 1st Battalion/327th Infantry contained information about the battalion's mission and contact with the enemy. The following was related to Munoz's death: "The following night the Tiger position was probed. This time, the Force retaliated with swift and deadly accuracy. Of the 5 VC probing the position, 4 were killed and 2 M-1 carbines and 1 MAT-49 were captured."

The sworn witness statement of Tiger Force medic Forrest Miller on January 18, 1974. The document was Exhibit 54 of the Coy Allegation. It included the following:

MILLER: Early that same morning, a young boy about 12 years old was found in the area, leading his two blind brothers around by the hand. The two blind boys were killed, and the boy was dusted off in a helicopter to the rear. I did not see who killed the two blind boys, but I did see the helicopter leave with only the young boy on it.
QUESTION: Do you know who killed the two blind boys?
MILLER: I do not know who did the actual shooting, but the order would have come from Hawkins or Doyle.
QUESTION: Do you feel that these personnel were doing anything that would have warranted their death rather than their removal to a rear area?
MILLER: Other than the fact that they were there, no.

The sworn statement of Manuel Sanchez Jr. on January 28, 1974. The document was Exhibit 57 of the Coy Allegation. It contained the following:

SANCHEZ: We saw two Vietnamese males running across a rice paddy, away from us. We yelled for them to stop, but they didn't. So I told our people not to fire and we started chasing them. There were several of us that chased them down and caught them. We brought them back to this knoll where we had stopped and turned them over to our Vietnamese interpreter. The prisoners were a man about 25 years old and a boy about 13–14. They both had regular village dress on.
Sanchez said he called battalion headquarters about the prisoners:
SANCHEZ: The response came back: "What do you do with a horse with a broken leg?" I didn't actually hear the transmission but a few minutes after the interpreter was done, someone, I don't know who, came over to me

and, in a joking manner, told me about the transmission that was received. Also, this same individual told me that this same Lt. or Capt. I mentioned earlier had told him and someone else to take the prisoners down the hill and take care of them. I went with the guy and several others down the hill, with the prisoners, and after we got to the bottom, the prisoners were stood side by side. Then, two of the guys shot the prisoners with their M16s. At the time of the shooting, the prisoners were not tied and the men who did the shooting were about five or six feet away from them. I then turned around and walked back up the hill.

QUESTION: Would you describe the terrain where this took place?

SANCHEZ: I believe this was the Song Ve Valley. It's the valley where everything happened to us.

Books

Bilton, Michael, and Kevin Sim. *Four Hours in My Lai.* New York: Penguin Books, 1992.

The Pentagon Papers. New York: Bantam Books, 1971.

Schell, Jonathan. *The Military Half.* New York: Knopf, 1968.

The Winter Soldier Investigation: An Inquiry into American War Crimes. Boston: Beacon Press, 1972.

CHAPTER 11

Main Sources

We interviewed Lu Thuan; Nyugen Dam; Kieu Trak and his wife, Mai Thi Tai; and dozens of villagers who lived in the Song Ve Valley during the summer of 1967. We talked at length with numerous Tiger Force members, including William Carpenter, Barry Bowman, Ken Kerney, and Douglas Teeters.

For the section about the shooting of the farmers, we drew on extensive interviews with numerous Tiger Force members and Vietnamese witnesses, and CID documents from the Tiger Force case. Kieu Trak said soldiers opened fire without warning. Tiger Force members told us they were frustrated and "out for revenge" after weeks of being hit by snipers in the Song Ve Valley.

Army Records

The sworn witness statement of Tiger Force medic Forrest Miller on January 18, 1974. The document was Exhibit 54 of the Coy Allegation. It included the following:

QUESTION: In June/July 1967, do you remember entering a hamlet where several Vietnamese working in a field were shot just outside the hamlet?

MILLER: Yes, this was near Duc Pho to the west, in the Song Ve Valley. We had received no incoming fire from the village, and the people in the field, about 10 persons both male and female, were shot. We never went out to the field to see if they were armed. Also killed were several water buffalo. I remember this well because we were held over in that area an extra week and the odor was unbearable.

QUESTION: Who gave the order to shoot the people in the field?

MILLER: It would have been either Hawkins or Trout who initiated the order, but the persons were shot by mutual agreement of the element.

The sworn witness statement of William Carpenter on January 18, 1973. The document was Exhibit 23 of the Coy Allegation. It contained the following:

QUESTION: Was Tiger Force ever given orders to the effect "Kill everything that moves?"

CARPENTER: Yes. Lt. Hawkins has given that order to the Tiger Force. I recall one incident in the area of the village where Ybarra killed and scalped the NVA in June/July 67, when we were walking into an inhabited hamlet that had several Vietnamese farmers, men and women, they were on our right flank, the lead element of this platoon came under fire from the front and Hawkins had the platoon shoot all of the farmers on our flank. We killed about ten of the farmers then stopped firing. The enemy on our front had departed, leaving several pieces of ammo and canteens behind in their position. We moved into the village and set up camp after that, nothing was done about shooting the farmers. No one went to see if the farmers had weapons or not. We knew the farmers were not armed to begin with but shot them anyway because Hawkins ordered it.

QUESTION: Who was there during this incident?

CARPENTER: The whole Tiger Force platoon, everyone that wasn't KIA'd or hospitalized.

The sworn witness statement of Michael Allums on January 17, 1974. The document was Exhibit 16 of the Coy Allegation. It included the following:

QUESTION: About the same period, July 1967, in an area west of Duc Pho, do you have any knowledge of Tiger Force members firing on some farmers that were working outside a hamlet?

ALLUMS: I'm not sure if this is the same incident, but I remember walking along a trail and some people being to our right flank. The people started to run from where they had been working in the field and the order was passed to open fire. I remember the incident so well as I was really put down and I did not open fire with an M79 I was carrying.

Books

Karnow, Stanley. *Vietnam: A History*. New York: Viking Press, 1983.

Schell, Jonathan. *The Military Half*. New York: Knopf, 1968.

The Winter Soldier Investigation: An Inquiry into American War Crimes. Boston: Beacon Press, 1972.

CHAPTER 12

Main Sources

We interviewed numerous Tiger Force members about the last days of the Song Ve Valley campaign, including William Carpenter, Barry Bowman, and Ken Kerney. We drew on interviews with Dennis Stout and the friends and family of Donald Wood. In addition, we talked at length to dozens of villagers from the Song Ve, including Nyugen Dam, Lu Thuan, and Kieu Trak.

For the section on the defoliation of the Song Ve Valley, we relied on the unit history of the 1st Battalion/327th Infantry and historical records about the defoliation in South Vietnam during 1967. We also drew on the interviews with Nyugen Dam and numerous villagers who recounted how they became sick shortly after U.S. planes sprayed the valley with defoliants.

Our account of the meeting between Lieutenant Donald Wood and Lieutenant Stephen Naughton was based, in part, on CID documents included in the Tiger Force case. Wood was clearly upset by the platoon's behavior in the field and reported the misconduct to Naughton, who was his supervisor. During the CID investigation, Wood told agents he complained to Naughton and a high-ranking battalion officer. Wood said he couldn't remember the officer's name. Officers were always rotating out of the 1st Battalion/327th Infantry. At any given time, there were more than twenty battalion officers stationed at Duc Pho.

Dennis Stout provided us with the perspective of his last days in Vietnam. By the end of July, Stout was disillusioned with the war and the Army's command structure. He said he witnessed atrocities in the field but was ostracized for reporting them. He said he promised himself he would collect as much evidence about the atrocities as he could — including locations and names of soldiers who committed the crimes — so he could report them when he was discharged from the Army.

Army Records

The sworn witness statement of Donald Wood on January 22, 1974. The document was Exhibit 45 of the Coy Allegation. It included the following:

> WOOD: A few days later, after we returned to Duc Pho, I discussed the incident with the battalion XO whom I cannot identify and was advised to return to my duties with the unit. After working with the Tiger Force for another mission which lasted several weeks, I was able to obtain a transfer and finished my tour with other units in the battalion.

The sworn witness statement of CID agent James Alexander on February 5, 1975. Alexander interviewed Naughton about Tiger Force and Wood's complaint. The document was Exhibit 124 of the Coy Allegation.

Books

Bilton, Michael, and Kevin Sim. *Four Hours in My Lai*. New York: Penguin Books, 1992.

Karnow, Stanley. *Vietnam: A History*. New York: Viking Press, 1983.

The Pentagon Papers. New York: Bantam Books, 1971.

Schell, Jonathan. *The Military Half.* New York: Knopf, 1968.

Topmiller, Robert J. *The Lotus Unleashed: The Buddhist Peace Movement in South Vietnam 1964–1966.* Lexington: University Press of Kentucky, 2002.

CHAPTER 13

Main Sources

We talked at length with numerous Tiger Force members about the move to Chu Lai and their early days in Quang Tin province. We interviewed dozens of Vietnamese who lived in Quang Tin in August 1967, including Colonel Nguyen Thai, a Vietcong soldier who set up ambushes against U.S. troops in the province.

For the section about the terrain of Quang Tin province, we drew on extensive interviews with Tiger Force soldiers and the Vietnamese people. Tiger Force soldiers told us that the terrain in Quang Tin was covered with triple-canopy jungles — so thick it was often difficult to see more than a few meters ahead.

For other parts of the chapter, particularly the historical context of the Vietnam War in July and August 1967, we drew on several books, newspaper articles, and interviews with historians. We also relied on the unit history of the 1st Battalion/327th Infantry, which included information about the move to Quang Tin and the unit's first weeks in the province.

Army Records

The unit history of the 1st Battalion/327th Infantry. It contained the following information: "At the termination of Operation Hood River on 10 Aug., the 1st Battalion (Airborne)/327th Infantry conducted an airlift of the companies from Quang Ngai Airstrip and truck convoy from Carentan base to Chu Lai. The following five days were spent in refitting activities and preparation of the coming operation."

The sworn witness statement of Gerald Morse on March 17, 1975. The document was Exhibit 315 of the Coy Allegation. It included the following:

MORSE: In the triple-canopy jungle, visibility, even in the daytime, was extremely limited. Sometimes you couldn't see ten yards ahead.

Books

Anderson, David. *Facing My Lai: Moving Beyond the Massacre.* Lawrence: University Press of Kansas, 1998.

Beattie, Keith. *The Scar That Binds.* New York: New York University Press, 2000.

Karnow, Stanley. *Vietnam: A History.* New York: Viking Press, 1983.

Langguth, A. J. *Our Vietnam: The War 1954–1975.* New York: Touchstone, 2000.

The Pentagon Papers. New York: Bantam Books, 1971.

Schell, Jonathan. *The Military Half.* New York: Knopf, 1968.

Topmiller, Robert J. *The Lotus Unleashed: The Buddhist Peace Movement in South Vietnam 1964–1966.* Lexington: University Press of Kentucky, 2002.

Valentine, Douglas. *The Phoenix Program*. New York: Morrow, 1990.
The Winter Soldier Investigation: An Inquiry into American War Crimes. Boston: Beacon Press, 1972.

CHAPTER 14

Main Sources

We interviewed numerous Tiger Force soldiers and officers, including William Carpenter, William Doyle, Ken Kerney, Barry Bowman, and Gerald Morse. We also relied on witness statements taken by CID investigators during the Coy Allegation.

Our account of the platoon's first days at Chu Lai was based on extensive interviews with Tiger Force soldiers who said they were "singled out" at the base, partly because of their reputation in the field. For the parts of the chapter about Chu Lai's history, we relied on Army documents, books, and interviews with historians.

For the section on Lieutenant Colonel Gerald Morse's first encounter with Tiger Force in the field, we drew on information provided by platoon members, particularly from William Doyle. In addition, we examined the battalion's radio logs, which detailed the platoon's daily movements.

For Morse's military record and background, we relied on Army personnel files and CID documents from the Coy Allegation.

Our account of the fight between Tiger Force and the Marines was based, in part, on information from Bill Carpenter.

Army Records

The witness statement of Captain Robert Morin on February 18, 1975. The document was Exhibit 333 of the Coy Allegation. It included information from CID agent Philip Lindley about his interview with Morin. Lindley said Morin recounted a story about Tiger Force capturing an unarmed elderly man. The soldiers allegedly tortured the man before drowning him in the Song Ve River in 1967.

LINDLEY: Morin did remember hearing the story at a party with a group of officers assigned to the battalion and Morin thought the battalion commander probably heard the account of the incident at the same time that he did. Further, Morin thought that either a Tiger Force platoon leader or a platoon sergeant from the Tiger Force had recounted the incident for the group.

Books

Fall, Bernard. *Street Without Joy*. Rev. ed. Mechanicsburg: Stackpole, 1994.
Herring, George. *America's Longest War: The United States and Vietnam*. New York: Knopf, 1996.
Karnow, Stanley. *Vietnam: A History*. New York: Viking Press, 1983.
Langguth, A. J. *Our Vietnam: The War 1954–1975*. New York: Touchstone, 2000.

NOTES

Olson, James S., and Randy Roberts. *Where the Domino Fell: America and Vietnam*.
  New York: St. Martin's Press, 1996.
The Pentagon Papers. New York: Bantam Books, 1971.
Schell, Jonathan. *The Military Half*. New York: Knopf, 1968.

CHAPTER 15

Main Sources
We interviewed numerous Tiger Force members about search-and-destroy missions
in the Que Son Valley and other parts of Quang Tin province. We also interviewed
friends and family members of Terrence Kerrigan.

For the section about the ambushes and dangers in the Que Son Valley and
skirmishes with the North Vietnamese Army, we drew on dozens of interviews
with Tiger Force soldiers. In addition, we examined the unit history of the 1st
Battalion/327th Infantry. By late August 1967, many Tiger Force members said
they came to the grim conclusion that the war was becoming a quagmire.

Our account of Private James Messer's death and the platoon's frustration was
based on extensive interviews with Tiger Force members.

For the section about bunkers, we talked at length with Tiger Force soldiers.
We also drew on interviews that CID agents conducted with platoon members
during the Coy Allegation.

For the section about the platoon's assault on a village along the Son Ly River,
we relied on a lengthy interview with Tiger Force medic Barry Bowman. During
the Coy Allegation, CID agents interviewed Bowman three times, but he never
told them about the attack — or that he executed a wounded prisoner. Bowman
discussed the shooting for the *Toledo Blade* series "Buried Secrets, Brutal Truths."
The four-day series ran October 19 to 22, 2003.

Our account of James Cogan shooting the old man was based on CID records
and interviews with Tiger Force soldiers. Carpenter told the CID in 1973 that
Cogan fired two shots into the elderly Vietnamese. But for the *Toledo Blade* series
"Buried Secrets, Brutal Truths," Carpenter said he was actually the one who fired
the second shot.

Army Records
The sworn witness statement of William Carpenter on January 18, 1973. The
document was Exhibit 23 of the Coy Allegation. It contained the following:

CARPENTER: Sometime in July or August 1967 we entered a village west
of Chu Lai and saw an unarmed 20-year-old man run from a hut with a
rucksack on his back. The Tiger Force opened up and killed the running
man, then searched the hut. There was an old man inside. He was the father
of the man we had just killed. Trout ordered Cogan to kill the old man and
Cogan took him behind the hut and shot him with a .45 pistol through the
mouth and left him laying on the ground. I saw that the old man was still

350

moving and told Cogan that that old man was alive. Cogan then went to the old man and shot him with the .45 again, this time in the throat, killing him. I watched this second shooting of the old man by Cogan and I heard Trout order Cogan to shoot the man in the first place.

The sworn witness statement of Barry Bowman on May 31, 1973. The document was Exhibit 41 of the Coy Allegation. It contained the following about Cogan shooting the elderly Vietnamese man:

BOWMAN: We approached a hooch when a young Vietnamese ran from the hooch. He was told to stop and as he continued to run he was shot and killed. I remember he had some kind of bag with him. Inside the hooch was an old man wearing a white hat and he was taken outside and behind the hooch, where one of the combat engineers shot him twice in the head with a .45-cal. pistol. He was still alive after he was shot the first time and the combat engineer had to shoot him a second time to kill him. I saw the incident myself.

QUESTION: Was the old man armed and were there any indications which lead you to believe that he was an enemy?

BOWMAN: There were no such indications and he was not armed. In my opinion this was also an unjustified killing.

For the section about Kerrigan following Trout's order to kill the Vietnamese man, we talked to Tiger Force soldiers and Kerrigan's friends and family members. We also depended on witness statements that were part of the CID investigation of Tiger Force.

A casualty report about James Messer's death. The document was Exhibit 436 of the Coy Allegation. It contained the following about the private: "Died on 22 August 1967 in Vietnam as the result of gunshot wounds received in hostile ground action."

The sworn witness statement of Forrest Miller on January 18, 1974. The document was Exhibit 54 of the Coy Allegation. It included the following about the attack on the bunkers:

QUESTION: How were the children killed?

MILLER: They were in bunkers, and we threw in hand grenades.

QUESTION: Would this have been the normal thing to do for the Tiger Force to kill the children found in the village?

MILLER: In any other area, no. However, in this area, a free-fire zone, yes.

The sworn witness statement of Kenneth Kerney on June 18, 1974. The document was Exhibit 112 of the Coy Allegation. CID agent Charles Fann wrote a report based on his interview with Kerney. It contained the following about the bunkers:

FANN: According to Kerney, they yelled to the people to come out by using short Vietnamese phrases that the soldiers had picked up. No interpreter was available to talk to the people. Kerney did not recall hearing an order to use hand grenades because the members of the Tiger Force knew what to do. He could not furnish an account of how many people were killed during the incident but did see bodies brought out of the bunkers. According to Kerney, a search of the bunkers failed to show any sign of Vietcong supplies or to substantiate that the village sympathizers were with the Vietcong. No return fire was received by the Tiger Force. The Tiger Force did not have access to gas grenades to flush the people from the bunkers. Kerney could not explain why it was necessary to get the people out of the bunkers.

The sworn witness statement of Charles Fulton on June 24, 1974. The document was Exhibit 120 of the Coy Allegation. It contained the following about the attack on the bunkers:

> FULTON: Once in the immediate area of the bunkers, one of the NCOs (the one that always wore the Tiger fatigues) who I think may have been Ssg. Haugh gave the order to throw hand grenades into the bunkers. I was among some of the guys that threw them into the bunkers. I threw mine into the tall one. I also remember one of the medics throwing hand grenades into the bunkers also. That bunker was flush with the ground. I don't know what happened after that for we continued on for about 25–30 meters and then stopped to set up our perimeter for we stayed there that night. I do remember that all during the night we kept hearing human sounds which came from the direction of the bunkers.

Books

Grossman, David. *On Killing: The Psychological Cost of Learning to Kill in War and Society.* Boston: Little, Brown, 1996.

Karnow, Stanley. *Vietnam: A History.* New York: Viking Press, 1983.

The Pentagon Papers. New York: Bantam Books, 1971.

Schell, Jonathan. *The Military Half.* New York: Knopf, 1968.

Shay, Jonathan. *Achilles in Vietnam: Combat Trauma and the Undoing of Character.* New York: Atheneum, 1994.

The Winter Soldier Investigation: An Inquiry into American War Crimes. Boston: Beacon Press, 1972.

CHAPTER 16

Main Sources

We interviewed numerous Tiger Force soldiers, including William Carpenter, Barry Bowman, Floyd Sawyer, and William Doyle. We also talked at length with friends and family members of Gerald Bruner. We drew from sworn witness statements taken by CID agents during the Coy Allegation.

For the biographical information about Bruner's childhood, we drew on numerous interviews with family members, including his wife, Karen, and brothers, Jack Bruner and Michael Stuckey. They provided us with Bruner's letters from Vietnam — letters in which he began questioning the U.S. objectives in the war.

For the section on Tiger Force soldiers abusing two prisoners, we relied on extensive interviews with numerous Tiger Force members, including Bowman and Sawyer. In an interview with us, Bowman said he was so upset by the killing that he told a chaplain. Sawyer told CID investigators he shot the prisoner because the detainee was trying to escape. In addition, Sawyer told CID agents he had no idea the prisoner was set up by Tiger Force. When we interviewed Sawyer, he said he killed the prisoner because he was fleeing. He said soldiers beat the prisoners — including the one he shot — and the platoon "killed a lot of people we shouldn't have." But he added, "I've worked so hard to shut it off that the whole thing is a blank spot in my life."

Our account of the confrontation between Doyle and Bruner in a farming village was based on interviews with Tiger Force members and CID documents. It is interesting to note that, before he died at age fifty-nine, Bruner made a tape about his four tours of duty in Vietnam for a Pearl Harbor commemoration ceremony. On the tape, he condemned the shooting of the farmer: "To me, this was what you call murder — they flat-out murdered the guy." In an interview, Doyle told us he would have killed the farmer himself — instead of ordering the execution — but his gun jammed. "You want to know the truth? I had my rifle on rock and roll and the goddamn thing misfired."

Army Records

The sworn witness statement of William Carpenter on January 18, 1973. The document was Exhibit 23 of the Coy Allegation. It included the following about the death of the prisoner:

> CARPENTER: I don't know whose idea it was to have the prisoners work. However, on one day I saw Sawyer beating one of the prisoners with a shovel handle, Sawyer struck this Vietnamese several times, knocking him to the ground, then Sawyer struck him a couple times while he was down. The next morning the Vietnamese prisoner that was beaten by Sawyer had to be mi-evacuated to a hospital. That same day, Sawyer and Ybarra were guarding the remaining prisoner. I was just a short distance away from Sawyer when I heard two shots. I turned to Sawyer and saw the prisoner lying about 10 feet from him. Sawyer was holding his M16. I approached Sawyer and he told me that the prisoner tried to run away so he shot him. This area where Sawyer shot the prisoner was located in open country and aside from that the prisoner couldn't hardly walk, much less run. I know the prisoner was in very bad physical condition and couldn't have run if he had wanted to. Sawyer was a sadist. I had previously watched him tie two prisoners up with "Det Cord" and then connected the Det Cord to a claymore trigger, then Sawyer wrapped a piece of Det Cord around a small tree and exploded it to

show the prisoners what he would do to them if they gave him a hard time. These prisoners that Sawyer tied up are the same ones I mentioned above.

QUESTION: Did someone else witness Sawyer shoot the prisoner and/or tie the two prisoners up with Det Cord?

CARPENTER: Yes. Ssg. Trout observed both instances, I recall him specifically. And as far as others seeing both incidents, the whole Tiger Force platoon was present in camp. I can't recall just who was watching either incident.

QUESTION: Were either of the above incidents reported to your superiors?

CARPENTER: Not to my knowledge. I do recall Lt. Hawkins was there and saw both incidents, however, I doubt if he reported it.

The sworn witness statement of Barry Bowman on May 31, 1973. The document was Exhibit 41 of the Coy Allegation. It contained the following about Floyd Sawyer shooting the prisoner:

BOWMAN: The following day word was passed around that the prisoner who had been beaten and injured with the shovel be given a chance to escape to prevent possible repercussions about his severe beating. Somebody, I can't recall who, told the prisoner that he was free to go and as he moved down the hill Sawyer shot him from behind with an M16 rifle. I was standing close and watched the whole thing. Sawyer put the rifle to his shoulder, fired one shot, and hit the prisoner in the head. Sawyer at the time was about 35–50 yards away from the prisoner.

QUESTION: Was Sawyer ordered to kill that man?

BOWMAN: I don't know. In my opinion, somebody with authority told him to get rid of the prisoner. I am sure Sawyer would not have shot the prisoner if he would not have been told to by someone with authority.

The sworn witness statement of Gerald Bruner on February 12, 1974. The document was Exhibit 132 of the Coy Allegation. It included the following about the shooting of the farmer:

BRUNER: I came back out and I saw one of Doyle's men hitting him, and at one point he was knocked to his knees. His family was crying and yelling so the men drug [sic] him away from them. The guy was then jerked to his feet, and at this time Doyle shot him in the forearm with his M16. I don't know which arm it was. About this time, the interpreter from my team came up to me and said that this man's brother was in the second hooch and we should get him because maybe Doyle's team would believe what the guy was telling them. I then went with my interpreter to the second hooch and in a bunker there, we found a young kid about 16 years old and what was apparently his wife, her parents, and the two brothers' parents. Also, I guess there were a couple of children.

About the time we started back towards the first hooch, with the family, we heard a burst of fire and I distinctly heard the sound of an M79 being

fired. As we approached the area, I could see the Vietnamese guy lying
facedown and there was smoke still in the air. I have no idea who did the
shooting. I started to take the young Vietnamese kid to my team, who was
separated from Doyle's, when a tall guy from Doyle's team came over and
took the kid from me. He hit the kid a couple of times and then drug [sic]
him over and threw him down on the ground next to his brother. I went
over to see what was going on, and I could see that the older brother was
dead — having been shot in the back several times and his skull was broken
open. I then asked a general question, to no one in particular, of what was
going on. Somebody standing there said that the guy had been told to run,
and when he did, he was shot. I don't know who the guy was that said this
but apparently he was as mad as I was at what was happening.

At the time I was trying to find out what had happened, some of Doyle's
team were trying to make the kid lie down next to his brother but he kept
trying to get up and appeared to be praying or something. All the while he
was doing this, they kept kicking and hitting him. Someone told Doyle's
interpreter to tell the kid to lie down or he'd get the same as his brother.
Then someone came up and put a .45 to the kid's head. At this time, the
kid's family came up and while Doyle's people were trying to keep them
back, I took the kid over to our team. There was kind of a pause, like
Doyle's team was discussing something, then this same tall guy came over
and hit the kid about three times. He grabbed the kid and started to take
him back by his brother when I told him to leave the kid alone. The guy
was pointing a .45 at the kid and I told him that if he "fired up" the kid, I
would do the same to him.

The sworn witness statement of Ralph Mayhew on October 5, 1973. The
document was Exhibit 126 of the Coy Allegation. It included the following about
the shooting of the farmer:

MAYHEW: The man indicated that there was no VC in the area, speaking
through an interpreter, nor had he seen any in the past. When he gave this
answer, Doyle shot the Vietnamese in the arm with his M16 rifle. Again, he
asked about the VC, to which he got the same answer that there was none.
This time, Doyle began beating him on the head with his M16 rifle, hitting
him several times, beating him to the ground. Then Doyle turned his back
and as he walked away he said, "Shoot him," at which time several members
of the group shot him with their M16s, and one man with an M79 grenade
launcher.

We also relied on Army records, including the unit history of the 1st Battalion/
327th Infantry, for parts of the chapter related to the hunt for NVA positions. In
August 1967, the U.S. military leaders had underestimated the strength of the NVA
presence in Quang Tin and other areas of the Central Highlands. When Tiger
Force teams embarked on search-and-destroy and reconnaissance missions, they
were regularly encountering enemy soldiers.

NOTES

Books

Bilton, Michael, and Kevin Sim. *Four Hours in My Lai*. New York: Penguin Books, 1992.

Karnow, Stanley. *Vietnam: A History*. New York: Viking Press, 1983.

The Pentagon Papers. New York: Bantam Books, 1971.

Schell, Jonathan. *The Military Half*. New York: Knopf, 1968.

Topmiller, Robert J. *The Lotus Unleashed: The Buddhist Peace Movement in South Vietnam 1964–1966*. Lexington: University Press of Kentucky, 2002.

CHAPTER 17

Main Sources

We talked at length to numerous Tiger Force members, including William Doyle and Daniel Clint. We also interviewed Gerald Bruner's friends and family.

We drew on our interviews and CID investigative records about the meeting between Bruner and Captain Carl James. When questioned by CID agents in 1974, James said he had no recollection of Bruner. But in an interview, James told us he remembered Bruner coming into his office at Chu Lai but couldn't remember details of the meeting. He complained that the CID investigation was the reason the Army held up his promotion for years. "If it wasn't for all that shit — Bruner and Tiger Force — things would have been different in my life."

Army Records

The sworn witness statement of Gerald Bruner on February 12, 1974. The document was Exhibit 132 of the Coy Allegation. It included the following about the meeting with James:

> BRUNER: When I went to the rear, Sgt. Trout carried a letter to the company commander about me, and I have no idea what was in the letter. When we got in, Sgt. Trout told me to get cleaned up, the company commander called for me. When I saw the company commander, he started yelling at me and said that he read this note that came in from the field. And that he didn't like the idea of me threatening his men. He suggested that I was going to see a psychiatrist. At that time, the first sergeant stopped in and said that he remembered me from A Company and that I had done a fine job and that they had no problems with me. The company commander then asked me if I had anything to say. That's when I tried to explain why I threatened another team member. I told him that I felt I was justified in doing it to save a Vietnamese's life whose brother had been killed by Doyle's team unnecessarily. I felt that if I hadn't threatened the tall guy, that they would have killed the other brother, too. After I explained that to him, he told me to go over to his tent. Then he showed up with a chaplain and they asked if I had any type of personal problems and I said no. Then the chaplain left. Then the company commander asked again why I got so disturbed.

Then I reported my story, indicating that I felt justified in the actions that I had taken.

Books

Karnow, Stanley. *Vietnam: A History.* New York: Viking Press, 1983.
Langguth, A. J. *Our Vietnam: The War 1954–1975.* New York: Touchstone, 2000.
The Pentagon Papers. New York: Bantam Books, 1971.
The Winter Soldier Investigation: An Inquiry into American War Crimes. Boston: Beacon Press, 1972.

CHAPTER 18

Main Sources

We interviewed friends and family members of Sam Ybarra and Kenneth Green, including Green's mother, Kathleen, and sister, Sherry Hodson. We talked at length with numerous Tiger Force members, including William Carpenter, William Doyle, Barry Bowman, Daniel Clint, and Harold Fischer.

For our account of Sam Ybarra and Kenneth Green's visit to the United States, we drew on information from their family and friends, including friends who socialized with them during their monthlong leave. During this leave, Kathleen Green said, her son was restless and suffered severe headaches. "He had a terrible temper and I thought when he went into the service he would get over that. But he didn't. If anything, Vietnam made it worse."

We drew on Tiger Force interviews, the unit history of the 1st Battalion/327th Infantry, and the platoon's radio logs for the section about Terry Oakden's death. Many of the Tigers vividly recalled the day. Not only was Oakden killed when he stepped on a mine but several platoon members were injured, including Daniel Clint, who wrote a short story about the explosion. "Things happen quickly in these situations," Clint wrote. "For us it was an assessment of who was and who was not injured. Sergeant Diaz had his leg completely shattered (he would later have it amputated above the knee). Oakden's head had suffered major trauma — there was no saving him. I heard the distant voices conferring, 'He's gone.'"

We drew on extensive interviews with Tiger Force members for the sections about the deaths of Jerry Ingram, Robin Varney, Kenneth Green, and Edward Beck. By the end of September, the Tigers were encountering snipers every day. The soldiers told us the deaths of four platoon members over forty-eight hours pushed some members over the edge. Harold Fischer recalled, "They all wanted revenge — especially Ybarra. We had to keep Sam away from friendly villagers because he would kill them. He would kill unarmed villagers when the opportunity presented itself, which sometimes was on a daily basis."

Tiger Force private Richard Ammons was so upset by Green's death that he wrote a letter to Green's father, expressing his sorrow:

I don't know exactly what to say but I would like you to know that "Boots" was a very close friend of mine and that I'm very sorry about what happened. He was a very likable man and everyone he came in contact with found him very easy to become friends with. Everyone thought he was one of the greatest guys in the force. I've been in Tiger Force for 15 months and I've known a lot of guys and saw quite a few in action. Ever since I've known Boots, when you needed help you could always count on him.

Mr. Green, I don't know if you found out how it happened or not so I'll tell you now. We walked into somewhat of a hasty ambush and Boots rushed for the enemy and was shot in the left thigh. Edward Beck ran to his aid and picked him up and tried to get him into some kind of cover. The enemy killed both before he could reach it. I'm very sorry that this happened and I just don't know how I can put into words how I felt when it happened. I also want you know that it was one of the hardest things in the world for me to do when I was called to identify his body. I'm so sorry.

Our account of Green's body being transported by chopper to Chu Lai was based on interviews with Leon Fletcher, who had tried to stop Green from volunteering for Tiger Force. He said the image of Green's body in the chopper continues to haunt him. "The blast from the chopper blade blew open the poncho and there was Ken. It just freaked me out. There was his bullet-ridden body, blood all over him. I had different nightmares about this for years. One of them was that he rose up in the helicopter and he grabbed me by my shirt and he would say, 'Why did you let me go to Tiger Force?' And another one was he would grab me by the shirt and say, 'Why didn't you come with me so you could have watched my back?' I still have those nightmares."

Army Records
The sworn witness statement of William Carpenter on January 18, 1973. The document was Exhibit 23 of the Coy Allegation. It included the following about Green's death:

QUESTION: After Green was killed, 29 Sep. 67, was there a noticeable effect in Ybarra's actions?
CARPENTER: He was visibly disturbed, he cried about Green's death, and on the day Green's personal effects were turned over to Ybarra, I heard him say that he would "even the score by killing more Vietnamese."

The sworn witness statement of Gerald Bruner on February 12, 1974. The document was Exhibit 132 of the Coy Allegation. It included the following about Oakden's death:

BRUNER: Approximately two weeks later, we were working in a different area up near Tam Ky and our team was told to occupy a certain area because there had been people sighted coming in our direction, but to stay away from a certain hill because it was booby trapped. However, Lt. Hawkins told us to go to the top of the hill because it was the best vantage point to see the terrain, but be careful. Approximately three minutes after occupying the hill, one of the team members stepped on a mine.

In the same interview, Bruner told CID agents about Hawkins and Lieutenant Edward Sanders firing rounds at a farmer.

> BRUNER: The next morning we were up on a hill and I observed Lt. Hawkins and an artillery officer firing their weapons. As they put it, they were "test firing" into a rice paddy. However, there was an old Vietnamese man plowing with a water buffalo in the rice paddy. The man suddenly stopped and ran for cover. They were laughing about it and this was when I approached Lt. Hawkins and flatly told him I wanted to leave the Tiger Force.

For our account of the psychology of combat, we drew on a *Frontline* interview with retired lieutenant colonel David Grossman, author of the book *On Killing*.

Books

Clint, Dan. *John Martinez 1967,* 2002.

Grossman, David. *On Killing: The Psychological Cost of Learning to Kill in War and Society.* Boston: Little, Brown, 1996.

Herring, George. *America's Longest War: The United States and Vietnam.* New York: Knopf, 1996.

Karnow, Stanley. *Vietnam: A History.* New York: Viking Press, 1983.

Langguth, A. J. *Our Vietnam: The War 1954–1975.* New York: Touchstone, 2000.

The Pentagon Papers. New York: Bantam Books, 1971.

The Winter Soldier Investigation: An Inquiry into American War Crimes. Boston: Beacon Press, 1972.

CHAPTER 19

Main Sources

We talked at length with numerous Tiger Force members, including William Carpenter, Rion Causey, Ken Kerney, Harold Fischer, and William Doyle. In addition, we talked to Gerald Bruner's friends and family. We also drew on the Army records about the campaign, including information in the unit history of the 1st Battalion / 327th Infantry and radio logs of Tiger Force's daily contact with the enemy.

Our account of Lieutenant Hawkins's last days as the platoon's commander was based on extensive interviews with soldiers and officers. Captain Carl James told us how he led Hawkins back to the officers' barracks after the second lieutenant became drunk. During the interview, James said Hawkins's drinking problem was one of the reasons he was relieved of duty. "I felt it was time for a change. You can burn out if you stay with a platoon too long. And he was burned out," James said.

For the section on Captain Harold McGaha's leadership, we drew on interviews with Tiger Force members and records from the CID's Tiger Force investigation. Many platoon members said McGaha was "aggressive" in the field and encouraged the Tigers to kill for body count. In the final days of Operation Wheeler, Lieutenant Colonel Gerald Morse also prodded his men for additional kills. During the CID's investigation, soldiers told agents someone using Morse's radio call sign "Ghost Rider" asked for 327 kills — the same number as the battalion's designation. The order via the radio was transmitted to the battalion's three line companies and Tiger Force. Army records show Tiger Force recorded the 327th kill on November 19. Several soldiers told us that they heard the message and that it led to the killing of unarmed civilians. But in an interview, Morse said he never asked for 327 kills. He said the accusation was unfounded.

We drew on interviews with Tiger Force members and CID records for the section about Ybarra beheading the baby. The atrocity eventually led to the Tiger Force investigation — four years later. It's interesting to note that some witnesses withheld information from CID investigators. For example, Harold Fischer never told CID agents he looked into the hut and saw the baby's body. In an interview, Fischer told us he held back information from CID agents because he was "afraid of Ybarra." In the end, CID agents failed to substantiate the atrocity because of a lack of cooperation from Tiger Force soldiers.

For the section on the attack on the village, we relied on extensive interviews with Tiger Force soldiers. Many of them told us that by October 1967, it was "open season" on villagers. Anyone in villages or huts was considered "the enemy," and few soldiers seemed concerned that no weapons were being seized. As Operation Wheeler continued, the platoon began counting dead civilians as enemy soldiers. They would include them in the body count when they radioed battalion headquarters. "We knew they were civilians, not VC," Causey said.

Our account of the execution of the young mother was based in part on James Barnett's sworn statement to CID agents. He told investigators that Sergeant Harold Trout ordered him to shoot the woman. Trout refused to talk to the CID in 1973. When we contacted Trout in connection with the *Toledo Blade*'s series "Buried Secrets, Brutal Truths," he talked about his time in Tiger Force — the patrols and ambushes. But Trout refused to discuss the CID investigation or war crimes.

Army Records

The sworn witness statement of Harold Fischer on November 30, 1972. The document was Exhibit 8 of the Coy Allegation. It included the following about the baby's death:

FISCHER: This incident occurred towards the end of Operation Wheeler. I recall that this operation started in September of 1967 and ended on or about 25 Nov. 67. I think that this incident with the baby happened during the middle of Nov. 67. We were in a village or hamlet which consisted of about three or four huts. I was standing about 15 meters away from one of the hooches when I saw Kerrigan walking towards me. He looked a little excited and as he passed by me he said that Sam had just cut the baby's head off. We didn't discuss the incident any further and Kerrigan went on his way.

QUESTION: What was your reaction to this?

FISCHER: I just shrugged it off. It was no big thing to me at the time. In the situation we were in, people were dying every day.

QUESTION: Do you really think that this happened the way Kerrigan told you?

FISCHER: Yes. Sam was a very cold-blooded person and he was capable of such an act. Also the way Kerrigan expressed himself I had no doubt that this incident occurred.

The sworn witness statement of William Carpenter on January 18, 1973. The document was Exhibit 23 of the Coy Allegation. It included the following about 327 kills:

CARPENTER: On one occasion in Nov. 67 during Operation Wheeler I overheard a radio transmission from Ghost Rider to the Tiger Force that they needed a certain number of additional bodies to make the number 327 which was the number that stood for our infantry battalion "327." I don't know if it was Morse, it could have been someone else, whoever the person was used his call sign. I don't recall just how many additional kills were needed. It was several I believe. I remember that the radio transmission was answered to the effect that "Do you want them before or after breakfast?"

Later during the interview:

CARPENTER: I remember that the NVA, VC, and Vietnamese civilians killed in the incidents that I have seen and detailed in this statement were included in the body count which was reported to the battalion headquarters.

The sworn witness statement of Lieutenant Stephen Naughton on February 5, 1975. The document was Exhibit 124 of the Coy Allegation. It contained the following:

QUESTION: Do you know anything about Capt. McGaha, who replaced him?

NAUGHTON: Only that he was good at karate and practiced it all the time.

QUESTION: What was Hawkins's reputation as the Tiger Force commander?

NAUGHTON: It was lousy. The man was incompetent in the field resulting in several members of the Tiger Force losing their lives, and was a heavy drinker and was always drunk in the field. His reputation after he left the Tiger Force was just as screwed up.

The sworn witness statement of James Barnett on November 27, 1974. The document was Exhibit 177 of the Coy Allegation. It included the following about the young mother's death:

QUESTION: How far were you from the woman when you shot her?

BARNETT: About 10 to 15 feet.

QUESTION: You are talking about that woman who was the wife of that VC or NVA?

BARNETT: Yes, she was the one who had the child.

QUESTION: Was she dead after you shot her?

BARNETT: She fell after I shot her and I turned around and left. I didn't check her if she was dead. I can't even recall the impact of the shots or the bullet holes in her chest. I know that I hit her and I assumed she was dead. I also knew at the time what damage an M16 round can do.

QUESTION: Why did you shoot that woman, Mr. Barnett?

BARNETT: Because I was told by Trout to do it and I carried out what he told me.

QUESTION: Did you have to carry out this order?

BARNETT: I felt at the time I had to do it because I was told to do it. Today I know better. I didn't have any idea what an unlawful order was while I was in RVN with the Tiger Force or that I could refuse such an order and not get into any trouble over it.

Books

Herring, George. *America's Longest War: The United States and Vietnam.* New York: Knopf, 1996.

Langguth, A. J. *Our Vietnam: The War 1954–1975.* New York: Touchstone, 2000.

Olson, James S., and Randy Roberts. *Where the Domino Fell: America and Vietnam.* New York: St. Martin's Press, 1996.

The Pentagon Papers. New York: Bantam Books, 1971.

The Winter Soldier Investigation: An Inquiry into American War Crimes. Boston: Beacon Press, 1972.

CHAPTER 20

Main Sources

We talked at length with Gustav Apsey, Captain Earl Perdue, and other CID agents involved in the Coy Allegation. We also drew on thousands of CID documents related to the four-and-a-half-year investigation, including more than one hundred sworn witness statements from Tiger Force soldiers and commanders. In addition, we examined hundreds of documents from the Colonel Henry Tufts Archive at the University of Michigan. Tufts was an important figure in CID history. In the 1960s, he spent a year reorganizing the agency to make it more efficient. He also oversaw high-profile investigations, including the My Lai Massacre. We talked at length with Dennis Stout, a former military journalist with the 1st Battalion/327th Infantry in Vietnam. In addition, we interviewed friends and family members of Sam Ybarra, including his wife, Janice Little, and mother, Therlene Ramos. We also talked to Ken Kerney, Harold Fischer, and friends and family members of Terrence Kerrigan.

Our account of Apsey's being assigned the Coy Allegation was based on extensive interviews with the lead agent and other Tiger Force investigators. It's interesting to note that the investigation was already one year old — with only a handful of interviews conducted — when Apsey was handed the case.

For the section on the history of war crimes and the My Lai Massacre, we drew on records in the National Archives in College Park, Maryland. During the Vietnam War, the Army investigated 242 war-crime allegations. We examined each case. In addition, we reviewed the records of the Working War Crimes Group, a special U.S. panel created in the wake of the My Lai Massacre. The group — consisting of six military officers — was established to review war-crime cases to prevent cover-ups. After journalist Seymour Hersh broke My Lai, President Nixon told the nation the massacre was an "isolated incident." In response to the public condemnation of My Lai and pressure from congressional leaders such as U.S. Representative Morris Udall, the CID promised to swiftly investigate war-crime allegations.

For the section on pressures facing the CID, we drew from the Colonel Henry Tufts Archive. We also relied on records of the Working War Crimes Group. In addition, we examined transcripts of the Winter Soldier hearings.

Our account of the Stout Allegation was based on numerous interviews with Stout and former battalion soldiers, as well as on hundreds of CID documents related to the case. It's interesting to note that after Stout told his story to a Phoenix newspaper, the Nixon White House was considering the possibility of seeking an injunction to prevent the news media from publishing war-crimes allegations. In a letter to a civilian, Major General Kenneth J. Hodson, the Army's judge advocate general, wrote, "On behalf of President Nixon, I am replying to your telegram of 11 December concerning the possibility of an injunction against the news media. Whether the United States Government could enjoin the news media from disseminating certain news depends upon the facts of any given case. The Department of Justice is considering the possibility of seeking such an injunction."

For the section on Sam Ybarra's life, we drew on his juvenile court record. We discovered Ybarra was found guilty of illegal consumption of alcohol on December 14, 1964, and sentenced to fifteen days in jail in lieu of a $100 fine. On February 13, 1965, Ybarra was convicted of disturbing the peace and illegal consumption. For that offense, he spent twenty-five days in jail in lieu of a $125 fine. On April 9, 1965, Ybarra was convicted of illegal consumption and received a six-month suspended sentence. Records show that Ybarra was sentenced to fifteen days in jail in lieu of a $200 fine after being found guilty of illegal consumption on October 10, 1965. Ybarra was convicted of carrying a concealed weapon and illegal consumption on January 8, 1966. After the hearing, Ybarra was released from jail so he could be inducted into the Army.

Army Records

The sworn witness statement of Private Gary Coy on February 3, 1971. The document was Exhibit 1 of the Coy Allegation. It included the following about the baby's beheading by a Tiger Force soldier:

COY: I was with the 3rd Platoon, the second element behind the 1st Platoon, which was leading the column. About this time the point of the column began to receive fire from one of the four huts to our front. We dispersed and took the huts under fire. Shortly after that we heard two explosions in the vicinity of the huts. After the firing stopped we were told to move into the village which consisted of the four huts. As we passed between the huts, I overheard two men arguing inside one of the huts. I stepped into the hut, I saw two or three bodies lying on the ground, one of the bodies was that of a woman. I also heard a baby crying. The two men were arguing about taking the baby with them or leaving it in the hut. I stepped outside and talked to a friend of mine called John Ahern (KIA: Mar–Apr 68). I stepped back into the hut. I didn't hear the baby crying, and then I noticed that the baby's throat had been cut and there was a lot of blood on its throat and front. I said, "What happened?" and one of the men that had been arguing said, "Sam did it." Then I turned around and walked out. Later I told Ahern about it, and he said, "It's just one of those things, there's nothing you can do about it."

QUESTION: Who is Sam?

COY: He was assigned to Tiger Force (similar to a Ranger unit) out of HHC, 1st Bn, 327th Inf Bde. He was about 68 inches tall, dark complected, of Indian background, I believe from New Mexico.

QUESTION: Do you know Sam's full name?

COY: No. All I know is that he had been in-country longer than a year.

The sworn witness statement of James Barnett on March 10, 1971. The document was Exhibit 6 of the Coy Allegation. It included the following statement by CID agent Frank Toledo, who interviewed Barnett:

Barnett stated that he considered Sam Ybarra a "gross person," however, did not elaborate, nor had he knowledge that Sam Ybarra had murdered any Vietnamese child. Barnett named a Sgt. Trout, later identified as SSG Harold G. Trout, RA 27 551 931, HHC, 1st Bn, 327th Inf, as being a Team Leader of Sam Ybarra during the tactical operation of 7–15 Nov. 67. Barnett also said that the actions of the men on a search-and-destroy mission depended upon who issued the order for the execution of the mission.

The following information was contained in the final report of an investigation known as the Stout Allegation:

Allegations made by Mr. Stout generated widespread local news coverage in Phoenix, AZ, in Dec. 69. Mr. Stout alleged that while in RVN from Sep. 1966–Sep. 67 he witnessed and was informed of numerous atrocities perpetrated by members of his unit, including rape, mutilation and torture of the enemy, murder, and other indiscriminate acts.

A March 2, 1972, letter from Colonel Henry Tufts to U.S. Representative Morris Udall about the Stout investigation. It included the following information:

In the course of this investigation, USACIDC identified, located, and re-
constructed Army records pertaining to the identification of former members of Mr. Stout's unit. Additionally, Army operation records concerning
combat activities of the unit during the time in question were located and
examined. As a result 112 former members of Mr. Stout's unit, located
throughout the United States and RVN, were identified and interviewed.
Investigation disclosed insufficient evidence to prove or disprove Mr. Stout's
allegations.

Sam Ybarra's military personnel records, or 201 file. Ybarra was court-martialed
on December 6, 1968, for being AWOL. He was sentenced to one month in jail
and fined $145. On February 12, 1969, he faced an Article 15 hearing for being in
an off-limits area. He was sentenced to a reduction in grade from private first class
to private second class. A special court-martial was held March 12, 1969, for two
violations of lawful general regulations — transporting a Vietnamese civilian without authority and being in an off-limits area, breaking restriction, wrongful appro-
priation of a two-and-a-half-ton truck, willful disobedience of a lawful order, and
disrespect to a superior officer. He was sentenced to six months' confinement with
hard labor (excess of one month suspended) and a fine of $433.

The sworn witness statement of Ken Kerney on November 16, 1972. The
document was Exhibit 110 of the Coy Allegation.

The sworn witness statement of Harold Trout on November 22, 1972. The
document was Exhibit 66 of the Coy Allegation.

Gustav Apsey's sworn statement. He interviewed Terrence Kerrigan on December 12, 1972. The document was Exhibit 11 of the Coy Allegation. It included the
following:

APSEY: Mr. Kerrigan appeared hostile and uncooperative throughout his
interview on 12 Dec. 72. He related that he and Ybarra were close friends
and that his abilities in combat equaled that of Ybarra and that he was the
only member of Tiger Force who dared to address Ybarra with the title of
"punk." He indicated several times that he disliked authority used by the
officers and NCOs in the Tiger Force, that the unit was an "ass-kicking
outfit" that fought the war as they saw fit and they didn't condone or associ-
ate with any outsiders and that everyone was afraid of them.

Books

Anderson, David. *Facing My Lai: Moving Beyond the Massacre.* Lawrence: University
Press of Kansas, 1998.

Beattie, Keith. *The Scar That Binds.* New York: New York University Press, 2000.

Belknap, Michal R. *The Vietnam War on Trial.* Lawrence: University Press of Kansas,
2002.

Bilton, Michael, and Kevin Sim. *Four Hours in My Lai.* New York: Penguin Books,
1992.

Hersh, Seymour M. *My Lai 4: A Report on the Massacre and Its Aftermath.* New York:
Random House, 1970.

Kimball, Jeffrey. *Nixon's Vietnam War.* Lawrence: University Press of Kansas, 1997.

Kissinger, Henry. *Ending the Vietnam War.* New York: Simon & Schuster, 2003.

Langguth, A. J. *Our Vietnam: The War 1954–1975.* New York: Touchstone, 2000.

Olson, James S., and Randy Roberts. *Where the Domino Fell: America and Vietnam.* New York: St. Martin's Press, 1996.

Sheehan, Neil. *A Bright Shining Lie: John Paul Vann and America in Vietnam.* New York: Random House, 1988.

Solis, Gary. *Son Thang: An American War Crime.* Annapolis: Naval Institute Press, 1997.

Spector, Ronald H. *After Tet: The Bloodiest Year in Vietnam.* New York: Vintage Books, 1993.

Vistica, Gregory. *The Education of Lieutenant Kerrey.* New York: St. Martin's Press, 2003.

The Winter Soldier Investigation: An Inquiry into American War Crimes. Boston: Beacon Press, 1972.

Periodicals

Phoenix Gazette articles about Dennis Stout recounting alleged atrocities committed by soldiers of the 1st Battalion/327th Infantry in Quang Ngai province. The stories ran in the newspaper on December 12 and December 13, 1969.

CHAPTER 21

Main Sources

We interviewed numerous Tiger Force members, including William Carpenter and Barry Bowman. We talked at length with Gustav Apsey, the lead investigator in the Tiger Force case, and other CID agents who took part in the investigation. We interviewed family and friends of Donald Wood, including his wife, Joyce, and brother, Jim. In addition, we talked to Gerald Bruner's wife, Karen, and other family members.

Our account of William Carpenter's meeting with Gustav Apsey was based on a series of interviews with the two men and extensive CID documents related to the Tiger Force investigation.

For parts of the chapter about soldier interviews, we drew on numerous CID records. Every time a CID agent interviewed a former Tiger Force member or officer, the agent had to file a report. We examined those reports, along with sworn witness statements and other accompanying information. In addition, we talked to soldiers and their families about the investigation.

For sections about CID agents interviewing soldiers, we drew extensively on thousands of Army documents related to the investigation. They included sworn witness statements, written reports by agents, and, in some cases, polygraphs.

Army Records

Weekly and monthly updates of war-crime cases that Apsey and other CID agents had to prepare for Colonel Henry Tufts, the White House, and the offices of the secretary of defense and secretary of the Army in 1972 and 1973.

The sworn witness statements of William Carpenter in 1973. The documents included Exhibits 23 and 24 of the Coy Allegation.

QUESTION: What kind of person was Ybarra?

CARPENTER: From my association with him and from my observations, I believe he is really mentally disturbed. He acted like he enjoyed killing.

QUESTION: Regarding the farmer that Hawkins shot on that night patrol. Can you add anything of value to that incident?

CARPENTER: I could see no reason for the killing. Hawkins was intoxicated as a result of drinking beer that the resupply chopper had delivered earlier in the day.

QUESTION: Were there other incidents of what you believed to be unjustified killing and mutilation while you were a member of Tiger Force?

CARPENTER: Yes, many.

QUESTION: Mr. Carpenter, I have been talking to you for over a week now and you have related numerous war crimes that happened in 1967. I would like to know why you are bringing them to light now?

CARPENTER: At the time these incidents happened in Vietnam, it was no big thing. I was assigned to an infantry element and it was our job to kill the enemy. The incidents that I have described I never reported because killing was the standard operating procedure of the Tiger Force. Another reason for not reporting them at the time was that Hawkins threatened to shoot me if I said anything. After I was discharged and reentered civilian life, my ideas about the Vietnam War changed, and I really regret that these things happened. I have nothing to hide and when you called me I told you that I had been thinking about telling someone in authority of what happened in Vietnam.

The sworn witness statement of Leo Heaney on February 15, 1973. The document was Exhibit 25 of the Coy Allegation. It contained the following about the shooting of the old man by the Song Ve River:

QUESTION: Can you describe this old man?

HEANEY: He was about 50 years old. I think he wore shorts and some kind of top. The baskets he carried contained fowl; I think they were geese. There is no question that the old man was unarmed.

QUESTION: Do you know the reason why this old man was killed?

HEANEY: Maybe he irritated them by his screaming. His screaming was loud enough to give our position away. There was no justifiable reason that the old man had to be killed. His screaming could have been restrained in many other ways. The fact that the old man was making too much noise could not have been the reason to kill him because the shots which killed him also gave our position away. My personal opinion is that he was killed because he irritated certain members of the CP element.

QUESTION: Was it routine at the time for the Tiger Force to go on night operations as the one you described?

HEANEY: Prior to my going on leave in May 1967, we very seldom went on night moves. During Hawkins's tenure, night moves became a common thing.

The sworn witness statement of James Hawkins on March 16, 1973. The document was Exhibit 63 of the Coy Allegation. Highlights of the interview were contained in a report filed by Gustav Apsey on March 28, 1975. Most of the report concerns the death of Dao Hue.

APSEY: Hawkins stated that he could not recall a resupply of beer and hot food on that day and that he had no knowledge of the old Vietnamese being detained by the Tiger Force and later released to him. Hawkins then denied that he killed the old Vietnamese and that he had been drunk that night. Hawkins was then confronted with part of the testimony given by three former Tiger Force members (Carpenter, Lee, and Heaney) concerning the alleged murder, and at this point, Hawkins suddenly lost his composure and appeared to be under emotional stress. He made the statement that to the best of his knowledge he didn't kill the Vietnamese and that he didn't know what to do about his situation and asked whether he should talk to a lawyer or not. He was then reminded that the decision to speak to a lawyer was his. Hawkins then appeared confused to the point that it was evident he was unable to make an intelligent decision whether to seek a lawyer or not and the questioning was discontinued at 16:30 hours. Hawkins requested time until the morning in order for him to reach a decision on what to do and he agreed to meet this agent at 10:30 hours, 17 March 73.

At 10:30 hours, 17 Mar 73, Hawkins arrived at Room 501, Holiday Inn, Tampa, Fl., with his legal representative, Cpt. Guyton O. Terry Jr. Hawkins was readvised of his legal rights in the presence of SA Weaver and stated that he was willing to answer specific questions only per advice of his counsel. Hawkins was then asked specific questions concerning the murder allegation and he declined to respond to each question per advice of his council [sic].

The sworn witness statement of James Barnett on April 27, 1973. The document was Exhibit 36 of the Coy Allegation. It included the following:

QUESTION: Were the Bn Commanders aware of the atrocities committed by the Tiger Force?

BARNETT: In my opinion, they knew what was going on. They should have known that we never turned in prisoners. However, I don't know of any specific incident which occurred which would show that the Bn Commanders had knowledge of what was going on.

QUESTION: Have you ever received orders to kill anything that moved?

BARNETT: The only such orders I heard came from the Tiger Force element leaders who received their orders from the platoon leader. We were always on search-and-destroy missions and it was generally understood to kill anything that moved. As far as we knew, the civilians had been moved out and what was left in our Areas of Operations were strictly enemy or enemy sympathizers. We were designated as a reconnaissance element but we did very little of that. We were utilized like a combat element just like the line companies. We were a small force, therefore more mobile and we were involved in far more combat actions than the line companies. I have heard Hawkins and Trout issue such orders. Matter of fact, Trout's favorite expression was "grease them." I have personally never heard a Bn Commander issue such orders. During that time, the most important achievement was a high body count. Our accomplishments were not measured by the amount of prisoners that were captured but by high body count figures. Everyone stressed a high body count from the Bn level on down.

The sworn witness statement of Barry Bowman on May 31, 1973. The document was Exhibit 41 of the Coy Allegation. It contained the following about Trout encouraging Bowman to shoot the wounded Vietnamese man:

BOWMAN: We were set up in a night perimeter in a village and it was well after dark when I heard shots. The Vietnamese CIDG Forces we had with us had opened fire on a Vietnamese male who had approached our positions. As a result, the Vietnamese was wounded and someone called for a medic. I went over to where the Vietnamese man was and saw that he was seriously wounded. I can't recall his injuries but I remember that he was near death. Trout was there and he said to me something like, "Come on and break your cherry, Doc," which meant that I should kill him because I hadn't done this sort of thing because I was rather new in the outfit. I declined this and then Trout took my .45-cal. pistol and shot and killed the Vietnamese. I can't recall how many times he shot him or where he hit him and I can't recall who else was present who may have seen this.

QUESTION: Did you object to or try to prevent this incident?

BOWMAN: No, I felt the man was going to die anyhow and that it was a mercy killing.

The sworn witness statement of CID agent Billy Joe Evans on November 20, 1974. The document was Exhibit 88 of the Coy Allegation. It included the following about James Cogan's mental state: "Mrs. Margie Lobdell, identified as the mother of Joseph Dean Cogan Jr., related that Cogan had been undergoing medical treatment for a mental problem and has encountered many difficulties in adjusting to civilian life after his separation from the U.S. Army."

The results of a CID-administered polygraph examination taken by Floyd Sawyer on August 13, 1973. They included the following: "Based on the polygraph charts it is concluded that the examinee was not truthful when he denied tying the prisoners with detonator cord. Based upon the polygraph charts it is concluded that the examinee was truthful when he denied beating a prisoner with a shovel and shooting a prisoner without justification."

The sworn witness statement of Harold Trout on October 17, 1973. The document was Exhibit 68 of the Coy Allegation. Highlights of the interview were included in a report filed by Gustav Apsey on March 28, 1975.

APSEY: On 17 Oct. 73 at the Ft. Benning FO, Third Region, USACIDC, Ft. Benning, Ga., Trout was advised by the undersigned of the offenses he is suspected of and his rights. After he declined to make a statement and elected to seek the advice of a lawyer, Trout was taken to the Benning SJA Office to obtain a lawyer.

On 1 Nov. 73 Capt. Robert H. Taylor SJA Office, Ft. Benning, Ga., advised that he is Trout's lawyer and that Trout would not make any statements concerning this investigation.

The sworn witness statement of Donald Wood on January 22, 1974. The document was Exhibit 45 of the Coy Allegation. It contained the following about the death of Dao Hue:

WOOD: I recall an incident which occurred in the following manner: One afternoon shortly after Hawkins had assumed command, probably in June or July 1967, we were camped outside of a small village west of Duc Pho when we received our ration of beer and soda. After the Tiger Force had consumed a large portion of the supply, later that same evening, Hawkins gave the order that Tiger Force was to cross the river and set up ambushes for the night. I argued with Hawkins about the order, protesting that this was dangerous because the men had been drinking. However, Hawkins, who also had been drinking, overruled my argument and insisted that his mission be carried out. We crossed the river in a column led by Hawkins, who was behind the point. I was second from last in line, feeling that this was the safest place to be considering the condition of most of the members of Tiger Force. Shortly after we reached the far bank of the river, everyone suddenly stopped, then spread out and hit the ground. As soon as I hit the ground, a machine gun fired behind me and I could see the tracers overhead in the direction of the column. Information filtered back that a prisoner had been taken up ahead, the column started forward and I started working my way forward and was about 10 to 15 meters from the front of the column when I heard shots coming from the front. I immediately thought of the prisoner and started to protest when Trout, who was behind me at the time, struck me on the side of the head, knocking me to the ground. As I struck the ground, I heard someone fire in my direction from the front of the column, I did not see who fired.

QUESTION: Did the Tiger Force Commander, Platoon sergeant, and battalion commander know that atrocities and mutilations were occurring within the unit?

WOOD: Hawkins and Trout knew.

QUESTION: Did Hawkins and Trout condone such practices?

WOOD: Hawkins did but I don't believe Trout did but he couldn't say anything one way or the other.

The sworn witness statement of Gerald Bruner on February 12, 1974. The document was Exhibit 132 of the Coy Allegation.

The sworn witness statement of Forrest Miller on January 18, 1974. The document was Exhibit 54 of the Coy Allegation. It contained the following:

QUESTION: Do you remember him (Ybarra) in possession of a string of human ears or gold teeth?

MILLER: I remember that quite a few of the Tiger Force members had such a collection. . . . Collection of ears and cutting off ears from the dead was done in Tiger Force, but I had no fascination for such things, and had no contact with anyone who did so.

QUESTION: Was it a practice of the Tiger Force to kill prisoners prior to a move rather than take them along, or remove them to a rear area?

MILLER: It was an unwritten law.

QUESTION: Did you see this practice in action while assigned to Tiger Force?

MILLER: Yes.

MILLER: I remember that a young male was shot in the back.

QUESTION: Do you remember the circumstances surrounding the death of the young man?

MILLER: I remember that he was not armed, and that he was shot in the back in cold blood.

QUESTION: For what reason was he shot?

MILLER: There was no legal reason for his death, nor was he running. He was told to *"Didi Mau,"* the Vietnamese expression to leave, get out of the area. As he walked away, he was shot in the back.

QUESTION: Who shot this man?

MILLER: I remember that the man (Doyle) was a man who had worked with Fidel Castro when he took over Cuba, or at least that is what he told me.

QUESTION: Did you, during your tour in Vietnam, place any significance in the mutilation of the Vietnamese bodies upon their death?

MILLER: I knew that under the Vietnamese belief, the mutilation of the body would prevent one from going to heaven. I feel that this was probably the reason that this practice was used by the troops. My feelings, however, were just the opposite, I felt that the enemy, seeing these mutilated bodies, might be angered enough to keep them going when they would have normally become weak.

The sworn witness statement of Cecil Peden on January 24, 1974. The document was Exhibit 54 of the Coy Allegation. It included the following about Varney:

PEDEN: I don't know when it occurred, but one day about evening, while on patrol, we stopped to rest, and men were put out along the trail to act as lookouts. At this time, our team had an NVA prisoner we received from another team, and I guess we were going to pass him to HQ's team. We had only had him for a short period. Well, when we stopped to rest, our Viet-

namese scout started to question the prisoner. Apparently the scout wasn't
getting the information he wanted because he was getting mad. Varney was
also standing there with the scout and prisoner. I was about 100 meters from
them, but I could hear the scout yelling at the prisoner. It was for this reason
that I looked at them to begin with. I then saw Varney hit the prisoner in
the face and the man was knocked to the ground. He stood up again and at
this time the scout took his bayonet point to the prisoner's throat and held
onto his hair with the other hand. I don't know exactly what happened
then, because there were other people standing around there. But either
Varney shoved the man's head forward onto the bayonet or someone else
pushed the man's head forward. The man fell to the ground and about this
time I turned around and started getting my gear ready to move out. Then
we moved out. I walked past the prisoner and he was dead, bleeding from
the throat.
QUESTION: Did you ever hear the nickname "One-Punch Varney"?
PEDEN: Yes, it was after this incident that people started calling him that.

The sworn witness statement of Benjamin Edge on January 18, 1974. The
document was Exhibit 69 of the Coy Allegation.
The sworn witness statement of Manuel Sanchez Jr. on January 17, 1974. The
document was Exhibit 16 of the Coy Allegation.
The sworn witness statement of Michael Allums on January 17, 1974. The
document was Exhibit 16 of the Coy Allegation. It included the following:
QUESTION: Mr. Allums, it has been alleged that a member of Tiger Force
murdered a Vietnamese infant by cutting its throat during Nov. 1967. Do
you have knowledge of that incident?
ALLUMS: Yes, I do know of the incident. I did not witness the actual
thing. As best as I remember, I was left in a defensive position and some
men went out on a patrol. I do not know who all went but I do know that
Sam Ybarra was in the group. This actually took place during Operation
Wheeler but I do not know the appropriate date. I did not witness the
incident, but someone told me about the incident. I cannot remember the
actual details. I remember being shocked with the details at the time. He did
tell me that he had killed the child and he had a band that he said he took
from the child. I remember being repulsed about the whole thing. I could
not accept the fact that he or anyone would kill a child. He was rather proud
of the incident and gloated about it. Ybarra kept the metal band and wore it
and I think he was wearing it the last time I saw him.
QUESTION: Did you believe Ybarra when he told you that he killed the
child?
ALLUMS: Yes, for sure. He would have been capable of such an act. I saw
him during the same time period, cut an ear off a male body approximately
20 to 25 years old. The body was the result of some action. I do not remember exactly what. Ybarra got down on his knees and using a straight-
line razor he started cutting the ear off. I turned my head and when he was

finished he was covered with blood on his hands and had the ear. He put the ear in a bag or something. I only know that later I saw some ears he had in a jar.

QUESTION: During this same period did you ever observe Ybarra in possession of a ration bag containing a string of human ears and human gold teeth?

ALLUMS: Yes, it was what we call an LRP bag, Long Range Patrol. I saw it at least once, maybe more times. He had quite a few ears in the bag and he kept a handful of gold teeth in a cloth bag. He did not keep them together or at least they were not together when I saw them. I remember Ybarra saying that the teeth had been kicked from bodies and that he was either going to take them or mail them home and melt them down.

QUESTION: You have indicated that quite a bit of the activities took place as we have talked about, but you actually only witnessed a very few. Why?

ALLUMS: When we would get fired on, I would look for cover. Ybarra, Green, and some of the others would charge forward. When I advanced, many times the mutilation had already occurred, or they would linger in an area with bodies after I had left.

QUESTION: Were any of the incidents reported to your knowledge?

ALLUMS: I do not know if any were reported at all. I doubt it, as the officers, both company and battalion, actually seemed to condone the acts. We, Tiger Force, were told by the officers that when we went into an area, anything moving, man, woman, or child, was to be killed as they were not supposed to be there. We were constantly being told how good we were, how our body count was always the highest and what a good job we were doing. I cannot be more specific as to the officers telling us to kill every-thing, but the company officers were of this attitude at all times.

Books

Herring, George. *America's Longest War: The United States and Vietnam*. New York: Knopf, 1996.

Kimball, Jeffrey. *Nixon's Vietnam War*. Lawrence: University Press of Kansas, 1997.

Kissinger, Henry. *Ending the Vietnam War*. New York: Simon & Schuster, 2003.

Langguth, A. J. *Our Vietnam: The War 1954–1975*. New York: Touchstone, 2000.

The Winter Soldier Investigation: An Inquiry into American War Crimes. Boston: Beacon Press, 1972.

Periodicals

Several *New York Times* stories about the Paris peace negotiations and treaty

CHAPTER 22

Main Sources

We talked at length with Gustav Apsey about the physical toll the investigation took on his life. We also interviewed CID agents who took part in the Tiger Force investigation. In addition, we interviewed numerous Tiger Force soldiers about the probe. We interviewed Sam Ybarra's family and friends, and drew on thousands of documents in the Colonel Henry Tufts Archive at the University of Michigan. We talked at length with friends and family members of James Barnett.

Our account of Ybarra's visit to Roosevelt to meet Green's mother was based on interviews with Kathleen Green and Janice Little. According to Little, who was married to Ybarra, her husband felt guilty about Green's death. She said Ybarra often blamed himself for his friend's demise. Green's mother, Kathleen, said Ybarra was "filled with sorrow" during his brief visit to her home.

Our account of CID agent Robert DiMario trying to undermine the investigation was based in part on an interview with Daniel Clint for the *Toledo Blade*'s series "Buried Secrets, Brutal Truths." The four-day series ran from October 19 to 22, 2003. It's interesting to note that Clint told us Tiger Force members committed atrocities, but he took DiMario's advice and kept quiet about war crimes. Clint, however, did hint to DiMario that there were serious problems with the fighting unit.

For the section about the meeting between Apsey and Barnett in Loretto, Tennessee, we drew on extensive interviews and CID records related to the Tiger Force case. Our account of Barnett sending his medals to the White House was based on interviews with family members and newspaper articles. It's interesting to note that Barnett's Silver Star is stored at the Gerald R. Ford Presidential Library.

For the section on Colonel Henry Tufts retiring from the CID, we drew on extensive interviews with his family, his friends, and CID officials. The records Henry Tufts removed from his CID office are part of the Colonel Henry Tufts Archive at the University of Michigan.

Army Records

The sworn witness statement of Ken Kerney on June 18, 1974. The document was Exhibit 112 of the Coy Allegation. It contained the following from CID agent Charles Fann:

FANN: Kerney confirmed that body mutilations were a common and accepted practice within the Tiger Force. . . . Kerney stated that Ybarra did have a human scalp braided on the front sight of his rifle.

FANN: In reference to the attack on the village near Chu Lai in which several children and other persons were killed by Tiger Force members with hand grenades because they refused to leave their bunkers, Kerney stated that information was received from S-2 that the village people were Vietcong sympathizers and that S-2 wanted something done about it.

FANN: According to Kerney, a search of the bunkers failed to show any sign of vietcong supplies or to substantiate that the village sympathizers were with the Vietcong. No return fire was received by the Tiger Force. FANN: Kerney stated that during his assignment with the Tiger Force, it appeared that the force was used as an assassin squad for the higher echelons of the command structure. Kerney further stated that since the war has ended and numerous war-crime allegations are now being made, the members of the Tiger Force have become scapegoats for the commanders who actually ordered that certain incidents occur.

The sworn witness statement of Charles Fulton on June 24, 1974. The document was Exhibit 120 of the Coy Allegation. It contained the following about the bunkers:

FULTON: It was approaching the end of the day and we came into a village. I didn't see anyone run into the bunkers for I was at the end of the column. Once in the immediate area of the bunkers, one of the NCOs who I think may have been Sgt. Haugh gave the order to throw hand grenades into the bunkers. I was among some of the guys that threw them into the bunkers.

The sworn statement by CID agent David Ayers, who interviewed Fulton. The document was Exhibit 121 of the Coy Allegation. It contained the following:

AYERS: Fulton stated in his written statement that he heard certain sounds coming from the direction of the bunker that had been hand-grenaded. When asked specifically about the sounds, he mentioned that they were sounds of people that had been hurt and were trying to get someone's attention in order to get help. Although faint, they were clear.

The sworn witness statement of Daniel Clint on January 26, 1973. The document was Exhibit 200 of the Coy Allegation. It contained the following:

QUESTION: What kind of person was Ybarra and Kerrigan?

CLINT: In my opinion, Ybarra appeared to have no scruples and no conscience. Kerrigan seemed more like a manipulator in that, during that time period, there was sort of a power struggle. Those who had the highest body counts were looked up to and those who didn't believe in killing just for the sake of killing were shunned. Kerrigan was one of those looked up to and that's all I have to say about it.

QUESTION: Do you ever remember being issued orders to kill everything that moved during search-and-destroy missions while assigned to the Tiger Force?

CLINT: Yes, just prior to leaving the 320th Arty base camp we were briefed by LTC Morse Bn Commander, who told us we were the most "professional killers" in RVN, but I can't recall the date. During the briefing, LTC Morse told us that we were to kill everything in the valley because the valley had allegedly been cleared and anyone left there was either VC or a VC sympathizer.

QUESTION: Were there any other occasions when you were instructed to kill everything that moved?

CLINT: Several, but I can't give you exact times and dates or the names and titles of those who issued the instructions.

QUESTION: During your assignment with HHC, 1st Bn, 327th Inf Bde, did you ever hear the expression used "Sam did it" and if so, what was it supposed to symbolize?

CLINT: It usually meant that Ybarra had killed someone, but most times it was more specific like "Sam blew the old man away" or something of that nature.

QUESTION: Is there anything you wish added or deleted from your statement at this time?

CLINT: Yes, I'd like to make it known that Sam Ybarra had a way of threatening people in the unit in a way that intimidated people.

The sworn statement of Anthony DeMario, who interviewed Daniel Clint. The document was Exhibit 201 of the Coy Allegation. It included the following:

DeMARIO: Upon signing his sworn statement, Clint related that he disliked Ybarra very much and had even contemplated killing Ybarra while Clint was on guard duty in Vietnam, but that Fischer talked him out of it.

The sworn statement of Forrest Miller on April 5, 1974. The document was Exhibit 55 of the Coy Allegation. It contained the following:

QUESTION: Were there any indications that these people were hostile forces, VC, or sympathizers?

MILLER: No.

QUESTION: Did you actually see any of these persons being hit by Tiger Force fire, or see bodies on the ground after the firing ceased?

MILLER: I saw them fall down, however, I did not go out and check them to see if they were dead.

QUESTION: SPC Miller, in your prior statement, you related an incident involving the killing of several children using grenades. Will you relate fully to me the circumstances of this incident?

MILLER: This incident occurred near Chu Lai RVN near the middle of August 1967. We were on patrol and entered this village, and upon entering, some children and other people ran into bunkers and would not come out. We told them to come out and they did not. Due to this fact, we threw grenades into the bunkers. We didn't take any prisoners from the group in that they were all killed.

QUESTION: Did you actually see these grenades being thrown into the bunkers?

MILLER: I was there and I know of the incident for fact.

The sworn witness statement of James Barnett on November 27, 1974. The document was Exhibit 177 of the Coy Allegation. It included the following:

BARNETT: Since my last statement on 27 April 73, I got to thinking about a lot of things that happened in RVN. Most of those incidents could be classified as war crimes today. I feel that a lot of this stuff could have been prevented by Trout or Hawkins, but those two actually condoned such practices and at times encouraged them by not saying anything about the way some of the incidents happened. There were several cases when Trout told us to shoot people. The reason I want to bring this to light now is mainly that I and others followed orders given by Trout to shoot people when it was not necessary. We carried out those orders and if I or some of the others that were involved were still in the Army today we could be subject to be tried for committing war crimes. I know that since I am a civilian now, the Army can't touch me. I intend to tell you about some incidents I have personal knowledge of and which involved either me directly or Trout. I know I wasn't the only one that carried out such orders to kill people when it was not necessary but I don't want to talk about other Tiger Force members because I feel it is their business to decide if they want to report such incidents or not.

During the interview, Barnett told Apsey that Trout ordered him to shoot a young mother after her husband escaped:

BARNETT: Trout, who was our element leader, got real mad about this and told us to burn the hooch down. We got the woman out of the house and she had a baby which was about six months old. Also somehow an old woman came into the picture, and I don't know where she came from. We then set the hooch on fire and totally destroyed it and a medic we had with us gave her a bunch of pills or capsules to take, which quieted her down. I don't remember who this medic was. Our entire element then moved out from there with the two women and the baby and went about 200–300 meters and stopped at another hooch. After finding that the house was secure, we set up security around it and remained in the general area there. Myself, Trout, and three others then took the two women and the child inside the hooch. Trout told me to tell my team to chow down and then I saw that Trout and the woman went down into the bunker inside the building. That bunker was a hole in the floor with dirt steps leading below into a room. I then left the hooch and told my people to eat. About five minutes or a little longer Trout appeared from the hooch by himself and mentioned something to the effect that "this was pretty good stuff," in other words he was insinuating that he had screwed her.

Before Tiger Force left the village, Barnett said, Trout told him to shoot the woman.

BARNETT: I asked Trout at this point if he was sure that this is what he wanted to do and he replied, "Grease her." The term "greasing" was one of Trout's favorite expressions. The element saddled up and I got myself ready to go by putting on my rucksack and then the element started moving out. I don't know how the woman came out of the building, but she was standing in front of the hooch when I saw her. I took my M16 rifle and pointed it at her and then shot her in the chest. She fell over and I turned around and saw that Trout was behind me and had seen the whole thing. We then left her lying there and then joined the rest of the element.

QUESTION: Would you describe the woman you shot?

BARNETT: She was about 22 or 23 yrs. old, medium build, and I think she had short hair or she had her hair rolled up. She had a pretty good-looking body that looked better than the average woman we encountered in the field. That is about all I can tell you about her.

QUESTION: You stated she was given pills by a medic when her hooch was burned down. Do you know what effect those pills had on her?

BARNETT: Like I said, she calmed down after she took them. I could see that she was high, like under the influence of drugs. I think she was given Darvons, but I am not sure about this because the medics carried all kinds of different pills.

QUESTION: Why did Trout and that woman go down into that bunker together?

BARNETT: I am sure that Trout had sex in mind when they went down there because I saw him playing with her breasts before that. I remember she had fairly large breasts for a Vietnamese woman.

The sworn witness statement of Kenneth Smith, who interrogated Carl James on November 6, 1974. The document was Exhibit 138 of the Coy Allegation. It included the following:

SMITH: James appeared to be extremely nervous and apprehensive regarding the purpose of the interview. After providing information necessary for an interview work sheet, James indicated prior to being advised of his rights that he may terminate the interview immediately if the allegations were not detailed to him. The undersigned determined that in order for James to have a clear concept of what he was suspected of, portions of the substantiation regarding Bruner's allegations would be reviewed with James. James was not allowed to read any portion of the investigative material.

During a review of the material, James made numerous comments as if speaking to himself, indicating he recalled Bruner, and then "the chaplain" was mentioned, he indicated aloud "that would be Tommy Thompson." James was warned against making such remarks until fully advised of his rights. Subsequently, during the rights advisement, James indicated that he would like to "waiver" the undersigned reading the rights, and was fully cognizant of his rights. However, the rights advisement was continued as required by the appropriate regulations. The rights advisement took place after James indicated that he now fully understood the allegations against him, as detailed on the face of DA Form 3881.

Subsequent to the rights advisement, James made several additional comments to the undersigned supporting the undersigned's belief that James had recall regarding the incident alleged by Bruner. At one point, James pointed to his head in a gesture indicating that Bruner had mental problems. James also indicated that he thought he recalled a letter hand carried by someone regarding Bruner, but wasn't sure.

The sworn witness statement of Kenneth Smith, who interrogated Carl James on January 20, 1975. The document was Exhibit 139 of the Coy Allegation. It included the following:

SMITH: James was allowed to review his written statement of Nov. 6, 1974, and related that the statement was true and correct. James related that at the time of the alleged incident, there was a lot of activity going on in their area, casualties were high, and that if Bruner did tell him of the incident, but not in the context that he understood it to be an atrocity, he may not have done anything about Bruner's allegation. Again, James stated that at this time, he does not recall anything about the incident and is unable to answer questions in any way but "I don't know," "Maybe," or "I'm not sure."

We drew on the combat psychology concepts from various writings by retired lieutenant colonel David Grossman and Dr. Jonathan Shay, author of *Achilles in Vietnam: Combat Trauma and the Undoing of Character.*

Books

Beattie, Keith. *The Scar That Binds.* New York: New York University Press, 2000.

Grossman, David. *On Killing: The Psychological Cost of Learning to Kill in War and Society.* Boston: Little, Brown, 1996.

Kimball, Jeffrey. *Nixon's Vietnam War.* Lawrence: University Press of Kansas, 1997.

Kissinger, Henry. *Ending the Vietnam War.* New York: Simon & Schuster, 2003.

Shay, Jonathan. *Achilles in Vietnam: Combat Trauma and the Undoing of Character.* New York: Atheneum, 1994.

The Winter Soldier Investigation: An Inquiry into American War Crimes. Boston: Beacon Press, 1972.

CHAPTER 23

Main Sources

We interviewed Gustav Apsey and numerous CID agents involved with the Tiger Force investigation. We also interviewed William Doyle and several Tiger Force soldiers, including James Hawkins, who described the Pentagon meeting in November 1975.

For the section on Apsey writing the final report, we drew on extensive interviews with the lead agent and other CID agents, including Captain Earl Perdue. They said Apsey spent weeks holed up in his office, dictating his findings into a tape recorder.

Our account of Hawkins and General William Maddox flying to the Pentagon to meet with the Army's top brass was based on an extensive interview with the former Tiger Force platoon leader in connection with the *Blade*'s series "Buried Secrets, Brutal Truths." The series ran October 19 to 22, 2003. Hawkins told us he read the document and was told by Maddox the case was being closed.

Army Records

The sworn witness statement of Bradford Mutchler on January 21, 1975. The document was Exhibit 323 of the Coy Allegation. It included the following information about Tiger Force:

QUESTION: Was the success of the TF and other companies in the battalion measured by a high body count?

MUTCHLER: Yes, that was one of the means by which the companies were evaluated. I attended all of the briefings prior to the missions and body count was often mentioned. This was the policy throughout all of the units and there definitely was competition between the line companies and the TF to see who could amass the greatest body count.

QUESTION: Did you ever hear rumors to the effect that members of the TF collected ears, gold teeth, and scalps?

MUTCHLER: I heard rumors to the effect but I never saw any of the items. It was something that no one really talked about out in the open and it was something that you just kept trying to "sweep under the rug" and forget because you really didn't want to know if it was true or not.

QUESTION: Would you define the term "free-fire zone" and state whether or not the term was used in the Bn and by the troops during your tour of duty in Vietnam?

MUTCHLER: It was used by everyone during my tour and it meant to open up and kill everything that moved.

QUESTION: What provisions were in effect in handling noncombatants and other unarmed persons that were encountered in such a free-fire zone and especially during the Song Ve Valley operations?

MUTCHLER: I don't recall any provisions made for noncombatants in the Song Ve Valley. It was just put out at the briefings that there was nothing in there that was friendly.

QUESTION: On 18 Jan. 73, you orally related that at mission briefings you heard orders given in the following manner: "There is nothing of ours in that area and we need a body count." Can you relate when, where, by whom, and to whom these orders were issued?

MUTCHLER: As the Bn Surgeon I attended all of the mission briefings. I heard that order, or similar orders, given at every briefing. I cannot recall specifically who gave that order, but I believe that it would have been the S-3 officer, the second in command of the battalion. These orders would have been given to everyone who attended the briefings which would have been the company and TF commanders.

QUESTION: Can you relate your interpretation of those orders?

MUTCHLER: In my opinion, it meant kill whatever was in the area. If it moves, kill it.

The sworn witness statement of Lawrence Jackson on January 17, 1975. The document was Exhibit 325 of the Coy Allegation.

The sworn witness statement of Colonel Manfred Kelman on January 17, 1975. The document was Exhibit 317 of the Coy Allegation. Kelman was once assigned to the 1st Battalion/327th Infantry.

The sworn witness statement of William Doyle on February 17, 1975. The document was Exhibit 135 of the Coy Allegation. It included the following comments by CID agent Bonnie Sapp:

SAPP: Doyle was contacted at his home in Saint Petersburg by Sapp, who informed Doyle that he was suspected of committing the offenses of murder and aggravated assault and informed Doyle of his rights against self-incrimination. Doyle stated that he understood his rights and then signed a waiver certificate (LA Form 3881). Throughout the subsequent interview, Doyle was evasive when asked questions relating to the offenses being investigated. Most of the time, he attempted to appear fairly congenial, but it was apparent that he was quite hostile.

SAPP: Doyle stated that while he was in Vietnam, he fought in the unit he wanted to fight in. He stated that the Tiger Force was his kind of unit — that he liked Hawkins, that Hawkins was fighting the same kind of war he was fighting, and therefore he joined the Tiger Force. Doyle would not comment further on what he meant by saying that he and Hawkins were fighting the same kind of war. He did say that one of the reasons he wanted to belong to the Tiger Force was because it was better equipped than the other units in the battalion, and therefore a man was safer in the Tiger Force.

SAPP: Doyle stated that Bruner was a wiseass who couldn't be depended on. He stated that Bruner was always trying to tell someone what to do, that he was obnoxious, that he was always trying to make peace instead of making war, and that he couldn't be led, but had to be driven.

SAPP: Doyle was asked if he considered Tiger Force as sort of an "elite unit within the elite," and he stated that he certainly would. He stated that there was always body count competition between the Tiger Force and other units in the battalion. According to him, at the end of each operation, the unit that had the highest body count would get the most beer and the best food, and usually the Tiger Force came out on top with the highest body count.

The sworn witness statement of James Alexander, who interviewed Stephen Naughton on February 5, 1975. The document was Exhibit 124 of the Coy Allegation.

The sworn witness statement of Colonel Gerald Morse on March 17, 1975. The document was Exhibit 315 of the Coy Allegation.

The daily radio logs detailing Tiger Force's daily contact with the enemy and battalion headquarters between May 1, 1967, and November 30, 1967. The document was Exhibit 438 of the Coy Allegation.

381

We used information from the CID "Report of Investigation" known as the final report. The report, which covered a period between May and November 1967, substantiated war crimes against Tiger Force soldiers. It included the following information:

Investigation disclosed that on an unknown date during the latter part of 1967, at an unknown location, James Barnett, by his own admission, shot with an M16 rifle a VN female detainee with the intention of killing her, at the orders of Trout, his element leader.

Investigation disclosed that during the hours of darkness, on or about 23 Jul. 67, in the Song Ve Valley, Nghia Thuan district, Quang Ngai province, during operation Hawkins (2LT Cdr 3 Jul.–Oct. 67) murdered an unarmed elderly VN male, by shooting him in the head with an XM-16E1 rifle (Car-15) and that Trout (TFRP Apr. 67–Mar. 68 and PSG in Jul. 67) struck the old man on the head with an M16 rifle.

Investigation disclosed that during the hours of darkness, on or about 24 July 67 in the Song Ve Valley, Trout murdered an unarmed wounded VN, by shooting him several times with a .45-cal. pistol, assigned to Barry Bowman (TFRP medic Jun.–Sep. 67).

Investigation based on the testimony of Mayhew and Sgt. Gerald W. Bruner disclosed that during Aug. or Sept. 67, at an unknown location, unidentified TFRP members executed a male VN detainee with M16 rifles at the orders of Doyle after the detainee was shot in the arm and beaten by Doyle during an interrogation. Also that the same detainee was repeatedly beaten and kicked by two unidentified TFRP members and that the same assailants assaulted another detainee at that location in a like manner, but stopped when Bruner interfered and threatened to shoot one of the assailants who had pointed a .45-cal. pistol at the detainee's head and that James later indicated he had knowledge of the incident. On or about 22 Sept. 67, presumably at Phan Rang, Bruner reported the above to the Cdr, HHC, 1/327, believed to have been James. No information was developed that any action was taken against anyone for the offense, whether or not James reported this to the higher authorities in accordance with MACV Dir 20–4, or that the Bn Cdr ever became aware of the incident.

Investigation disclosed, based on Miller's testimony, that in Aug.–Sept. 67, at an unknown location, unidentified TFRP members threw hand grenades into bunkers and killed an undetermined number of occupants.

Investigation disclosed that during the morning hours on or about 27 Jul. 67, in the Song Ve Valley, Sanchez witnessed the execution of two male detainees by two or three unidentified TFRP members with M16 rifles. Investigation further indicated that this execution was ordered by the officer-in-charge (Hawkins).

Investigation disclosed, based on Bruner's testimony, that on or about 21 Sept. 67, near Tam Ky during Operation Wheeler, Sanders and Hawkins, indiscriminately and in jest, fired M16 rifles at an unarmed VN farmer who was plowing in a rice field. The farmer ran for cover and was not injured.

Investigation disclosed that between Jun.–Nov. 67 at unknown dates and locations, Ybarra on numerous occasions cut ears from dead VN bodies; possessed a set of human ears and a jar containing two ears; possessed a string with human ears which he wore on several occasions around his neck and a gag with 15–20 gold teeth, suspected to have been removed from dead bodies.

Investigation also disclosed an undetermined number of unidentified TFRP members . . . were observed in possession of human ear, scalp, and gold teeth collections. Investigation also indicated that those practices were carried out because TFRP members believed that the VN were superstitious of dead bodies that were mutilated.

Investigation disclosed that during the latter part of 1967, at an unknown location west of Chu Lai, Cogan (attached combat engineer from Co A, 326th Eng. Bn, 1st Bde, 101st Abn Div) executed an old unarmed VN male by shooting him twice in the head with a .45-cal. pistol.

The daily radio logs detailing Tiger Force's contact with the enemy and battalion headquarters between May 1, 1967, and November 30, 1967. The document was Exhibit 438 of the Coy Allegation.

Books

Beattie, Keith. *The Scar That Binds.* New York: New York University Press, 2000.

Herring, George. *America's Longest War: The United States and Vietnam.* New York: Knopf, 1996.

Kimball, Jeffrey. *Nixon's Vietnam War.* Lawrence: University Press of Kansas, 1997.

Kissinger, Henry. *Ending the Vietnam War.* New York: Simon & Schuster, 2003.

Valentine, Douglas. *The Phoenix Program.* New York: Morrow, 1990.

The Winter Soldier Investigation: An Inquiry into American War Crimes. Boston: Beacon Press, 1972.

INDEX

Index

chanting of, 160, 190, 191
civilian killings and, 39, 60, 92, 120, 150
Clint and, 268, 376
in combat, 60, 90, 141, 147, 152, 153, 155, 159, 160, 161, 196–98
Communism and, 19
on death, 149
death of, 313
drinking of, 4, 7, 8, 9, 11, 93, 227, 271–72, 313, 363
family of, 7–8, 11, 145, 162, 174, 313, 330, 336, 357, 362, 374

farmers' killings and, 122–23
Fischer and, 189, 207, 231–32
Green and, 9–12, 21–22, 60–61, 62–63, 82–83, 112, 160, 271, 337, 374
Green's death and, 188, 189–90, 191, 207, 358
Kerrigan and, 145, 179, 234
killings by, 64, 239, 266, 335, 336, 337, 357, 376
on leave, 161–62, 173–79

new tour of, 136–37
postwar life of, 3–8, 270–72, 313
prisoner killings and, 63–65, 112, 266, 336, 353
psychology of, 64, 228
sources on, 328–30, 336, 357, 362, 363, 365, 374, 375
Tiger Force and, 13, 14, 15–17, 228, 330
on Vietnamese people, 47
Wood and, 39, 127
Youngdeer, Robert E., 4, 329

ABOUT THE AUTHORS

Michael Sallah and Mitch Weiss were awarded the 2004 Pulitzer Prize for Investigative Reporting for their work on the *Toledo Blade's* Tiger Force series. Sallah has received numerous state and national awards for his investigative work and was formerly named Best Reporter in Ohio by the Society of Professional Journalists. He is currently the investigations editor for the *Miami Herald*. Weiss spent twelve years with the Associated Press, where he won various state and national awards. He is now editor with the *Charlotte Observer*.